D0935462

CHURCH AND STATE IN MODERN IRELAND

1923—1970

CHURCH AND STATE IN MODERN IRELAND

1923—1970

J. H. WHYTE

GILL AND MACMILLAN

First published 1971 by
GILL AND MACMILLAN LTD
2 Belvedere Place
Dublin 1
and in London through association with
MACMILLAN AND CO. LTD

© J. H. Whyte, 1971

7171 0486 9

Cover design by Des Fitzgerald

Printed and bound in the Republic of Ireland by
CAHILL AND CO LIMITED

CONTENTS

CONTENTS

INTRODUCTION

First, I must define my terms. The 'State' which is under consideration in this book is the twenty-six-county area which has existed as a distinct entity under a variety of names—the Irish Free State, Eire, the Republic of Ireland—since 1922. In the body of the book I shall follow current usage in the twenty-six counties and refer to this State *tout court* as 'Ireland'. This usage can sometimes cause confusion, for it appears to imply that the State of Ireland and the island of Ireland are identical, thus ignoring the existence of the six-county area of Northern Ireland, in which more than one-third of the island's inhabitants live. But on the other hand it makes for brevity, and in the present study, which is not concerned with Northern Ireland, there should be no ambiguity.

By 'Church', I mean the Church of the great majority in the twenty-six counties—the Roman Catholic Church. The relation between the State and the various minority denominations makes an interesting subject, and I have traced elsewhere the relations between the State and the largest of these minorities, the Church of Ireland.[1] But though an interesting subject, it is a distinct one, and it will not be touched on here except where it illuminates relations between the State and the Church of the majority. I shall refer to Roman Catholics throughout as 'Catholics'. I hope that members of other denominations, who feel that they are just as entitled to use the term 'Catholic' as are members of the Roman Communion, will nevertheless take no offence at this usage. Like the use of the term 'Ireland' for the twenty-six-county State, it makes for brevity, and in the context of this book there can be no ambiguity.

This book has three main purposes. The first is to provide a general account of Church–State relations in Ireland since 1923.

1. 'Political Life in the South', in Michael Hurley, S.J. (ed.), *Irish Anglicanism, 1869–1969*, Dublin 1970. Some non-Irish readers may wish to have it explained that the Church of Ireland is the title of the Irish branch of the Anglican communion.

The second is to provide a more detailed examination of the most celebrated episode in Church-State relations during that period—the long-drawn-out difficulties between the Catholic hierarchy and successive Ministers for Health over the shaping of the health services, difficulties which began with the Health Act 1947, reached their most dramatic moment with the mother and child scheme of 1950-1, and came to an end only with the Health Act 1953. The third purpose is to attempt an answer to the question 'How much influence does the Catholic hierarchy wield in Irish politics?'. In arranging the book, however, I have not attempted to divide it into three sections corresponding to these three purposes. An attempt to do so at the drafting stage proved more confusing than helpful. The health-services episode is so much intertwined with the general narrative that it does not lend itself to separate treatment: one cannot describe the general course of Church-State relations without constant reference to the difficulties over the health services; and one cannot explain the difficulties over the health services without constant reference to the general situation at the time. I have therefore interwoven the narrative about the health-services issue with the general narrative. As far as my third purpose is concerned—to assess the influence of the Catholic hierarchy in Irish politics—I have attempted to draw together my conclusions in the final chapter.

Although a full account of the sources used is provided at the end of the book, a word might be in order here about the evidence on which it is based. Unpublished documents play only a minor part in it. Neither Church nor State in Ireland has opened its archives for so recent a period as this, and, although I have obtained copies of some important unpublished documents (such as the text of the mother and child scheme, which, despite all the fuss which it provoked in 1950-1, has never been made public before), they have been of help only at particular points. The main types of source-material are two. First, I have read very extensively in published sources—newspapers, periodicals, books, pamphlets, parliamentary debates, government publications. These provide a surprising amount of information for someone who is prepared to search them thoroughly. Second, I have conducted an extensive programme of interviewing. The interviewing has been most systematic for the health-services episode, where I have talked to virtually all the leading participants on all sides. Apart from the health-services question, I have used interviews to clarify particular points: for instance, I have talked to several people concerned with the legal adoption issue which came to the fore in 1948–52.

A work based on such sources is bound to have its limitations. Some may wonder whether, in the absence of access to archives, I have not missed important episodes. There may have been highly significant encounters between Church and State of which I have remained entirely ignorant because they were not made public at the time and because they were not recalled in interview by my informants. To this objection I can, in the nature of the case, have no convincing answer. I do not myself believe that events of real importance will have been so completely concealed: my experience, when comparing interview evidence with published evidence, is that nearly all the events which participants in Church-State negotiations remember left some trace in the public record at the time. This makes me hopeful that, even when an episode was *not* recalled by my informants in interview, I shall none the less have picked up some trace of its existence from published sources. But I cannot be certain of this. It is only when the archives are opened, at some future date, that it will be possible to see how important are the episodes of which I am unaware.

However, though I expect that some day this book will be superseded by a more definitive study based on archives, I hope I have discovered enough to produce a work of some interest. And, by tackling the subject at a time when many of the participants are still alive and available to be interviewed, I may have been able to discover and preserve some items of information which would be gone for ever if we waited till the archives were opened. For people do not put everything they think onto paper. It is possible that some of my informants have revealed more to me in conversation—about their attitudes, more likely, than about the actual course of events—than would ever be evident to a scholar working solely from documents in the future.

An explanation should be given for the choice of opening and closing dates. The selection of 1923 as the opening date may cause some surprise: why not 1922, when the Irish Free State was

established, or even 1919, when Dail Eireann proclaimed the
independence of Ireland? The reason is that 1923 marks a more
important dividing line for the kind of issue with which the
Church was concerned. In the period just before that date, the
Church was preoccupied with the problem of legitimacy: of
deciding what attitude to adopt towards the competing regimes
claiming jurisdiction in Ireland. Between 1919 and 1921 the
struggle was between the British administration and the
revolutionary government established by Sinn Fein; in 1922–3 it
was between the newly-established Irish Free State government
and the Republicans who opposed it in arms. This problem of
legitimacy bore no relation to the themes which have been
dominant in Church-State relations since 1923: to have discussed it would have meant including an additional chapter,
of considerable length, in which issues would have been raised
which hardly appeared again in the rest of the book.

In choosing my closing date I have had no such elaborate considerations in mind. I have wished simply to come as close to the
present day as possible, and in preparing the manuscript I have
been able to take into account events up to 30 September 1970.

In conclusion, it is a pleasure to thank all those who have
helped me in the preparation of this book. First of all I must
mention the thirty-nine people who were kind enough to allow
me to interview them. I list them in the note on sources at the
end of this book, but I should like to express my gratitude here
for their courtesy and co-operation. I must also thank the many
other people, both clerical and lay, who have discussed my
subject-matter with me more informally. Next, I must thank the
friends and colleagues who have read my typescript at one stage
or another: Dr John Bossy, Mrs Miriam Daly, Dr Cornelius
O'Leary, Mr Desmond Roche, Professor Richard Rose, Mrs
Maureen Wall, and Professor Howard Warrender. All have given
me valuable advice, although of course none is responsible for
the form which my text has finally taken. Especially, I must thank
my wife—for critically examining my text, for helping me to
check the typescript and proofs, for assisting with such reading in
Irish as was required for this book, and, most of all, for creating
the conditions in which it was possible to bring this work to a
conclusion.

GLOSSARY OF IRISH TERMS

The following list, which is included for the benefit of non-Irish readers, provides an indication of the meaning of the various Irish terms which are to be met with in this book. Many such terms are correctly written with accents, as shown below. In the body of this book, however, I have followed a convention widespread in English-language works on Ireland, and have omitted accents from Irish words.

Term	Literal meaning	Connotation in Irish politics
Árd-Fheis	great meeting	term used for the annual conferences of parties, etc.
Árus an Uachtaráin	house of the president	residence of the President of Ireland in Phoenix Park, Dublin.
Clann na Poblachta	children of the republic	a left-wing political party
Clann na Talmhan	children of the land	an agrarian political party
Cómhar	co-operation, alliance	an Irish-language periodical
Cumann na nGaedheal	society of the Irish	a political party of the period 1923–33
Dáil	meeting	lower house of the Irish parliament
Éire	Ireland	
Fianna Fáil	warriors of destiny	Ireland's largest political party

xi

Term	Literal meaning	Connotation in Irish politics
Fine Gael	family of the Irish	Ireland's second largest political party
Fírinne	truth	A Catholic society of the nineteen-fifties
Muintir na Tíre	people of the land	a rural development organisation
Oireachtas	assembly	the Irish parliament
An Ríoghacht	the kingdom	a Catholic social study organisation
Seanad	senate	upper house of the Irish parliament
Tánaiste	second, heir	deputy prime minister
Taoiseach	chief, leader	prime minister

CHAPTER I

SOME TRADITIONS OF IRISH CATHOLICISM

It might be helpful to begin this chapter with a word about the formal organisation of Irish catholicism. One peculiarity emerges at once: in Ireland, ecclesiastical and political jurisdictions do not coincide. Politically, the island has been divided between two jurisdictions since 1921, but ecclesiastically it continues to be subject to a single hierarchy, taking decisions for the whole island. The Catholic Church is not unique in thus ignoring the political divisions of the island: the principal Protestant denominations—the Church of Ireland, the Presbyterian Church in Ireland and the Methodist Church in Ireland—are also organised on an all-Ireland basis.

The Catholic Church in Ireland is organised into four provinces (Armagh, Dublin, Cashel and Tuam) and twenty-eight dioceses. It does not follow that the hierarchy always numbers exactly twenty-eight: on the one hand, two or three of the archbishops and bishops at any given time may have coadjutors or auxiliaries who also have a right to attend the meetings of the hierarchy; on the other hand, there may be sees vacant, and, since 1954, the smallest diocese, Ross, has no longer had a bishop of its own but has been administered by the Bishop of Cork. But the total number of archbishops and bishops has never been far from twenty-eight.

While each bishop is the authority for matters concerning his own diocese, matters concerning Ireland as a whole are dealt with in full meetings of the Irish hierarchy. During most of the period covered by this book, these meetings took place twice a year, in June and October. Since the Second Vatican Council, there has been such an increase in the volume of business that the bishops have found it necessary to hold a third meeting each year, in April; but until the nineteen-sixties, an extra meeting in April

I

was rare and occurred only in the most pressing circumstances. A standing committee of the hierarchy meets quarterly, in January, April, June and October. The standing committee consists of the four archbishops, the two bishops who are acting as secretaries to the hierarchy, and one further bishop from each province, elected by the bishops of that province.[1] The fact that the hierarchy meets infrequently, and at fixed times of the year, may have its effect on relations between Church and State. It may mean that a government, or a private interest group, which is seeking a decision from the hierarchy on some point of importance to it, has to wait weeks or even months until the next meeting falls due. It may also mean that, if a government or private interest group takes some action to which the bishops object, the next meeting of the hierarchy may not fall due until it is too late to do anything but enter an *ex post facto* protest. We shall come across examples of both these contingencies in ensuing chapters.

As well as these biannual or triannual meetings of the hierarchy, there take place at much rarer intervals National Councils, which representatives of the lower clergy and of the religious orders also attend, and which frame statutes amplifying, for Ireland, the canon law of the universal Church. So far, such National Councils have been held in 1850, 1875, 1900, 1927 and 1956.

Irish bishops are appointed by a process which appears to be largely one of co-option. Since 1925, the formal procedure has been as follows. At intervals of about three years, each archbishop calls together the bishops of his province and they draw up a list of priests whom they consider suitable for the episcopate. In compiling this list, they are required to seek confidential advice from among their parish priests, but each bishop may use his own discretion as to how many priests he consults, and as to whether he accepts their opinions. The list, when completed, is forwarded to Rome, and in addition the bishops are entitled to send further recommendations to Rome whenever a see falls vacant.[2] The Holy

1. The information in the preceding sentences is derived from interviews kindly given to me by two members of the hierarchy. Early in 1970 it was announced that the hierarchy was now meeting three times a year, in March, June and October: *Irish Times,* 12 March 1970.
2. See the Decree of the Sacred Congregation of the Consistory on the recommendation of candidates for bishoprics in Ireland, printed in *Acta et Decreta Concilii Plenarii . . . 1956,* 137–41.

See is not obliged to choose from among the names forwarded to it, and, since the establishment of a papal nunciature in Ireland in 1930, it has had an alternative source of information available on the merits of candidates. But with the exception of the first holder of the office, Mgr Paschal Robinson, all the nuncios have been non-Irish, and common sense suggests that they would not often have sufficient knowledge of the personalities involved to offer serious alternatives to the candidates proposed by the bishops. The civil government has no part in the formal nominating procedure, and, despite rumours to the contrary in one or two rare instances, I have been unable to find any case where it has made even informal representations to the ecclesiastical authorities.

So much for the organisation of Irish catholicism: now for a word about its traditions. The purpose of this chapter is not to outline all the characteristics of Irish catholicism, but simply to pick out certain features which seem important in explaining how Church-State relations have developed during the period covered by this book. Five features in particular seem worth mentioning, which were strongly marked in 1923, and have remained important for all or at least most of the period since. None of these five features has aroused much controversy during the last five decades, and so they will not receive much mention in ensuing chapters. But to omit all reference to them would mean depriving a reader, especially a reader unfamiliar with Ireland, of essential background information. Between them they provide an impression of the value-system within which Church-State relations have been worked out.

1. *The hold of the Catholic Church on the loyalty of the people.*

A first approach to demonstrating the strength of catholicism in Ireland can be made through the census figures. Even before independence, the census of 1911 showed that in the area of the present republic 89·6 per cent of the population was Catholic. Since independence, the proportion has risen with every count: 92·6 per cent in 1926, 93·4 per cent in 1936, 94·3 per cent in 1946 and 94·9 per cent in 1961.[3] The figures show that Ireland is

3. *Census of Population of Ireland, 1961*, VII, 1.

overwhelmingly, and increasingly, homogeneous in religion. Yet census figures by themselves might not mean much. There are other countries where probably an even higher proportion of the population is Catholic at least in name—Italy, Spain, Portugal, some of the Latin American countries. But in these other countries a large proportion of nominal Catholics have lost all contact with the organised Church. Ireland is unusual in having a large majority, not just of Catholics, but of committed and practising Catholics.

Before the period covered by this book began, this was already a well-marked feature of Irish catholicism. Observers from every point of view were struck by the piety of the people. A French writer, Louis Paul-Dubois, commented as follows:

No one can visit Ireland without being impressed by the intensity of Catholic belief there, and by the fervour of its outward manifestations. Watch the enormous crowds of people who fill the churches in the towns, the men as numerous as the women; see them all kneeling on the flagstones, without a sound or gesture, as though petrified in prayer! Go to early mass on Sundays in Dublin and watch three or four priests simultaneously giving the Sacrament to throngs of communicants too great for the size of the churches.[4]

Paul-Dubois was a sympathiser with Catholic Ireland; but his views are echoed by a hostile observer who described himself as neither Protestant nor Catholic.[5]

It is a fatal mistake to begin by under-estimating the piety of the Irish, or by representing it as an unreal and insincere thing; nothing could be more absurd. It is thoroughly real and sincere. . . . No other country in the world, I believe, can boast such piety as Ireland; they are of all people the most completely drilled and absorbed in the Christian religion, as it is distorted by the churches.[6]

For a middle view one can go to Sir Horace Plunkett, a Protestant whose comments on Irish catholicism mingled praise with criticism. He wrote: 'In no other country in the world, probably,

4. L. Paul-Dubois, *Contemporary Ireland*, 492–3.
5. Filson Young, *Ireland at the Cross Roads*, 64.
6. *Ibid.*, 68–9.

is religion so dominant an element in the daily life of the people as in Ireland.'[7]

Half a century later, observers are still making the same kind of comment. Paul Blanshard, whose book *The Irish and Catholic Power* is a sustained attack on Irish catholicism, concedes at the outset that Ireland is 'the world's most devoutly Catholic country' and, speaking of the domination of the Catholic outlook, he adds that 'the majority of the Irish people do not resent this domination. They accept it as an organic and established part of Irish life'.[8] A French Catholic visitor, Jean Blanchard, finds Ireland 'an outstanding country owing to the depth and unity of its faith'.[9] A friendly but not uncritical American writer, Mr Donald Connery, starts his chapter on 'Church and State' with the words: 'Religion matters in Ireland more than in any other country in the English-speaking world.' He goes on:

The impression of total catholicism can begin on the flight to Dublin, for if it is an Aer Lingus plane it will be named after a saint. There may be several priests or nuns among the passengers, and then in the capital there are more to be seen on the streets, and in the shops and restaurants. There appear to be churches at every turn, but this may only be because the Irish churches (Catholic churches, at any rate) are busy places, with people moving in and out at all hours, weekdays and Sundays. . . . A visitor to Ireland notices that the bookshops are full of religious works and that Catholic publications are thick on the news-stands. . . . Volunteers of the St Vincent de Paul Society and other Catholic charities collect contributions on the streets. The newspapers tell of the thousands of pilgrims who have climbed Croagh Patrick or of the hundreds flying off to Lourdes and other holy places on special pilgrimage flights.[10]

In support, Mr Connery quotes the impressions of Mr Lionel Fleming, an Irish Protestant journalist returning home after a distinguished career abroad:

Back here, I am struck by the preoccupation with clerical things; well remembered, yet half forgotten. It is natural for the hairdresser to

7. Sir H. Plunkett, *Ireland in the New Century*, 94.
8. P. Blanshard, *The Irish and Catholic Power*, 27.
9. J. Blanchard, *The Church in Contemporary Ireland*, 29.
10. D. Connery, *The Irish*, 130–31.

make conversation by talking of the late proceedings of the Vatican Council, though if any hairdresser did so in London I would have thought him round the bend. Hats off on the top of the bus as it passes a Catholic church. Fish on Fridays. The collecting-box for the missions in the local shops. Grottoes along the country road.[11]

Such statistics as are available support the impressions of observers. Jean Blanchard quotes a figure of 80 to 90 per cent as the practice rate in the diocese of Dublin[12]—and, since rural practice rates are generally higher than urban ones, one may guess that the figures for other dioceses are if anything higher. One unpublished survey is said to have shown that almost one hundred per cent of the Catholics in the villages and rural areas studied were weekly or more frequent mass-goers.[13] A count of mass-goers in the city of Limerick in 1959 indicated that almost all those bound by the law of the Church to attend mass appeared to be doing so.[14]

It is true that observers sometimes question how far the impressive outward piety of the Irish corresponds with internal conviction. The number of Irish Catholics who fall away from their faith when they move to other countries gives some colour to these doubts. At the beginning of the century, Sir Horace Plunkett noted: 'We have only to look at the extent of the "leakage" from Roman catholicism amongst the Irish emigrants in the United States and in Great Britain, to realise how largely emotional and formal must be the religion of those who lapse so quickly in a non-Catholic atmosphere.'[15] An English sociologist, after surveying the literature on defections among Irish Catholics in Britain, suggests that 'the catholicism of the Irishman is internalised only to a very slight degree. In general his religious life is made up of social and ritual forces which through the person of the priest bind him to God'.[16] Even at home in Ireland, some wonder how deep the fervour goes. Mr Donald Connery writes:

11. *Ibid.*, 131, quoting *Irish Times*, 11 July 1966.
12. J. Blanchard, *op. cit.*, 31.
13. C. K. Ward, 'Socio-religious research in Ireland', *Social Compass* (XI, 3/4) 1964, 26, citing research by Rev. Fachtna Lewis, O.F.M.
14. *Ibid.*, 26.
15. Sir H. Plunkett, *op. cit.*, 111.
16. J. A. Jackson, *The Irish in Britain*, 149.

'Just as the image of a submissive, Church-controlled society comes into focus, however, the counter-evidence begins to appear. You notice that much of the famous piety of the Irish Catholics is often a matter of lip service by people going through the motions; that church-going is little more than a social ritual for many people (a Sunday morning obligation before the pleasures of the pub).'[17]

Yet the very strength of these customs is an indication that Irish catholicism is something more than mere custom. It may be true that some Irish Catholics go to mass only out of habit; but it seems unlikely that the habit would persist unless, to many Irishmen, it was something more than that. And anyone who observes Irish devotional patterns will acknowledge that there is far more than mere conformity involved. The Church obliges its members to go to mass on Sundays; it does not require them to attend mass on weekdays and yet many thousands do so. It obliges its members to go to communion at least once a year; the queues for communion in the churches, Sunday after Sunday, show that many Irish Catholics are not content with just 'getting by'. The large and, until very lately, increasing numbers of vocations to the priesthood is another index of vitality.[18]

One facet of this loyalty of Irish Catholics to their Church is the tradition that they do not criticise their clergy in public. This tradition, it is true, has in its full strength been of comparatively short duration. There seems to have been more plain speaking between clergy and laity in the nineteenth century than after 1900;[19] and since about 1950 there have been increasing signs, as later chapters will show, that the tradition is breaking down. But at least for the greater part of the period covered by this book, the tradition was powerful, and coloured the course of Church-State relations. Whatever they may have said in private, Irish

17. D. Connery, *op. cit.*, 133.
18. The situation up to 1961 is surveyed in Rev. J. Newman, 'The priests of Ireland: a socio-religious survey', *Irish Ecclesiastical Record* (5th series, XCVIII, 1) July 1962, 1–27. The annual returns published in the *Irish Catholic Directory* since that date show that the total number of priests in Ireland has continued to rise, but that the number of ecclesiastical students and, more recently, the number of ordinations have started to drop.
19. See John A. Murphy, 'Priests and people in modern Irish history', *Christus Rex* (XXIII, 4) Oct. 1969, 235–59.

Catholics paid public respect to what their bishops said, and, in appearance at least, Irish Catholic opinion was remarkably monolithic on most matters where the Church's belief or practice was relevant.

2. *A tradition of independence of clerical guidance on some issues.*

Yet despite Irish Catholics' tradition of public deference to their pastors, bishops and clergy have never been able to count on the obedience of their flocks on all issues. Religious loyalties are strong, but other forces have sometimes proved stronger still. One example in the past has been provided by agrarian crime. For most of the nineteenth century, Irish farmers suffered from a shockingly oppressive land system. Most of them were tenants at will, which meant that they had no security against eviction, no security against arbitrary increases in rent, no incentive to improve their holdings. In their struggle to secure reforms they had the active help of the Catholic clergy, who indeed were often the local leaders of successive farmers' agitations. But the Church insisted that agitation must be carried on by peaceful means. It could never be right, for instance, to take human life, or forcibly to resist the law.[20] Yet all through the nineteenth century, such methods were used. Oppressive landlords were shot. Tenants who accepted farms from which another farmer had been evicted had their cattle maimed or their houses burnt about their heads. On this matter, it seems, what the clergy considered permissible, and what public opinion was prepared to tolerate, just did not coincide.

In the twentieth century this problem has faded into the background. Between 1870 and 1923 a series of land acts first restricted the landlord's right to evict, and then provided for the buying out of the landlords by their tenants. Today, Ireland is a country of owner-farmers. Even today, however, disputes can still occur between farmers over the ownership of land, and, when this happens, it sometimes appears that the drastic traditions of the nineteenth-century land war are not yet dead. As late as 1960, the Bishop of Kerry had to make certain kinds of agrarian outrage

20. See e.g. the declaration of the Irish bishops published in *Irish Ecclesiastical Record* (3rd series, III) 1882, 440.

reserved sins in the parishes of Ballymacelligott and Tralee.[21] This, however, was an exceptional event, and agrarian crimes in Ireland are now mainly a matter of history. They are worth recalling here simply as an illustration that Church authority had its limits.

Apart from the land, there was another group of issues on which the bishops could not count on complete obedience from their flocks. This comprised questions in which national feeling was deeply involved. Three episodes in particular can be mentioned, in the sixty years before 1923, in which large numbers of Catholics simply defied the rulings of the Church.

The first of these episodes was the Fenian movement of the eighteen-sixties. British rule in Ireland was perhaps never more unpopular than at that time. The population was pouring out of the country, the land system was oppressive, there was a multitude of other grievances from the lack of provision for education to the over-endowment of the Church of Ireland, and yet no British government had made any serious effort to put through a reform programme since the eighteen-thirties. Constitutional agitation had failed, and so, when the Fenian organisation spread across the country in the eighteen-sixties with a view to launching an insurrection, it received widespread support. The Fenians, however, were a secret society, and the Catholic Church opposes secret societies. The Fenians were condemned, accordingly, by the Irish hierarchy in 1863 and eventually by Rome itself in 1870.[22] But despite these denunciations, the bulk of their support came from Irish Catholics, and, if their rising in 1867 was a failure, the immediate causes of this were bad organisation and bad weather, not the opposition of the Church. After the failure of 1867, the Fenian organisation continued in existence, now known as the Irish Republican Brotherhood, and, despite repeated condemnations from the Church, it survived to organise the 1916 rising.

The second episode centred round the fall of Parnell in 1890. Charles Stuart Parnell, for ten years the unchallenged leader of

---

21. *Irish Weekly Independent*, 24 March 1960. A reserved sin is one which can be absolved only by the bishop himself or by a priest specially deputed by him.

22. E. R. Norman, *The Catholic Church and Ireland in the Age of Rebellion*, 86–134.

the Irish parliamentary party, became involved in a particularly unsavoury divorce case, and the Irish parliamentary party met to decide whether he should continue as leader. Before it could reach a decision, two things happened. The Liberal party in England made clear that, if Parnell continued as leader, it could not continue to support the Irish party's claim for home rule. The standing committee of the Irish hierarchy declared that the proceedings in the divorce case made Parnell unfit to be the Irish leader. The majority of the party rejected him, but some stayed loyal to him, and subsequent elections showed that a substantial minority of the Catholic electorate agreed with them. Memories of Parnell's past services, and resentment at interference by the English Liberals, swayed them more than did the arguments of prudence and of loyalty to the Church.[23]

The third episode was very recent when the period covered by this book begins: it was the Civil War of 1922–3. Between 1919 and 1921 a guerilla army, with very wide backing among the Irish people, had fought for complete separation from Britain and the establishment of an Irish republic. By the end of 1921 the British were sufficiently worn down to offer dominion status for twenty-six of the thirty-two counties in Ireland. Dissension then arose on the Irish side on whether this offer should be accepted. By a narrow majority the Dail, or Irish Parliament, agreed to do so, and a government was set up for the new dominion or Irish Free State. But a large minority of the Dail, and perhaps a majority of the fighting men, were so opposed to the British terms that they took up arms against the new Free State government rather than accept it. In this Civil War, the hierarchy intervened emphatically on the side of the Free State. A joint pastoral of 10 October 1922 declared that the Irish Free State Government was the legitimate government, and that to resist it by force of arms was grievously wrong. 'Such being divine law, the guerilla warfare now being carried on by the Irregulars is without moral sanction, and, therefore, the killing of National soldiers in the course of it is murder before God, the seizing of public and private property is robbery, the breaking of roads, bridges and railways is criminal destruction, the invasion of homes

23. F. S. L. Lyons, *The Fall of Parnell, passim.*

and the molestation of citizens a grievous crime.'[24] Words could hardly be stronger, but despite this condemnation the Republicans fought on, and it was defeat in the field, not the denunciation by the hierarchy, which led them to abandon the fight in April 1923.

In all three of these episodes, it was national feeling which led men to defy the warnings of the Church. The majority of Fenians, Parnellites and Republicans considered themselves good Catholics. They were prepared to accept the claims of the Church in other matters, such as education. But the Fenians felt so intensely that the British government was tyrannical that on this point they rejected the judgment of the Church. The Parnellites felt equally strongly about an English political party attempting to veto their leader, and the Republicans could not bring themselves to accept the continued British hegemony which they believed dominion status to involve.

Since 1923, this trait in Irish catholicism—the ability to profess loyalty to the Church while rejecting its guidance on particular issues—has been less important in Irish politics. It has arisen mainly in regard to the Irish Republican Army. After the defeat of the Republicans in the field in 1923, most of them accepted constitutional politics, and in 1927 their representatives entered the Dail as the Fianna Fail party. But a minority of intransigent republicans survived. They retained the name Irish Republican Army, refused to recognise the *status quo* in either Northern Ireland or the twenty-six counties, and planned to reunite Ireland by force. The I.R.A. was formally condemned by the Irish hierarchy in 1931 and again in 1956,[25] but none the less it lasted on. Again the phenomenon was seen of personally devout Catholics rejecting the teaching of the bishops, like Sean South, an I.R.A. leader noted for his piety, who was killed in a cross-border raid in 1957.[26] However, though the I.R.A. provides the main illustration of this feature of Irish catholicism in the years after 1923, we shall come across traces of it in other circumstances, particularly when we are surveying the record of Fianna Fail governments.

This ability of Irish Catholics to remain loyal to the Church on

24. *Irish Catholic Directory, 1923*, 610.
25. *Irish Independent*, 19 Oct. 1931, 19 Jan. 1956.
26. See below, p. 123.

some matters and not on others is an interesting characteristic, and it is to be hoped that some day an investigator will seek an explanation for it. One historian, Mr John A. Murphy of University College, Cork, has suggested that it was due to an individualistic tradition in Irish piety: 'The private and devotional nature of Irish catholicism provided a solution to the dilemma of the Catholic revolutionary: he could argue . . . that while the priest's spiritual authority must be respected, politics was none of his business.'[27] But whatever the causes, the phenomenon existed, and it marks out Ireland from other Catholic countries. Elsewhere, a rejection of clerical views on one issue has led on to a questioning of clerical views in general, and a feature of every other Catholic country has been the strength of anti-clerical parties, at least on occasions when elections have been free enough to show the drift of public opinion. This has been evidenced in Spain, Portugal, Italy, Austria, Malta, Belgium, and the countries of eastern Europe and Latin America. Ireland is exceptional among Catholic countries in that it has never produced an anti-clerical party. The reason is not that Irish Catholics are uniformly docile, but that they are able to compartmentalise their loyalties, and to accept the Church's authority unquestioningly in one sphere at the very time that they challenge it in another.

3. *A tradition of aloofness between Church and State.*

So much for relationships between the clergy and their flocks; now for relationships between the clergy and the State. During the nineteenth century, relations between the Catholic hierarchy and the British government were marked by a certain distance on both sides. To use the phrase 'separation of Church and State' might be misleading, for the term has a definite meaning in some countries, such as France and the United States, where it connotes, among other things, that the State gives no aid to denominational education, a situation which did not obtain in Ireland. But to speak of 'aloofness between Church and State' would be accurate enough as an epithet: it conveys the Church's reluctance to

27. John A. Murphy, 'Priests and people in modern Irish history', *Christus Rex* (XXIII, 4) Oct. 1969, 254.

become entangled with the State, even though there might be advantages attached. A proposal at the beginning of the nineteenth century that the State, in return for granting Catholic emancipation, should have a veto on the appointment of bishops, was, though acceptable at Rome, rejected by the Irish Catholic bishops and laity.[28] Proposals in the eighteen-forties and again in the eighteen-sixties that the Irish Catholic Church should accept an endowment from the State, along with the Church of Ireland and the Presbyterian Church, were rejected by the Catholics.[29] When disestablishment of the Church of Ireland came in 1869, the Catholic bishops made no claim to replace the Church of Ireland as the established Church.

A recent writer, Dr E. R. Norman, has suggested that this tradition was out of line with papal teaching in the nineteenth century.[30] And it is true that the principle of separation of Church and State was repeatedly condemned by nineteenth-century popes—by Gregory XVI in his encyclical *Mirari Vos* of 1832, by Pius IX in his Syllabus of Errors of 1864, by Leo XIII in two of his encyclicals.[31] In most European countries the Catholic Church was both established and financially supported by the State, sometimes alone, sometimes concurrently with Protestant denominations. When disestablishment did occur, as in France in 1905 or Portugal in 1911, it was treated by pope and bishops as a violation of the Church's rights.[32] There were, it is true, some countries, such as the United States, Britain and most of the British colonies, where the Catholic Church neither possessed nor sought any special position. But these were countries where Catholics were only a small minority of the population, for the most part later immigrants to a country whose institutions were already formed, and where they had to be content with whatever status the majority was willing to concede. If, in the nineteenth century, relations between the State and the Catholic Church in

28. R. B. McDowell, *Public Opinion and Government Policy in Ireland, 1801-46*, 92-6.
29. For the proposal in the eighteen-forties see K. B. Nowlan, *The Politics of Repeal*, 224-6, and in the eighteen-sixties see E. R. Norman, *The Catholic Church and Ireland in the Age of Rebellion*, 301-19, 337-8.
30. E. R. Norman, *op. cit.*, 282, 287, 300.
31. E. Gilson, *The Church Speaks to the Modern World*, 79, 176, quoting the encyclicals *Immortale dei* and *Libertas praestantissimum*.
32. O. Premoli, *Contemporary Church History (1900-1925)*, 114, 179-81.

Ireland resembled the Anglo-American pattern rather than the continental European one, this could be ascribed to force of historical circumstances, and an observer might wonder whether, once Ireland obtained her independence, she would not go over to the continental tradition of having an established and endowed Church.

This, however, is not what happened. When independence came, it appeared that the tradition of aloofness between Church and State in Ireland was so strong that there was no desire to change it, even now that the State was a mainly Catholic one. This was illustrated by the constitution of the new State. The 1922 constitution did not even mention the Catholic Church, let alone accord it a special position. Article 8, the article on religion, read as follows:

Freedom of conscience and the free profession and practice of religion are, subject to public order and morality, guaranteed to every citizen, and no law may be made either directly or indirectly to endow any religion, or prohibit or restrict the free exercise thereof or give any preference, or impose any disability on account of religious belief or religious status, or affect prejudicially the right of any child to attend a school receiving public money without attending the religious instruction at the school, or make any discrimination as respects State aid between schools under the management of different religious denominations, or divert from any religious denomination or any educational institution any of its property except for the purpose of roads, railways, lighting, water or drainage works or other works of public utility, and on payment of compensation.

This was about as comprehensive a declaration of neutrality between denominations as the State could make. It is true that, in framing this article, the authors of the constitution were limited by article 16 of the treaty with Great Britain, which imposed, in almost the same words as those used in the constitution, an obligation on the Irish Free State to ensure religious equality. But it does not follow that this obligation was accepted reluctantly. Article 8 of the constitution went through the Dail almost without debate,[33] and it seems to have aroused no criticism either from the hierarchy or from any other quarter.

33. *Dail Debates*, I, 694-5 (25 Sept. 1922).

Since 1922, the tradition of aloofness between Church and State has generally been maintained. It is true that, as we shall see, the constitution of 1937 contained an acknowledgement of the 'special position' of the Catholic Church, but, as we shall also see, it is doubtful how far, if at all, this has altered the juridical position of the Church.[34] In any case this recognition of a special position in 1937 came out of the blue, as a result of Mr de Valera's own decision; there was no agitation beforehand in Ireland for such a change. In other ways, Church and State remain independent of each other, neither of them seeking advantages, nor demanding obligations, from the other. No concordat between the Irish State and the Catholic Church has ever been negotiated, nor, so far as is known, has one ever been suggested. The Church remains a voluntary body in its finances, dependent on donations from the faithful for the salaries of its priests and the upkeep of its churches and seminaries. In 1948, for instance, when the hierarchy decided that the national seminary of Maynooth required a large capital sum for expansion, it did not seek a government grant, but instead raised the money by direct appeal to the Catholics of Ireland.[35] The State has no say in the appointment of bishops, who are appointed by Rome on the basis of lists drawn up by the bishops in Ireland.[36] The Church forbids its clergy to take an active part in politics,[37] and the priest-deputy, who has played so important a part in the politics of some continental countries, is unknown in Ireland. The State gives no special recognition to canon law, and, although its provisions may be admitted in evidence in particular cases—for instance, in the event of a dispute between two clerics—it is treated as a foreign law, whose provisions have to be proved by expert evidence.[38]

The relative lack of contact between Church and State in Ireland helps to explain the relative harmony of their relations. It

34. See below, p. 55, note 119.
35. *Irish Weekly Independent*, 16 Oct. 1948. A year later, the hierarchy acknowledged the receipt of £643,000: *ibid.*, 15 Oct. 1949.
36. See above, pp. 2–3.
37. *Acta et Decreta Concilii Plenarii . . . 1956*, statutes 21–5, 39. Similar provisions can be found in the decrees of preceding National Councils.
38. e.g. in a case of 1925: Rev. James Callaghan v. The Right Rev. Charles O'Sullivan, Bishop of Kerry. This case is referred to in J. Blanchard, *The Church in Contemporary Ireland*, 66.

means that a number of potential issues which have caused trouble in other countries—disputes over State payment for the clergy, or over State interference in the appointment of bishops—have never arisen in Ireland. The field of contact, and hence the field of potential conflict, is narrower than in, say, Italy or Spain.

4. *A grip on education of unique strength.*

At the same time, this 'aloofness between Church and State' must not be exaggerated. In social welfare services, for instance, the Church has a stake which might seem extensive to visitors from Protestant countries. The State does not attempt to provide all such services itself. Many hospitals, orphanages, reformatories, and other welfare institutions are run by religious orders, with the aid of government grants, and, to varying extents, under government control.

This interpenetration of Church and State is seen most clearly in the field of education. The basic attitude of the Catholic Church to education is the same in all countries. It is argued that the right to educate rests primarily with the parents; that the State has the right to lay down standards and to provide schools, but that it has no right to impose a particular form of education on children in defiance of parents' wishes; that the Church has, so far as Catholic parents are concerned, the right to lay down conditions to ensure the Catholic upbringing of their children.[39] In practice, the Church insists that, wherever possible, Catholic parents send their children to Catholic schools, and it also claims, in the name of parental rights, that parents who send their children to Catholic schools should not be under financial disadvantage.

The Church has had varying success in different parts of the world in implementing this programme. In some countries, such as Soviet Russia, the Church has been forbidden to operate schools altogether. In others, such as the United States, Australia, or France under the Third Republic, it has been free to operate schools but has received no direct support from public funds. In others again, such as England and Northern Ireland, Catholic schools receive substantial aid from the State but not quite so much as the schools directly maintained by local authorities.

39. See, e.g., J. Messner, *Social Ethics*, 409-12.

There are just a few countries where the full Catholic claim has been conceded. Catholic literature tends to pick out four countries where the school system is satisfactory from the Catholic point of view: Scotland, the Netherlands, the province of Quebec, and Ireland.

In all these countries, Catholic schools are on an equal footing financially with others.[40] In Scotland, denominational schools are fully maintained by local authorities and yet the denominations retain control over the appointment of teachers, and thereby over the religious character of the school. In the Netherlands, local authorities are obliged to give the same financial assistance to a denominationally-run school as they give to schools directly run by themselves. In Quebec, there are no state schools, but parallel systems of Protestant and Catholic schools between which funds are divided in proportion to the number of school children in each. In Ireland, primary and secondary schools are privately-owned, and in law any school-owner who fulfils the requirements may apply for government grants; in practice, virtually all such schools are associated with one denomination or another, and all denominations receive equal treatment.

If, however, the position in Quebec, Scotland, and the Netherlands could be considered as par from the Catholic point of view, the position that has developed in Ireland could be described as par plus. For in Ireland the Church secured rights, while still under British rule, which went beyond those attained anywhere else.

In the first place, Irish education is not merely denominationally controlled: it is clerically controlled. The denominational schools in Scotland are run by local authorities elected by the community at large; those in the Netherlands and Quebec are run by school boards elected by the members of the denomination concerned. In Ireland, however, local control of a primary school rests not with an elected board, but with a single officer, the school manager, who in the case of a Catholic school is usually the parish priest. Secondary schools are equally free from elected local control. A

40. Details of the Scottish, Dutch and Quebec systems are taken from J. Mescal, *Religion in the Irish System of Education,* 169–74, and Catholic Education Council for England and Wales, *The Case for Catholic Schools,* 80–6, 95–106. The Irish system is described in J. Mescal, *op. cit.,* and T. J. McElligott, *Education in Ireland.*

minority of Catholic secondary schools are owned by laymen,
but most are owned by dioceses or by religious orders. The only
schools in Ireland run by local authorities are technical or, as they
were renamed in 1930, vocational schools. These are under the
control of Vocational Education Committees, chosen by the
council of the county, county borough or urban district
concerned.

In the second place, Ireland is the only country, so far as I know,
where the Catholic hierarchy has applied the principle of separate
education for Catholics at university level. In some countries,
such as England and Australia, there are no Catholic universities,
so the problem does not arise. There are a number of countries,
on the other hand, where one or more Catholic university
institutions do exist—France, Germany, Italy, the United States,
Canada, Belgium, the Netherlands, to name only some. But in
none of these countries does the hierarchy insist that all Catholic
university students attend Catholic institutions, nor would there
be room for them in the Catholic universities if they all tried to
go there. In nineteenth-century Ireland, however, the only
universities available were Trinity College, Dublin, founded in
1591 and with a deeply Protestant ethos, and the three Queen's
Colleges of Belfast, Cork and Galway, founded in 1845 with an
undenominational charter. The Irish Catholic hierarchy was so
suspicious of these institutions that it warned Catholics against
attending them, and kept up an unremitting campaign for the
establishment of a university acceptable to Catholics. Finally, in
1908, the British government accepted this demand, and established a university—the National University of Ireland—which,
while formally undenominational, was nevertheless designed to
ensure a considerable influence for the Catholic hierarchy in its
governing bodies, and which, through its constituent colleges in
Dublin, Cork and Galway, would provide enough places to
cater for something approaching the whole of the potential
Catholic university population.[41]

This is not the place to explain how it was that the Irish
hierarchy first asserted, and then made good, these extensive
claims in the field of education. Suffice it to say that they were the

41. For an introduction to this question see T. W. Moody, 'The Irish university
question of the nineteenth century', *History* (XLIII, no. 148) June 1958, 90–109.

fruits of a long struggle, waged with remarkable perseverance against great opposition.[42] What had been won with such labour was not going to be lightly cast aside, and, already before independence, the hierarchy had developed a tradition of keen sensitivity to any suggestion that the degree of clerical control in education might be reduced. In 1904, following a proposal for the setting up of a Department of Education in Ireland, a joint statement from the bishops protested against any change in managerial control of primary schools.[43] In 1907, a government proposal for the setting up of an Irish Council, which would have control over, among other things, education, was abandoned, partly because of the hierarchy's hostility to any reduction in its control over education.[44] In 1919, an education bill which proposed greatly increased grants for Irish education—but also tighter government control—was abandoned largely because of the opposition of the Irish hierarchy.[45]

Thus when native governments took over in Ireland they well knew that, of all subjects, the one on which the Catholic hierarchy was most sensitive was education. It does not follow that they disagreed with these claims, and in fact successive Ministers for Education can be quoted as defending the merits of the *status quo*. Professor John Marcus O'Sullivan, Minister for Education from 1925 to 1932, defended the limitations on his own powers:

A system has grown up here . . . that in some respects at least did satisfy some of our deepest and most lasting aspirations. It may not be as logically rounded off as some of the systems we find in other portions of Europe, but it was possibly none the less healthy on that account. I am not complaining that we have not control of the monopoly of education . . . quite the contrary. Personally, I strongly believe that if anything of the kind were possible, it would be wrong that we should aim at it.[46]

42. The story, so far as primary education is concerned, is worked out in D. Akenson, *The Irish Education Experiment.* No comparable study exists for secondary education, but an outline of developments can be found in N. Atkinson, *Irish Education.*
43. *Irish Catholic Directory, 1905,* 458–61 (under date 22 June 1904).
44. F. S. L. Lyons, *John Dillon,* 297.
45. *Irish Catholic Directory, 1921,* 498 (under date 9 Dec. 1919).
46. Cited in J. Mescal, *Religion in the Irish System of Education,* 56.

His successor and political opponent, Mr Thomas Derrig, said of the managerial system: 'In my opinion, it is of great value to the community.'[47] A subsequent Fianna Fail Minister for Education, Mr Sean Moylan, stressed that, though the State met nearly all expenditure on education, it made no claim to ownership of schools.[48] The Minister for Education in the inter-party governments of 1948–51 and 1954–7, General Mulcahy, made it clear that he accepted the Catholic viewpoint on education:

The State approach to education in the Irish Republic is one which unreservedly accepts the supernatural conception of man's nature and destiny. It accepts that the proper subject of education is man whole and entire, soul united to body in unity of nature, with all his faculties natural and supernatural, such as right reason and revelation show him to be. It accepts that the foundation and crown of youth's entire training is religion. It is its desire that its teachers, syllabuses and text books in every branch be informed by the spirit underlying this concept of education, and it is determined to see that such facilities as ecclesiastical authorities consider proper shall be provided in the school for the carrying on of the work of religious education.[49]

However, even if any of these ministers had disagreed with the Church's claims in education, they would have realised that to express such doubts in public would have brought a storm about their heads. Since independence, as before, the bishops have reacted sharply to any hint that clerical control of education might be reduced. An example can be found in the hierarchy's response to the campaign, waged intermittently since 1926 by the Irish National Teachers' Organisation, to secure the transfer to local authorities of responsibility for the cleaning, heating and sanitation of primary schools. These matters had been since British times the responsibility of the clerical manager of each school, and it was the contention of the I.N.T.O. that under this system the condition of the schools often left much to be desired. In proposing that local authorities take over these burdens, the I.N.T.O. insisted that it had no desire to undermine

47. *Ibid.*, 100.
48. *Irish Catholic Directory, 1954*, 737 (4 Nov. 1953).
49. J. Mescal, *op. cit.*, 136–7.

the managerial system, and indeed argued that the poor condition of the schools was that system's greatest danger. But the bishops looked without favour on its proposals, and eventually, in 1952, a letter from the hierarchy formally requested the I.N.T.O. to desist from its campaign.[50] If so mild a proposal could meet with such firm opposition, it is not surprising that more extensive reforms in the educational system were not even broached.

In the last few years there have been rapid changes in the climate of Irish opinion, and since 1963 a number of important reforms in the educational system have been put through with the acquiescence and even approval of the Catholic hierarchy.[51] But this change is of very recent date. Over most of the period since independence, the remarkable feature of educational policy in Ireland has been the reluctance of the State to touch on the entrenched positions of the Church. This is not because the Church's claims have been moderate: on the contrary, it has carved out for itself a more extensive control over education in Ireland than in any other country in the world. It is because the Church has insisted on its claims with such force that the State has been extremely cautious in entering its domain. This has given Church-State relations in Ireland an unusual characteristic. Taking the world as a whole, one can say that education has caused more trouble between Church and State than any other single topic. In self-governing Ireland, it has only rarely been an issue.

5. *The authoritarian strain in Irish culture.*

One last characteristic of Irish catholicism remains to be mentioned. It is not a specifically religious characteristic, but rather a feature of Irish life in general whose effects spill over into the religious sphere. It is what may be called the authoritarian strain in Irish culture.

Ireland is a curious mixture. On the one hand, it is a genuinely democratic State, with a government answerable to a freely elected parliament, a competitive party system, freedom of speech and of association and an independent judiciary. And

50. T. J. O'Connell, *History of the I.N.T.O.*, 437–40.
51. See below, pp. 339–43.

B

yet on the other hand, an autocratic style in the use of authority has been noted by commentators on many different aspects of Irish life. Mr Donald Connery, the American writer already quoted, has observed it in Irish politics: 'It is striking how much authority is confined to the few men who constitute the power *élite* and how autocratically they wield it. The government ministers have such power and so little effective opposition that they tend to become arrogant.'[52] The anthropologists Arensberg and Kimball have noted it in father-son relationships among Irish small farmers. After remarking that farmers' sons may still be called 'boy' at the age of forty-five or fifty, they continue: 'It goes without saying that the father exercises his control over the whole activity of the "boy". It is by no means confined to their work together. Indeed, the father is the court of last resort, which dispenses punishment for deviations from the norm of conduct in all spheres. Within the bounds of custom and law he has full power to exercise discipline.'[53] An educationalist, Mr Charles McCarthy, considers that a similar phenomenon has existed, at least in the past, among primary school teachers. They were trained, he says, in 'a residential training college which was conducted on remarkably authoritarian lines . . . . The special stamp which is so noticeable in Irish culture was largely the work of these very able men and women who were prepared for teaching in this strict and authoritarian way'.[54] The same authoritarian cast of mind perhaps lies behind another phenomenon which we shall note in subsequent chapters—the impatience with which civil servants tend to treat the interest groups in their sphere of competence.[55] Such autocratic methods, whether in the family, in government or in the school, do from time to time arouse resentment among those to whom they are applied, but on the whole the remarkable thing about Irish life has been how far people have acquiesced in being thus treated

52. D. Connery, *The Irish*, 109.
53. C. M. Arensberg and S. T. Kimball, *Family and Community in Ireland*, 55.
54. C. McCarthy, *The Distasteful Challenge*, 109–10. Perhaps to describe Mr McCarthy as an educationalist does not do justice to his manifold talents. As General Secretary of the Vocational Teachers Association he is also a prominent figure in the trade union world, and a member of the National Industrial Economic Council.
55. See below, pp. 97–8, 129, 336.

by those who have authority over them. As the former *Irish Times* journalist, Mr Brian Inglis, has put it: 'The Irish are not, contrary to common opinion, a belligerent race. They are not "agin the government"; they are certainly more amenable to authority than the British.'[56]

Even to attempt an explanation for this trait would take us far away from our main theme. Whether it is rooted in the deeply-stratified structure of Gaelic society, as a historian might argue, or whether it is a consequence of the roles played by different groups within the small-farmer society from which so many Irishmen spring, as an anthropologist might contend,[57] is a debate into which we need not enter here. It is also important to note that this characteristic, like so many others in Irish life, is rapidly disappearing.[58] But it has certainly been important in the past. It may help, for instance, to explain the tradition of public deference to the clergy already mentioned in this chapter, and the acquiescence by public opinion in clerical control of education. If readers, including Catholic readers, from other cultures are sometimes surprised at the degree of compliance which subsequent chapters will show the Irish hierarchy to have secured, they will find it easier to understand if they remember that deference to authority has been a feature not just of Irish ecclesiastical life, but of Irish life in general.

56. B. Inglis, *West Briton,* 196.
57. 'The relations between young and old in the community, like those between parent and child within the family, are understandable in the light of the roles of the broad age groups.': C. M. Arensberg, *The Irish Countryman,* 121.
58. This is stressed by C. McCarthy, *op. cit.,* 109. One sociologist who did his fieldwork about 1950 already noted a marked change in family life from the more authoritarian pattern of the previous generation: A. Humphreys, *New Dubliners,* 121, 146.

CHAPTER II

THE CATHOLIC MORAL CODE BECOMES ENSHRINED IN THE LAW OF THE STATE, 1923-37

Irish bishops, in the years after the Civil War, appear to have been deeply pessimistic about the state of their country. Despite occasional tributes to the continuing piety of their people, the stress in their public statements is on the falling off of standards. The Archbishop of Armagh, Cardinal Logue, warned clerical students at Maynooth in 1924 that they would 'have to meet a divided people . . . who had lost much of their reverence for religion and the Church'.[1] Bishop Hoare of Ardagh spoke in the same year of 'the very low level of degeneracy' reached in Ireland.[2] Bishop Foley of Kildare and Leighlin said in 1925 that it would be uphill work to restore the standards that had been lost.[3] Archbishop Byrne of Dublin, in his lenten pastoral of 1926, wrote of the lower moral fibre of the people.[4] Many pastoral letters deplored the growing craze for pleasure, and the slackening of parental control.

The bishops found cause for dismay in many different areas. Their pastorals abound in denunciations of intemperance, gambling, perjury, crimes of violence and many other evils. But there was one sphere in particular which aroused their alarm. By far the most prominent topic in their published statements was the decline in sexual morality. The bishops evidently believed that the traditional standards of their people were under unprecedented pressure. New mass media—the cinema, the radio, and above all the English sensational newspapers, whose circula-

---

1. *Irish Catholic Directory, 1925,* 582 (under date 24 June 1924).
2. *Ibid.,* 589 (3 Aug. 1924).
3. *Ibid., 1926,* 566 (29 March 1925).
4. *Ibid., 1927,* 568 (14 Feb. 1926).

tion in Ireland appears to have increased during the twenties[5]—
were bringing unfamiliar values to the attention of their flocks.
Bishop McNamee of Ardagh was reported as drawing attention
to this in 1927: 'In many respects the danger to our national
characteristics was greater now than ever. The foreign press was
more widely diffused amongst us; the cinema brought very
vivid representations of foreign manners and customs; and the
radio would bring foreign music and the propagation of foreign
ideals.'[6] Archbishop Gilmartin of Tuam drew a similar picture
about the same date:

In recent years the dangerous occasions of sin had been multiplied. The
old Irish dances had been discarded for foreign importations which,
according to all accounts, lent themselves not so much to rhythm as
to low sensuality. The actual hours of sleep had been turned into hours
of debasing pleasure. Company-keeping under the stars of night had
succeeded in too many places to the good old Irish custom of visiting,
chatting and story-telling from one house to another, with the Rosary
to bring all home in due time. Parental control had been relaxed, and
fashions bordering on indecency had become a commonplace; while
bad books, papers and pictures were finding their way into remote
country places.[7]

Of all the new fashions in post-war Ireland, the one which the
bishops seem to have feared most was the mania for dancing
which spread across the country, and which led to a rash of
small dance-halls, unhygienic, ill-supervised, and offering dances
which went on all through the night. It was not easy for the
bishops, when addressing audiences composed of both sexes
and all ages, to say too bluntly what they feared, but it was
clear that what worried them was not the dances themselves so
much as what was likely to happen after them. In the words of
a joint statement on the dance-hall evil, issued by the hierarchy

5. I have seen no comparative figures of pre- and post-war circulations, but the
fact that English papers were increasing their Irish circulation seems to have been
generally accepted. See, e.g., R. S. Devane, S.J., 'Suggested tariff on imported
newspapers and magazines', *Studies* (XVI) Dec. 1927, 545, and 'Ireland: events in
the Free State', *Round Table* (XVIII) Mar. 1928, 379.
6. *Irish Catholic Directory, 1928,* 605 (29 Sept. 1927).
7. *Ibid.,* 557 (8 Dec. 1926).

in 1925: 'The surroundings of the dancing hall, withdrawal from the hall for intervals, and the back ways home have been the destruction of virtue in every part of Ireland.'[8]

There were, of course, variations in stress between one bishop's statement and another's. The Irish hierarchy included men of marked character and individuality, and, besides, problems varied between one diocese and the next. In the north-west, bishops were still concerned about the distilling of poteen, a local industry which both Church and State sought to root out because of the evils which followed from drinking this raw spirit.[9] In Dublin, Archbishop Byrne was concerned at the practice, which he detected among some of his flock, of sending their children to non-Catholic schools.[10] The most energetic episcopal statements used to come from Bishop O'Doherty of Galway. In one sermon, for instance, after deploring the craze for dancing, he advised fathers: 'If your girls do not obey you, if they are not in at the hours appointed, lay the lash upon their backs. That was the good old system, and that should be the system to-day.'[11] The lead given to the hierarchy by successive Archbishops of Armagh also varied in emphasis. Cardinal O'Donnell (Archbishop of Armagh 1924-7) was more flexible in temperament than either his predecessor Cardinal Logue (Archbishop 1887-1924) or his successor Cardinal MacRory (Archbishop 1929-45), and might, had he lived longer, have initiated a slightly more liberal policy. But the difference would only have been one of nuance. On the whole, the remarkable feature of the Irish bishops' views was how unanimous they were. They summed up their fears in the joint pastoral issued after the National Council of Maynooth in 1927:

8. *Irish Independent,* 7 Oct. 1925.

9. See K. H. Connell, *Irish Peasant Society,* 47 note 1, for measures taken by the Bishops of Derry, Raphoe and Clogher. For a denunciation by the Bishop of Galway see *Irish Independent,* 9 April 1924.

10. See, e.g., his pastorals of 1927 and 1930, quoted in *Catholic Bulletin* (XVII, 4) April 1927, 350-1 and *ibid.,* (XX, 4) April 1930, 358.

11. *Irish Catholic Directory, 1925,* 568 (8 April 1924). According to another report of this sermon, the bishop added: 'It had been suggested that the present day attraction for dancing was physical exercise. He did not believe it. If physical exercise were needed why did not the devotees of dancing go out and skip with a rope.' See *Irish Independent,* 9 April 1924.

These latter days have witnessed, among many other unpleasant sights, a loosening of the bonds of parental authority, a disregard for the discipline of the home, and a general impatience under restraint that drives youth to neglect the sacred claims of authority and follow its own capricious ways. . . . The evil one is ever setting his snares for unwary feet. At the moment, his traps for the innocent are chiefly the dance hall, the bad book, the indecent paper, the motion picture, the immodest fashion in female dress—all of which tend to destroy the virtues characteristic of our race.[12]

This preoccupation of the Irish Catholic Church with sexual morality was not a new phenomenon. Already before the first World War, some observers thought that it had gone too far. An anti-clerical Catholic, W. P. Ryan, wrote: 'After several changes theologians had fixed the number of deadly sins as seven; Irish parish priests in practice made courtship an eighth. For lovers to walk the roadside in rural Ireland when the average priest was abroad was a perilous adventure.'[13] Sir Horace Plunkett remarked that 'in many parishes the Sunday cyclist will observe the strange phenomenon of a normally light-hearted peasantry marshalled in male and female groups along the road, eyeing one another in dull wonderment across the forbidden space through the long summer day'.[14] A more hostile writer declared that 'the complete and awful chastity of the people' had reached the point that it had become 'a dreadful evil. . . . So searing has this iron morality become that even the pleasant and wholesome social intercourse of young people had been banned and killed'.[15] However that may be, the bishops seem to have felt, in the years before the war, that they had the situation in hand. Their pastoral letters in the years 1911–15 show some concern about immoral literature imported from England, and in 1911 a Vigilance Association was founded to campaign against this danger;[16] but on the whole their published statements during that period show that they regarded intemperance as the most serious pastoral problem, and dangers to sexual morality were

---

12. *Acta et Decreta Concilii Plenarii . . . 1927*, 141–2.
13. W. P. Ryan, *The Pope's Green Island*, 79.
14. Sir H. Plunkett, *Ireland in the New Century*, 116.
15. Filson Young, *Ireland at the Cross Roads*, 76–7.
16. *Irish Catholic Directory*, *1912*, 526, 532, 535–6 (22 Oct., 5, 12, 19 Nov. 1911).

mentioned with nothing like the frequency that was reached after the war.[17]

It was not only the bishops who showed an increased concern about sexual morality in the post-war period. They were supported by many of the priests, and, indeed, by many lay people as well. A priest, writing in a context that clearly refers .to this period, has remarked: 'Most of us can recall from our boyhood days the regular and vehement denunciations from pulpit and altar of the small dance-halls which were dotted so profusely about the country-side. Preachers both "ordinary" and "special" waxed eloquent about those "dens of iniquity, haunts of the devil and vestibules of hell." '[18] A priest working in America was struck on his visits to Ireland by 'the enormous emphasis upon the so-called danger of company keeping, the listing of it in the catechism as a danger to purity and as something to be confessed, and the thundering against it in pulpits'.[19] Almost every area of the country has its folklore about local puritans. In county Kerry, the playwright Bryan MacMahon has recalled the campaign of priests in the twenties and thirties against crossroads dancing: 'Wooden roadside platforms were set on fire by curates: surer still, the priests drove their motorcars backward and forward over the timber platforms; concertinas were sent flying into hill streams, and those who played music at dances were branded as outcasts.'[20] In Clones, county Monaghan, the parish priest brought fame to his town by insisting that men sit on one side of the aisle, and women on the other, in the local cinema.[21] In Cork city, Sean O'Faolain recalls that the worst censors were to be found among the laity:

Cork's too-good people have, as a matter of local history, almost ruined their theatre. They recently formed themselves into a Society of St Jude and exercised an unofficial censorship over plays. As a result

17. The best way of getting a general view of the bishops' pastorals and other published statements is to go through the 'Record of Irish ecclesiastical events' published in each issue of the *Irish Catholic Directory*. I have examined these from the issue of 1905 (covering the events of 1904) onwards.
18. Rev. Michael I. Mooney, 'The parish hall', *The Furrow* (IV, I) Jan. 1953, 3.
19. Quoted in John A. O'Brien (ed.), *The Vanishing Irish*, 231.
20. *Ibid.*, 212.
21. T. P. Coogan, *Ireland since the Rising*, 202.

of the closing down of the theatre when it ventured to show some play that displeased these good folk, English touring companies were for years shy of visiting Cork. But there is a long tradition behind that sort of pussyfoot mentality. When I was a boy and Maud Allan came to Cork to do classic dances, pious young men stood at the theatre door and took down the names of every prominent Catholic citizen who dared attend her display. . . . I lay it to his eternal credit that the Bishop (with the tough commonsense and humanity of his country birth), has consistently frowned on these Manichaeans.[22]

The pressure appears to have been mounting through the nineteen-twenties. In some areas it may not have reached its peak until the nineteen-thirties or even the forties. The American anthropologists Arensberg and Kimball, who did their field-work in county Clare in 1932–4, reported: 'Certain observers profess to find the puritanical outlook on sexual matters on the increase in the countryside. The country people themselves purport to see a change in their outlook.'[23] A contributor to *The Bell* in 1941 asked the question: 'Why . . . does the habit of evading sex not only continue in Ireland but get worse and more aggressive?'[24] Another writer in the same periodical, a few years later, described the evolution in his own village in terms racy enough to be worth extended quotation:

During 1929 to '32 there were at least twice as many boys and girls between the ages of 19 to 25 years in this village as there are to-day. There was less employment and less money but we had plenty of enjoyment that cost us very little. . . . We had a choice of four or five kitchen dances every Sunday night within a two mile radius of home. One in every four was able to play some instrument, one in ten was able to sing—at least we thought we were. The rest were able to dance, some of them good step dancers. We had great fun and ourselves making it. . . .

In 1931 we got a new P.P. He condemned dancing in every form, even the kitchen dances were sinful and against the wishes of our Church. Boys and girls should not be on the road after dark. The C.C. was sent out to patrol the roads and anybody found or seen on the

22. S. O'Faolain, *An Irish Journey*, 83, 86.
23. C. M. Arensberg and S. T. Kimball, *Family and Community in Ireland*, 199.
24. C. B. Murphy, 'Sex, censorship, and the Church', *The Bell* (II, 6) Sept. 1941, 73.

roads had to give their names. The people who allowed boys and girls into their home to dance were committing a grave mortal sin. The people who had a dance after a 'Station' were putting God out of their homes and bringing in the devil. Where there was dancing there could be no grace. Dancing was the devil's work. And so was company keeping. Woe to that father or that mother who allowed their daughter to go out at night. Woe to that boy and that girl who met and went to that lonely wood or that lonely place. They were damning their souls. Perhaps the change seemed more sudden in our parish as our old parish priest, may he rest in peace, had never interfered with the amusement of young people, but . . . the change came in every parish. . . .

One night in 1947 I drove a party to and attended a dance in Caighwell in St. Michael's Hall. . . . On the right just inside the door was a civic guard in uniform. On the left was the C.C. Along the wall on the left side was a row of girls sitting up straight with their hands crossed on their knees. There wasn't even a genuine smile on any of them. On the right was a row of men some sitting and the ones who weren't were well back off the beautiful maple well-polished floor. On the walls on both sides were large official-looking notices: Don't Throw Cigarette Ends or Lighted Matches on the Floor. Don't Leave Hats, Caps, etc., on Seats. Don't Stand on the Seats. Respectable Girls Don't Sit on Gentlemen's Knees, etc.

. . . I took a chance and picked what I thought was a fairly lively partner. As far as dancing went we got on all right, but I couldn't even get her to smile. I might as well be dancing with the broom. Most of the dancers went round the hall one way and that meant that she was facing the P.P. going one way and facing the C.C. going the other, so I tried going across in the middle. It actually worked. When she found that she couldn't be seen from the stage or the door she began to laugh and chat just as if she was at a real dance. I heard afterwards that if a girl appeared to enjoy herself at any of these dances she could be accused of having taken drink. On the way home some of my passengers asked me if I had enjoyed the dance. I don't remember all I said, but I told them we had more fun and freedom at the Corpus Christi Procession in Esker.[25]

What caused this preoccupation with the safeguarding of sexual morality in post-independence Ireland? First, it should

---

25. John Kavanagh, 'Emigration: a letter', *The Bell* (XIX, 10) Nov. 1954, 54–8. Some readers may like to know that P.P. stands for Parish Priest and C.C. for Catholic Curate.

be pointed out that there were objective signs of a decline in moral standards. An indicator is the illegitimate birth rate, which showed an upward trend during the first quarter-century of independence. In 1921-3, illegitimate births totalled 2·6 per cent of all births in the twenty-six counties.[26] From there the figure crept upward till it reached a momentary peak of 3·5 per cent in 1933-4. There was a temporary drop back to 3·2 per cent in 1939, and then the figure rose again to the record, for Ireland, of 3·9 per cent in the years 1944-46.[27] (It subsequently dropped to the remarkably low figure of 1·6 per cent in the years 1958-61, only to rise again to 2·6 per cent in 1969, the last year for which, at the time of writing, figures are available.)[28]

All the same, these figures hardly prove an epidemic of immorality in modern Ireland. Even supposing that many Irish girls go to England to have illegitimate babies, the figures remain low by international standards.[29] Some observers, therefore, have suspected that the Irish Catholic preoccupation with sexual morality is subjective rather than objective in origin: that it is motivated not by evidence that this is a serious problem in Ireland, but by some kind of inner necessity that obliges Irish people to harp on the subject.

A whole crop exists of explanations along these lines for the puritan streak in Irish catholicism. Some writers attribute it to the Celtic temperament.[30] This is too vague an explanation to be of much help: in particular, it does nothing at all to explain why this characteristic of Irish Catholics should have been at its most intense in the twenties, thirties and forties of the present century. Other writers refer to the 'Jansenist' or 'Augustinian'

26. *Annual Report of the Registrar-General for Saorstat Eireann, 1924,* ix.
27. Figures from *Annual Reports of the Registrar-General.*
28. The *Annual Reports of the Registrar-General* are replaced after 1952 by annual *Reports on Vital Statistics.* These, however, ceased to give the illegitimate birth rate after 1954. Thereafter, the illegitimate birth rate can be found in the *Quarterly Returns of Marriages, Births, and Deaths,* published by the Department of Health. The return for the fourth quarter of each year includes an annual summary.
29. K. H. Connell, *Irish Peasant Society,* 119; *Reports of the Commission on Emigration and other Population Problems,* 101.
30. e.g. A. Ussher, *The Face and Mind of Ireland,* 91; John A. O'Brien (ed.), *The Vanishing Irish,* 209.

strain in Irish catholicism.[31] But again the problem of timing arises: why should Ireland have been more 'Augustinian' at this period than before or since? The anthropologists Arensberg and Kimball have offered an explanation in terms of their own discipline. They argue that, at any rate in the small-farmer society which comprises a great part of Ireland, sexual role and social role are so closely linked that a woman who violates sexual norms brings about a ramifying series of difficulties for herself and her kin.[32] One can see that, in such a society, sexual immorality would invite exceptionally severe censure from public opinion, but the theory seems too mechanistic to fit all the facts. As the sociologist Father Alexander Humphreys has pointed out, there are other peasant societies with social structures similar to Ireland's, yet none of these other societies are so noted for an ascetic sexual morality.[33] The ideas and values of the people, as well as the structure of their society, must be brought into any complete explanation.

A recent attempt to harmonise economic factors and popular values in a single explanation has been made by Professor K. H. Connell.[34] Professor Connell points to the peculiar demographic features of the Irish countryside: the high average age of marriage, the large proportion who never marry at all. The basic causes of this, he stresses, are economic. The Irish farmer learnt by bitter experience in the nineteenth century the perils of subdivision. He therefore passes on his farm intact to one of his sons. But this means that there will be no holdings for his other sons, who, unless they emigrate, will be forced therefore to remain unmarried. Professor Connell argues that the role of religion has been to reconcile the Irish peasantry to this fate. His article has aroused controversy, but it has one merit over other explanations: it does fit the chronology. For the demographic peculiarities to which he refers were growing more marked in Ireland until quite recently. The average age of marriage in Ireland, in

31. e.g. M. Sheehy, *Is Ireland Dying?*, 18, 37; A. Humphreys, S.J., *New Dubliners*, 25–6.

32. C. M. Arensberg and S. T. Kimball, *Family and Community in Ireland*, chapter XI.

33. A. Humphreys, *op. cit.*, 26 note.

34. 'Catholicism and marriage in the century after the famine', in K. H. Connell, *Irish Peasant Society*, 113–61.

so far as it can be deduced from the census returns, appears to have reached its peak about the time of the census of 1936.[35] The proportion of men never marrying at all may have reached its maximum later still. The percentage of men still unmarried in the age group 55–64, for instance, reached its highest level— 30·0 per cent—in the census of 1946. All through the twenties and thirties, then, and into the forties, the proportion of Irishmen, at least in the countryside, who were doomed by circumstances to perpetual celibacy was on the increase. This presented a real pastoral problem, and it would have been surprising if there had not been some reaction from the Church.

One weakness of all the explanations so far examined, however, is that they proceed on the assumption that Ireland was unique. This assumption requires at least to be verified. It is not easy to find comparative material from other countries, because the evolution of national attitudes to moral questions is not a subject to which historians have devoted much attention. But there is evidence to suggest that the erosion of traditional standards in the years after the 1914–18 war caused anxiety in many different countries. Distrust of the dance-hall craze, for instance, was not confined to Ireland, and action against these halls was reported from territories so diverse as Italy, Turkey, Hungary, Cuba and the German State of Thuringia.[36] The increasing traffic in obscene literature aroused sufficient concern for an international conference on the subject to be held at Geneva in 1923, attended by the representatives of thirty-five states.[37] A recent study of Dutch catholicism in the period 1925–35 reveals a preoccupation with sexual morality which in some ways parallels that of Ireland.[38] It may indeed be true that a sense of the vulnerability of traditional values was particularly strong among Irish Catholics, for they were, as a community, unusually exposed to external cultural influences. Unlike the various nationalities of continental Europe they had, on the whole, no language of their own to insulate them from such influences. Apart from a few Irish-

---

35. A. Humphreys, *op. cit.,* 69.
36. *Irish Weekly Independent,* 8 Jan. 1927; R. S. Devane, S.J., 'The dance-hall', *Irish Ecclesiastical Record* (5th series, XXXVII) Feb. 1931, 190.
37. M. Adams, *Censorship,* 23–4.
38. M. van der Plas, *Uit het Rijke Roomsche Leven,* esp. chapters 1 and 8.

speaking communities along the western seaboard, they were simply a fragment of the vast English-speaking language group, exposed to the shoddiest products of Hollywood or Fleet Street. But even so, there appears to have been a difference only of degree, not kind, between the anxieties expressed in Ireland and those found in many other countries. If a full survey were undertaken, it might appear that the Irish Catholic preoccupation with sexual morality in the twenties, thirties and forties of this century was only an extreme example of a trend to be found among the more traditionally-minded people all over the world.

So much for the preoccupations of the Church during these years: now for the response of the State. The governing party in Ireland down to 1932 was Cumann na nGaedheal, under the leadership of William T. Cosgrave. Mr Cosgrave and his colleagues came from that section of Sinn Fein which had accepted the treaty with Great Britain of December 1921. There was no reason why such a government should be specially deferential to the Church. Several of its members had belonged to the Irish Republican Brotherhood, which the Church had repeatedly denounced. It is true that the hierarchy had condemned their opponents during the Civil War, but this was an inevitable result of the bishops' views on where legitimate authority lay in Ireland, and it has never been suggested that it was the result of any sort of bargain between the government and the bishops. Indeed a cynic might argue that the bishops' support of the government during the Civil War actually made the government more independent of the Church, because it meant that the hierarchy had deprived itself of room for manoeuvre—it could no longer transfer its support to the other side. Several early actions of the government, indeed, suggested a willingness to reduce ecclesiastical influence. The last British home rule bill for Ireland, in 1920, had provided that the Senate of an Irish Parliament should include four Catholic bishops, as well as two Church of Ireland ones; but the new government appointed no clerics to the Senate of the Irish Free State.[39] Educational changes, though not extensive, had the effect, so far as they went,

39. W. Alison Phillips, *The Revolution in Ireland*, 308.

of tightening State control over the school system in which the Churches were so involved. The semi-independent boards which had hitherto controlled elementary and intermediate education, and on which the clergy had been well represented, were abolished, and replaced by a government department.[40] A change in the financial regulations governing secondary schools obliged schools run by religious orders to employ a proportion of lay staff.[41] The degree to which Church influence appeared to be weakened in the infant Irish Free State was noted, with pleased surprise, by several Unionist commentators.[42]

It is true that by the late twenties, in the opinion of some observers, there was a revival of this influence. Dr Conor Cruise O'Brien has written that 'the specific influence of the Catholic Church in politics was growing more palpable again', and Mr Sean O'Faolain has described these years, more bitterly, as 'a time when the Catholic Church was felt, feared and courted on all sides as the dominant power'.[43] It would not be surprising if there were some truth in this view. With the end of the Civil War, and the adoption of constitutional politics by most of the defeated Republicans, it became possible for the hierarchy to take an attitude of neutrality between the two main parties in the State, and the government could no longer count so confidently on the bishops' good will. And as the decade went on, it needed support increasingly from whatever quarter it came. Cumann na nGaedheal never succeeded in winning an absolute majority of seats in any general election. Up to 1927 this did not greatly matter, because the principal opposition group refused to enter the Dail, and so the government was left to face only a small Labour party, one or two other small and transient groups, and a few independents. But in 1927 most of the Republicans entered the Dail, and the government's position thereafter was precarious. Catholic priests were prominent among the

40. D. Gwynn, *The Irish Free State 1922–1927*, 386.
41. *Ibid.*
42. W. Alison Phillips, *op. cit.*, 308; *ibid.*, 326, quoting *Quarterly Review*, Oct. 1923; 'The Irish Free State: an ex-Unionist view', *Round Table* (XVI) Dec. 1925, 42.
43. C. C. O'Brien, 'Passion and cunning: an essay on the politics of W. B. Yeats', in A. N. Jeffares and K. G. W. Cross (eds.), *In Excited Reverie*, 249; S. O'Faolain, *Vive Moi!*, 264.

supporters of Cumann na nGaedheal,[44] and the government could not afford to do anything which might dampen their enthusiasm.

However, if the government proved on the whole willing to listen to the Church, there is no need to explain this as simply due to political necessity. Ministers were products of the same culture as the bishops, and shared the same values. There was only one Protestant in the government, Ernest Blythe, and his austere Ulster outlook seems to have fitted in well enough with the Catholic puritanism of his colleagues. All the other members of the government were Catholics—several of them, including Cosgrave himself, known as fervent Catholics—and they were probably just as ready as any bishop to see that traditional standards were maintained. Certainly there is no sign of resentment or constraint in their handling of topics where both Church and State had an interest.

From its early days, the government proved willing to use the power of the State to protect Catholic moral values. It would probably be fair to take as examples the Censorship of Films Act 1923, which established a film censor with power to cut or refuse a licence to films which, in his opinion, were 'subversive of public morality'[45]; the Intoxicating Liquor Act 1924 which reduced the hours of opening for public houses; and the Intoxicating Liquor Act 1927 which made provision for reducing the excessive number of licensed premises in Ireland. A particularly clear example is supplied by the government's attitude to divorce. At the time the Irish Free State was established, no divorce courts existed in Ireland, and an Irish resident wishing to obtain a divorce had to do so by way of a private bill in Parliament at Westminster. With the establishment of the new State, jurisdiction in this matter passed to the Irish Parliament, and three private divorce bills were actually presented. Mr Cosgrave's government reacted to this in the sharpest manner: it carried a motion in the Dail requiring standing orders to be amended so as to make it impossible for such bills in future even to be introduced.[46] In his speech introducing this motion, Mr Cosgrave

44. W. Moss, *Political Parties in the Irish Free State*, 136, 170.
45. Censorship of Films Act 1923, s. 7 (2).
46. D. O'Sullivan, *The Irish Free State and its Senate*, 161–5.

made no bones about the fact that he was upholding the values of the Catholic majority:

I have no doubt but that I am right in saying that the majority of people of this country regard the bond of marriage as a sacramental bond which is incapable of being dissolved. I personally hold this view. I consider that the whole fabric of our social organisation is based upon the sanctity of the marriage bond and that anything that tends to weaken the binding efficacy of that bond to that extent strikes at the root of our social life.[47]

The government's most famous measure to safeguard traditional moral values was the Censorship of Publications Act 1929. This act did two main things. First, it provided for a Censorship of Publications Board of five persons, with power to prohibit the sale and distribution of any book which it considered 'in its general tendency indecent or obscene', and of any periodical which it considered to 'have usually or frequently been indecent or obscene'.[48] Secondly, it made the publishing, selling or distribution of literature advocating birth-control an offence.[49] The board provided for under the act was established in February 1930. It consisted of one Protestant, three Catholic laymen and one Catholic priest, with the priest as chairman.[50]

One other measure of the Cosgrave government might be mentioned here, because, although it was not concerned with a moral issue, it does illustrate the relationship of Church and State. This was the Vocational Education Act of 1930. This act provided for an expansion of what had hitherto been labelled technical education. Technical education was, as pointed out in the last chapter, the only part of the Irish educational system which was controlled by local authorities and not by religious denominations. This arrangement was continued by the new act. However, this does not mean that the measure was disapproved of by the hierarchy. Thirty years' experience of the operation of technical education had shown that, whatever the

47. *Dail Debates*, X, 158 (11 Feb. 1925).
48. Censorship of Publications Act 1929, ss. 3, 6, 7.
49. *Ibid.*, ss. 6, 7, 16.
50. M. Adams, *Censorship*, 64–5.

letter of the law might say, clerical leadership was in practice accepted here as in other educational fields. The committees of local authorities which administered technical education habitually co-opted clergy as members, and frequently elected a priest to be their chairman.[51] This custom has continued, and it is still common to find a priest as chairman of a Vocational Education Committee.[52] There was another safeguard also. This was not published at the time, but I have it on the authority of a subsequent Minister for Education that the then Minister for Education, Professor John Marcus O'Sullivan, gave the bishops a written assurance that the vocational education system would stick strictly to its authorised field, and would not be allowed to develop so as to impinge upon the field covered by the denominationally-run secondary schools.

It is hard to assess whether the wording and precise content of these measures was to any degree influenced by the hierarchy. The Cosgrave government's usual device, in an issue of the kind that would interest Church as well as State, was to set up a committee or hold a conference, at which all interests concerned, including of course the Catholic hierarchy, or Catholic societies approved by the hierarchy, could present their views. The government would wait for a consensus to emerge, and then legislate accordingly. The Intoxicating Liquor Act 1927 was based on the recommendation of a commission of enquiry into the licensing laws established in 1926.[53] The Vocational Education Act arose from the report of the Commission on Technical Education, published in 1927.[54] The Censorship of Publications

51. An examination of *Thom's Directory of Ireland, 1928* disclosed the name of the chairman for 59 of the technical instruction committees then operating in Ireland. Of these, 27 were priests, one (in Bray) was a Church of Ireland rector, and 31 were laymen.

52. The disappearance under the act of 1930 of many small urban technical instruction committees, which tended to elect laymen as chairmen, has actually increased the proportion of clergymen chairing such committees. An examination of *Thom's Directory of Ireland, 1958* disclosed the names of 27 chairmen of vocational education committees. Of these, five were laymen and 22 were priests.

53. *Dail Debates*, XVIII, 522 (16 Feb. 1927: speech of Mr Kevin O'Higgins introducing the bill).

54. *Ibid.*, XXXIV, 1735ff. (14 May 1930: speech of Professor J. M. O'Sullivan introducing the bill).

Act 1929 derived from the report of the Committee on Evil Literature published in 1927,[55] and, controversial though that measure was, it appears to have hit fairly accurately the centre of gravity of Irish opinion at that time, being criticised by some for going too far and by others for not going far enough.[56] The Intoxicating Liquor Act 1924 arose out of a conference of the interests affected. As the Minister for Justice, Mr Kevin O'Higgins, explained: 'On the 12th of last month a rather large conference was held, at which I brought together representatives of all the interests—temperance associations, of which there are four or five; representatives of the licensed trade throughout the country, and the city traders; representatives of clubs; representatives of hotels, theatres, and so on. . . . What I aimed at was to strike a reasonable mean between the conflicting views.'[57] The Censorship of Films Act 1923 did not arise from any formal enquiry or conference, but it did follow a visit to the minister from a deputation representing various bodies interested in moral welfare—'the Irish Vigilance Association, the Priests' Social Guild, the Catholic Church in Ireland, the Protestant Episcopalian Church in Ireland, the Presbyterian Church.'[58] Even the decision to prohibit the introduction of divorce bills did not come completely without preparation. It was preceded by a report from the Joint (i.e. Dail and Senate) Committee on Standing Orders, clarifying the issues.[59]

So much for the attitudes of Cumann na nGaedheal on matters of Church and State. Now what about their principal opponents? These were the Republicans, who had rejected the treaty with Great Britain of December 1921, who had been prepared to fight their fellow-countrymen in the Civil War of 1922–3 rather than accept it, but who had eventually been beaten by force of arms. From 1923 to 1927 the Republicans, while being prepared to fight elections, refused to enter the Free State parliament, which they looked on as a British-invented puppet

55. M. Adams, *op. cit.*, 39.
56. *Ibid.*, chapters 2 and 3.
57. *Dail Debates*, VII, 2711 (19 June 1924).
58. *Ibid.*, III, 751 (10 May 1923).
59. D. O'Sullivan, *The Irish Free State and its Senate*, 164

institution. But as the years went by the policy of abstention looked increasingly futile.[60] In 1926 the Republican movement split, some extremists sticking to the policy of abstention, but the majority, under Eamon de Valera, being now prepared to treat abstention or participation as a matter of expediency.[61] Mr de Valera's followers formed a new party, Fianna Fail, and in 1927 they entered the Dail. From then on, until they came to office in 1932, they provided the main parliamentary opposition.

The observer might have expected Fianna Fail to be a very anti-clerical party. It was formed from those who, during the Civil War, had been condemned by the hierarchy, and often refused the sacraments by the clergy. Undoubtedly the experience left bitter memories, and some Republicans remained estranged for years from the Catholic Church. But on the whole, the Irish capacity for opposing the clergy in politics while considering one's self a loyal son of the Church reasserted itself, and Fianna Fail proved just as ready as Cumann na nGaedheal to uphold, by law if necessary, the traditional values of the Catholic Church. Mr de Valera in particular was a devout Catholic of conservative religious views. One of his biographers has described his outlook at this time:

With his religion went a puritanical morality which made him indifferent to taunts for airing his views. In Leinster House [where Dail and Senate are located], for instance, a bar was connected with the members' dining-room, and he raised the question soon after entering the chamber as to whether the bar could be separated or else abolished altogether. He himself, it was said, neither drank nor smoked. . . . His strictures extended beyond the evils of drink to the evils of jazz, the evils of betting on the races, the dangers from indecent books.[62]

60. The fullest analysis of this evolution in Republican opinion is to be found in an unpublished thesis: P. Pyne, *The Third Sinn Fein Party, 1923–1926*, chapters 3 and 5. Mr Pyne has published a summary of his argument in two articles in *Economic and Social Review* (I, 1 and 2) 1969–70.

61. At the crucial conference of Republicans, in March 1926, a motion reaffirming the principle of abstention was carried against Mr de Valera by 223 votes to 218: M. Bromage, *De Valera and the March of a Nation*, 219. But the next general election showed that the great majority of Republican electors in the country followed Mr de Valera, for his supporters won 44 seats and the extreme Republicans only five.

62. M. Bromage, *op. cit.*, 228–9.

After that, it is no surprise to hear that Mr de Valera promised to facilitate the passage of the Censorship of Publications Bill.[63] The bill, it is true, received criticism from some members of Fianna Fail, but less than it suffered from some of the government's back-benchers.[64]

Indeed there are indications that, in the last few years of Cumann na nGaedheal rule, Fianna Fail was trying to build up an image of being the more truly Catholic party of the two. As one of its leading members, Mr Sean T. O'Kelly, put it in 1929: 'We of the Fianna Fail Party believe that we speak for the big body of Catholic opinion. I think I could say, without qualification of any kind, that we represent the big element of Catholicity.'[65] This might seem a desperate claim to establish on the part of people who had been under the ban of the Church only a few years before, but Fianna Fail had some evidence on its side. It could claim that its vote was largest in the most purely Catholic parts of the country—the four counties with the highest percentage of Catholics, Clare, Galway, Mayo and Kerry, were also the ones in which, at the two general elections of June and September 1927, Fianna Fail received the highest percentage of votes.[66] Another claim which Fianna Fail could make was that their opponents received the support of Freemasons. The Catholic Church forbids its members to join the Masonic Order, on the ground that it is a secret society, and so to accuse a group of Catholic politicians of receiving Masonic support is to imply that they are only dubiously Catholic. Now this might seem a far-fetched charge, but the continuing power of Freemasonry in Ireland caused considerable discussion in the nineteen-twenties. A Jesuit wrote a book on the subject.[67] Three Catholic periodicals —the *Catholic Bulletin,* the *Catholic Pictorial* (later the *Catholic Mind*), and the *Irish Rosary*—were able to keep alive largely on anti-Masonic propaganda. A Catholic society, the Knights of St Columbanus, was founded in 1922 to counter discrimination against Catholics by Freemasons and others, and soon came to

63. M. Adams, *Censorship,* 43.
64. *Ibid.,* 43 and notes.
65. *Dail Debates,* XXX, 821 (5 June 1929).
66. See maps in E. Rumpf, *Nationalismus und Sozialismus in Irland,* 67, 127, 128.
67. E. Cahill, S.J., *Freemasonry and the Anti-Christian Movement.*

be accused of organising discrimination itself.[68] It is possible that disappointment with the economic results of the Irish revolution caused this wave of anti-Masonic feeling: the twenty-six counties had achieved political freedom, but economic power still seemed to be where it had always been, in the hands of a small, mainly Protestant, well-to-do class, and the easiest way of explaining this was by attributing it to Masonic clannishness. However this may be, Fianna Fail speakers cashed in on the anti-Masonic feeling in Ireland. They argued that the government depended for its support on the Freemasons.[69] And indeed it is quite likely that most Freemasons favoured Cumann na nGaedheal. In general, Cumann na nGaedheal appealed to the propertied elements in the country,[70] and, as Freemasons are generally propertied, no doubt they tended to give Cumann na nGaedheal their support.

There were several occasions in the last years of the Cosgrave government when Fianna Fail spokesmen seized a chance to appear more zealously Catholic than their opponents. One such episode occurred in 1929, when the government announced that an exchange of diplomatic representatives had been arranged with the Vatican. It might not seem easy to appear more Catholic than the government on such a question, but there was one loophole in the government's position. The young Minister for External Affairs, Mr Patrick McGilligan, in his eagerness to complete the arrangements, had omitted to inform the Irish bishops, who, naturally, were none too pleased to learn such an item of news from the newspapers. Mr McGilligan freely concedes in interview that this was an error on his part, occasioned, not by any desire to snub the bishops, but by the fact that the government's sights were set on other things: the primary motive in setting up this and other diplomatic missions

68. The earliest criticisms that I have seen of the Knights of St Columbanus for obtaining jobs and business for their own members are to be found in the *Irish Statesman,* 29 Dec. 1928, and the *Star,* 19 Jan. 1929: both quoted in *Catholic Bulletin* (XIX, 2) Feb. 1929, 108–13.

69. For a charge of Masonic dictation in the Mayo library case, to be described below, see *Dail Debates,* XXXIX, 455 (17 June 1931). For charges of Masonic support for Cumann na nGaedheal candidates at by-elections, see *Irish Weekly Independent,* 15 June 1929, 31 May 1930.

70. W. Moss, *Political Parties in the Irish Free State,* 58, 68, 183.

was to assert the Irish Free State's right to be represented independently of Great Britain. However, the omission somehow became generally known, and Fianna Fail took advantage of it. Mr Sean T. O'Kelly, the Fianna Fail front-bench spokesman on external affairs, probed on the matter:

> I would like to know . . . whether those who are very intimately and seriously concerned in this matter, those whose views ought to be given very serious consideration in a matter of this kind, were consulted, for instance, the Primate of All Ireland or the Archbishop of Dublin. . . . I would be glad if the Minister would be kind enough to inform us whether these people were consulted and, if so, whether they are satisfied with the arrangement.[71]

Mr McGilligan was obliged to admit that he had had no approval from the hierarchy.[72] Mr O'Kelly had put himself in the position of appearing to show more concern for the rights of the bishops than did his opposite number in the government.

Another such episode occurred the following spring, when a prominent member of Fianna Fail, Mr Paddy Little, introduced a private member's bill to amend the law relating to legitimacy.[73] The measure itself was a sensible one: it provided that children born illegitimate should be legitimated if their parents subsequently married. It was also unimpeachably orthodox: as Mr Little pointed out, the proposal simply followed canon law.[74] The Minister for Justice, Mr Fitzgerald-Kenney, was, however, none too pleased at its introduction. As he explained: 'I have seen a deputation from the bench of Irish Bishops on this matter, and I undertook to prepare a Bill. The heads are ready and I was going to introduce it at the earliest opportunity, but on the last day of the last sitting Deputy Little forestalled me, and in consequence this Bill is here and not mine.'[75] In short, Fianna Fail had moved with more alacrity than Cumann na nGaedheal to meet the bishops' wishes, and it was the Fianna Fail measure which, after amendment, became the Legitimacy Act 1930.

The exchanges between government and opposition over the

71. *Dail Debates*, XXX, 820–1 (5 June 1929).   72. *Ibid.*, 877.
73. *Ibid.*, XXXIV, 241 (27 March 1930).
74. *Ibid.*, 242.   75. *Ibid.*, 254.

nunciature and the Legitimacy Bill are not important and indeed slightly farcical, but another question arose shortly afterwards in which Fianna Fail played the Catholic card and in which the points at issue were more serious. The episode was sparked off by the appointment of a Miss Letitia Dunbar-Harrison to be County Librarian of Mayo. Miss Dunbar-Harrison was a Protestant and a graduate of Trinity College. She owed her selection to a recently-established body, the Local Appointments Commission, which had been set up by the government in 1926 as part of a reform programme in local government. The L.A.C. took over from local authorities the task of making most appointments in the local government service, the intention being to eliminate jobbery and favouritism in this field. Though its choices were officially termed 'recommendations', local authorities were obliged by law to accept them.[76]

When the Mayo Library Committee met to give formal approval to her appointment, however, it refused to do so.[77] Those present at the meeting to consider her appointment consisted of a Catholic bishop, five Catholic priests, a Christian Brother, a Protestant rector, and four laymen.[78] This body decided, by ten votes to two, not to accept Miss Dunbar-Harrison, the only dissentients being the Protestant rector and one (probably Catholic) layman.[79] The argument against the new librarian was that her background and education unfitted her for the task of supervising the reading matter of a mainly Catholic community. In the words of the Dean of Tuam, Monsignor E. A. D'Alton:

We are not appointing a washerwoman or a mechanic, but an educated girl who ought to know what books to put into the hands of the Catholic boys and girls of this county. The views of Catholics and Protestants, especially of late years, on such subjects as birth control and divorce are at variance. At the Lambeth Conference we had an episcopal blessing pronounced on birth control, and one of the most

76. J. Collins, *Local Government,* 32, 64–5.
77. *Catholic Bulletin* (XXI, 1), Jan. 1931, 1–18.
78. *Ibid.,* 11.
79. The layman's name was Dr MacBride, and he was a graduate of the Royal University, which preceded the National University: this sounds like a Catholic background. *Ibid.,* 11.

distinguished clergymen in England is going in for trial marriages. Supposing there were books attacking these fundamental truths of Catholicity, is it safe to entrust a girl who is not a Catholic, and is not in sympathy with Catholic views, with their handling?[80]

The government reacted energetically to this defiance. It gave Mayo County Council a chance to repudiate the decision of its library committee, and, when it refused to do so, dissolved the county council.[81] A commissioner was appointed to administer the county, and he invested Miss Dunbar-Harrison with her post.[82] But a boycott of library services then started in Mayo: nearly all the library centres in the county closed down, and most of them sent their books back to the librarian.[83] Eventually the government was obliged to transfer Miss Dunbar-Harrison to another position,[84] and in the following year the incoming Fianna Fail government restored Mayo County Council to its functions.[85]

The attitude of Fianna Fail during this episode was interesting. As the Republican Party, the party which consciously looked to the Protestant patriot Wolfe Tone for its inspiration, it might have been expected to rally to the support of Miss Dunbar-Harrison, and to uphold the right of a Protestant to a position in the public service without any kind of religious test being applied. This was not what happened. When the matter was debated in the Dail, in June 1931,[86] a succession of Fianna Fail speakers rose to castigate the government. Mr de Valera personally defended the people of Mayo:

If it is a mere passive position of handing down books that are asked for, then the librarian has no particular duty for which religion should be regarded as a qualification, but if the librarian goes round to the homes of the people trying to interest them in books, sees the children in the schools and asks these children to bring home certain

80. *Ibid.*, 2.   81. *Irish Times*, 20, 29 and 31 Dec. 1930.
82. *Ibid.*, 7 Jan. 1931.
83. *Dail Debates*, XXXIX, 433–6 (17 June 1931: speech of Mr R. Walsh).
84. *Irish Times*, 7 Jan. 1932, reported that she would shortly take up duty at the Military Library, General Headquarters, Dublin.
85. *Department of Local Government and Public Health. Report, 1932–3*, 13.
86. *Dail Debates*, XXXIX, 418–552 (17 June 1931).

books, or asks what books their parents would like to read; if it is active work of a propagandist educational character—and I believe it to be such if it is to be of any value at all and worth the money spent on it—then I say the people of Mayo, in a county where, I think—I forget the figures—over 98 per cent. of the population is Catholic, are justified in insisting upon a Catholic librarian.[87]

Not content with that, Mr de Valera widened the issue, and asserted that a Protestant ought not to be appointed a dispensary doctor in a mainly Catholic area. 'The Catholic community', he said, 'does want to be assured that the doctors appointed locally to minister to their people, who will be at their sides at the most critical moment, at the time of death, shall be members of the same religious faith as themselves.'[88]

The defence offered by the government to these criticisms must have been a disappointment to believers in the principle of equal opportunity for people of different faiths. Neither of the ministers who spoke in the debate even mentioned the point that it might be the government's duty to ensure fair play for Protestants.[89] The Minister for Local Government, General Mulcahy, justified his dissolution of Mayo County Council on the narrow ground that the Council had broken the law and the law must be upheld.[90] On the religious issue he merely remarked: 'My view is that there are people in this country responsible for dictating to us what safeguards ought to be taken in the matter of religion, and that I do not regard either Mayo County Council or the Fianna Fail Party as the people who can tell us that.'[91] The 'people responsible for dictating to us what safeguards ought to be taken in the matter of religion' were clearly the Catholic hierarchy, so the minister's argument was in effect that, as the Catholic hierarchy had not objected, then Miss Dunbar-Harrison's appointment was all right. The implication is that, if the Catholic hierarchy *had* protested against the appointment of a Protestant librarian, the minister would have felt obliged to take heed.

87. *Ibid.*, 518.   88. *Ibid.*, 517.
    89. *Ibid.*, 491–501 (speech of Mr Cosgrave), 528–47 (speech of General Mulcahy).
90. *Ibid.*, 528–31.   91. *Ibid.*, 536.

It should in fairness be added that Mr de Valera, when he came to office, did not act on the doctrines which he had propounded in the Mayo library debate. Logically, his position entailed the establishment of parallel networks of libraries and dispensaries, one set for Catholics and the other for Protestants.[92] He did not attempt to set up anything so impracticable. Nor does it seem that the Local Appointments Commission has been frightened off giving posts to Protestants—such discrimination would in any case be a violation of guarantees to be found in both the 1922 and the 1937 constitutions. My enquiries confirm that Protestants have been appointed as county librarians and as dispensary doctors since 1931. The number of such appointments appears to be small, but they are sufficient to show that these careers are not closed to the religious minority. The importance of the Mayo library case, then, lies not in what was done but in what was said. It illustrates the Fianna Fail attitude to matters of Catholic interest. Despite the fact that they had been condemned by the hierarchy only a few years previously, members of Fianna Fail felt themselves just as well qualified to act as spokesmen for Catholic interests as were their political opponents.

This stance was maintained by Fianna Fail after it came to office in 1932. In its attitude to the Church it proved to be correct, almost deferential. It provided a State reception at the Eucharistic Congress of 1932.[93] It made a practice, when a new factory or a new housing estate was being opened, of asking the bishop of the diocese to bless it.[94] Some, at least, of its members were assiduous in attending Catholic functions. Mr de Valera and Mr Sean T. O'Kelly attended the centenary celebrations in Paris of the Society of St Vincent de Paul in 1933, and Mr de Valera went on to make a Holy Year pilgrimage to Rome.[95]

92. He acknowledged this: *ibid.*, 519.

93. *Irish Independent*, 22 June 1932.

94. e.g., the sites of new sugar factories at Tuam, Thurles and Mallow were blessed by the Archbishop of Tuam, the Archbishop of Cashel and the Coadjutor-Bishop of Cloyne respectively: see *Irish Catholic Directory, 1934,* 643 (24 and 25 Nov. 1933, for Tuam and Thurles), and *ibid., 1935,* 570 (2 Dec. 1933, for Mallow). New housing estates at Kilkenny and at Muine Bheag were blessed by the Bishops of Ossory and of Kildare and Leighlin respectively: *Irish Weekly Independent,* 7 Oct. 1933, 2 March 1935.

95. *Irish Independent*, 20 May 1933.

The Irish national pilgrimage to Lourdes in the same year was attended by a minister (Mr P. J. Ruttledge) and a parliamentary secretary (Mr P. J. Little).[96] The hierarchy, for its part, appeared ready to let bygones be bygones. The men in power, even if they had defied the hierarchy in 1922, were now the legitimate government of the country, and were entitled to be treated as such. Besides, embarrassment over past differences was diminished by the fact that the hierarchy which Fianna Fail faced now was not quite the same as had condemned the Republicans in 1922. Of the twenty-six members of the hierarchy at the time of the joint pastoral of October 1922, only fifteen were left by the time Fianna Fail came to office in 1932, and their number was diminishing all the time.

Indeed, some of the published statements of Mr de Valera and his colleagues imply that, to them, the only true Irishmen were Catholics. On taking office the new government sent a message of 'respectful homage and good wishes' to Pope Pius XI, and assured him of 'our intention to maintain with the Holy See that intimate and cordial relationship which has become the tradition of the Irish people'.[97] A few weeks later, at the beginning of the Eucharistic Congress in Dublin, Mr de Valera received the Papal Legate with a reference to 'our people, ever firm in their allegiance to our ancestral faith'.[98] In his St Patrick's Day broadcast to the United States in 1935, Mr de Valera said: 'Since the coming of St Patrick, fifteen hundred years ago, Ireland has been a Christian and a Catholic nation. All the ruthless attempts made down through the centuries to force her from this allegiance have not shaken her faith. She remains a Catholic nation.'[99] The same attitude can be detected, perhaps, in the preamble to the 1937 constitution: 'We, the people of Eire, humbly acknowledging all our obligations to our Divine Lord, Jesus Christ, Who sustained our fathers through centuries of trial . . .'. These are moving words, but one might ask: *whose* fathers were sustained through centuries of trial? The words fit the situation of Irish Catholics, whose ancestors endured the penal laws,

96. *Irish Catholic Directory, 1934,* 625 (10 Sept. 1933).
97. *Irish Independent,* 15 March 1932.
98. *Ibid.,* 22 June 1932.
99. *Catholic Bulletin* (XXV, 4) April 1935, 273.

but they might not be felt as appropriate by Irish Protestants. This tendency to equate 'Irish' and 'Catholic' seems to have been special to Fianna Fail, and particularly to Mr de Valera himself. It is not so evident in the speeches of Mr Cosgrave and his colleagues in the preceding government.

In legislation, Fianna Fail proved as willing as its predecessors to employ the power of the State in safeguarding Catholic moral standards. In the budget of 1933, a tax was placed on imported daily papers. Though the measure was justified simply as a revenue-raising device,[100] it was obviously welcome to those who believed that cheap English papers were corrupting the people, and it received the plaudits of Archbishop Harty of Cashel and Archbishop Gilmartin of Tuam.[101] Two years later, the government plugged one gap in the mounting wall of protective moral legislation which had hitherto been left un-filled. The censorship act of 1929 had made it illegal to advocate the use of contraceptives, but the actual sale and import of these articles had not yet been interfered with. The government remedied this by carrying the Criminal Law Amendment Act 1935, section 17 of which prohibited the sale and importation of contraceptives. In the same year the government dealt with another matter which aroused episcopal anxieties, by carrying the Public Dance Halls Act 1935. The bishops had at first tried to deal with the dance-hall problem by direct advice and in-struction to the faithful. In 1925 the hierarchy had issued a joint warning on the dance-hall evil, with an instruction that it was to be read to the faithful four times a year until further notice.[102] Some bishops went further: Bishop O'Doherty of Galway forbade his flock to attend dances on Saturday nights;[103] and even Cardinal O'Donnell of Armagh, who was by no means the most rigid member of the hierarchy in his general outlook, threatened excommunication if the evils connected with certain dance-halls in County Louth were not remedied.[104] But by the

---

100. *Dail Debates*, XLVII, 751 (10 May 1933: speech of Minister for Finance, Mr. S. MacEntee).
101. *Irish Weekly Independent*, 20 and 27 May 1933.
102. *Irish Independent*, 7 Oct. 1925.
103. *Irish Catholic Directory, 1926*, 561 (22 Feb. 1925).
104. *Ibid.*, 582 (16 Aug. 1925).

end of the nineteen-twenties, it seems, these measures were coming to be felt as inadequate. Bishop Morrisroe of Achonry, in his lenten pastoral of 1929, called for legislation on the dance-hall question, stating: 'Though not formally Catholic, our Government at the same time legislates for Catholics in the main, so that its laws, while not oppressive to any section, should take special account of the needs of the overwhelming portion of its subjects.'[105] The hierarchy may have approached the government about this time, for one clerical writer believes that the Public Dance Halls Act was introduced at the suggestion of 'some members of the hierarchy'.[106] The act provided that a licence from the local district court was necessary for all public dances, and laid down criteria which the District Justice was to employ in deciding whether to grant such a licence.[107] The act does not seem to have been a great success. One writer has complained that it stamped out informal dances in private houses, where the young people danced under the eyes of their elders, and diverted them to commercial dance halls where there was less supervision.[108] At the time, several bishops complained that there was no uniformity in applying the act between one District Justice and another,[109] and before long some of the bishops reverted to dealing with the matter by direct instruction to the faithful.[110] But, however inadequate the act may have been in practice, in intention it was undoubtedly one more attempt to enforce Catholic moral standards by legislation. It was one more measure in the line marked out by the censorship of books and films, the ban on the advocacy of birth-control and on the import of contraceptives.

The coping-stone of this development was reached in the constitution of 1937. The reasons for introducing a new con-

105. Quoted in R. S. Devane, S.J., 'The dance-hall', *Irish Ecclesiastical Record* (5th series, XXXVII) Feb. 1931, 173.
106. Rev. Michael I. Mooney, 'The parish hall', *The Furrow* (IV, 1) Jan. 1953, 3.
107. Public Dance Halls Act 1935, s. 2.
108. Rev. Michael I. Mooney, *op. cit.*, 4.
109. See, e.g., *Irish Weekly Independent*, 5 March 1938: pastorals of Archbishop Gilmartin of Tuam, Bishop Doorly of Elphin, Bishop Morrisroe of Achonry.
110. e.g., Bishop Finegan of Kilmore forbids Catholics to go to a dance after 11 p.m.: *Irish Weekly Independent*, 9 Nov. 1935; Bishop O'Brien of Kerry lays down regulations: *ibid.*, 29 Feb. 1936; Bishop Fogarty of Killaloe says 11 p.m. is the right time for dances to end: *ibid.*, 25 Feb. 1939.

stitution were, indeed, political and not religious. Mr de Valera had always opposed the 1922 constitution, the product of a forced bargain with the British, and he wanted to replace it with a document that would be indisputably Irish.[111] The main difference between the two constitutions was that, whereas that of 1922 made Ireland a dominion of the British Crown, and provided for the monarch as head of the state, the 1937 constitution made no reference to any outside links, and provided that the head of state be a president elected by the people. In many other ways the two documents were similar: each provided for an executive responsible to the legislature, for an independent judiciary, for a two-chamber parliament in which the upper house had a limited power of delaying bills, and for election by proportional representation.

There was, however, one other important difference between the constitutions, apart from the elimination of the Crown. This was in the treatment of fundamental rights. The 1922 constitution had been a typical liberal-democratic document which would have suited a country of any religious complexion. The only article on religion was one which briefly guaranteed religious freedom and equality.[112] The other personal rights guaranteed were what might be described as a stock list—freedom from arbitrary arrest, inviolability of the home, freedom of speech and of association, and the right to free elementary education.[113] The corresponding articles of the 1937 constitution, however, were obviously marked by Catholic thought. Not much is yet available to the public about the framing of the 1937 constitution—it was clearly very much Mr de Valera's own creation,[114] and we shall have to await the forthcoming second volume of his authorised biography for details of where he drew his inspiration—but some of his source-material can be deduced from the text. In particular, the influence of the *Code of Social Principles*, published at Malines in 1929 by a Catholic organisa-

111. M. Bromage, *De Valera and the March of a Nation,* 249.
112. Article 8: quoted above, p. 14.
113. Articles 6, 7, 9, 10.
114. M. Bromage, *op. cit.,* 249. Mr de Valera's pride of authorship was obvious in the Dail debates on the draft constitution. He received almost no assistance from his ministers in piloting the measure. It was he who explained its provisions, and decided whether to accept or reject modifications suggested by other deputies.

tion, the International Union of Social Studies, can be detected in several of the articles.[115]

Four articles in particular bear the stamp of Catholic teaching. Article 41, on the Family, starts with the sonorous declaration:

1. 1° The State recognises the Family as the natural primary and fundamental unit group of Society, and as a moral institution possessing inalienable and imprescriptible rights, antecedent and superior to all positive law.

2° The State, therefore, guarantees to protect the Family in its constitution and authority, as the necessary basis of social order and as indispensable to the welfare of the Nation and the State.

A little further on is drawn a practical consequence from this declaration:

3. 1° The State pledges itself to guard with special care the institution of Marriage, on which the Family is founded, and to protect it against attack.

2° No law shall be enacted providing for the grant of a dissolution of marriage.

In other words, Mr de Valera had set up a new hurdle against the introduction of divorce in Ireland. Henceforward, to legalise divorce in Ireland would mean not merely passing a statute, but passing an amendment to the constitution as well, which entails an appeal to the people in a referendum.

Article 42, on Education, succinctly summarises Catholic teaching on the prior rights of the parents:

1. The State acknowledges that the primary and natural educator of the child is the Family and guarantees to respect the inalienable right and duty of parents to provide, according to their means, for the religious and moral, intellectual, physical and social education of their children.

The limited nature of the State's rights in education is stressed. For instance:

115. V. Grogan, 'Towards the new constitution', in F. MacManus (ed.), *The Years of the Great Test,* 171.

3. 1° The State shall not oblige parents in violation of their conscience and lawful preference to send their children to schools established by the State, or to any particular type of school designated by the State.

2° The State shall, however, as guardian of the common good, require in view of actual conditions that the children receive a certain minimum education, moral, intellectual and social.

Article 43, on Private Property, echoes Catholic teaching on man's right to ownership:

1. 1° The State acknowledges that man, in virtue of his rational being, has the natural right, antecedent to positive law, to the private ownership of external goods.

A following section concedes that these rights ought 'to be regulated by the principles of social justice', and grants the State the right to delimit their exercise in accordance with 'the exigencies of the common good'.

It is in Article 44, on Religion, that Mr de Valera's ideas on Church-State relations are most fully expressed. The article maintains, in words close to those used by the 1922 constitution, the guarantees of equality and non-discrimination which that constitution had enshrined:

2. 1° Freedom of conscience and the free profession and practice of religion are, subject to public order and morality, guaranteed to every citizen.

2° The State guarantees not to endow any religion.

3° The State shall not impose any disabilities or make any discrimination on the ground of religious profession, belief or status.

4° Legislation providing State aid for schools shall not discriminate between schools under the management of different religious denominations, nor be such as to affect prejudicially the right of any child to attend a school receiving public money without attending religious instruction at that school.

5° Every religious denomination shall have the right to manage its own affairs, own, acquire and administer property, movable and immovable, and maintain institutions for religious or charitable purposes.

C

6° The property of any religious denomination or any educational institution shall not be diverted save for necessary works of public utility and on payment of compensation.

But this declaration is preceded by another section to which, in the 1922 constitution, there was no counterpart:

1. 1° The State acknowledges that the homage of public worship is due to Almighty God. It shall hold His Name in reverence, and shall respect and honour religion.

2° The State recognises the special position of the Holy Catholic Apostolic and Roman Church as the guardian of the Faith professed by the great majority of the citizens.

3° The State also recognises the Church of Ireland, the Presbyterian Church in Ireland, the Methodist Church in Ireland, the Religious Society of Friends in Ireland, as well as the Jewish Congregations and the other religious denominations existing in Ireland at the date of the coming into operation of this Constitution.

In short, Mr de Valera deliberately introduced into the constitution a distinction between belief-systems which had not been there before. It is true that the wording was imprecise, and that it was not easy to see what practical effect, if any, it might have. But Section 1.1° indicated that, as between religion and irreligion, the State was in some sense not neutral. Sections 1.2° and 1.3° indicated that, as between different forms of religion, it was in some sense not neutral either. While all denominations existing at the time of the coming into force of the constitution were accorded recognition, the Catholic Church was singled out from the others by being accorded a 'special position'.

It should in fairness be pointed out, before Mr de Valera is accused of introducing a sectarian constitution, that there were two points on which these articles did not measure up to what Catholic authorities might have desired. The first of these points arose in Article 41, on the Family. Though this article prohibited divorce, it did not in all respects bring the matrimonial law of the State into line with that of the Church. Cases sometimes arise in which a person is validly married in the eyes of the State but not in those of the Church, or vice versa. Marriage in a registry office, for instance, was legalised in British times and continues to be recognised by the Irish State; but in the eyes of the Church, a Catholic who marries in a registry office has contracted no true marriage. This means that, if he should subsequently leave the partner with whom he went through the marriage ceremony in the registry office, he is in the eyes of the Church entitled to marry another person in a Catholic church, and yet in the eyes of the State this second ceremony would be bigamy. Such cases have occurred.[116] Or again, the grounds for nullity recognised by civil and by canon law do not coincide, and a case has occurred in which a marriage declared void by the ecclesiastical courts has been upheld by the civil courts.[117] Suggestions have from time to time been made that the State ought to bring its law in line with the Church, at any rate for Catholics,[118] but this has never yet been done.

The other point on which Mr de Valera's provisions have sometimes been criticised for not being Catholic enough is to be found in Article 44. The phrase recognising 'the special position' of the Catholic Church is extremely vague. The authorities still argue over whether it has any juridical effect.[119] Mr de Valera indicated, when the constitution was passing through the Dail, that his purpose in this section was simply to recognise a sociological fact. 'There are', he said, '93 per cent of the people in this part of Ireland and 75 per cent of the people of Ireland as a whole who belong to the Catholic Church, who believe in its teachings, and whose whole philosophy of life is the philosophy that comes from its teachings. . . . If we are going to have a democratic State, if we are going to be ruled by the representatives of the people, it is clear their whole philosophy of life is going to affect that, and

116. e.g. the Hunt case: *Irish Times*, 12 Dec. 1945; another case in October 1946 mentioned in Rev. W. Conway, 'Marriage in Ireland: Church and State', *Irish Ecclesiastical Record* (5th series, LXVIII) Dec. 1946, 361; and a case in 1964 mentioned in D. Fennell (ed.), *The Changing Face of Catholic Ireland*, 17.

117. Begley v. Begley, 1955: outlined in J. Blanchard, *The Church in Contemporary Ireland*, 70.

118. e.g. D. Fennell (ed.), *op. cit.*, 17–18.

119. J. Newman, *Studies in Political Morality*, 425 ff., argues that it does have a juridical effect, but his colleague at Maynooth, Rev. Enda McDonagh, argues that it does not: see E. McDonagh, 'Church and State in the constitution of Ireland', *Irish Theological Quarterly* (XXVIII, 2) April 1961, 131–44. Professor J. M. Kelly, in *Fundamental Rights in Irish Law*, 247 note, considers that most ·udges would probably agree with Fr McDonagh.

that has to be borne in mind and the recognition of it is important.'[120] To some Catholics, Article 44 did not go far enough in stressing the distinction between what they considered the true Church on the one hand, and erroneous denominations on the other. Mr de Valera admitted in the Dail that 'it might be said that this does not go, from the Catholic point of view, the distance that would be desired by a number,'[121] and a recent newspaper report by a well-informed journalist suggests that neither Cardinal MacRory, the then Archbishop of Armagh, nor Pope Pius XI were altogether satisfied with the text.[122] A few years later, as we shall see in a subsequent chapter, an agitation broke out for the strengthening of the reference to the Catholic Church in Article 44.[123]

However, even if Mr de Valera's constitution did not go quite so far in the direction of recognising Catholic values as some churchmen might have wished, it certainly went much further than the 1922 constitution had done. It can be considered one more instance of the movement which had been going on, regardless of which party was in power, since the establishment of the State to enshrine Catholic principles in the law of the land.

At this point the question might be raised: did this movement arouse any resistance? Although the two main parties appeared united in its support, were there any other forces which opposed it? Such opposition was certainly not to be found in the only other party with a continuous existence throughout this period— the Irish Labour Party. The Labour party was, on moral issues, just as conventional as its two larger rivals. In the Mayo library debate, for instance, it voted with Fianna Fail and against the government:[124] in other words, when faced with an issue in which both parties claimed that their attitude was consistent with Catholic principles, Labour chose the more intransigently Catholic of the two.

120. *Dail Debates*, LXVII, 1890 (4 June 1937).
121. *Ibid.*, 1891.
122. John Horgan in *Irish Times*, 23 Sept. 1969. Mr Horgan did not publish his authority but he has been kind enough to inform me of his source, and it is one deserving of respect.
123. See below, pp. 163–5.
124. *Dail Debates*, XXXIX, 547–52 (17 June 1931).

It is possible that among ordinary Catholics in Ireland there was more resistance to the imposition of the Church's standards than one would deduce from observing the politicians whom the people elected. I have heard it suggested that there has always been more criticism of the clergy in Ireland, especially in the countryside, than has appeared in print. An English observer remarked on this in 1941: 'A curious and perhaps unexpected feature of Irish life, however, is that urban opinion is more clerical and controlled than rural, which is often quite outspokenly independent.'[125] But though this may be so, there was no sign of overt protest during the period covered by this chapter. Emigration may have acted as a safety-valve. It is sometimes suggested that the causes of emigration from Ireland have not been entirely economic, and that some emigrants have left because they resented the drabness of life which the clergy have helped to produce.[126] If the most discontented were likely to leave, then there was less likelihood that those who remained behind would be stirred to protest.

If Catholics remained inarticulate, some opposition to the trend of public policy might have been expected from Protestants. Protestant ethical principles did not always coincide with Catholic ones, and the State, in imposing Catholic principles by law, was thereby obliging Protestants to accept constraints which their own consciences did not demand of them. Many Protestants, for instance, did not believe that divorce or the use of contraceptives were in all circumstances wrong. On censorship, Protestants were more likely than Catholics to argue that the individual should decide for himself what books he can read without harm, and that the State should not do it for him. And indeed protests on these lines can be found. The Protestant-owned *Irish Times* campaigned for divorce facilities,[127] criticised the Censorship of Publications Bill,[128] and allowed correspondence to appear against the Criminal Law Amendment Bill.[129] Individual Protestant deputies and senators also objected to government policy on

125. J. Hawkins, *The Irish Question Today*, 17.
126. e.g. John A. O'Brien (ed.), *The Vanishing Irish*, 80, 115, 188.
127. See, e.g., its leading articles of 23 Feb. 1924, 12 June 1925.
128. M. Adams, *Censorship*, 40–1.
129. *Irish Times*. 25 June–19 July 1934 *passim*.

these issues.[130] One Protestant deputy criticised the recognition of the special position of the Catholic Church embodied in Article 44 of the 1937 constitution.[131]

Protestant opposition on these issues, however, appeared rather half-hearted. Though Protestant deputies put with dignity and moderation the case for freedom of conscience, their speeches in the Dail read more as if made for the record than with any real determination to influence the views of the majority. This self-effacing attitude was probably inevitable. As a small minority facing a huge and apparently monolithic Catholic majority, Protestants must have felt that they had no hope of influencing the majority's point of view. Again, to fight a campaign on an issue of sexual morality was a task of some delicacy: in the twenties and thirties, such things were not discussed with anything like the same freedom as they are today. Furthermore, the legal code built up under the new State was more irksome in theory than in practice. Any Protestant (or for that matter any Catholic) who wanted to read a banned book or secure a supply of contraceptives could do so easily enough, by having them mailed in under plain cover: it was unlikely that small quantities would be detected in the customs. To secure a divorce was more troublesome, but anyone really anxious to obtain one could do so by domicile in England. Finally, the experience of Protestants on another issue may have convinced them of the futility of seeking to modify the policies favoured by the majority. The imposition of compulsory Irish in the schools aroused much Protestant resentment. There were many protests against it, by Church of Ireland bishops and others;[132] the *Irish Times* even suggested that Protestants vote against government candidates at the next election unless the policy was modified.[133] It was not

130. e.g. on divorce: *Dail Debates*, X, 159–63 (11 Feb. 1925: Professor Thrift), 178–9 (Mr Alton); *Seanad Debates*, V, 450–2 (11 June 1925: Mr Bagwell), 455–9 (Mr Douglas); *Dail Debates*, LXVII, 1885–6 (4 June 1937: Dr Rowlette). On the Censorship of Publications Bill, M. Adams, *op. cit.*, 39–64, cites a number of criticisms by Professor Alton, Professor Thrift and Senator Sir John Keane. On the Criminal Law Amendment Bill see *Dail Debates*, LIII, 2017–20 (1 Aug. 1934: Dr Rowlette), *Seanad Debates*, XIX, 1249–53 (6 Feb. 1935: Mr Bagwell).

131. *Dail Debates*, LXVII, 1891–2 (4 June 1937: Dr Rowlette).

132. For an anthology of Protestant criticisms of the language policy, accompanied by a hostile commentary, see *Catholic Bulletin* (XVII, 1) Jan. 1927, 7–18.

133. *Irish Times*, 13 Nov. 1926.

surprising that Protestants should have felt so strongly on the subject. Most of them were still Unionist in outlook, and had little sympathy with nationalistic arguments for Ireland having a language of her own. They also faced the practical problem that they had far more difficulty than Catholics in finding qualified teachers of Irish for their schools. Yet despite the fact that there was no point of Catholic moral teaching involved, and that some Catholics shared their distaste for the compulsory Irish policy, they were unable to make any more impression on the majority here than on directly ethical issues such as divorce or contraception.

There was only one quarter from which systematic opposition came to the policy of giving Catholic moral standards the backing of the State. This was a small and loosely-organised group of literary men. The outstanding figure among them was W. B. Yeats. Among his friends and collaborators were men from Catholic backgrounds such as Oliver St John Gogarty and, in the younger generation, Sean O'Faolain and Frank O'Connor; and others from Protestant backgrounds such as Lennox Robinson and George Russell.[134] But though the members of this circle could all be classified sociologically as Protestant or Catholic, most of them had drifted away from their religious allegiances, a fact which helped to give their criticism of Irish catholicism its radical character. Yeats and his friends kept up unceasing attack against what they considered the narrowness and philistinism of the society around them. In the nineteen-twenties their main organ was the weekly *Irish Statesman*. When it ceased publication in 1930, Yeats' next device was to establish an Irish Academy of Letters, whose object, described by Frank O'Connor, was to provide 'a solid body of informed opinion that might encourage young writers and discourage the Catholic Church from suppressing them'.[135] But the kind of criticism made by Yeats and his friends made little impact on the Ireland of their day. Yeats, then a senator, delivered a famous speech in defence of the right to divorce in 1925,[136] but he seems chiefly to have aroused

---

134. Two recent autobiographies are helpful for this circle: S. O'Faolain, *Vive Moi!*, and F. O'Connor, *My Father's Son*.
135. F. O'Connor, *op. cit.*, 98.
136. *Seanad Debates*, V, 434–43 (11 June 1925).

disgust among those not already of his way of thinking.[137] The group's main campaign was waged against the Censorship of Publications Bill of 1929, but despite the persistent and often acute criticisms of the *Irish Statesman* they were unable to impede its passage. In return the group themselves were under bitter criticism from the kind of Catholics whom they condemned. The *Catholic Bulletin,* in the intervals of pursuing Freemasons, specialised in attacking Yeats and his friends, whom it categorised as 'the sewage school'. A prominent Jesuit, Father P. J. Gannon, denounced the foundation of the Irish Academy of Letters and denied the capacity of most of its members to give a truthful picture of Irish life.[138] Yeats died in 1939, and it was not till long afterwards that the kind of criticism which he made of Ireland began to receive a response. The apostolic succession was maintained by a little periodical, *The Bell,* whose first editor was Yeats' protégé Sean O'Faolain. *The Bell* during its years of existence (1940–54) kept liberal criticism of Irish society alive until, as we shall see in a subsequent chapter, in the fifties a more open climate of opinion began to emerge in Ireland.

The years 1923–37 reveal, so far as religious values are concerned, a remarkable consensus in Irish society. There was overwhelming agreement that traditional Catholic values should be maintained, if necessary by legislation. There is no evidence that pressure from the hierarchy was needed to bring this about: it appears to have been spontaneous. The two major parties, bitterly though they differed on constitutional or economic issues, were at one in this. Mr Cosgrave refused to legalise divorce; Mr de Valera made it unconstitutional. Mr Cosgrave's government regulated films and books; Mr de Valera's regulated dance halls. Mr Cosgrave's government forbade propaganda for the use of contraceptives; Mr de Valera's banned their sale or import. In all this they had the support of the third party in Irish politics, the Labour party. The Catholic populace gave no hint of protest. The Protestant minority acquiesced. The only real opposition

---

137. *The Catholic Bulletin* (XV, 7) July 1925, 642, described his speech as 'satanic arrogance'.
138. *Irish Times,* 14 Nov. 1932.

came from a coterie of literary men whose impact on public opinion was slight.

The acknowledgement of the special position of the Catholic Church by the constitution of 1937 may be taken, despite the ambiguity of the phrasing, to mark the culmination of this process. The Irish State appeared wholly committed to the maintenance of Catholic values, and it was difficult to see what further evolution in Church-State relations was possible. If further development did take place after 1937, this was because the concept of what was involved in a State being committed to Catholic values was changing. It was coming to comprise a particular attitude not only to moral issues but to social issues as well. This development will be examined in the next chapter.

CHAPTER III

THE CATHOLIC SOCIAL MOVEMENT BECOMES A FORCE IN IRELAND, 1931-44

One feature of Irish catholicism in the first quarter of the twentieth century was the weakness of its social movement. In this it contrasted with many areas of the continent, where Catholics had developed a network of organisations with a social purpose: co-operatives, friendly societies, farmers' organisations, youth movements, adult education movements, trade unions. The motivation behind this growth was various. In part, it was negative: to save Catholic workers and farmers from falling into the clutches of the socialists. In part, it was positive: the generous response of many Catholics to the social evils of their day. The extent and success of the movement varied also. In much of southern and eastern Europe it was weak. In the Catholic parts of Germany and Switzerland, in Austria, France and parts of Italy, it was powerful. Its most complete development was probably to be found in Belgium and the Netherlands. But taking Europe as a whole, the rise of this movement was one of the most important developments among Catholics in the years 1880-1920.[1]

Intellectually, the movement was underpinned by a growing number of study circles, specialist periodicals, and congresses such as the *semaines sociales,* which started in France in 1904 and were soon imitated in other countries.[2] At an early stage the ideas which germinated in these quarters were summed up and ratified at the highest level in the Church, when Pope Leo XIII issued his encyclical on the social question, *Rerum Novarum,* in 1891.

1. For accounts of the development of the Catholic social movement see M. P. Fogarty, *Christian Democracy in Western Europe;* Joseph N. Moody (ed.), *Church and Society;* S. H. Scholl (ed.), *150 Ans de Mouvement Ouvrier Chrétien;* H. Daniel-Rops, *A Fight for God.*
2. H. Daniel-Rops, *op. cit.,* 158-9.

Rerum Novarum was on the whole a cautious document, which left a wide range of social and economic policies open to Catholics. But it did rule out some extreme courses. As against socialism, it asserted man's right to private property. As against individualism, it asserted the State's right to intervene against bad working conditions. In place of the class warfare of the socialist, and the unrestricted competition of the individualist, it proposed an ideal of class harmony as the goal towards which Christians should aim. Its teachings, despite the many questions which it still left open, were sufficiently definite to provide a platform for further discussion, and for the next generation social Catholics were busy elaborating the doctrine of *Rerum Novarum,* and applying it to the particular circumstances of their various countries.

It would be wrong to imply that this social movement among continental Catholics was without echoes in Ireland. In the countryside especially, priests were often active in projects for social reform. The rural co-operative movement was a particular favourite, and one writer estimated in 1904 that priests had identified themselves with over 600 local co-operative societies.[3] Several local industries owed their existence to the energy of local priests or religious houses, the most famous being the woollen industry at Foxford, county Mayo, established by Mother Morrogh Bernard of the Sisters of Charity.[4] The Gaelic League, which could be considered in part a movement for social betterment, also had many friends among the clergy.[5] In the towns, much charitable work was done by the voluntary lay workers of the Society of Saint Vincent de Paul, which had been introduced from France in the nineteenth century. After 1921, their efforts were supplemented by an organisation of Irish origin, the Legion of Mary, which has since spread all over the world.[6]

Yet, despite the efforts of individual priests and laymen, the social record of Irish catholicism remained unremarkable. The charitable work of the Saint Vincent de Paul Society alleviated many cases of distress, but it did nothing to alter the system which

3. M. O'Riordan, *Catholicity and Progress in Ireland,* 208.
4. *Ibid.,* 210–30, 405–19.
5. C. Plater, S.J., *The Priest and Social Action,* 118.
6. D. Fennell (ed.), *The Changing Face of Catholic Ireland,* 63–72.

made that distress possible. In Dublin, the main force for social change in the years before the First World War was the volcanic James Larkin, who organised the unskilled labourers to fight against the inhuman conditions in which they worked; but Larkin was not a practising Catholic, and the attitude of priests to him ranged from aloofness to hostility.[7] In the countryside the rural co-operative movement was pioneered by a Protestant, Sir Horace Plunkett, and, though he received the support of priests, the clergy did not play so prominent a role in the co-operative movement as they did in parts of continental Europe. Plunkett himself noted that the record of Irish clergy compared unfavourably with that of the clergy in Belgium, France, parts of Germany and Austria, and northern Italy.[8] And indeed some Irish priests were prepared to admit as much. A Jesuit, Father Lambert McKenna, wrote in 1913: 'Of Catholic social work properly so called, there is little, very little indeed in Catholic Ireland. In this respect as in so many others, we are thirty or forty years behind the times.'[9] Another priest, Father (later Monsignor) John Kelleher, writing in 1915, strongly hinted that his fellow-clergy should be doing more than they were.[10]

On the intellectual front, also, there was little to report. A study circle, the Leo Guild, was founded in Dublin in 1912,[11] but seems to have been moribund within a few years. Pamphlets on social questions were published, in the decade before independence, by Father Patrick Boylan, Mr James P. Kerr of Belfast, Father Lambert McKenna, S.J., and a young lecturer at University College, Cork, Dr Alfred O'Rahilly.[12] The Jesuit periodical *Studies*, which began publication in 1912, included in its early issues a number of articles on social questions. But there were no periodicals specialising in social issues, no study weeks, no

7. Emmet Larkin, 'Socialism and Catholicism in Ireland', *Church History* (XXXIII) Dec. 1964, 462–83.
8. Sir H. Plunkett, *Ireland in the New Century*, 103–4.
9. Quoted in C. Plater, *op. cit.*, 122.
10. Rev. J. Kelleher, 'Priests and social action in Ireland', *Studies* (IV) Sept. 1915, 169–70, 179.
11. C. Plater, *op. cit.*, 122.
12. Rev. P. Boylan, *Catholicism and Citizenship in Self-governed Ireland*; James P. Kerr, *A Catechism of Catholic Social Principles*; Rev. L. McKenna, S.J., *The Church and Labour*; A. Rahilly, *A Guide to Books for Social Students and Others.* Dr Rahilly began signing his name 'O'Rahilly' in 1920.

equivalent of the Catholic Social Guild which the numerically weaker English Catholics established in 1909.

There were good reasons why the Catholic social movement should have been relatively weak in Ireland. Father Edward Cahill, S.J., one of the pioneers of the movement in Ireland, put the case reasonably in an article published in 1930: 'In Ireland a Catholic social movement in the ordinary sense was practically impossible up to very recent times. The land struggle, the fight for educational freedom, the national contest, the work of church building and religious organisation, engaged the energies of the priests and people during the nineteenth and the first quarter of the twentieth centuries.'[13] There is much truth in this, and it does mark out Ireland from those countries where the Catholic social movement was strongest. These latter countries—Germany, France, the Low Countries—were ones where national independence was not an issue at the end of the nineteenth century, and in which energies were not diverted into a fundamental political struggle. They were countries where no social problem remained to be solved so basic as the Irish land question remained up to the Wyndham Act of 1903. They were ones also where the Church, whatever its troubles, had never suffered an obliteration of its external structure such as had happened in Ireland under the penal laws, and where consequently the Catholic people had never had to put their efforts into rebuilding, from the ground up, the basic institutions—churches, presbyteries, schools, charitable institutions.

On the intellectual side, the weakness of the Catholic social movement in Ireland can be explained by reference to the general intellectual weakness of Irish catholicism. This was a phenomenon which struck even friendly observers. The French writer Louis Paul-Dubois remarked in 1907: 'Among the Catholics of Ireland, even among the liberal classes, there are but few to be found who possess any real culture. We find, on the contrary, a certain form of intellectual apathy very widespread, a distaste for mental effort, a certain absence of the critical sense.'[14] The Cork solicitor

13. E. Cahill, S.J., 'The Catholic social movement', *Irish Ecclesiastical Record* (5th series, XXXVI) Dec. 1930, 585.

14. L. Paul-Dubois, *Contemporary Ireland*, 496. This was published in 1908; the French original was published in 1907.

John J. Horgan records in his memoirs that, when he published a book on *Great Catholic Laymen* in 1905, it was 'one of the first books on a religious subject by a Catholic layman to come out of Ireland'.[15] The clergy did somewhat better: they included scholars such as the historians Monsignor James McCaffrey and Monsignor E. A. D'Alton, and from 1906 they supported the *Irish Theological Quarterly*. But on the whole, as Father Michael O'Riordan admitted in 1904, Irish Catholics associated educational superiority with Protestants and secularists rather than with themselves.[16] This was partly a reflection of social conditions: the educated class in Ireland was largely Protestant, and in so far as it had Catholic members, these were often newly-arrived, and more concerned to absorb the manners of their Protestant counterparts than to build up a Catholic culture. It was also the result of the policies of Church and State with regard to higher education. Opinions can differ as to which carried the more responsibility: the Church for discouraging Catholics from entering the universities available before 1908, or the State for refusing until then to establish a university which the Catholic bishops would accept. But wherever the responsibility lies, the fact remains that, before the Irish Universities Act of 1908, it was almost impossible for a Catholic university-trained élite to emerge in Ireland.

By the late nineteen-twenties, however, the factors which had hitherto delayed the development of a Catholic social movement in Ireland were becoming less important. Ireland was now a self-governing country, and, even if the form of self-government was not satisfactory to all its citizens, at least sufficient had been achieved for attention to turn from the winning of political independence to the building up of the country. The physical plant—churches, schools, and other buildings—which the Church had spent so much energy during the nineteenth century in providing, was now substantially complete. On the intellectual side, the National University of Ireland had been functioning since 1908, and a university-trained Catholic leadership was coming into existence. It is not surprising to find, then, in the

15. J. J. Horgan, *Parnell to Pearse*, 127.
16. M. O'Riordan, *Catholicity and Progress in Ireland*, 490.

later nineteen-twenties, signs that the Catholic social movement was at long last taking root in Ireland. A federation of study circles, *An Rioghacht* (The Kingdom), was founded in 1926, and soon became more extensive than the Leo Guild of 1912 had ever been.[17] In 1928, the Catholic Young Men's Society in Dublin organised the first study week for the examination of Catholic social principles.[18]

The best date to choose, however, for marking the take-off of the Catholic social movement in Ireland is 1931. The reason is that that year saw the publication, on 15 May, of Pope Pius XI's encyclical *Quadragesimo Anno*. As its name implies, *Quadragesimo Anno* was issued to commemorate the fortieth anniversary of *Rerum Novarum,* and its purpose was to adapt and develop the doctrine which *Rerum Novarum* had outlined. The basic teaching of the two encyclicals, then, was the same: both stressed harmony between different social groups as the Christian answer to the doctrine of class war. *Quadragesimo Anno,* however, was more precise than *Rerum Novarum* about how this aim might be attained. The solution it proposed was that the members of each industry or profession be organised in 'vocational groups' or 'corporations', in which employers and workers would collaborate to further their common interests. As well as being an alternative to class conflict, this development would, the Pope believed, have a further advantage. It would restore the State, burdened by an excessive number of duties, to its rightful place, which is not to do everything itself, but to direct, watch, urge and restrain subsidiary organisations. For, the Pope argued, there is a basic principle in social philosophy, the principle of subsidiary function: 'It is an injustice and at the same time a grave evil and disturbance of right order to assign to a greater and higher association what lesser and subordinate organisations can do.'[19]

The idea of a corporate order was not, of course, one which the Pope had thought up for himself. There was a long tradition of

17. J. Waldron, 'An Rioghacht—a retrospect', *Irish Monthly* (LXXVIII, no. 924) June 1950, 274–80.
18. *Irish Independent,* 21 April 1928. *Standard,* 27 April 1929, mentions that this had been the first Catholic social week in Dublin.
19. *Quadragesimo Anno,* paragraph 79. I am using the translation in Terence P. McLaughlin (ed.), *The Church and the Reconstruction of the Modern World: The Social Encyclicals of Pius XI.*

corporate thinking in Europe, especially in France and in Austria, and by no means confined to Catholics.[20] Nonetheless, there were reasons why the proposal should have appeared specially attractive at this time. The encyclical was published at the depth of the great depression. Millions of industrial workers were unemployed. Thousands of employers faced ruin. Thousands of farmers were burning produce which they could not sell. The reputation of the prevailing economic system, capitalism, had never been worse, and men all over the world were seeking a new social order. Communism made many converts in the nineteen-thirties. So did totalitarian movements of the right, such as the Nazis in Germany. But there were features of these movements which made many who were far from in love with capitalism wonder whether the remedy was not worse than the disease—the brutality, the suppression of liberty, the strident harping on class or national conflict. In this situation, caught between the anarchy of traditional capitalism on the one hand, and the totalitarianisms of left and right on the other, Catholics believed that the Pope had shown them a way out. All over the world, a new self-confidence, and a new precision in the formulation of objectives, can be seen in the Catholic social movement after 1931.

In Ireland, thanks to the previous weakness of the Catholic social movement, its progress after 1931 was even more obvious than it was in many other countries. An early sign of its development was the foundation of *Muintir na Tire* (People of the Land) in 1931 by Father John Hayes, a priest of the diocese of Cashel, then a curate at Castleiny, county Tipperary. Father Hayes actually founded his movement one week before the publication of *Quadragesimo Anno*, but his ideas fitted closely with those of the new encyclical, to which he appealed as a justification for his movement.[21] *Muintir na Tire* started as an economic organisation, a producers' co-operative, modelled on the *Boerenbond* which the Flemish clergy had done so much to build up over the previous forty years.[22] But soon the emphasis began to shift. From 1933 *Muintir na Tire* was holding rural week-ends (based on the

20. See, e.g., Matthew H. Elbow, *French Corporative Theory, 1789–1948;* Alfred Diamant, *Austrian Catholics and the First Republic.*
21. S. Rynne, *Father John Hayes,* 107–8.
22. *Ibid.,* 104, 107.

semaines rurales of the French Catholic farmers' movement) at which participants could discuss the problems of the Irish country-side and seek for remedies.[23] From 1937, these were supplemented by rural weeks, residential study congresses held in the premises of some college or secondary school.[24] *Muintir na Tire* changed from being a marketing organisation to being a movement for the social uplift of the Irish countryside. The parish was adopted as the unit of organisation, and the parish guilds were left with freedom to choose whatever project they felt would be of most benefit in their particular circumstances. Father Hayes' biographer gives examples:

The Murroe guild built the first parish hall under the auspices of Muintir na Tire. The Athy guild distributed over sixty pairs of boots to the children of the unemployed. Seven acres of trees were planted by the Tuam guild, the main object being to give useful work to men who would have been otherwise unemployed. The Clogheen guild in county Cork harried the County Council about the state of their roads; made a survey of the housing needs of the parish and instituted a prize scheme for plots and allotments. Other guilds made registrations of the unemployed, arranged for lectures from the County Committee of Agriculture, Vocational Education Committee and other groups willing to supply speakers.[25]

However, though the methods of the organisation were flexible, and Father Hayes himself hated to be tied down by written constitutions, the underlying ideology can be labelled 'vocation-alist'. The parish councils were elected on a vocational basis. The council in Father Hayes' own parish, for instance, had twenty-five members representing five sections: farmers, farm labourers, trade unions, business and professional men, and unemployed.[26] At the rural week-ends and rural weeks a talk on vocational organisation was almost a rule. Father Hayes' own speeches were studded with references to the teaching of *Quadragesimo Anno*. *Muintir na Tire* was a growing organisation. The number of parishes sending representatives to rural weeks numbered fifty in 1939, 100 in 1942, 200 in 1949.[27] It can be considered one of the most import-

23. *Ibid.*, 113.   24. *Ibid.*, 144.   25. *Ibid.*, 157.
26. J. Toner, O.P., *Rural Ireland*, 40.   27. *Ibid.*, 34.

ant of the channels through which the new precision in Catholic social teaching became known in Ireland.

Other organisations spread the same teaching. The Guilds of Regnum Christi, founded in Dublin in 1933, were intended primarily to aid the personal sanctification of their members, but were organised on a vocational basis, with a separate guild for each vocation or calling.[28] The idea of social study weeks, which the Catholic Young Men's Society had started in Dublin in 1928, spread to the countryside, and a newspaper report of 1940 remarks that Galway was the fifth diocese in Ireland to arrange such an event.[29] The most important of the crop of study sessions were the Social Order Summer Schools, held each year in the Jesuit college at Clongowes Wood, county Kildare, from 1935 until 1940. The Clongowes summer schools, taking place as they did in a residential setting, gave opportunities, not merely for respectful attention to lectures by eminent speakers, but for argument and discussion. They attracted attendance from men prominent in politics, the professions, and the trade unions, and are still remembered by those who took part as lively and enjoyable affairs.

In the press, the most notable advocate of the new trend in Catholic social teaching was a weekly newspaper, the *Standard*. The *Standard* had been founded in 1928. It was ailing when, in 1938, it was taken over by a new team of directors, containing representatives of all the main political parties then active.[30] The new board stated as their aim 'the creation of a united public opinion in the cause of Catholic reconstruction'.[31] This was general enough, but under the new ownership the words were given precision. The editor was Peadar O'Curry, and his principal contributor was Dr Alfred O'Rahilly, Professor of Mathematical Physics in University College, Cork. Though the title of his chair would not lead one to expect it, Professor O'Rahilly was one of the most prolific writers in Ireland on economic and religious topics, and while opinions might differ about the content of his

28. R. Burke-Savage, S.J., 'The Church in Dublin: 1940–65', *Studies* (LIV, no. 216) Winter 1965, 298, for the date of foundation; *Manual of the Guilds of Regnum Christi* for their objects and organisation.

29. *Irish Weekly Independent*, 27 April 1940.

30. *Standard*, 16 Dec. 1938.   31. *Ibid.*

articles, he was always a lively and provocative writer. Dr Conor Cruise O'Brien in an article published in 1945, assessed his impact on the *Standard*:

The Professor is, among other things, one of the most remarkable journalists since the German-American terrorist, Johann Most, who used for seven years to write a four-page daily single-handed. Professor O'Rahilly probably does not write all of the *Standard* every week but it would be feeble merely to say that he has impressed his personality upon it. It is he who has given it a social policy, consisting of his own monetary theories, he who fights its battles with H. G. Wells and others, he who orients its attitudes to science and philosophy and life. Under his occupation the *Standard* shifted to something that might almost be described as the Left. Its circulation soared to 50,000 (1939 figures).[32]

The *Standard* under Dr O'Rahilly's aegis showed a distinct tendency to corporatism. An issue of 1942, for instance, had for its heading 'Catholic Statesmen Seek Peace and Order', and under this caption were portraits of the three statesmen thus referred to: Pétain, Salazar and Franco.[33] It should not be thought, however, that the paper was hostile to democracy: it praised, for instance, features of the Swiss and Swedish systems.[34] It was well-written, and on subjects such as censorship or education it would offer discriminating criticism at a time when most Irish papers allowed no criticism at all. It is impossible to measure its influence precisely, but the circulation figure of 50,000, mentioned by Dr Conor Cruise O'Brien for 1939, is large for a country the size of Ireland. It means that in proportion to the country's

32. Donat O'Donnell, 'The Catholic press. A study in theopolitics', *The Bell* (X, 1) April 1945, 37. Donat O'Donnell is Dr Conor Cruise O'Brien's pen-name. The circulation figure of 50,000 reported by Dr O'Brien matches well with a figure of 45,020 reported in reply to a parliamentary question in 1947: *Dail Debates*, CVI, 1523 (11 June 1947).
   There is another Catholic weekly in Ireland, the *Irish Catholic*, but I have not given it the same consideration as the *Standard*, partly because its circulation at this time was smaller (30,000 according to the same Dail reply in 1947), and partly because it was more of a straight newspaper than the *Standard*, and less the advocate of a particular point of view.
33. *Standard*, 20 Feb. 1942.
34. For praise of the Swiss system see *Standard passim* during the general election campaign of 1943. For praise of Sweden see article by Alfred O'Rahilly in *Standard*, 30 Oct. 1942.

population it had a much bigger circulation than some weeklies that are acknowledged as influential in Britain, such as the *New Statesman* or the *Economist*. The anxiety shown by the Irish Labour Party when, as we shall see, the *Standard* launched an attack on it in 1944, is an indication that it was an influential paper.

One writer might be mentioned, whose application of what he considered to be Catholic principles led to conclusions which many of his fellow-Catholics found drastic. This was Father Denis Fahey of the Holy Ghost Fathers. Father Fahey taught philosophy and church history to the young members of his order, a position which gave him ample opportunity to develop his distinctive ideas. Most of them are already set out in his first book, *The Kingship of Christ according to the Principles of St Thomas Aquinas*, published in 1931. Father Fahey started from the general principle that there was one correct social order, willed by God, which it was the duty of all mankind to strive to attain. This social order had been most nearly achieved in the thirteenth century,[35] but since then the Protestant Reformation, the French Revolution, and the Russian Revolution had marked successive steps away from it. These steps had indeed been so calamitous that they could not be dismissed as the result of chance: the last two, at least, were the fruit of deep-laid conspiracy.[36] The ultimate author of this conspiracy was Satan, but its immediate agents were the Freemasons. The reader may wonder how the Freemasons, an essentially bourgeois movement, could have been linked with the Communist revolution in Russia, but the question gave no trouble to Father Fahey. To him, both Freemasons and Communists were instruments of the Jews.[37]

In later books, Father Fahey elaborated these doctrines. He married them to monetary reform theories derived from Professor O'Rahilly,[38] and to theories about the evils of commercial farming derived from English writers such as Lord Portsmouth.[39] He

35. D. Fahey, *The Kingship of Christ according to the Principles of St Thomas Aquinas*, 37.
36. *Ibid.*, 71–3.   37. *Ibid.*, 143, 157.
38. Especially in *The Mystical Body of Christ and the Reorganisation of Society*.
39. Especially in *The Church and Farming* and in the appendix to *Money Manipulation and the Social Order*.

came to believe, I have been told, that it was contrary to the natural law to eat white bread. But his basic principles did not change, and neither did the immediate conclusion that he drew from them. This was that in Ireland, where a majority of the population had a true grasp of order, it was their duty to put their principles into operation. In particular, as most Irishmen accepted that the Roman Catholic Church was the one true Church, they should see that that fact was proclaimed in the constitution of their country.[40]

It is doubtful if Father Fahey was a figure of much influence in the thirties. The religious order to which he belonged is an important one, running some of the leading secondary schools in Ireland as well as providing many missionaries overseas: but although all its scholastics for many years passed through Father Fahey's hands, by no means all of them accepted his views.[41] He is of most interest as marking the extreme wing of Irish Catholic thought at this time, the man whose vision of a truly Christian social order entailed the most thoroughgoing changes in the conditions actually existing in his day. But he was not an entirely isolated figure. Many of his ideas came from Father Edward Cahill, S.J., the founder of *An Rioghacht,* in particular his belief in a conspiracy of Freemasons and Jews against the Church.[42] And one influential member of his own order certainly sympathised with him. His first book contains a warmly commendatory introduction from the Very Reverend J. C. McQuaid, then Superior of Blackrock College, and now Archbishop of Dublin.[43]

The growing interest in Catholic social teaching can also be seen in the statements of the Irish bishops. True, the preoccupation with matters of personal morality remained strong throughout the thirties, and even at the end of the decade dance-halls were still the most frequent single topic for mention in episcopal

40. e.g. *The Kingship of Christ according to the Principles of St Thomas Aquinas,* chapter IV; *The Mystical Body of Christ in the Modern World,* appendix VIII of the 1st edn.; *The Mystical Body of Christ and the Reorganisation of Society,* 353–60.

41. Personal information from a Holy Ghost Father, a former student of Fr Fahey's.

42. e.g. D. Fahey, *The Kingship of Christ according to the Principles of St Thomas Aquinas,* 143, commends E. Cahill, S.J., *Freemasonry and the Anti-Christian Movement.*

43. D. Fahey, *The Kingship of Christ according to the Principles of St Thomas Aquinas,* 7–12.

pastorals. But along with this now traditional subject, there were increasingly frequent references in the pastorals to the Church's social teaching. In 1937, for instance, Bishop Kinane of Waterford pointed to the recent strikes in his city as illustrating the need for corporate organisation. Bishop Casey of Ross lamented that so little had yet been done in Ireland to implement the Pope's social teaching. Cardinal MacRory of Armagh wanted it to be understood that his opposition to communism did not mean that he was satisfied with existing social conditions.[44] In the same year, the hierarchy established a Chair of Catholic Sociology and Catholic Action at Maynooth, and appointed Father Peter McKevitt, a priest of the diocese of Armagh, to fill it.[45]

Three bishops in particular can be mentioned for their interest in social questions. The senior was the Most Reverend John Dignan, Bishop of Clonfert from 1924 to 1953. For the first dozen years of his episcopate, Dr Dignan was not particularly noted for his interest in social issues. His most famous public statement in that time was a lecture at Maynooth in 1933 in which he made an onslaught on Trinity College, Dublin.[46] In 1936, however, Dr Dignan accepted from the Fianna Fail government the chairmanship of the new National Health Insurance Society, which was taking over the administration of health insurance under the National Insurance Acts from the jungle of small societies which had hitherto divided the work between them.[47] The government's choice of Dr Dignan for this post was an interesting one. It may have felt that it could count on his good will because during the Civil War Dr Dignan, then a parish priest, had sympathised with the Republicans.[48] As far as the bishop himself was concerned, the appointment gave him a practical knowledge of the workings of the social services which made him the hierarchy's leading authority on the subject.

44. *Irish Independent*, 8 Feb. 1937.
45. *Irish Catholic Directory, 1938*, 606 (under date 22 June 1937); *ibid.*, 630 (12 Oct. 1937).
46. Later published as a pamphlet: Most Rev. J. Dignan, *Catholics and Trinity College*.
47. *Irish Weekly Independent*, 18 July 1936.
48. He made this clear when replying to an address presented to him by the Sinn Fein clubs of his diocese after his consecration: *Irish Weekly Independent*, 7 June 1924.

The second bishop to be mentioned here is the Most Reverend Michael Browne, Bishop of Galway since 1937. He had previously, from 1921, been Professor of Moral Theology at Maynooth. At the time of his consecration he was forty-one years old, and the youngest member of the hierarchy.[49] Even today he is still not the oldest bishop, though he is the senior in date of consecration. Dr Browne is well over six feet tall, with strongly-marked features: the cliché 'a commanding presence' is apt when applied to him. Since his consecration he has, as we shall see, been involved in a number of controversies. Some might question whether his manner of stating his case is not sometimes needlessly brusque. But his readiness to put his views bluntly in public is welcome at least to the historian. It means that, in contrast to some other members of the hierarchy, there can be no doubt about what Dr Browne thinks or about the direction in which he uses his influence. The record shows him to have consistently opposed what he considers the undue extension of State power in Ireland.

The third bishop to be mentioned here deserves a more extended discussion. He is the Most Reverend John Charles McQuaid, who was appointed Archbishop of Dublin in November 1940, and ever since has probably been the most-talked-about Irish prelate. This is partly because of the importance of his diocese. The senior appointment in the Irish Church is the see of Armagh; it is the Archbishop of Armagh who presides over meetings of the Irish hierarchy and who, in the twentieth century, has always received the cardinal's hat. But in every other way Dublin is the more important diocese. It is easily the largest in Ireland. In 1940, out of 4,331 priests in Ireland, the Dublin diocese contained 718. Only three other dioceses (Cork, Down and Connor, and Limerick) contained as many as 200.[50] The Catholic population of the diocese was nearly 600,000, or nearly a quarter of the total Catholic population of the twenty-six counties. Decisions taken in the Dublin diocese, then, have an impact on a larger number of Catholics than decisions taken in any other diocese, and, indeed, circumstances may arise in which

49. *Irish Independent,* 11 Aug. 1937.
50. *Irish Catholic Directory, 1941,* 623.

a determined line taken in the Dublin diocese can effectively reduce the freedom of choice open to other bishops. To add to its importance, Dublin contains by far the largest number of charitable institutions, hospitals and schools in the country, many of them run by religious orders. It contains the headquarters of most national organisations, religious and secular. Since Dublin is the seat of government, the archbishop is usually deputed by the hierarchy to handle any negotiations it may have with the government.

In any circumstances, an appointment to the see of Dublin would arouse interest. In 1940, circumstances were such that it made even more of an impact than usual. The previous archbishop, Dr Byrne, had been in failing health for years. The new archbishop, Dr McQuaid, aged forty-five, was young and energetic. He was also a surprise appointment. His selection broke the almost universal rule in Ireland that bishops are chosen from the secular clergy, for he was, and still is, the only member of the Irish hierarchy to come from a religious order or congregation. He had from 1931 to 1939 been headmaster of Blackrock College, an important secondary school near Dublin run by the Holy Ghost Fathers. At the time of his appointment as archbishop he had recently retired from the position of headmaster to take charge of the senior boys in the school.[51] Politically, his appointment was interesting because there were links between Fianna Fail and Blackrock. Mr de Valera had once been a pupil there, and he sent his sons there.[52] There have indeed been persistent rumours, often with circumstantial detail, that Dr McQuaid's appointment to the see of Dublin was in some way influenced by Mr de Valera. Such interference would be inconsistent with the Irish tradition, which is that governments do not seek to influence episcopal appointments, and I have reason to believe that the rumours are inaccurate. Certainly Dr McQuaid's subsequent record has shown that he is far from being in the pocket of Fianna Fail or any other political party. But the existence of such rumours added to the stir which his appointment made.

This is not the place to assess Dr McQuaid's total impact on his

51. R. Burke-Savage, S.J., 'The Church in Dublin: 1940–65', *Studies* (LIV, no. 216) Winter 1965, 297.

52. M. Bromage, *De Valera and the March of a Nation*, 22, 251.

diocese—his work for church-building, for diocesan administration, for religious instruction in schools.[53] Even in the field which concerns us, those mixed areas in which both Church and State have an interest, his impress has been marked. Right from the start Dr McQuaid showed that he had a special interest in social welfare. When the members of Dublin Corporation came, soon after his consecration, to offer him an address of welcome, he perhaps disconcerted them by urging that they build more houses for the poor.[54] A little later, he was reported as giving £500 to the victims of an incident in which a German aircraft had mistakenly dropped bombs on Dublin.[55] In 1942, he set up the Catholic Social Welfare Bureau, whose chief activity was to be the care of emigrants to Britain—an important problem about which little had hitherto been done in Ireland.[56] In the same year he co-operated with the government in opening two youth training centres,[57] and in the following year the government appointed him to preside over a committee on youth unemployment.[58] Also, in 1943 he gave £1,000 to the Sisters of Mercy to aid them in the anti-tuberculosis work that they were undertaking.[59] In 1944, at a time when an increase in venereal disease was causing concern in Ireland, he initiated a movement to develop V.D. clinics in the Dublin voluntary hospitals.[60]

Dr McQuaid's most striking contribution to social welfare in Dublin was the creation of the Catholic Social Service Conference in April 1941. There was already a great deal of charitable work being done in Dublin by various Catholic societies, but it was unco-ordinated. With the distress caused by wartime shortages of food, of clothing, and above all of fuel, it was more important than ever that charitable work should be efficient. The first step was taken by Dr McQuaid in January 1941, within weeks of his consecration. He called together a group of social workers and asked them to submit proposals for the co-ordina-

53. R. Burke-Savage, S.J., *op. cit.*, for a discussion of these and other activities.
54. *Irish Weekly Independent*, 18 Jan. 1941.
55. *Irish Catholic Directory, 1942*, 661 (4 June 1941).
56. *Ibid., 1943*, 629 (17 June 1942).
57. *Irish Weekly Independent*, 5 Sept. 1942.
58. *Commission on Youth Unemployment, Report*, viii.
59. *Irish Weekly Independent*, 19 June 1943.
60. *Journal of the Medical Association of Eire*, June 1944, 61.

tion and expansion of Catholic welfare work in the diocese. In accordance with the plan that they drew up, a federation was established of existing Catholic organisations and eventually thirty-nine different bodies were represented.[61] Their work was co-ordinated under several departments: food, clothing, maternity welfare, housing, youth, fuel, employment.[62] The largest proportion of the conference's funds was absorbed by the food department which was soon providing at nominal sums 250,000 meals a month.[63]

The C.S.S.C. transformed the quality of social work in Dublin. A single large organisation provided a focus for charity, and many thousands of pounds were subscribed annually in the collections taken up each autumn by order of the archbishop. It enabled fresh resources to be tapped: for instance, nuns were asked to take charge of food centres in places unconnected with their convents, and although this marked a new departure for some religious orders, they agreed to do so.[64] The food department did particularly important work and the archbishop was able to claim that 'in this city no one need suffer the dread of hunger'.[65] From 1944 onwards, Dr McQuaid in his annual appeals mentioned the cost of administration. It started at 3 per cent[66] and later fell to $2\frac{1}{2}$ per cent:[67] these remarkably low figures were attainable only by the harnessing of voluntary effort. The C.S.S.C. also received grants from central and local government funds—in 1941–3 these covered £9,850 out of a total outlay of £43,750[68]—but the bulk of the income, and all the energy and labour, came from voluntary sources. This may have been important at a later date when controversy arose around the extension of government social services. If Dr McQuaid appeared reluctant to countenance the extension of State services, it must be remembered that the success of the C.S.S.C. had given him a model of what the

61. *Handbook of the Catholic Social Service Conference*, 10, 59–60.
62. *Ibid.*, 10–11.
63. *Ibid.*, 17.
64. *Ibid.*, 18.
65. *Irish Catholic Directory, 1947*, 723 (22 Sept. 1946).
66. *Ibid., 1945*, 705 (24 Sept. 1944).
67. *Ibid., 1947*, 722 (22 Sept. 1946).
68. *Handbook of the Catholic Social Service Conference*, 13–14.

most fruitful balance of State and voluntary enterprise would be.

One further example can be given of Dr McQuaid's interest in social questions. Late in 1942, an Anti-Tuberculosis League, composed of doctors, social workers and representatives of public bodies, was initiated to combat the growing tuberculosis menace.[69] Preparations went ahead and on 15 February 1943 a meeting was held in the Royal Hibernian Hotel to mark the formal inauguration of the League. Before the proceedings had gone very far, however, a priest of the Dublin diocese, Monsignor Daniel Molony, rose and read a letter from the Archbishop of Dublin. The archbishop wrote that it was his 'definite opinion' that the campaign should be carried out by the existing Irish Red Cross Society. He pointed out that the Red Cross Society enjoyed government patronage, was already nation-wide, and had a large membership of trained workers, and he added that at the end of the war it would 'find ample opportunity for devoting its trained energies to an anti-tuberculosis campaign with undistracted attention.'[70] The archbishop's intervention aroused some resentment: the chairman of the meeting, Senator Dr Rowlette, complained that the organisers had been given no warning of such a proposal,[71] and it is noteworthy that when, ten years later, the anti-Catholic writer Paul Blanshard visited Ireland, this was one of the examples he was given of 'how Catholic pressure works'.[72] On this point I have had the benefit of a discussion with Dr McQuaid, and can state that it was not his intention to bring pressure on anyone. He merely wished to express what he considered well-founded objections. But it is true that an objection from such a quarter was hard to resist. Any Catholic member of the proposed organisation would feel that if he went ahead he would be putting himself in open opposition to his archbishop, and, in the then climate of Irish opinion, that was more than he might wish to face. Three weeks after the meeting in the Royal Hibernian Hotel, it was announced that

69. *Journal of the Medical Association of Eire*, Dec. 1942, 66–7; *Irish Times*, 17 Feb. 1943.
70. *Irish Independent*, 16 Feb. 1943.
71. *Ibid.*
72. P. Blanshard, *The Irish and Catholic Power*, 186–7.

the proposed Anti-Tuberculosis League would fuse with the Irish Red Cross Society.[73] The incident illustrated not only Dr McQuaid's interest in social questions, but his readiness to suggest fairly precisely how he thought social policy should be shaped. It was, perhaps, a portent for the future.

It was not only among Churchmen and among Church organisations that interest in Catholic social teaching was growing after 1931. The same development could be seen in the political parties. The three main parties will be examined in turn.

Cumann na nGaedheal was involved in rapid changes after its defeat in the general election of 1932. First, the new Centre party, catering mainly for farmers and led by Mr Frank Mac-Dermot and Mr James Dillon, arose alongside it.[74] Then, a uniformed organisation, the Blueshirts, grew up to protect Cumann na nGaedheal and Centre party meetings from being broken up by their political opponents.[75] Next, in September 1933, a union was negotiated between these three groups— Cumann na nGaedheal, Centre party and Blueshirts—under the presidency of the Blueshirt leader, General Eoin O'Duffy.[76] The new party was christened Fine Gael, or the United Ireland party.

Fine Gael was the first Irish party to respond to the new wave of Catholic social teaching inaugurated by *Quadragesimo Anno*. It was in need of an ideology and the encyclical provided one. Even before the union of September 1933, General O'Duffy had begun to talk of the desirability of a corporate State in Ireland.[77] The establishment of industrial and agricultural corporations was written into the programme of Fine Gael.[78] The pages of *United Ireland*, the party's weekly journal, began to carry articles

73. *Irish Times*, 6 March 1943.

74. D. O'Sullivan, *The Irish Free State and its Senate*, 299. This book covers much more ground than its title suggests, and is in effect a political history of Ireland from 1922 to 1940. It is invaluable as a repository of facts and dates, though its virulent anti-de Valera bias means that it must be treated more cautiously with regard to interpretations.

75. *Ibid.*, 321–2, 329.   76. *Ibid.*, 335.

77. *Irish Times*, 11 Aug. 1933. I owe this reference and the next to Mr. Maurice Manning. Cf. his forthcoming book, *The Blueshirts*, 84.

78. *Irish Times*, 13 Nov. 1933.

arguing that power should be diffused among vocational groups, on the lines recommended by *Quadragesimo Anno*. The main exponents of the new teaching were two academics, Professor Michael Tierney of University College, Dublin, and Professor James Hogan of University College, Cork. Though neither wished to see the abolition of Parliament, both envisaged that, under a vocational order, the power of the Dail would be diminished.[79]

The conversion of Fine Gael to corporatist doctrines proved, however, to be short-lived. Of the leaders, General O'Duffy was the only one who showed enthusiasm for the idea. Mr Cosgrave, Mr MacDermot, Mr Dillon and other prominent figures displayed much less interest. General O'Duffy's leadership of the party did not last long, for personal differences with his colleagues led to his resignation in September 1934.[80] In 1935, he founded a new party, the National Corporate Party,[81] but made little or no attempt to organise it.[82] In 1936, on the outbreak of the Civil War in Spain, he took an Irish Brigade to fight for General Franco,[83] and that was his last political activity. Meanwhile, Mr Cosgrave had quietly taken over the leadership of Fine Gael, and under his direction the party once again became a parliamentary opposition, no longer suggesting that the parliamentary system be modified by a corporate order, and showing little interest in vocational organisation even in the economic sphere. Indeed, during the decade after O'Duffy's departure from the leadership of Fine Gael it was in the other parties that the impact of Catholic social teaching was most obvious.

The next party to be considered is the Irish Labour Party. It was much smaller than either Fine Gael or Fianna Fail: during the twenties and thirties it obtained an average of about ten per cent of the first preference votes at general elections.[84] During

79. M. Manning, *op. cit.*, chapter XIII, contains an analysis of their ideas.
80. D. O'Sullivan, *op. cit.*, 408.   81. *Ibid.*, 435.
82. M. Manning, *op. cit.*, 200, found no newspaper reports of meetings in the year after its foundation.   83. E. O'Duffy, *Crusade in Spain, passim*.
84. C. O'Leary, *The Irish Republic and its Experiment with Proportional Representation*, 50–1, shows the Labour proportion of the first preference vote as fluctuating between 5·7 per cent in the general election of 1933 and 12·6 per cent in the general election of June 1927.

the revolutionary period, 1916–23, it had appeared for a time quite militant, passing resolutions at its annual conferences congratulating the Bolsheviks on their revolution,[85] calling for workers' control of industry,[86] and demanding public ownership of all land.[87] During the next ten years it was a moderate body, concentrating on immediate objectives such as the extension of social insurance, improvement of educational opportunity, and better conditions for workers in state-run enterprises. When Fianna Fail came to office in 1932, Labour gave it general support,[88] and during the next two years a number of reforms for which Labour pressed were implemented. Widows' and orphans' pensions were introduced; more employment was provided as a result of the government's industrialisation programme; and a notable speeding-up occurred in the building of houses. Indeed the government's radicalism became a source of embarrassment to Labour, for it was soon difficult to distinguish between Labour's policy and Fianna Fail's.[89]

The Labour party's solution to this problem was to adopt, at its annual conference of 1936, a new party constitution. This was designed, as Senator Thomas Johnson explained in introducing it, 'to indicate that the Labour Party was taking a line more to the left than it had done hitherto.'[90] It pledged the party to work for the establishment of a 'Workers' Republic', and it stated that party's belief in 'the public ownership by the people of all essential sources of wealth.'[91] Such language was not new to the Labour party: it could be considered a reversion to its militant past. The phrase 'Workers' Republic' derives from the party's founder, James Connolly, and there had been much talk of sweeping nationalisation in the immediate post-war period. But what went without comment in 1920, at the height of a

85. *Irish Labour Party and Trade Union Congress. Report of the 25th Annual Meeting* . . . *1919*, 136; *Report of the 27th Annual Meeting* . . . *1921*, 175.

86. *Ibid., Report of the 25th Annual Meeting* . . . *1919*, 112.

87. *Ibid., Report of the 26th Annual Meeting* . . . *1920*, 137; *Report of the 27th Annual Meeting* . . . *1921*, 179.

88. *Irish Labour Party. Second Annual Report* . . . *for 1932*, 14.

89. See, e.g., the complaint of Mr Frank Robbins that Fianna Fail had stolen most of their programme: *Irish Labour Party. Fourth Annual Report* . . . *for 1933–34*, 70.

90. *The Labour Party. Fifth Annual Report* . . . *for 1934–35*, 107.

91. *Ibid.*, appendix.

revolutionary era, would be scrutinised more closely in 1936, at a time when the recent publication of *Quadragesimo Anno* had drawn attention again to the Church's social teaching. The acceptance of a 'Workers' Republic' as an objective could be said to imply class war which had been condemned by the Church; and the advocacy of public ownership could be read as an endorsement of socialism, which had also been condemned by the Church.

Criticism came from within the Labour party itself. It was expressed by an affiliated union, the Irish National Teachers' Organisation, whose secretary, Mr M. P. Linehan, was a well-known lecturer on Catholic social teaching. The course of events can best be stated in the words of the I.N.T.O. executive committee's report for 1940:

It may now be stated that for more than two years the question of alterations in the Labour Party Constitution have [*sic*] been engaging the attention of the Executive. The new Labour Party Constitution was adopted at a Party Conference in 1936. It was only after its publication in pamphlet form, when there was a fuller opportunity to study its various clauses, that doubts began to be expressed regarding the propriety of certain of the Aims and Objects set forth in the Constitution, especially in their relation to the teaching and practice of the Catholic Church.

Early in 1937 the matter was raised at the Executive, and it was decided to seek authoritative advice thereon. A letter was sent to the hierarchy who referred the whole matter to a Committee of Experts, and later informed the Executive that there were definitely in the Constitution certain things which were opposed to Catholic teaching. These had reference mainly to the 'Workers' Republic'—which was set out as the ultimate aim of the Party, and to certain clauses which appeared to interfere with the rights of private property.

As a result of subsequent discussions and correspondence, a series of amendments were placed on the Agenda for the following (1938) Conference of the Party by the Executive, with the object of deleting the objectionable features from the Constitution. It became apparent, however, after discussions and interviews with the Administrative Council of the Party, that these amendments would not be carried at that Conference. The Executive thereupon decided to withdraw them and to give the Council and the members of the Party a fuller opportunity of considering them. The amendments were again placed on the Agenda for the 1939 Conference and a circular-letter setting forth the arguments in favour of their adoption was issued to the Affiliated Unions and Branches. The Administrative Council itself, however, asked and obtained from Congress permission to redraft the Constitution, and made it plain that in doing so the objectionable clauses would be omitted. Thus the object which the Executive had in view was achieved. The new draft Constitution has now been issued, and the Executive are glad to be in a position to report that there is nothing in the revised version to which objection can be taken on religious grounds. The new draft is in accord with that suggested by the Committee of Experts to whom the question was originally submitted by the Hierarchy. The Executive believe that it is due to their action and efforts that these desirable changes have been made, and their action in the matter has received the express commendation of the general body of the Bishops.[92]

In the amended constitution of April 1940, the phrase 'Workers' Republic' was replaced by 'a Republican form of government', and the statement about public ownership was rephrased as follows: 'The Labour Party believes in a system of government which, while recognising the rights of private property, shall ensure that, where the common good requires, essential industries and services shall be brought under public ownership with democratic control.'[93] The decision to allow the constitution to be rewritten in this way was not universally popular in the party, and it was carried on division at the annual conference by 89 votes to 25.[94] A Protestant member, Mr Sam Kyle from Belfast, protested that they were granting an outside body the right to say that the movement must act in accord with their ideas and not its own.[95] But however that may be, the change seems to have done the Labour party no harm at all with the Irish public. At the local elections in 1942 it made extensive gains, winning 100 out of the 630 county council seats, as against 37 out of 757 county council seats at the previous local elections in 1934.[96] In the general election of 1943 it achieved

92. *Irish National Teachers' Organisation. Annual Directory . . . for 1940*, 20–1.
93. *The Labour Party. Ninth Annual Report . . . 1939*, 169.
94. *The Labour Party. Eighth Annual Report . . . 1938*, 112.
95. *Ibid.*, 108.
96. *The Labour Party. Report of the Administrative Council for the Year 1942*, appendix III.

its highest proportion of first preference votes at any general election since the treaty[97] and increased its parliamentary strength to seventeen, as compared with nine at the previous general election in 1938. Fine Gael simultaneously dropped from 45 seats at the general election of 1938 to 32 at the general election of 1943, and Labour believed that it was within striking distance of becoming the principal opposition party.

The Labour party, however, had not yet secured itself against attacks on the religious front. During 1943–4 it was racked by a dispute with the largest trade union in Ireland, the Irish Transport and General Workers' Union. The cause of the dispute, the authorities seem agreed, was personal.[98] The president of the I.T.G.W.U., William O'Brien, was a long-standing enemy of the veteran Labour leader James Larkin. Until the nineteen-forties, O'Brien had been one of the most powerful men in the Labour party and Larkin had not been a member at all. But in 1941 Larkin was admitted as a member of the party, and in 1943 he was a successful candidate at the general election. O'Brien tried to prevent Larkin being recognised as an official candidate, and it was his failure to do so which brought the dispute to a head.[99] But the terms in which the dispute was presented are interesting. Larkin had at one time been a communist and the I.T.G.W.U. represented itself as concerned for the purity of the Labour party from communist infiltration, which the party's official leadership was too weak-kneed to oppose. William O'Brien had not always been so anti-communist. In 1918, as president of the Labour party, he had welcomed the Bolshevik revolution.[100] But by putting the case on these grounds, O'Brien mobilised the support of militant Catholic opinion. His most vocal supporter was the Catholic weekly, the *Standard*, whose pages during the first half of 1944 are full of revelations, well or

97. C. O'Leary, *The Irish Republic and its Experiment with Proportional Representation*, 51, calculates it as 15·7 per cent.

98. Emmet Larkin, *James Larkin*, 299; J. J. Judge, *The Labour Movement in the Republic of Ireland*, *passim*. A main argument of Dr Judge's unpublished thesis is that O'Brien aimed throughout to dominate the Irish trade union movement.

99. E. Larkin, *op. cit.*, 301; *The Labour Party. Official Statement relating to the disaffiliation from the Labour Party of the Irish Transport and General Workers' Union*, 2–3.

100. *The Irish Labour Party and Trade Union Congress. Report of the 24th Annual Congress . . . 1918*, 9.

D

ill-founded, of communist penetration into the Labour party. The quarrel did the Labour party serious damage. The I.T.G.W.U. disaffiliated itself and five Labour deputies who were members of the I.T.G.W.U. resigned from the party.[101] For six years, 1944 to 1950, two rival groups, Labour and National Labour, sat independently in the Dail, and all hope that Labour might overtake Fine Gael as the main opposition party disappeared.

Meanwhile, the growing interest in Catholic social thought had also been affecting Fianna Fail. Proof of this can be found in the 1937 constitution, which has already been discussed in the previous chapter; but there is one section of this constitution, directly derived from *Quadragesimo Anno*, which seems more appropriately discussed here. This was the section dealing with the composition of the Senate. On this matter it is possible to trace the source of Mr de Valera's ideas more easily than in most parts of the constitution, for in 1936 he had set up a commission to advise him on how a second house of the legislature should be composed.[102] The commission was unable to come to an agreed conclusion and produced three minority reports as well as several reservations to the majority report.[103] It was one of the minority reports drawn up, as it happened, by members several of whom had links with Fine Gael,[104] which most attracted Mr de Valera, and which he made the basis of his own proposals. The minority report proposed that most of the Senate be chosen by vocational groups.[105]

Under the terms of the constitution, senators are of three kinds. Eleven are nominated by the Taoiseach, or prime minister. Six are elected by the graduates of Irish universities—three from the National University of Ireland, and three from Trinity College, Dublin. The remaining forty-three—and this is where the vocational element comes in—are selected by five panels of candidates, consisting of persons 'having knowledge and practical

101. E. Larkin, *op. cit.*, 301.
102. D. O'Sullivan, *The Irish Free State and its Senate*, 490.
103. *Ibid.*, 491.
104. The signatories were: D. A. Binchy, Sir John Keane, E. Lynch, Frank MacDermot, J. Moynihan, A. O'Rahilly, M. Tierney, R. Wilson.
105. *Irish Times*, 8 Oct. 1936.

experience of' the subjects germane to the panel concerned. The panels are respectively: the cultural and educational; agricultural; labour; industrial and commercial; and administrative.[106] Subsequent legislation, filling in the details, provided that candidates for these panels were to be nominated partly by deputies and outgoing senators, but partly also by vocational bodies within the field of the panel concerned.[107] The Irish Trade Union Congress, for instance, could nominate for the Labour panel, or the Irish Agricultural Organisation Society for the Agricultural panel.[108]

In practice, the vocational principle in Senate elections has not worked well. Though the nominations come in part from vocational bodies, the actual electorate for the forty-three panel members is entirely political—it consists of deputies, outgoing senators, and county and county borough councillors.[109] Voting is almost entirely along party lines, so that candidates secure election not because of their eminence in a vocation but on the strength of their party ties.[110] Nonetheless, the fact that the Senate's electoral system is vocational in form shows how influential the idea of vocational organisation had become in the Ireland of 1937. And, though it has not been implemented, there is provision in the constitution for direct election of part of the Senate by vocational groups to be introduced at a later date.[111]

The following year, the government took a further step towards the building up of a vocational order in Ireland. This was the establishment of a commission to 'examine . . . the practicability of developing functional or vocational organisation in the circumstances of this country', and 'the means best calculated to promote such development'. The suggestion that such a commission be established was made by two senators

---

106. The constitution (Article 18.7.1°) gives a longer description to each of these panels; but the titles here given are those in general use.

107. Seanad Electoral (Panel Members) Acts, 1937, 1947, 1954.

108. For a description of the nomination process see J. McG. Smyth, 'Seanad Eireann—3', *Administration* (XVI, 2) Summer 1968, 180–91.

109. Seanad Electoral (Panel Members) Act, 1947, s. 44.

110. For analyses of how the Senate electoral system works in practice, see B. Chubb, 'Vocational representation and the Irish Senate', *Political Studies* (II, 2) June 1954, 97–111, and T. Garvin, *The Irish Senate*, chapters III and V.

111. Article 19.

whose previous links had been with Fine Gael, Frank Mac-
Dermot and Michael Tierney, in a motion introduced in the
Senate on 13 July 1938.[112] Mr deValera accepted their motion and
the commission was appointed on 10 January 1939.[113] It was a
strong team of twenty-five members, drawn from many walks of
life—industrialists, trade unionists, people connected with agriculture, and people with a knowledge of social work and social
theory. The members included Father Hayes of *Muintir na
Tire*, Professor Alfred O'Rahilly, Professor Michael Tierney,
and Father E. J. Coyne, a Jesuit well known for his writings on
social questions. The religious minorities were well represented
too—forming a quarter of the total, according to Dr Harvey, the
Church of Ireland Bishop of Cashel, who was himself a
member.[114] The chairman of the commission was Dr Browne,
the Bishop of Galway. The drawback to appointing so large a
body was that it would be likely to work slowly and in fact it was
not until 1944 that its report was completed. But the fact that the
government was prepared to nominate a strong commission to
investigate this subject seemed to show that Fianna Fail, as well
as the other parties, had been affected by the growing interest
in Ireland in Catholic social teaching.

The Fianna Fail regime, indeed, was proving to be, from the
hierarchy's point of view, in many ways a model administration.
As we saw in the last chapter, it enacted a constitution acknowledging the 'special position' of the Catholic Church, and it was
ready to impose by law the Church's standards on such matters
as divorce and contraception. As we have seen in this chapter,
it promoted the papal ideal of vocational organisation. This was
a remarkable record for a party whose leaders had been excommunicated on the Civil War issue, and it illustrates the
Irish Catholic capacity for preventing disagreement with the
bishops on one issue from spilling over into disagreement on
others.

It would be misleading, however, to close this chapter by

---

112. *Seanad Debates*, XXI, 300.
113. *Commission on Vocational Organisation. Report*, 1.
114. *Irish Times*, 11 Sept. 1944.

suggesting that on all issues government and hierarchy were at one. Some questions did arise during the first decade of Fianna Fail rule, on which the government and some at least of the bishops did not see eye to eye. None of these was serious enough to be considered a conflict of Church and State, but they were sufficient to show that the independence of judgment which had led those who now headed Fianna Fail into conflict with the hierarchy during the Civil War had not been altogether abandoned.

One such issue was provided by the government's economic policy. By engaging in a tariff war with Britain, the government brought much hardship on farmers who had depended on the British market, and some of the bishops believed they were entitled to condemn this policy on moral grounds as unjust to the suffering farmers. Cardinal MacRory, speaking in Mr de Valera's presence at Slane, county Meath, on 15 August 1932, declared that it was 'a shame and a sin' to prosecute the economic struggle with Britain without attempting to negotiate a settlement.[115] Bishop Cohalan of Cork stated that the government's policies were putting unjust burdens on farmers.[116] Bishop Fogarty of Killaloe attacked the government's 'tariff madness', and lamented that the farmers had been ruined.[117] These, however, were only a minority of the hierarchy. Most bishops remained silent on the economic issue, and one or two, such as Bishop MacNeely of Raphoe and Bishop Dignan of Clonfert, even hinted that they sympathised with Fianna Fail.[118]

An issue on which perhaps a larger proportion of the bishops disagreed with the government was the danger of communism. There is no doubt that many of the bishops thought that there was a real danger of communism taking root in Ireland. Under the Cosgrave regime, when they condemned the I.R.A. in their

115. *Ibid.*, 16 Aug. 1932.   116. *Irish Weekly Independent*, 30 May 1936.
117. *Ibid.*, 5 Nov. 1932, 27 May 1933.
118. Dr MacNeely, in his lenten pastoral for 1933, said that the people had been true to themselves in the recent general election. As the election had produced an increased majority for Fianna Fail, it may be deduced that the bishop favoured that party: *Irish Catholic Directory, 1934,* 585 (26 Feb. 1933). Dr Dignan, in his pastoral at the same time, attacked the control exercised by international finance, which in the circumstances could be considered an endorsement of Fianna Fail's aim of economic independence: *Irish Weekly Independent,* 4 March 1933.

joint pastoral of 1931, they had also condemned its associated organisation, Saor Eire, for being communistic.[119] The Cosgrave government had almost simultaneously proclaimed Saor Eire and the I.R.A. to be illegal organisations,[120] but the incoming government revoked the ban,[121] and although Saor Eire faded away, the I.R.A. remained active, and communist influence within it remained strong enough to cause alarm. Warnings against communism were a prominent topic in the lenten pastorals for the years 1933 to 1937.[122] Some of the bishops spoke out against it on other occasions, such as confirmation services.[123] The raciest condemnation came, as might be expected, from the eccentric Bishop of Galway, Dr O'Doherty. Preaching at Kinvara in May 1933, he warned the congregation against joining a secret society like the I.R.A., and backed up his argument with an interpretation of the role of secret societies in Irish history which was remarkable for the number of Irish folk-heroes that it managed to assail:

I could say a lot of things about the history of secret societies and semi-secret societies. Who fought in '98? Was it the United Irishmen? It was not; it was the men of Meath and Wexford who fought.

What about the men of '48? They hatched a cabbage garden plot. What did Emmet do? He led a rabble through the streets of Dublin. The same applied to '67. Who went out in 1916? Who faced the 'Black and Tans' in this country? Was it any of the secret societies? It was not; it was the decent young men of the country. What did cut-throat Tone do? We hear a lot of talk about these people, and they are held up as heroes, so-called heroes; but secret societies or those who belonged to them never were of any benefit to the country.[124]

The bishops seem to have had some popular support for their alarm, at least in Dublin, where mob anti-communism was a feature of the nineteen-thirties. In 1933, a crowd shouting 'God

119. *Irish Independent,* 19 Oct. 1931.
120. D. O'Sullivan, *The Irish Free State and its Senate,* 265.
121. *Ibid.,* 295.
122. See the summaries in the *Irish Catholic Directory* for each year.
123. e.g. Archbishop Harty of Cashel, Bishop Collier of Ossory, Bishop Fogarty of Killaloe: *Irish Independent,* 22 May 1933; Bishop O'Brien of Kerry: *ibid.,* 26 May 1933.
124. *Irish Times,* 24 May 1933.

bless the Pope' stormed the headquarters of the Revolutionary Workers' Group in Great Strand Street, Dublin.[125] In 1936, a communist meeting in Rathmines town hall was broken up, it was said by the Catholic Young Men's Society.[126] But Mr de Valera refused to share these fears. In the Dail he argued that the communist threat in Ireland was negligible[127] and alleged that the bishops had been misled by information from General O'Duffy, who had been chief of police before he became the Blueshirt leader.[128] It was not until June 1936, after several brutal murders attributed to the I.R.A., that the government proclaimed it an unlawful association.[129]

Hardly had this been done than another event occurred on which the government and the bishops appeared to take divergent views. This was the outbreak of the Spanish Civil War. To many Catholics, General Franco was a Christian crusader, rescuing Spain from communist revolution. The Irish bishops as a whole seem to have accepted this interpretation. A joint statement in October 1936 protested against the atrocities being committed against the Church in Republican Spain, without mentioning any atrocities that might have been committed by Franco's forces.[130] Many of the lenten pastorals of 1937 referred to the events in Spain, in terms favourable to Franco's side.[131] In October 1937, the Irish hierarchy sent a sympathetic reply to the letter which the Spanish hierarchy had addressed to the Catholic bishops of the world, asserting the justice of Franco's cause.[132] In this attitude, the Irish bishops had the support of at least considerable sections of Irish public opinion. In the Dail, Fine Gael urged that Franco's regime be recognised as the government of Spain.[133] Outside Parliament, an organisation calling itself the Irish Christian Front was founded in August 1936 to combat communism in Ireland and send help to 'the

125. *Irish Weekly Independent*, 1 April 1933.
126. *Ibid.*, 18 Jan. 1936.
127. *Dail Debates*, L, 2496–2501 (1 March 1934), 2510–13 (2 March 1934).
128. *Ibid.*, LI, 1222 (20 March 1934).
129. D. O'Sullivan, *op. cit.*, 444.
130. *Irish Catholic Directory, 1937*, 627 (13 Oct. 1936).
131. *Irish Independent*, 8 Feb. 1937.
132. *Irish Catholic Directory, 1938*, 631–2 (12 Oct. 1937).
133. *Dail Debates*, LXIV, 1194 (27 Nov. 1936: motion by Mr Cosgrave).

Patriot Soldiers of Spain.'[134] It was strong enough to hold impressive rallies in Dublin,[135] and in January 1937 the first of the ambulance units which it organised for service in Spain was sent off, blessed by the Auxiliary Bishop of Dublin.[136] Meanwhile, General O'Duffy is said to have recruited about 700 men for service with Franco's forces; while this is not a large number it compares favourably with the 200 who are said to have gone from Ireland to fight on the republican side.[137] A church-door collection organised by the Irish hierarchy for the suffering Catholics of Spain brought in nearly £44,000.[138] Journals which opposed the prevailing pro-Franco line found themselves under pressure. A talented monthly, *Ireland To-day*, abruptly ceased publication in March 1938, as the result, it is said, of pressure organised by priests who objected to its publication of articles favouring the republican side in Spain.[139] The *Irish Times*, which tried to hold the balance even between the two parties in Spain, came under similar pressure but defied it and survived.[140] Even the Labour party, which, as ostensibly the most left-wing party in the country, might have been expected to show most sympathy for the Spanish republicans, was muted

134. *Irish Christian Front*, 1.

135. *Irish Weekly Independent*, 5 Sept. 1936, 10 April 1937.

136. *Irish Catholic Directory, 1938*, 579 (13 Jan. 1937).

137. T. P. Coogan, *Ireland since the Rising*, 265. Mr Coogan does not give his sources, but his figure for O'Duffy's forces corresponds with those given in O'Duffy's own book: *Crusade in Spain*, 155, 239.

138. *Irish Catholic Directory, 1938*, 582 (3 Feb. 1937).

139. P. Blanshard, *The Irish and Catholic Power*, 187; M. Sheehy, *Is Ireland Dying?*, 150–1. Mr Blanshard says that *Ireland To-day* 'published some articles against Franco during the Spanish Civil War, and immediately priests went into the shops telling the proprietors to "take that red magazine out of the window". Gradually its friends and advertisers began to slip away, and it soon died.' Mr Blanshard is a polemically anti-Catholic writer, and I would not take him as authoritative on anything without some support from another source. In this case, however, his claim is supported by a remark in one of the articles which appeared in *Ireland To-day* itself: 'It is now common knowledge in Ireland that even this cautious, and thoughtful periodical, has been submitted to a violent series of . . . attacks delivered in the name of religion'. See S. O'Faolain, 'The priests and the people', *Ireland To-day* (II, 7) July 1937, 37. Mr Blanshard describes this periodical as 'a progressive critical journal of first-rate quality', and, having been through its files, I would agree with him.

140. P. Blanshard, *op. cit.*, 187. Here, Mr Blanshard's evidence is supported by the memoirs of a member of the *Irish Times* staff: L. Fleming, *Head or Harp*, 170.

and uncertain. Its leaders seem to have avoided referring to the events in Spain, and when, at the party's annual conference in 1938, a young delegate from the Trinity College branch, Mr Conor Cruise O'Brien, made an attack on Franco, he provoked protests from a section of the delegates.[141]

The Fianna Fail government, however, refused to take part in an anti-communist crusade. It issued a statement deploring the excesses reported to have been committed in Spain, but that was as far as it would go.[142] Mr de Valera refused, in the face of strong protests from Fine Gael, to withdraw recognition from the republican government.[143] In February 1937 he piloted through the Dail the Spanish Civil War (Non-Intervention) Act, which forbade, among other things, Irish citizens to enlist on either side, and which therefore had the effect of drying up recruitment for O'Duffy's Irish Brigade, as well as for the smaller number of Irishmen fighting on the other side. There was, it is true, no formal contradiction between Mr de Valera's attitude and that of the bishops—it was possible to argue that Ireland should be neutral while still sympathising with one particular side—but there was an unmistakable difference of stress. To judge by what some of the bishops said in their pastorals, they might have preferred Ireland to adopt an attitude of non-belligerent support for Franco, similar to that taken by Salazar's regime in Portugal. But that was not what they got from Mr de Valera.

One bizarre episode in Church-State relations must be mentioned before closing this chapter. This was the application of wartime censorship to ecclesiastical pronouncements. During the Second World War, a censorship was imposed to ensure that the papers printed nothing which might compromise the country's neutrality. Statements which even appeared to imply partisanship for one side or the other were rigorously suppressed. The principle was applied just as strictly to statements from ecclesiastical quarters as to any others. For instance, Bishop Morrisroe of Achonry, in his lenten pastoral for 1941, included the following comment on the war in Europe:

141. *Irish Weekly Independent*, 9 April 1938.
142. *Ibid.*, 29 Aug. 1936.
143. *Dail Debates*, LXV, 833 ff. (19 Feb. 1937).

We know what the Poles are suffering and we know how the Dictator has treated the Church in Germany. Can we look with indifference on God dethroned from His rightful place in the universe? Can Catholics view with easy minds the possibility of a victory which would give brute force the power to control Europe and decide the fate of small nations?

Thoughtless persons give no heed to these prospects yet they may become very real. Such an attitude of indifference to the religious outlook of the future is treason to our faith. This mentality is caused by the persuasion that anything that injures a hereditary enemy is good for us. Even if true, political expediency should not weigh in the balance against Christianity.[144]

This clearly implied a hope that Germany would not win the war, and the papers were forbidden to publish it.[145] Mr de Valera, when challenged in the Dail, made no apology for this decision: 'That passage was censored in accordance with the general directions which had already gone out to all the newspapers. The newspapers themselves, if they were to act in accordance with the general instructions which they had received, would have themselves censored it. . . . If there are instructions given out in that particular way it is quite right that the censor should act uniformly.'[146] Nor was this a unique case. A few weeks earlier, a statement from the *Osservatore Romano* refuting rumours that the Pope favoured Hitler and Mussolini was censored, on the ground that the rumours to which it referred had not been published in Ireland.[147] A report of a Vatican Radio broadcast drawing attention to the unsatisfactory treatment of the Catholic Church by Nazi Germany was also censored.[148] A few months later, a farmers' journal was forbidden to publish in full a letter from Bishop Collier of Ossory. On this occasion, the reason was not that the statement jeopardised the neutrality of the country, but that it might harm the agricultural policy of the government. The letter was an appeal to farmers for more

144. Quoted by Mr James Dillon in *Dail Debates*, LXXXII, 1444 (3 April 1941). The author of the pastoral was identified as the Bishop of Achonry by Mr. P. McGilligan: *ibid.*, 1503.
145. *Ibid.*, 1444.
146. *Ibid.*, 1485.
147. *Ibid.*, 1439 (speech of Mr Dillon).
148. *Ibid.*, 1441 (speech of Mr Dillon).

tillage. This accorded with government policy; but, apparently, it included a passage comparing the price paid to the Irish farmer unfavourably with the price paid for imported wheat, and this the censorship decided to delete, on the basis that it 'might have been used as an excuse for the non-sowing of wheat by a certain type of farmer.'[149]

None of these acts of censorship was particularly important. By and large, Irish bishops remained free to say what they liked to the Irish people, and even on the occasions when censorship was used, the fact that deputies could raise the matter in the Dail and quote the offending passages meant that the prohibition could be evaded. But these incidents do prove (if proof were necessary) that Fianna Fail did not treat everything that came from a bishop as sacrosanct. As the forties wore on, there was a question-mark over Church–State relations. In the late twenties and the nineteen-thirties, Fianna Fail had appeared quite ready to co-operate with the bishops in maintaining Catholic standards of morality, especially in sexual matters. But interest was now changing. There was less concern about dance-halls or evil literature, and more about building up a social order which would be in accord with Catholic principles. So far, Fianna Fail had seemed quite well disposed towards such a design. But no one had yet worked out in detail just what a Catholic social order would mean in Ireland. When they did so, it was uncertain how a Fianna Fail government would respond. The precedents showed that Fianna Fail could be respectful, even deferential, to the Church; but they also showed that it had a mind of its own.

149. *Ibid.*, LXXXVI, 314–5 (26 March 1942: question by Mr P. Cogan and reply by Mr. F. Aiken, Minister for the Co-ordination of Defensive Measures).

CHAPTER IV

THE ISSUE TAKES SHAPE:
VOCATIONALISM VERSUS BUREAUCRACY, 1944-6

In the second half of 1944, two documents were published which brought the increasing demand for a Catholic social order in Ireland into sharper focus. One of these documents was a fat volume of over five hundred pages—the *Report of the Commission on Vocational Organisation*. The other was a slim pamphlet of only forty pages—*Social Security: Outlines of a Scheme of National Health Insurance,* published over the name of Dr Dignan, Bishop of Clonfert. The first ranged over the whole of Irish economic life; the second dealt with one particular problem. But each performed the same function, of working out with much more precision than had been attempted hitherto just what the reshaping of Irish society on Catholic social principles would entail, and each aroused wide interest in Ireland.

The Vocational Organisation Report, published in August 1944,[1] was the fruit of a great deal of work. Its five hundred pages began with a survey of the history of vocational organisation and continued with an account of its extent in twelve foreign countries—Italy, Portugal, Sweden, New Zealand, Denmark, Finland, Britain, Belgium, the Netherlands, France, Germany, and Russia. This part of the report showed that, despite the differences in regime between these countries, a considerable amount of vocational organisation existed in all of them. The next, and longest, part of the report contained a survey of the state of vocational organisation in Ireland. In compiling this section, the commission sent out a questionnaire to 333 bodies and heard oral evidence from 174.[2] The result is

1. *Irish Times,* 18 Aug. 1944.
2. *Commission on Vocational Organisation. Report,* 2. In citing this report I use page and not paragraph numbers.

a unique mass of information on Irish associational life: professional organisations, trade unions and employers' organisations, farmers' organisations, banks and the stock exchange, and civil service. The final section of the report contained the commission's recommendations.

The report is particularly important for two things: first, its analysis of what was wrong with the Ireland of its day; and second, its proposed remedies. Its analysis of ills is embedded in the central, descriptive section of the report, which is by no means the piece of detached and passionless commentary that it appears on the surface to be. On the contrary, it turns out, on examination, to contain a sustained criticism of the way in which government departments handled the interest groups in their area of activity. The two departments most in contact with economic interest groups—the Departments of Agriculture and of Industry and Commerce—were the ones most closely scrutinised. The Department of Industry and Commerce came in for particularly hard knocks. There was very considerable agreement among the interest groups concerned that it did not consult them sufficiently.[3] They complained that they were not consulted about the drafting of legislation or of statutory orders affecting them, and that deputations were sometimes refused an opportunity to put their point of view. A particular grievance was that the department did not make public the import licences which it issued, with the result that some firms were placed under serious disadvantages in competition with others.[4] The Federation of Irish Manufacturers complained that it was not consulted at the time of the Anglo-Irish trade treaty of 1938, although the British government consulted its opposite numbers in Britain.[5] The commission, in fairness, quoted the department's reasons for not consulting interest groups more widely. The department argued that in some negotiations—for instance, the setting up of a new industry—secrecy was essential, and that in others, the self-interest of industrialists conflicted with the national interest as seen by the department.[6] But the commission clearly felt that the weight of the argument was against

3. *Ibid.*, 207.   4. *Ibid.*
5. *Ibid.*, 198.   6. *Ibid.*, 206–7.

the department and that it ought to show more readiness to consult outside interests.[7]

The Department of Agriculture came out somewhat better in the commission's report. Much of the detailed administration was done by the County Committees of Agriculture, which consisted of people with a practical knowledge of, or special interest in, agriculture, and which therefore, could be considered a kind of vocational body.[8] In general, the department appeared ready to use vocational bodies where these were efficient, rather than setting up its own machinery to handle every problem. The issue of fat cattle export licences was delegated to a body representative of the exporters themselves.[9] Voluntary societies for the improvement of particular breeds were given grants, and 'the Secretary of the Department stated in evidence before us that these bodies accomplished useful work more economically than the Department could perform it'.[10] The Department of Agriculture had also done what the Department of Industry and Commerce had always failed to do, and set up consultative councils on various aspects of agricultural policy. However, even the Department of Agriculture did not escape criticism from the commission. It was all very well setting up consultative councils, but the important question was how often they met. The commission did a little research here, and it found that of five such councils existing in August 1941, one had not met at all in the preceding three years, two others had met only once, and the remaining two had met seven times and eight times respectively.[11] The commission's conclusion was that 'there is little real collaboration between the Department and organised agriculturalists. Broadly speaking, agriculture is regulated on bureaucratic lines.'[12]

Bureaucracy, indeed, was the main evil which the commission detected in Irish government. A passage towards the end of the report lucidly summarised what was wrong.[13] It pointed out that officials entered the civil service very young, and with no technical knowledge of industry or business. Once in the service, they found themselves working a system which called for very

7. *Ibid.*, 208.   8. *Ibid.*, 142, 307.   9. *Ibid.*, 294.
10. *Ibid.*, 132.   11. *Ibid.*, 141.   12. *Ibid.*, 142.
13. *Ibid.*, 424–5.

complete recording of all decisions, which generated bulky files and which made for slowness of decisions. The fact that a minister might be questioned in the Dail for the actions of any of his officials made the latter extremely careful and more ready to do nothing than to take a risk. At the same time, responsibility was diffused, owing to the fact that many officials might take a share in formulating proposals. True, a minister was theoretically responsible for the actions of all his officials, but the size and complexity of a modern department was such that the effectiveness of his control was diminished, and officials exercised considerable power without corresponding responsibility. The commission summed up the weaknesses of the system as follows:

These conditions result in certain features which would be regarded as defects in business or industrial management. They are (i) a rigidity shown in the tendency to interpret regulations in a narrow legalistic manner, to adhere fixedly to precedent and to refuse to create a new precedent or to experiment; (ii) a lack of personal responsibility and of inducement to produce results: where remuneration is not dependent on results, either negatively or positively, there is a temptation to adopt the easiest or most convenient course rather than the best; (iii) a lack of close and effective contact between the official and those affected by his decision: those officials who make decisions are located in Dublin and cannot be expected to have first-hand knowledge of all the details covering the matters upon which they have to give decisions.[14]

The commission did not believe, however, that the remedy for these evils was a simple reversion to *laissez-faire*. It recognised that the great increase in State intervention in recent years had been 'for the most part demanded by the public for the protection and promotion of the common good.'[15] The choice was not between State control and *laissez-faire*, but between one kind of State control and another. 'Bureaucracy is not identical with State control. It is but one form or method of State control.'[16] This was where the commission's positive recommendations came in.

The commission recommended that as an alternative to

14. *Ibid.*, 425.　　15. *Ibid.*, 422.　　16. *Ibid.*, 426.

bureaucratic control the State should act as much as possible through vocational bodies. It noted that this already happened in the professions, which largely regulated themselves through vocational bodies, without expense to the taxpayer and yet safeguarding the rights of the State.[17] What it asked was that the same principle be applied in agriculture, commerce and industry. In amplification of this proposal, it drew up an elaborate framework of interlocking authorities. Each profession and industry was to have its own vocational organisation, where these did not already exist.[18] Professions or industries with overlapping interests were to have joint councils—for instance a Council of Law, chosen by barristers, solicitors and judges, or a Cereals Council bringing together representatives of grain-growers, millers, and consumers of grain such as bakers, brewers and distillers.[19] Above these were to be six assemblies of wider range, one to each main area of economic activity—agriculture, industry, commerce, transport, finance and the professions.[20] Finally, these six authorities were to elect members to a supreme organ, the National Vocational Assembly, in the following proportions:—

National Agricultural Conference	40
National Industrial Conference	20
National Commercial Conference	10
National Transport Council	10
National Finance Council	10
Professional Commission	10
Co-opted by the elected members	20
Total ..	120[21]

The report went at some length into the functions of these organisations. The details differed with each one. But in general, the aim was to ensure that, as far as possible, decisions affecting an industry or profession were taken by the industry or profession concerned. For example, an industrial board would handle collective bargaining in the industry, would act as a research and planning authority, and would also act as admin-

17. *Ibid.*, 427.   18. *Ibid.*, 319–420 *passim.*   19. *Ibid.*, 331, 376.
20. *Ibid.*, 325, 346, 361, 392, 402, 412.   21. *Ibid.*, 442.

istering authority for such things as factory inspection.[22] The board of a profession would maintain a register of qualified members, and handle complaints against the conduct of individual members.[23] The job of middle-tier bodies, such as the National Agricultural Conference or the National Industrial Conference, was to act as a court of appeal from lower bodies, to settle their conflicts and co-ordinate their plans.[24] The National Vocational Assembly was to have the same tasks in regard to middle-tier bodies.[25] The functions of parliament and government were to be left unchanged. The commission stressed that 'we have suggested an economic vocational structure which can exist alongside and parallel with a political structure that is not based on vocationalism'.[26] But it did urge that government departments should make a point of consulting the appropriate vocational bodies before introducing legislation or issuing statutory orders.[27]

Two months after the appearance of the Vocational Organisation Report, Dr Dignan, Bishop of Clonfert, published his pamphlet on *Social Security: Outlines of a Scheme of National Health Insurance.*[28] The bishop's interest in the subject arose from his work as Chairman of the National Health Insurance Society and the pamphlet was originally read as a paper to the society's committee of management. It was much more limited in scope than the Vocational Organisation Report, for it dealt simply with one particular problem, the reorganisation of the social services. It covered, however, somewhat wider territory than its title implies, as it dealt not just with health insurance, but with the restructuring of the other social services as well. It claimed to be based on Christian principles[29] and it can be considered an attempt to work out in detail the application of Catholic social teaching to a particular sector of Irish life.

Dr Dignan's proposals, like the Vocational Organisation Report, can be analysed under two headings: criticism of existing structures, and proposals for reform. Dr Dignan's comments on the existing social services were severe. In particular he at-

22. *Ibid.*, 360–1.   23. *Ibid.*, 323–4.   24. *Ibid.*, 347, 362.
25. *Ibid.*, 443–5.   26. *Ibid.*, 318.   27. *Ibid.*, e.g. 427–8.
28. The paper is dated 11 Oct. 1944, and was summarised in the press on 18 Oct. 1944.   29. Most Rev. J. Dignan, *Social Security*, 7.

tacked the medical assistance service on which a large section of the population depended for medical treatment. This service had been part of the harsh Poor Law of British times, and although the nomenclature had changed, the bishop believed that the spirit in which the law was administered had not greatly changed. The poor physical condition of the dispensaries in which treatment was provided epitomised, he believed, the faults of the system. 'The dispensary', he wrote, 'is the core, the hub and heart of the degrading Poor Law system. To understand the system you have only to visit a dispensary. Most of them have no proper accommodation, no sanitary arrangements, no waiting rooms, and from the medical point of view they have few conveniences or appliances to help the doctor to diagnose or to treat.'[30] But indeed he criticised the whole legal framework on which the medical assistance service rested: 'The whole Poor Law legislation, the Medical Charities Act and similar legislation should be blotted out from our Statute Book and—from our memories. The system is tainted at its root and it reeks now, as it did when introduced, of destitution, pauperism and degradation.'[31]

Dr Dignan's remedy for these evils was to propose a radical overhaul of all Irish social services. He advocated that the existing services be unified and transferred to an insurance basis. Social insurance schemes already existed in Ireland, for sickness benefit, widows' and orphans' pensions, and unemployment benefit, and most employees were eligible for them.[32] Dr Dignan proposed that these schemes be unified and expanded, that medical treatment be henceforth provided as a benefit under the social insurance scheme and that the self-employed—who formed a very large proportion of the labour force in Ireland[33]—be allowed to join the scheme as voluntary contributors.[34] Dr Dignan appears to have favoured insurance-based social services

---

30. *Ibid.*, 12.   31. *Ibid.*

32. *First Report of the Department of Social Welfare, 1947–1949,* 10, 29, 35. This publication contains an admirable historical account of the development of each social welfare scheme in Ireland.

33. In 1946 there were 74,000 employers, 272,000 persons working on their own account, and 662,000 employees. Persons assisting relatives came to 213,000. See *Census of Population of Ireland, 1946,* VI, 1.

34. Most Rev. J. Dignan, *op. cit.*, 27.

because they fitted in best with Catholic teaching on the rights of the family. 'By the natural and divine law, the father of the family is bound to maintain his home for himself, his wife and his family: no authority, not even the State, can relieve him of this duty and privilege. Care must be taken then in any scheme of Social Services claiming to be Christian not to attempt to relieve him of this obligation to support his family: all we should do is to assist him so that he can the better meet his family and social obligations.'[35] Insurance schemes, he implied, fulfilled this condition: by granting the head of the family benefits in return for contributions, they supported him in his role of family provider, while assistance directly provided by the State would only undermine that role.

Another of Dr Dignan's proposals was that the expanded social insurance scheme should be administered, not by a government department, but by an enlarged version of the National Health Insurance Society. His reason for this was partly the practical one that he believed the existing National Health Insurance Society to have proved its efficiency, but it was also based on the principle of vocational organisation so much emphasised in Catholic social teaching. He argued that the society's committee of management, consisting as it did of representatives of all those concerned—government, employers and workers—was 'the nearest approach to Vocational Organisation in this country'.[36]

In appraising the Vocational Organisation Report and the Dignan plan, the same comment can be made on both—that they were more cogent when criticising existing Irish institutions than when offering alternatives. The Vocational Organisation Commission's criticisms of Irish bureaucracy—its inbred-ness, its addiction to routine, its suspicion of outside interest groups—were based on evidence from large numbers of witnesses and have a ring of truth. Dr Dignan's strictures on Irish social services were based on his experiences in the National Health Insurance Society and expressed widely shared opinions.[37] Indeed, only

35. *Ibid.*, 7–8.   36. *Ibid.*, 31.
37. For other criticisms of the dispensary system made at this time see W. R. F. Collis, *The State of Medicine in Ireland*, 16–17; *Journal of the Medical Association of Eire*, July 1944, 9.

a few years later a minister was to denounce the low standard of dispensary buildings in terms stronger than any used by the bishop.[38] The criticisms contained in the two documents were, in short, derived from empirical observation and they carried weight.

When it came to making recommendations, however, the desire to derive their conclusions from observed fact seemed to desert the authors of these documents. The Vocational Organisation Commission carried out no pilot studies to see whether the numerous authorities whose establishment it recommended would be doing a useful job of work. It made almost no reference even to the considerable amount of information it had collected about the working of vocational organisation in other countries. The elaborate pyramid of boards, conferences and assemblies which it recommended seemed to have been built up with more concern for symmetry than for ensuring that each of these bodies met a real need. Dr Dignan, for his part, evaded important difficulties in presenting his scheme. He skated over the crucial question of finance, making no effort to work out in detail how much his proposals would cost, or to show that they would give the country better value for money than the existing social services.[39] He ignored the objection that centralisation of social services under an enlarged National Health Insurance Society might only lead to a new bureaucracy growing up alongside the one whose operations he deplored. He also failed to grapple with one difficulty which besets any social insurance scheme: the problem of how to deal with those who are in need but who, for one reason or another, have fallen behind with their contributions. It would be inhumane to leave such people entirely without aid; but on the other hand to help them too readily would encourage other contributors to default. In practice, there is only one way out: to grant assistance, but to accompany it with a searching enquiry to ensure that the applicant is not imposing on the taxpayer—in other words, to provide something like the Poor Law which the bishop abhorred. It is almost

38. *Dail Debates*, CXVI, 1813 (1 July 1949: speech of Minister for Health, Dr N. Browne).

39. The bishop's remarks on finance can be found in Most Rev. J. Dignan, *op. cit.*, 33–7.

an axiom of social policy that, where social services are based on insurance, a social assistance service, operated with a means test, has also to be provided for those who fall through the insurance net.[40] If it is really desired to abolish invidious distinctions between the destitute and the rest, and to allow all to receive treatment on the same terms, there is only one way to do it—and that is to provide a free-for-all service financed out of general taxation, like the National Health Service in Britain.[41]

The fundamental weakness of both documents, perhaps, was that they applied too dogmatically the then dominant tenets of Catholic social teaching. This teaching was summed up in Pius XI's encyclical *Quadragesimo Anno*, in which the dangers of excessive State power, the desirability of diffusing power among intermediate groups, and the advantages of doing this by means of vocational organisation, were all stressed. The Vocational Organisation Report and the Dignan plan were designed accordingly to apply these principles to Ireland. In the case of the Vocational Organisation Report, at least, the retort can at once be made that this is what the commission was appointed to do and that it can hardly be blamed for doing it as conscientiously as possible. This is true enough and perhaps the responsibility should be placed further back, on those who urged that such a commission be set up, and on the government which agreed to do so. But the fact remains that, by stressing vocational organisation, these documents were stressing a problem that was not of the first importance for Ireland. Public administration certainly had its weaknesses in Ireland, but no one drawing up a list of problems facing the country would have put this top of the list. There were far more serious weaknesses in Irish society—low productivity and high emigration being two obvious examples.

If the Catholic social movement had been of longer standing in Ireland, these deficiencies might have been avoided. A tradition might have grown up of examining Irish problems in the light of Catholic social principles, and of evolving a body of middle-

40. J. H. Richardson, *Economic and Financial Aspects of Social Security*, 47.
41. These criticisms of the Dignan plan are derived from discussions with former officers of the Department of Local Government and Public Health, and they are, I understand, among the objections raised within the department at the time to Dr Dignan's proposals.

range doctrine in which these principles were applied to the Irish situation. But because the Catholic social movement had developed only recently in Ireland, no body of middle-range doctrine had yet grown up. Exponents of Catholic social thought had to turn elsewhere for such doctrine—and this meant, in the mid-nineteen-forties, turning in the first place to the encyclical *Quadragesimo Anno*. But *Quadragesimo Anno* had been written with the experience of industrialised nations on the continent primarily in mind. It was intended to provide a guide for Catholics in those countries, who, caught in a welter of ideologies, were seeking a middle way between the competing claims of communism, fascism and unreconstructed capitalism. But in Ireland the challenge of unchristian ideologies was not the problem, and to behave as if it was meant diverting attention from the problems which were really there. The Vocational Organisation Report and the Dignan plan reflect the relatively low level of development which the Catholic social movement had so far attained in Ireland. They are intellectually undistinguished documents, and they help to explain the undistinguished intellectual level on which ensuing controversies between Church and State were conducted.

Despite their shortcomings, however, the Vocational Organisation Report and the Dignan plan were sincere attempts by public-spirited men to grapple with what they believed to be important issues. One might, then, have expected the government, even if it did not accept their recommendations, at least to welcome these documents as expressions of civic concern. In fact, the government's reaction to them was most unfriendly.

When the Vocational Organisation Report came out, it was greeted on the government's part by silence. Weeks passed before any minister referred to the report in public at all. At last, in November 1944, three months after publication, Dr James Ryan, Minister for Agriculture, speaking at a Catholic social week in Dublin, mentioned the document. He did so only to rebut the complaints which the commission had made against his department:

Referring to a statement in the Vocational Commission Report to the effect that in the future the exporting and marketing of farm produce must be carried on by a large central organisation, and that this could be done more efficiently by those conversant with their respective ends of the producing business rather than by civil servants, he said that he and his predecessor had been trying to get the creameries to combine to do their own marketing for a long number of years.

Central marketing had been carried on for a time and had been looked on with disfavour by most of the creameries, with the result that it had to be administered by civil servants. In the end they got down to it on one condition and that was that a civil servant should be the chairman.

Parts of the Commission's report painted a picture which gave the impression that civil servants were bureaucrats and were interfering where they should not interfere. It was really the other way round. They were compelled to interfere by the people in business, and the same applied to the other ministers. The higher civil servants were very anxious to get out of the business and let the people do it themselves.[42]

Several weeks later, Mr Sean Lemass, the Minister for Industry and Commerce, gave his view of the report. The commission had criticised his department even more severely than Dr Ryan's, and his reaction was correspondingly sharp:

I have read the report of that commission on more than one occasion and I have been unable to come to any conclusion as to whether the querulous, nagging, propagandist tone of its observations is to be attributed to unfortunate drafting or to a desire to distort the picture. The commission spent a great deal of energy upon its researches, and a very long time in preparing its report, and I think it is unfortunate that the report, when published, should be such a slovenly document. I think that that is a fair description of it, because it contains an extraordinary number of misstatements of fact which could easily have been rectified by a telephone inquiry to the Department or organisation concerned. In some respects, its recommendations are self-contradictory.[43]

These bitter words provoked an equally bitter response. The Bishop of Galway, chairman of the commission, was clearly

42. *Irish Independent*, 31 Oct. 1944.
43. *Seanad Debates*, XXIX, 1323-4 (21 Feb. 1945).

angered by these criticisms and challenged the minister to substantiate his accusations. An acrimonious controversy followed, in which Mr Lemass produced a list of twenty-seven alleged errors, and the bishop countered them one by one, claiming that they were not really errors at all.[44] Anyone who reads through the controversy will, I think, agree that Mr Lemass's complaints were niggling and that the bishop had almost wholly the better of the argument. But the episode evidently rankled, because twenty years later in a newspaper interview, Mr Lemass still felt sore enough about the subject to refer to the report disparagingly: 'The present Bishop of Galway was the chairman of that Commission, and he set out with one main ambition— to produce a Report in less time than was ever achieved before. So a lot of the material that went into the Report was not subjected to any very critical examination.'[45]

It still remained to be seen what action, if any, the government as a whole would take on the Vocational Organisation Report. On 23 March 1945, the Minister for Education mentioned in the Dail that each department had been asked to furnish observations on the sections of the report affecting it, and that the government had not yet fully considered them.[46] The process appears to have taken some time, for over two years later, on 16 April 1947, Mr de Valera stated in reply to a parliamentary question that 'it is not yet possible for me to indicate finally the extent to which the recommendations of the commission will be implemented by the Government'.[47] On the same occasion he listed a number of ways in which the commission's proposals had already been carried into effect:

As examples of recommendations already implemented, I might cite the Hire Purchase Act, 1946; the Industrial Relations Act, 1946; the Auctioneers and House Agents Act, 1947, which became law a few weeks ago; and the Consultative Medical Council set up by the Minister for Health, which held its inaugural meeting last week. The consolidation of laws, on which the commission also made recom-

44. *Irish Independent*, 8, 23 and 28 March 1945.
45. *Irish Times*, 18 Feb. 1966, quoting an interview in *The Word*.
46. *Dail Debates*, XCVI, 1761.
47. *Ibid.*, CV, 570.

mendations, has been under active consideration for several years past, and a number of consolidating measures have been passed both before and since I received the report of the commission. Last May both Houses of the Oireachtas, at the instance of the government, adopted additional standing Orders to facilitate the passage of consolidation bills.[48]

The most notable feature of this list of measures is that most of them were minor and all of them were peripheral to the commission's main recommendations. The most important of them was the Industrial Relations Act 1946, which improved the machinery for industrial conciliation in Ireland by setting up a Labour Court; but useful though this measure has been, it fell far short of setting up the vocational structure which the commission had recommended. Already, in July 1946, Mr de Valera had made clear his government's general attitude to the report. 'Our general position', he said, 'with regard to vocational organisation is that we believe that if it is going to be of real value to the community it will have to be a natural growth . . . We feel that if it is going to be something that is not artificial, that if it is going to have its foundations in the lives of our people, it should come from below and not be superimposed from the top.'[49] It seems fair to paraphrase this as an avowal that the government would take no active steps to encourage vocational organisation. Mr de Valera's words only brought into the open what the government's inaction was already making clear —that it was quietly shelving the Vocational Organisation Report.

If ministerial response to the Vocational Organisation Report was chilly, it was almost virulent to the Dignan plan. The relevant member of the government was the Minister for Local Government and Public Health, Mr Sean MacEntee. Mr MacEntee was (and still is) noted for having one of the sharpest tongues in Irish public life, and he gave it full rein on this occasion. The day after the Dignan plan was published, a letter from his private secretary appeared in the newspapers. It said: 'Mr MacEntee read with surprise the statement in yesterday morning's papers that a scheme for an extension of the social

48. *Ibid.*, 569–70.   49. *Ibid.*, CII, 142 (2 July 1946).

services in the State had been submitted by the National Health Insurance Society to the Minister. . . . If by a scheme for an extension of social insurance is meant a proposal substantially worked out in detail, supported by factual argument and embodying estimates of the expenditure involved and concrete proposals for defraying the cost, the Minister can categorically state that no such scheme has been submitted to him.'[50] Three weeks later, in reply to a request in the Dail for a statement, he was equally tart: 'In recent years', he stated, 'many papers on public health and associated problems have been brought to my notice, but I have not deemed it appropriate to make a statement in the Dail in relation to any of them. I am not aware of any reasons why an exception should be made in the case of the paper to which the Deputy's question relates.'[51] Two months later again, the leader of the Labour party, Mr William Norton, raised the matter once more in the Dail, but the minister's reply showed that the passage of time had done nothing to mollify him:

Mr MacEntee: . . . I have had the paper examined in my Department. The examination revealed that the paper in general did not take due cognisance of the several very complex fundamental difficulties which the author's proposals involved, that many of these proposals were impracticable, and that accordingly no further action on the basis of the paper would be warranted.

Mr Norton: Would the Minister say whether an estimate of the cost was prepared in his Department? Can the Minister now, as a matter of information on a subject which is exciting widespread discussion, give the House and the country any indication as to what the cost of providing those benefits would be?

Mr MacEntee: I have nothing to add to the very comprehensive answer which I have given . . .

General Mulcahy: Would the Minister inform the House, either now or at some other time, under what heading he found the proposals impracticable?

Mr MacEntee: Under almost every heading on the paper.[52]

50. *Irish Times*, 19 Oct. 1944.
51. *Dail Debates*, XCV, 626 (8 Nov. 1944). This reply was read on Mr MacEntee's behalf by his parliamentary secretary, Dr F. C. Ward.
52. *Ibid.*, 1489 (24 Jan. 1945).

At this point the Bishop of Clonfert wrote direct to Mr MacEntee, asking for detailed objections to his paper. The minister replied, after a three weeks' delay, regretting that pressure of business prevented him giving the bishop's letter the attention it required, and hoping to write again in a week or so.[53] When after four weeks no further letter had arrived, the bishop brought the matter into the open. In a speech at Loughrea he publicly requested the minister to state his grounds for opposing the scheme, and asked him to reply in a speech which he was due to give the following day.[54] Mr MacEntee rose to the challenge. In a speech to a Fianna Fail meeting, on 13 March 1945, he traversed the whole dispute between himself and Dr Dignan. The National Health Insurance Society, he pointed out, had been set up by the Minister for Local Government and Public Health. The minister appointed its chairman and committee of management, and had absolute power to remove them. 'It is obvious from this', Mr MacEntee continued, 'that the persons appointed by the Minister to hold office in the Society or to be members of its Committee of Management must be persons who will be meticulous to confine themselves to those functions which the Minister appointed them to discharge and, especially, will not arrogate to themselves functions which attach to the Minister or, if not particularly to him, then to the Government as a whole'. Notwithstanding, the committee of management had issued a document in which the chairman proposed to supersede in regard to all health services the Minister for Local Government and Public Health and the existing authorities. Although published by the society, 'for whose proper functioning the Minister is responsible to Parliament', it was not submitted to the minister for his views nor was his consent sought for its publication. In these circumstances, it would be a derogation of his office to allow controversy to arise between him and his appointee, and he did not propose to answer the bishop's question further.[55]

By this startling pronouncement, Mr MacEntee shifted the ground of controversy. It was no longer a question of whether

53. He wrote to the minister on 26 Jan., and received a reply dated 14 Feb.: see Dr Dignan's speech at Loughrea, *Irish Independent,* 13 March 1945.
54. *Ibid.*
55. *Irish Independent,* 14 March 1945.

the Dignan plan was good or bad, but of whether the bishop had any right to publish it without the minister's consent. Dr Dignan took the minister up on this point. He argued that Mr MacEntee was claiming wider powers than he was entitled to. 'The Minister', he conceded, 'has the statutory right to appoint and to remove me from the chair', but, he added, 'I repudiate the claim that I occupy the chair at "his will and pleasure". I am not "the agent" of the Minister, and when he says that I must not fail to observe my obligations to him "in any regard", I consider this is tantamount to his claiming complete, almost autocratic authority over the chairman.'[56] Mr MacEntee, however, had the last word. When, in August 1945, Dr Dignan's term of office came to an end, he was not reappointed. Instead, the chairmanship was given to a civil servant, Mr D. J. O'Donovan, whom departmental discipline could be trusted to keep in line.[57] Mr MacEntee had not told the public just what his objections to the Dignan plan had been, and, in fact, he never did so.

Some explanation is required for the unconciliatory attitude which Fianna Fail ministers took towards the Vocational Organisation Report and the Dignan plan. Simply as a matter of tactics, quite apart from considerations of courtesy, it might have seemed unwise to treat them with so much contempt. In an overwhelmingly Catholic country, documents purporting to deal with problems by reference to Catholic principles might be expected to obtain a friendly reception from the public, and to reject them so completely meant handing them over as weapons to the government's critics. If such calculations of prudence seemed no longer to weigh with Fianna Fail, part of the explanation may be found in the uniquely strong position in which the party found itself at this time.

In May 1944, Fianna Fail had been victorious at the sixth general election in succession. It had been in office for a dozen years, and the opposition parties were appearing less and less able to mount an effective challenge. The largest opposition party, Fine Gael, appeared to be in full decline. In four of the

56. Statement published *ibid.*, 27 March 1945.
57. *Ibid.*, 3 Aug. 1945.

five by-elections of 1945 it did not even present a candidate,[58] and though the reason given at the time was that it did not wish to 'disturb the country',[59] the real reason, I am told on excellent authority, was that it simply could not find candidates prepared to stand.[60] Labour, the next largest opposition party, had, as we saw, in the last chapter, appeared to be doing well in 1942 and 1943; but the split of January 1944 put paid to its chances of becoming the major opposition group. Its splinter group, National Labour, was even weaker. The only remaining party, Clann na Talmhan, was a sectional grouping based on the small farmers of the west. It was not until a new party, Clann na Poblachta, gained two spectacular by-election victories in October 1947 that any new threat to the government emerged.[61] For three years, from the middle of 1944 to the middle of 1947, Fianna Fail seemed invincible. It would not have been surprising if hubris had set in, and this may help to account for the brusqueness with which ministers dismissed the Vocational Organisation Report and the Dignan plan.

Behind Fianna Fail, one can perhaps detect the influence of the civil service. This is not an easy factor to document, because in Ireland, as in Britain, the convention prevails that civil servants are anonymous, and that statements of policy are made by the minister or at least in his name. But it would not have been surprising if civil servants had reacted unfavourably to the Vocational Organisation Report and the Dignan plan. After all, both documents—the Dignan plan implicitly, and the Vocational Organisation Report explicitly and at length—criticised the way in which the civil service did its job. And a corner of the veil is lifted in the unpublished minutes of evidence of the Vocational Organisation Commission, deposited in the National Library of Ireland. The Commission interviewed several of the permanent heads of departments, and pressed them for their views on vocational organisation. Their reactions varied from

58. For details see Dail Eireann, *Copies of the Public Notices of the Results of the Elections and of the Transfers of votes in respect of: (a) General Election, 1948. (b) General Election, 1951. (c) By-elections, 1944 to 1952 (inclusive)*, 10–11.
59. *Irish Weekly Independent*, 17 Nov. 1945.
60. Information from a member of Fine Gael who was senior in the party in the nineteen-forties.
61. *Irish Weekly Independent*, 8 Nov. 1947.

the comparative open-mindedness of the Secretary of the Department of Education, Mr J. O'Neill,[62] through the non-committal politeness of the Secretary of the Department of Industry and Commerce, Mr R. C. Ferguson,[63] to the freezing lack of sympathy of Mr J. J. McElligott, the austere and formidable figure who for twenty-six years held the post of Secretary of the Department of Finance.[64] But in general the civil service witnesses gave the impression of being reluctant to accept vocational organisation if it entailed upsetting their established methods of doing business.

However, some kind of rationale had to be offered to the public for rejecting the proposals in the Vocational Organisation Report and the Dignan plan, and it is worth examining the arguments used to the outside world. Apart from finding fault with innumerable points of detail, there is one theme which recurs in ministerial (and civil service) comment on these proposals. This is that any diffusion of authority to vocational groups would derogate from the principle of ministerial responsibility. The most belligerent expression of this point of view was to be found in Mr MacEntee's reply to Bishop Dignan, which showed that in the minister's view, the chairman of a semi-official body within the minister's sphere of authority should make no statement of policy without first clearing it with the minister. But Mr MacEntee's view was by no means unique. It was expressly defended in the Senate by the Tanaiste (i.e. deputy prime minister), Mr Sean T. O'Kelly.[65] The Minister for Education, Mr Thomas Derrig, in rejecting a Fine Gael motion for the establishment of an advisory council on education, used the argument that, if the council were to have any authority, it would clash with the principle that the minister was responsible to the Dail.[66] The same kind of objection recurs in the evidence given by civil servants before the Vocational Organisation Commission. The Secretary of the Department of Industry and

62. *Vocational Commission. Minutes of Evidence.* N.L.I. MS 929, 2528 ff.
63. *Ibid.*, 2420 ff.
64. *Ibid.*, N.L.I. MS 928, 2290 ff. Mr McElligott was Secretary of the Department of Finance from 1927 to 1953: see his entry in *Who's Who*.
65. *Seanad Debates*, XXIX, 1909 (20 March 1945).
66. *Dail Debates*, XCVI, 2147-9, 2153-4 (18 April 1945).

Commerce, when asked if there could not be more consultation with vocational bodies over matters such as the issue of licences, replied at once that he would like to see how that would fit in with ministerial control.[67] When asked if economic planning could not be shared with vocational bodies, he replied that 'it might weaken the Executive'.[68] The Secretary of the Department of Agriculture, when asked for his views on consultative councils, said that from the department's point of view, they might be a useful buffer between it and public opinion. 'But then', he added, 'I think that that would not be right. I think that for any action the Minister takes, or for any policy or change of policy he adopts in normal times, he should be subjected to criticism, if necessary, in the Dail and elsewhere in the country and he should not be able to shelter behind a body like the consultative council.'[69] The clash of viewpoints was brought out most clearly in an exchange between the chairman of the commission, Bishop Browne, and the Secretary of the Department of Finance, Mr McElligott. The bishop was trying to persuade Mr McElligott that some decentralisation of decision-making was desirable; Mr McElligott was insisting that current civil service practice was made inevitable by the doctrine of ministerial responsibility:

Mr McElligott . . . Outside concerns can deal with correspondence in a rather summary way. In Government departments we have to proceed on somewhat different lines because on any action of a Government Department a Parliamentary question may be addressed to the Minister and there may be a whole day's debate in the House about it. The matter might be raised on the adjournment or by some other means and the attention of the Government and of the country might be directed to it. A Civil Servant runs that risk whenever he answers a letter from outside. He must also see that any reply sent in is in conformity with the policy of his Minister and the general policy of the Government. It might take him some time to ascertain what, on the surface, may seem to be a simple matter. The question asked may raise issues of principle and it may take some time to ascertain what the policy of the Minister or the Government is.

67. *Vocational Commission. Minutes of Evidence.* N.L.I. MS 929, 2443.
68. *Ibid.*, 2460.
69. *Ibid.*, N.L.I. MS 930, 3010.

Chairman: It would be a great help to the Civil Service if the Ministry were not committed on points of administration like that? . . . If administration in detail were freer from this publicity?

Mr McElligott: That goes back again to the question of representative democracy to which you attach so much importance. I submit that all the actions of the Civil Service are conditioned by this representative democracy to which you attach importance.

Chairman: Respect for democracy is not a purely personal view of mine. It is shared by the Constitution and, I presume, by the Civil Service. Democracy is entirely a question of policy and it is not democracy if you cannot leave any discretion to a government?

Mr McElligott: Democracy, to my mind, presupposes the responsibility of the Government to representatives of the people.

Chairman: For policy?

Mr McElligott: The Government consists of Ministers and the Ministers are at the heads of different Departments. For the actions of their Departments they are answerable to the representatives of the people in the Dail and the Seanad.[70]

The interpretation of the doctrine of ministerial responsibility presented by Mr McElligott could not altogether be sustained. It was certainly more rigid than that obtaining in the country where that doctrine originated. In Britain, numerous public bodies existed with varying degrees of freedom from direct ministerial control—the British Broadcasting Corporation, the London Passenger Transport Board, the Unemployment Assistance Board, and dozens of others[71]—and a leading authority on British constitutional law summed up the position in 1936 by stating that it was false 'to assume that for every act that is done by a public authority some one is responsible to Parliament'.[72] The same could equally have been said for Ireland, where a similar crop of semi-autonomous public bodies had developed: the Electricity Supply Board, the Irish Sugar Company, Aer Lingus (the Irish airline) and many others. If such bodies could be tolerated, there was no constitutional reason why a wide range of partially self-governing vocational bodies could not

70. *Ibid.,* N.L.I. MS 928, 2320–1.
71. W. I. Jennings, *Cabinet Government* (1936 edn.), 72–84.   72. *Ibid.,* 80.

also be tolerated. Ministers and civil servants, in appealing to the doctrine of ministerial responsibility as a reason why vocational organisation should not be fostered in Ireland, were failing to see the implications of their own existing practice. The intellectual shortcomings of the exponents of vocational organisation in Ireland have already been noted; but those of their opponents were, if anything, worse.

By the mid-nineteen-forties a rift had emerged in Ireland between two philosophies of government. One could be labelled 'vocationalist', and called for the diffusion of responsibility among vocational groups. The other could be called 'bureaucratic', and defended the centralisation of authority in government departments. Neither philosophy was the fruit of indigenous development. The 'vocationalists' derived their ideas, via the encyclical *Quadragesimo Anno*, from the Catholic social movement on the continent, while the 'bureaucrats' defended their position by reference to the British-derived doctrine of ministerial responsibility. On both sides, these imported ideas were urged with a rigour that would probably have surprised those who had evolved them in their countries of origin.

The controversy aroused considerable interest in Ireland, and the 'vocationalists', in particular, attracted support from a variety of quarters. The *Irish Times,* for instance—which, as a Protestant-owned and ex-Unionist paper, had no reason for automatically welcoming documents issued over the signatures of Catholic bishops—welcomed the Dignan plan in a friendly editorial,[73] and devoted a considerable amount of its meagre war-time ration of newsprint to summarising the Vocational Organisation Report.[74] The organs of the Catholic social movement showed a particular interest in the documents. The *Standard* gave extensive coverage to them both.[75] The annual conference of *An Rioghacht* welcomed the Dignan Plan.[76] The *Muintir na Tire* rural week and the Dublin Catholic social week both devoted their next sessions after the publication of the Vocational Organ-

73. *Irish Times,* 18 Oct. 1944.
74. *Ibid.,* 21 Aug. 1944 ff.: a series of six articles.
75. *Standard,* 25 Aug. 1944 ff.; 20 Oct. 1944.
76. *Ibid.,* 2 March 1945.

isation Report to a consideration of its proposals.[77] The most permanent response came in the Dublin diocese where, in May 1945, representatives from a number of Catholic organisations formed the Catholic Societies Vocational Organisation Conference, to press for the implementation of the Vocational Organisation Report.[78] Through its constituent societies the C.S.V.O.C. had the support, in name at least, of thousands of Catholics in the Dublin area, and it was for some years an active pressure group.

The opposition parties also welcomed the documents. For them, the criticisms contained therein of the way in which Fianna Fail was running the country provided useful ammunition, and they took what opportunities offered of using them as sticks with which to beat the government, Fine Gael tending to stress the Vocational Organisation Report and Labour the Dignan plan. In March 1945, General Mulcahy, leader of Fine Gael, introduced a motion in the Dail for the establishment of a Council of Education, as urged in the Vocational Organisation Report.[79] In July 1945, Senator Luke Duffy of the Labour party introduced a discussion in the Senate of the Dignan plan.[80] In July 1946, General Mulcahy challenged the Taoiseach in the Dail to state his attitude to the Vocational Organisation Report.[81] In September 1947, the Labour party produced a social security scheme which paid tribute to the Dignan plan.[82]

Despite the varied nature of 'vocationalist' support, however, the situation had in it the elements of a clash between Church and State. The fact that the most articulate exponents of the 'vocationalist' point of view were two bishops, backed by a number of Catholic organisations, while on the other side the most determined defenders of the 'bureaucratic' viewpoint were ministers and civil servants, served to ensure this. It is true that Bishop Browne, in defending the Vocational Organisation Report, and Bishop Dignan, in issuing his social security plan,

77. *Irish Weekly Independent*, 11 Aug. 1945; *Standard*, 12 Oct. 1945.
78. *Standard*, 1 June 1945.
79. *Dail Debates*, XCVI, 1744 (23 March 1945).
80. *Seanad Debates*, XXX, 300 (18 July 1945).
81. *Dail Debates*, CII, 32 (2 July 1946).
82. *Irish Weekly Independent*, 13 Sept. 1947.

both made it clear that they were only offering proposals, which the government had the right to reject.[83] But they both implied, in controversy with ministers, that the government, in rejecting these proposals, was in danger of rejecting Catholic social teaching. Dr Dignan publicly asked Mr MacEntee, after the latter had in the Dail dismissed his scheme as impracticable: 'The scheme is built on Christian principles of social justice and charity. Does the Minister mean that a social and economic system based on these principles is impracticable in Ireland?'[84] And Dr Browne stated, in controversy with Mr Lemass, that it was his duty to defend the principles in the report, 'because they have been taught to us by Pope Pius XI'.[85] So far, Dr Dignan and Dr Browne had been the only bishops to speak, but on an issue where Catholic social principles were believed to be at stake, they could probably count on the sympathy of the whole bench of bishops. Sooner or later, a clash between 'vocationalist' and 'bureaucratic' outlooks was likely to occur again, and when it happened there was a danger that it might bring about a direct confrontation between Church and State.

---

83. See Dr Browne's speech at Galway, *Irish Independent*, 8 March 1945, and the phrase in Dr Dignan's foreword to his plan: 'There is nothing sacrosanct about it, for I write as Chairman of the National Health Insurance Society and not as Bishop of Clonfert.': Most Rev. J. Dignan, *Social Security*, 3.

84. *Irish Independent*, 13 March 1945.

85. *Ibid.*, 8 March 1945.

CHAPTER V

THE FIRST CLASH: THE HEALTH ACT, 1947

A shrewd observer might, after the disputes over the Vocational
Organisation Report and the Dignan plan, have anticipated a clash
between Church and State in Ireland. He would probably,
however, have had more difficulty in foretelling the area in which
the clash would come. A possible guess might have been education. Taking the world as a whole, education has caused more
conflict between Church and State than any other subject, at least
where the Church concerned has been the Catholic Church. In
Ireland, there was particularly wide scope for conflict, in view of
the extensive claims which the Church had established in the past.
And in fact an issue did arise, linked with education, at just this
time on which bishops and ministers did not see eye to eye.

The issue was that of teachers' salaries. In 1944 the Irish National
Teachers' Organisation (the trade union of primary school
teachers) put in a claim for an increase in pay.[1] Tough negotiations
dragged on through 1945 and into 1946, but the gap between
teachers and government was never closed, for the most that the
government felt able, in the economic circumstances of the time,
to offer was still less than the least the teachers were prepared
to accept. Finally, in March 1946, the I.N.T.O. declared a strike.
It was an ingenious form of strike: the teachers in Dublin were
called out, while the teachers in the rest of the country remained
at work and supported their Dublin colleagues by a contribution
from their salaries.[2]

In this dispute the teachers had episcopal backing. At the outset
they had written to the hierarchy for support and had received a
friendly reply informing them that the bishops had recommended

1. T. J. O'Connell, *History of the I.N.T.O.*, 210.
2. *Irish Times*, 21 March 1946.

their claim to 'the sympathetic consideration of the Government Departments concerned'.[3] Dr McQuaid, the Archbishop of Dublin, was particularly active on the teachers' behalf. He took a hand in the negotiations and at one stage intervened to prevent them breaking down.[4] When the strike was finally called, he showed where his sympathies lay by allowing a letter to be published in which he stated that the clerical managers and religious superiors had 'full sympathy with the ideal of a salary in keeping with the dignity and responsibility of your profession as teachers', and added that they would not penalise teachers who joined in the strike.[5] According to one newspaper report, the publication of this letter swayed some teachers who had not made up their minds whether to join the strike or not into doing so.[6]

The government's reaction to the strike, however, was to dig in its heels. Mr Thomas Derrig, the Minister for Education, speaking in the Senate the day after the strike began, described it as 'a definite challenge to the authority of the State', and added that the government would not be doing its duty as a government if it yielded to the people on strike.[7] An offer by Archbishop McQuaid to mediate was turned down.[8] The strike lasted through the summer and into the autumn without any sign of concession from either side. Finally, at the end of October, the teachers conceded defeat and returned unconditionally to work.[9]

This long-drawn-out affair could be represented as a dispute between Church and State. The fact that the government had taken one side while the hierarchy in general, and Dr McQuaid in particular, had taken the other, gave it such a complexion. This, however, would not be an accurate interpretation of the episode. The point at issue—whether the State could afford to meet the teachers' demands or not—was clearly a political question, on which the government was bound to have the last word. The hierarchy never claimed to do more than commend the claims of the teachers to the government and Dr McQuaid

3. *Irish School Weekly* (XLVI, nos. 47 and 48) 18 and 25 Nov. 1944, 467.
4. T. J. O'Connell, *op. cit.*, 214, 240.
5. *Irish Independent*, 20 March 1946.
6. *Irish Times*, 21 March 1946.
7. *Seanad Debates*, XXXI, 1047, 1050 (21 March 1946.)
8. *Irish School Weekly* (XLVIII, nos. 17 and 18) 4 and 11 May 1946, 192–3.
9. *Irish School Weekly* (XLVIII, nos. 43 and 44) 2 and 9 Nov. 1946, 505.

was careful in the various statements that he made to stress that he was not encroaching on the rights of the government or of any other party to the dispute.[10] The dispute, in fact, was one over finance; it only appeared to be linked with the sensitive area of education because it happened to be teachers' salaries and not anybody else's that were under consideration. In all the essentials of the education system, the Fianna Fail government left the *status quo* alone, and it was not here that difficulties between Church and State came to a head.

Collision came about in quite a different area—that of the health services. This was not something that an observer in the mid-nineteen-forties would have been likely to anticipate. There was indeed one precedent for the hierarchy showing an interest in this area: at the time that the National Insurance Bill of 1911, which provided for health and unemployment insurance for certain categories of industrial workers, was going through Parliament, the Irish hierarchy issued a statement criticising it on the ground that it was designed for an industrial and not an agricultural country and that as far as Ireland was concerned the expenditure proposed could be laid out to better advantage.[11] But this episode was, by the nineteen-forties, thirty years in the past, and since then the hierarchy had not, so far as is known, felt any need to make representations on any matter connected with health services. Nor had those services aroused much public interest or controversy.

Some explanation, then, is required of why, in the nineteen-forties, health services should suddenly have become a delicate issue. It seems best to approach this by first describing the health services as they existed at that period, by next outlining the pressures which were building up for reform, and by then describing the personnel and traditions of the government department which had oversight of the issue.

The public health services as they existed in the early nineteen-forties were a patchwork that had grown up over the preceding hundred years. The most extensive was the medical assistance

10. See e.g. his statement when the strike began (above, note 5), his offer to mediate (above, note 8), and his statement when the strike ended (above, note 9).
11. *Irish Catholic Directory, 1912,* 544 (20 June 1911).

service which, under legislation dating back to 1851, provided free medical treatment for those who were 'unable to provide by their own industry or other lawful means' the treatment which they or their dependents required.[12] The phrase was a loose one, and eligibility had to be assessed by officials appointed by the local authority.[13] But it was estimated that roughly one third of the population came within its scope.[14] The medical assistance service was provided in the first instance by over 600 dispensary doctors, who were stationed in a network all over the country.[15] They were paid a salary for their services, but were also entitled to take private patients, and generally did so.[16] For more seriously ill patients, the local authorities maintained hospitals where those assessed as eligible for free treatment could obtain it.[17]

The medical assistance service had important merits. It provided free treatment for that section of the population which most needed it. Through the network of dispensary doctors it ensured that there was a qualified doctor living in every part of the country, even the most remote. A defect was that patients had no choice of doctor: they had to accept the dispensary medical officer in whose district they lived, whether they got on well with him or not. In many parts of the country this must have been unavoidable: the dispensary doctor was the only doctor within reach, and had it not been for the dispensary system there would have been no doctor available at all. But this was not true everywhere. Especially in the towns it would have been possible to provide a measure of choice. There was, however, no agitation in the early nineteen-forties for such freedom of choice to be introduced. It is curious, in view of the stress put a few years later by exponents of Catholic social teaching on the importance of free choice of doctor, that no comment was aroused by the fact that, for the poor, free choice of doctor had never existed.

Parallel to, and independent of, the medical assistance service was the service provided for insured workers by the National

12. Department of Health, *Outline of Proposals for the Improvement of the Health Services* [1947], 5, 11.
13. B. Hensey, *The Health Services of Ireland*, 15.
14. Department of Health, *op. cit.*, 12.
15. *Ibid.*
16. W. R. F. Collis, *The State of Medicine in Ireland*, 16.
17. Department of Health, *op. cit.*, 12.

Health Insurance Society. With some exceptions, 'insured workers' at this period meant manual workers plus those non-manual workers who had an income of less than £250 *per annum*. The number of such workers in the early forties was around 600,000.[18] The main provision made for them by the National Health Insurance Society was the payment of cash benefits in case of sickness, disability, or maternity.[19] The Irish health insurance system was unusual in that it did not include provision for treatment as well as cash benefits—the reason being that many insured workers would be entitled to treatment under the medical assistance service.[20] By 1942, however, the National Health Insurance Society had amassed a considerable surplus of funds; and from that year it began, on a limited scale, to finance treatment for insured persons.[21]

The patchwork of Irish health services was completed by a number of schemes administered by local authorities, and covering varying proportions of the population for various contingencies. There was a school medical service which provided for the inspection of children in national schools, though in 1947 it was reported that the most it could aim at was an inspection every three years.[22] There was a tuberculosis service, under which free treatment for the disease was available to those who could not pay for it themselves.[23] There was a maternity and child welfare service which, however, had been developed only by some local authorities, and which was described by a white paper as being 'for all practical purposes confined to the poorer classes'.[24] Finally mention must be made of the work of voluntary agencies. These were especially important in Dublin, where the outpatient departments of the voluntary hospitals in effect operated a duplicate dispensary scheme, giving free treatment not only to the poor but also to many who would not have come within the scope of the public assistance services.[25]

18. Most Rev. J. Dignan, *Social Security*, 27.
19. *Ibid.*, 14–15. There was also a marriage benefit for women members.
20. *Annual Register 1911*, 281.
21. B. Hensey, *op. cit.*, 16.
22. *Department of Health, op. cit.*, 15.
23. *Ibid.*
24. *Ibid.*
25. W. R. F. Collis, *op. cit.*, 29.

The Irish health services, then, can be summarised as follows. The poorest third of the population were comprehensively catered for, receiving free treatment through the public assistance service. For the remaining two thirds of the population, some services had been developed, but according to no consistent plan. The degree of public aid that they could obtain varied with their income, with the extent to which their local authority had developed its services, and with the nature of the ailment from which they suffered. By and large, those in the wealthier two-thirds of the population appear to have met most of their medical needs from their own pockets.

There were various reasons why, in the early nineteen-forties, pressure for improvement of these services should have begun to mount. In the first place, disconcerting trends were shown by some of the Irish health statistics during the war years. This was particularly obvious in two important series—the tuberculosis death rate and the infant mortality rate. Even before the war, the tuberculosis death rate, though declining, had been declining less fast than in many other countries. An article by Professor T. W. T. Dillon, published in 1942, showed that during the period 1927–37 the rate of decline in the tuberculosis death rate was lower in Ireland than in any of the other nineteen countries for which he had collected statistics.[26] During the war the rate actually rose again, moving from 109 per 100,000 of the population in 1938 to 147 in 1942.[27] As far as infant mortality was concerned, the Irish rate in the years before the war had not caused much alarm; if it was higher than the rate for England and Wales, it was lower than the rates for either Scotland or Northern Ireland. But during the war it, too, caused concern; while the rates for England and Wales, for Scotland, and for Northern Ireland all declined, that for the twenty-six counties actually rose from 66 per 1,000 births in 1939 to 83 in 1943.[28] The reasons for these unsatisfactory figures could largely be found in social conditions. Both rates were much worse in the cities than in the small towns and the

26. T. W. T. Dillon, 'The Statistics of Tuberculosis', *Irish Journal of Medical Science*, July 1942. I have to thank Mrs Brian Farrell, daughter of the late Professor Dillon, for lending me offprints of this and other articles by her father.
27. *Annual Report of the Registrar-General, 1944*, xxi.
28. *Ibid.*, xxxii.

countryside.[29] This probably reflected bad housing and lack of fresh air and fresh food. War-time shortages of food and fuel doubtless were more acutely felt in the towns also. As far as infant mortality is concerned, a major cause of the upturn in the figures was an outbreak of gastro-enteritis in Dublin which killed many babies.[30] The ultimate solution to these health problems probably lay in improved living conditions in the larger towns. But this was necessarily a long-term solution; in the meantime improved medical services became a matter of urgency.

The other main factor disposing Irishmen to look more critically at their health services was the wave of discussion that followed the publication in Britain of the Beveridge Report in December 1942. The Beveridge Report, by laying down a programme through which poverty could be abolished in an entire nation, attracted attention far beyond its country of origin. Many of the social security programmes developed in continental countries after the war, for instance, were deeply influenced by it.[31] But there were good reasons why it should have made more of an impression in Ireland than in any other country save Britain itself. There was mobility of labour between Ireland and Britain. If the standard of British social services rose still further beyond those in Ireland, emigration was likely to reach even greater heights. Again, such emigrants as did return to Ireland were likely to become centres of discontent if nothing was done to narrow the gap. Now the Beveridge plan did not itself cover health services, but Sir William Beveridge made it clear that his plan would work only if a national health service were established, paying for medical treatment out of general taxation, and thus removing the burden of health costs from the social insurance scheme.[32] So the acceptance of the Beveridge plan in Britain

29. For instance, the tuberculosis death rate of 147 in 1942 was compounded from a rate in the larger towns of 197, in the smaller towns of 161, and in the rural districts of 126: *Ireland: Statistical Abstract, 1945,* table 23. The infant mortality rate of 83 in 1943 was compounded from a rate in the larger towns of 115, in the smaller towns of 87, and in the rural districts of 67: *ibid.,* table 17.

30. *Dail Debates,* CI, 1760 (13 June 1946: speech of Mr Sean MacEntee).

31. P. Durand, *La Politique Contemporaine de Sécurité Sociale,* 117–63. The importance which this French expert accords to the Beveridge Report is shown by his heading for this section of his book: 'Les positions internationales en matière de sécurité sociale depuis le rapport de Beveridge.'

32. *Social Insurance and Allied Services. Report by Sir William Beveridge,* 158–9.

brought with it the acceptance of greatly expanded public health services[33]—and hence, inevitably, pressure for the improvement of health services in Ireland.

Signs of such pressure were evident in Ireland from early in the nineteen-forties. In 1941, the Royal Irish Academy of Medicine published a report on the tuberculosis problem, and proposed a network of T.B. dispensaries and sanatoria to meet it.[34] In February 1943 the Anti-Tuberculosis League was founded, in which, as we saw in chapter III, the Archbishop of Dublin so dramatically intervened.[35] In the same year, a well-known Dublin pediatrician, Dr W. R. F. Collis, published *The State of Medicine in Ireland,* a thoughtful survey of the subject, proposing that health services be unified under an autonomous board.[36] In 1944, Dr Dignan published his celebrated plan, which we have already discussed in the previous chapter. About the same time the Medical Association of Eire published its own plan for reorganised medical services, based largely on the insurance principle.[37] In the same year an organisation of former tuberculosis patients, the Post-Sanatoria League, was founded to demand better financial provision for T.B. sufferers.[38] The tide was turning towards reform, and the only question was what shape reform would take.

The answer to this question largely depended on the government department concerned. This was, until 1947, the Department of Local Government and Public Health. Mr Sean MacEntee was the minister at its head from 1941. Mr MacEntee, a senior member of Mr de Valera's government, had been in the cabinet, first as Minister for Finance, and then as Minister for Industry and Commerce, ever since Fianna Fail came into office in 1932. He was a man capable of forming strong views on many topics and (as Dr Dignan found out) by no means tongue-tied in expressing them. However, though an influential figure politically, his importance in the development of health policy was only indirect.

33. Formally recognised by the British government in its white paper on *A National Health Service,* February 1944.
34. *Journal of the Irish Free State Medical Union,* July 1941, 12.
35. See above, p. 79.
36. W. R. F. Collis, *The State of Medicine in Ireland,* 13–15.
37. *Journal of the Medical Association of Eire,* Dec. 1944, 66–71.
38. *Irish Times,* 28 Sept. 1944.

His department was a sprawling one with varied responsibilities, and in March 1944 he made an administrative change which simplified his task but at the same time reduced his influence. While retaining control of local government matters for himself, he formally delegated his responsibilities on the public health side of the department to his parliamentary secretary, Dr Conn Ward.[39]

Dr Ward was, then, the effective political head of the department in public health matters during the period in which reforms were being planned. He had held the same post—Parliamentary Secretary to the Minister for Local Government and Public Health—ever since Fianna Fail came to office in 1932. In his first dozen years in office he had made little mark, but it seems fair to say that until Mr MacEntee became minister he was not allowed much scope. He showed powers of decision once he was given his head, and the main criticism of him would be that he was unnecessarily combative. A time came when he needed friends, and he did not find them even in his own party, let alone in the opposition.

Of the civil servants within the department, the one who my informants agree had most influence was the Chief Medical Adviser, Dr James Deeny.[40] Dr Deeny was appointed to his post in 1944. He had previously been a private practitioner in Lurgan, county Armagh, and had made a reputation by scientific papers on epidemiology. He came to the department, therefore, completely without administrative experience. All my informants agree on the transformation which his arrival made. From his first moments in the department, it appears, he threw out ideas in reckless profusion, leaving his colleagues in a state of permanent mental turbulence. The late Dr Ward described him to me as a genius, whose recruitment was one of the best things that had ever happened to the public service—a comment which is the more interesting because at the time, I understand, their relations

39. *Dail Debates*, XCIV, 609 (14 June 1944: speech of Mr MacEntee on his departmental estimates).
40. My estimate of Dr Deeny (and of Mr MacEntee and Dr Ward) is based on conversations with a number of former officials of the Department of Local Government and Public Health, as well as on interviews with Dr Deeny himself and with the late Dr Ward.

were not always unruffled. Dr Deeny felt deeply the benefits which a vigorous public health policy could bring. It seems to have been he, more than any other individual, who was responsible for the shape which health legislation took in Ireland.

Individuals, however, work through institutions, and the traditions of the Department of Local Government and Public Health as a whole appear to have been important in deciding the direction which health policy in Ireland took. The department had an innovating tradition. Indeed a case could be made for saying that it was the most enterprising of all Irish government departments. At a time when most departments had been content to jog along, administering the machinery inherited from the British with only piecemeal changes, the Department of Local Government and Public Health had put through important reforms. It had attacked jobbery in local government by the establishment of the Local Appointments Commission in 1926.[41] It had sought to make local administration more efficient by the introduction of city and county managers, in stages between 1929 and 1940.[42] It had promoted economy by setting up a combined purchasing scheme for local authorities in 1921.[43] But valuable though these reforms undoubtedly were, they had one common feature—they increased centralisation. Local authorities were left with less autonomy than they had had before. On the public health side of its functions, the department had been less active, but even here, its centralising tendencies were visible. The hospitals sweepstake, set up in 1930 by a group of voluntary hospitals to increase their revenue,[44] was quickly brought under departmental control,[45] and by the nineteen-forties voluntary hospitals were complaining of increasing interference in their management by the department.[46] Along with this centralising tradition went an impatience of outside advice. The Irish Free State Medical Union (later the Medical Association of Eire and now the Irish Medical Association) complained repeatedly of

41. J. Collins, *Local Government,* 64.
42. *Ibid.,* 30–1, 52–5.
43. *Ibid.,* 31.
44. Under the Public Charitable Hospitals (Temporary Provisions) Act 1930.
45. Under the Public Hospitals Act 1933.
46. *Journal of the Irish Free State Medical Union,* Feb. 1940, 14; May 1940, 49.

the department's refusal to consult it in matters where its members had legitimate interests.[47] It contrasted its treatment at the hands of the Irish department with the cordial relations that the British Medical Association maintained with the British Ministry of Health.[48] We have already seen the short work which the minister at the head of the department made of Dr Dignan, the Bishop of Clonfert, when the latter offered suggestions on how the health services might be improved. The Department of Local Government and Public Health perhaps exhibited more purely than any other department the 'bureaucratic' attitude which was outlined in the last chapter. It showed a readiness to concentrate authority, a lack of interest in the maintenance of autonomous groups, a reluctance even to consult outside groups, that made a sharp contrast with the 'vocational' principles which were being propagated by exponents of Catholic social teaching. It is perhaps no accident that the sharpest conflict between the 'bureaucratic' and 'vocational' attitudes should have arisen in a field controlled by this department.[49]

The first response of the Department of Local Government and Public Health to the mounting pressure for reform was provided by the Public Health Bill 1945. As this bill was the direct forerunner of the Health Act 1947, which provoked the first controversy between the hierarchy and the government, it is worth discussing in some detail. It was a wide-ranging measure, proposing changes in the law on a variety of matters from drainage and water supply to the provision of hospitals and the duties of medical officers of health. However, it was more than just a consolidation statute. In two areas in particular, it initiated fresh policy. These two areas covered the points on which the Irish health

47. *Ibid.*, Jan. 1940, 1; Feb. 1940, 13; May 1940, 49.
48. *Ibid.*, Nov. 1939, 49; July 1940, 76.
49. A civil servant who read this chapter in draft commented to me that there was a considerable difference between the various sections of the Department of Local Government and Public Health, some (including those most concerned with health) being rigorous in their supervision and others allowing more local autonomy. Perhaps it would be more accurate, then, to talk of the 'bureaucratic' tradition of certain sections of the department, rather than of the department as a whole. This, however, does not affect my main point, which is that the office tradition of the civil servants concerned was important.

record was particularly unsatisfactory: they were mother and child welfare, and infectious diseases (which included tuberculosis). To combat infectious diseases, the bill gave the most sweeping powers. The relevant part began with the laconic sentence: 'The Minister may by order declare that a disease is infectious.'[50] It went on to permit the minister, without any restrictions on his discretion, to make such regulations as he wished for the prevention and treatment of those diseases which he had declared to be infectious.[51] In the Dail, Dr Ward indicated that he had in mind regulations for the compulsory cleansing and disinfestation of persons, and the examination of persons suspected of being sources of infection.[52] Another section authorised Chief Medical Officers of counties or county boroughs to order the detention of persons whom they considered a probable source of infection, and laid down that a person who resisted such detention, or who was insubordinate to an officer of the hospital in which he was detained, committed an offence.[53] Dr Ward, in introducing the measure, defended these provisions as essential in the combat against infectious disease. He instanced known cases of carriers of disease who had refused to submit to treatment and who remained at large, infecting other people.[54]

As far as mother and child welfare was concerned, the changes envisaged were equally sweeping. Dr Ward proposed that the existing schemes for maternity and infant welfare and for inspection of schoolchildren be extended, improved and unified, so that there would be a single scheme for mothers and all children up to the age of sixteen.[55] The scheme was to be free for all who wished to avail themselves of it, regardless of means.[56] It would be provided by the dispensary doctors, who would be helped by the recruitment of full-time nurses.[57] To ensure that the scheme was of maximum benefit, school inspections were to be compulsory. As Dr Ward explained, experience had shown

50. Section 18 (1) of bill as introduced.
51. Section 20 (1) of bill as introduced.
52. *Dail Debates*, XCVIII, 1715 (12 Dec. 1945).
53. Section 29 (1) and (4) of bill as introduced.
54. *Dail Debates*, XCVIII, 2083-4 (14 Dec. 1945).
55. *Ibid.*, 1709 (12 Dec. 1945).
56. *Ibid.*
57. *Ibid.*, 1709-10.

that if parents were free to withhold their children from inspection, it was precisely those children who most needed the inspection who were most likely to be withheld—the verminous, the malnourished, the children with skin infections.[58]

In view of the sensitivities which these proposals for mother and child welfare subsequently raised, it is worth noting that Dr Ward made no effort to play down the scope of his plans. On the contrary, in his second-reading speech he described the sections dealing with the mother and child welfare scheme as 'by far the most important' in the bill.[59] The newspapers picked up the hint he had given them. The principal headline in the *Irish Press* the following day was: 'FREE CARE FOR MOTHERS AND CHILDREN. Dr. Ward moves new Health Bill in Dail.'[60] The *Irish Independent* gave the story its second headline: 'Care of Children up to Age of 16/SCHEME IN NEW HEALTH BILL/Free Service to Mothers.'[61] The *Irish Times* also gave the story front-page treatment.[62] The Irish public had been given full warning of the changes that were on the way.

The surprising nature of the new proposals can be brought out by comparing them with changes in progress elsewhere. The nineteen-forties were a period of reforms in health services all over the world. Country after country made great extensions in the scope of State medical services. In Britain, New Zealand and Australia, comprehensive health services catering for the entire population were introduced.[63] In France, social insurance was extended to cover the entire gainfully occupied population of the country, both employed and self-employed.[64] In other countries, such as Belgium or the Netherlands, the reforms, while not so drastic as this, meant the extension of State-supported medical services to a larger proportion of the population.[65] But diverse though the provisions in other countries were, the changes proposed for Ireland seem in some respects to have been unique.

58. *Ibid.*, 1708.　　59. *Ibid.*, 1709.　　60. *Irish Press*, 13 Dec. 1945.
61. *Irish Independent*, 13 Dec. 1945.
62. *Irish Times*, 13 Dec. 1945.
63. 'Post-War Trends in Social Security: Medical Care: I', *International Labour Review* (LX, 2) Aug. 1949, 111, 113.
64. H. C. Galant, *Histoire Politique de la Sécurité Sociale Française 1945-52*, chaps. III–V.
65. 'Post-War Trends in Social Security', *op. cit.*, 117–18.

To begin with, there was the absence of provision for free choice of doctor. Free choice was fundamental in the schemes of other developed countries. The British National Health Service and the schemes in New Zealand, Australia and the continent of Europe provided for choice of doctor.[66] It was only in the under-developed countries of Asia, Africa and Latin America that free choice was at all usually denied,[67] and there the absolute shortage of doctors would probably have made it a dead letter anyway.

Secondly, the Irish scheme was notable for its stress on compulsion. This was certainly not unknown elsewhere: in France and Mexico, for instance, engaged couples were legally obliged to undergo a pre-marital medical examination,[68] and in several countries the award of social security benefits to expectant mothers was conditional on their observance of regulations for medical supervision.[69] But in most countries the stress appears to have been on making services available: it was then up to the individual to decide whether he would use them or not. British legislation, for instance, provided, like the Irish proposals, for medical inspection of schoolchildren, but in contrast to the Irish project it specifically provided that where a parent objected to his child receiving treatment, the child was not to be 'encouraged or assisted' to avail himself of it.[70] I have not been able to find in the literature on comparative health services any other scheme in which compulsion was so much emphasised as in the Irish bill of 1945.

Thirdly, the Irish scheme was notable for its centralised control. True, the bill contained provision for the minister to be assisted by consultative councils.[71] But the councils were to be purely advisory; they were to be selected by the minister himself, and it was not even mandatory on the minister to establish them, so they were of little value as a check on his power. True also, the

66. 'Post-War Trends in Social Security: Medical Care: II', *International Labour Review* (LX, 3) Sept. 1949, 239-41.

67. *Ibid.*, 242.

68. 'Report II: Protection of Mother and Child by means of Social Security', *International Social Security Association. Ninth General Meeting . . . 1949. Proceedings*, 42.

69. *Ibid.*, 44.

70. Education Act 1944, Section 48 (4).

71. Section 12 of the bill as introduced.

actual administration of health services was to be in the hands of elected county and county borough councils. But these councils were to operate according to regulations made by the minister, and in any case their autonomy had already been weakened by the establishment of the city and county manager system. On the continent of Europe, by contrast, the administration of health insurance schemes seems to have been invariably decentralised to bodies in which those insured were directly represented.[72] In Britain, the administration of the National Health Service was diffused among Regional Hospital Boards, Area Executive Committees and local authorities, and, since the first two of these bodies included representatives of the doctors and other professional interests, the British scheme could be said to include an element of vocational representation.[73] In Australia and New Zealand, the administrative structure was closer to that proposed for Ireland,[74] but in those two countries the provision for choice of doctor made an important safeguard for liberty. In short, one can say that in the Public Health Bill 1945, the bureaucratic, centralising traditions of the Department of Local Government and Public Health had passed all bounds. The scheme produced by this department in an overwhelmingly Catholic country was probably further away from Catholic social principles than any scheme produced anywhere in the world at this time.

This is not to imply, of course, that the policy-makers in the department were crypto-atheists, seeking craftily to undermine the basis of Catholic Irish society. Of the department's senior officers, the only one who was not a Catholic, so far as I have been able to ascertain, was the Deputy Chief Medical Adviser, Dr Sterling Berry. He was the son of a Church of Ireland bishop, was nearing retirement age, and was, I understand, of slight influence on departmental policy. Dr Ward was a staunch Catholic, whose brother is a parish priest, and one of whose

72. A quick way of ascertaining the outline structure of the social services in each country is to look at the right-hand column, headed 'Administrative Organisation', in the charts for each country contained in the United States government publication, *Social Security Programs Throughout the World*.

73. For details of its structure see A. Lindsey, *Socialized Medicine in England and Wales*, esp. 85, 245.

74. See the tables for Australia and New Zealand in *Social Security Programs Throughout the World*.

daughters is a nun, a respected social worker in Belfast. Dr Deeny was also a staunch Catholic, and had participated in the Social Order summer schools at Clongowes before the war. The essential Catholicity of the department's officials was innocently illustrated for me by one of the framers of the Public Health Bill 1945, who told me, in all seriousness, that he planned to model the health services on the structure of the Catholic Church—with the dispensary doctors in the place of parish priests, the county medical officer in the place of the bishop, and the county hospital playing the part of a diocesan seminary. This engaging conception did not, however, prevent his plans from subsequently arousing the furious opposition of exponents of Catholic social teaching.

So much for the plan formulated by the Department of Local Government and Public Health; now for the reactions which it aroused. In the Dail, the bill received unrelenting opposition from Fine Gael. The second reading debate in December 1945 was prolonged over three days, largely because of the number of Fine Gael speeches. For the committee stage, in March and April 1946, no fewer than 642 amendments were put down, filling 59 pages of print.[75] This was a record number of amendments for an Irish bill,[76] and Fine Gael was largely responsible for them, as it provided nearly 500.[77] The committee stage extended over fifteen days, and would have gone on for longer had not Fine Gael walked out of the house on the fifteenth day in protest against what it considered an attempt by the government to rush discussion.[78] The debate on the report stage showed signs of being almost as lengthy and acrimonious when it was brought to an abrupt end in circumstances which will shortly be described.

The Fine Gael case against the bill was, in effect, that it violated Catholic social teaching. The centralising and bureaucratic spirit

75. *Public Health Bill 1945—Committee—Amendments.*
76. *Irish Press,* 4 March 1946.
77. Dr Ward mentioned (*Dail Debates,* C, 166: 20 March 1946) that the opposition had put down 516 amendments. The Labour Party stated (*The Labour Party. Report of the Administrative Council for the Year 1945,* 20) that it put down 25. Most of the remainder can be assumed to have come from Fine Gael.
78. For the protest by the Fine Gael leader, General Mulcahy, see *Dail Debates,* C, 1897 (12 April 1946). The fact that a walk-out had occurred was referred to a few minutes later by Major Vivion de Valera: *ibid.,* 1910.

which it betrayed, and in particular the provisions for compulsory inspection and detention, were subjected to repeated criticism. General Mulcahy described the bill as introducing 'an unprecedented series of attacks on public liberty'.[79] Mr John A. Costello thought that it was unconstitutional.[80] Mr Patrick McGilligan claimed that he was upholding the 'Christian tradition that there are individual rights which no State can take away'.[81] The government was accused of ignoring the proposals of the Vocational Organisation Report[82] and of the Dignan plan.[83] Indeed more than one speaker felt that the bill could not be approved by the Catholic hierarchy. General Mulcahy believed that the parliamentary secretary 'must be at loggerheads with the Church',[84] and Mr McGilligan said that he would like to know whether the Church authorities had been consulted.[85]

Outside the Dail, opposition to the bill was expressed in the *Standard*. This, it will be remembered, was the leading organ for the exposition of Catholic social principles at this time. An ably written article argued that the powers being taken to deal with infectious diseases were excessive:

If epidemics had been devastating the country for a number of years, and if the Public Health Department had found itself equipped with inadequate powers to cope with the situation, then the new measures would be justified. But no such situation has arisen. Bureaucracy is claiming power which is not justified by public necessity. The sick are being put in the category of criminals. They have not even the advantage that a criminal enjoys of seeking justice from the courts.

The compulsory inspection of schoolchildren was attacked on similar grounds:

Worse still, perhaps: the responsibility that parents must exercise over their children is openly challenged. The State, as the Constitution points out, only steps in 'in exceptional cases, where the parents, for

79. *Dail Debates*, XCVIII, 1731 (12 Dec. 1945).
80. *Ibid.*, 1945 (13 Dec. 1945).
81. *Ibid.*, C, 1138 (3 April 1946).
82. *Ibid.*, XCVIII, 1731-2 (Speech of General Mulcahy, 12 Dec. 1945).
83. *Ibid.*, C, 1821-2 (Speech of Mr McGilligan, 11 April 1946).
84. *Ibid.*, XCVIII, 1738 (12 Dec. 1945).
85. *Ibid.*, 2028 (14 Dec. 1945).

physical or moral reasons, fail in their duty towards their children'. It is in the light of this moral principle that we must view the practice of submitting all school children to a periodical medical examination. Under the new regulations this examination will be compulsory and universal. It will be extended to schools hitherto exempt from its operation.

This means that the State accepts the presumption that parents are unwilling or incompetent to safeguard the health of their own children . . . Again we claim that there is no evidence of widespread neglect or of any serious threat to the health of the community which would justify setting aside the parents in a matter of such radical importance.[86]

At this stage, however, opposition to the bill seems to have been limited to Fine Gael inside the Dail and to the *Standard* outside it. In particular two other bodies, which were later to show themselves highly sensitive to ethical arguments against ministerial health plans, displayed no reaction to this one. The first of these bodies was the Medical Association of Eire. The *Journal* of the Association carried little news of discussion within the profession on the bill. Its own editorials were quite friendly. It complained of lack of consultation with the profession in the drafting of the bill, but had little criticism to make of its substance.[87] It summarised opinion within the Association by saying that, apart from criticisms on particular points, 'we think that in general the Association approves of the Bill'.[88]

The other body which made no move at this point was the Catholic hierarchy. This might easily be explained on the ground that its attention was not directed to the bill. After all, the bishops are busy men, and they cannot be expected to scrutinise every measure that is brought before the Dail. However, I am in a position to state—and this is perhaps the most interesting fresh fact discovered in the course of research for this book—that the matter was not simply overlooked by the hierarchy. The late Dr Ward informed me, in an interview which I had with him only a few months before his death in 1966, that, faced with criticisms in the Dail that his bill was unchristian, he took the

86. *Standard,* 14 Dec. 1945.
87. *Journal of the Medical Association of Eire,* Jan. 1946, 1: May 1946, 65; Dec. 1946, 176.
88. *Ibid.,* May 1946, 65.

matter up with the Archbishop of Dublin. He received in reply two letters, which he showed me, and whose substance he appeared anxious to have published, in his own vindication. In the first of these the archbishop said that, so far as he could see, the text of the measure was satisfactory, and in the second he went a little further and described the bill as 'substantially good'. Dr McQuaid was speaking for himself, but in the second letter he did mention that the matter had been discussed at a meeting of bishops, and he would presumably not have been so reassuring to Dr Ward if he had found the other bishops unfriendly to the bill.[89]

At this point, then, it seems, the bishops were not prepared to make an issue of the health services. Dr Ward's bill already contained in outline the mother and child proposals which were to cause such a furore a few years later, and yet at this stage the bishops appeared ready to accept their enactment without protest. If the Public Health Bill 1945 had become law, the whole course of Church-State relations in Ireland might have been altered.

The Public Health Bill 1945, however—for reasons quite unconnected with the hierarchy—never did become law. On 29 May 1946 Dr Ward was in the Dail, defending his measure which was then half way through the report stage with his usual pugnacity, and presumably believing that he was in sight of the end. What he evidently did not know was that on the previous day the Taoiseach, Mr de Valera, had received letters accusing Dr Ward of corruption in his political and business activities in his home county, Monaghan.[90] The letters came from a Dr McCarvill, a prominent Dublin specialist, and his *locus standi* in the matter was that his brother had just been dismissed from the managership of a bacon factory which Dr Ward owned in Monaghan. Clearly such serious charges against a parliamentary secretary could not be left unexamined. Consideration of the Public Health Bill was suspended, and on 5 June Mr de Valera

89. The letter was dated February 1946, so the meeting of bishops to which Dr McQuaid referred was presumably not a full gathering of the hierarchy (since none was due at that time of year), but the January meeting of the Standing Committee.

90. The letters were read in the Dail and Senate by Mr de Valera on 5 June: *Dail Debates*, CI, 1319-33; Seanad Debates, XXXI, 1927-39.

moved resolutions in the Dail and Senate to set up a tribunal of enquiry.[91] The tribunal of three judges began to hear evidence on 14 June, and its report was signed on 6 July. It found that most of the charges against Dr Ward were baseless, but it did consider that one of them—that of making incomplete returns to the income tax authorities of the profits from his bacon factory—had been proved.[92] This was enough to make it impossible for him to continue in office, and he forthwith resigned.[93]

These events by themselves need not have caused the abandonment of the Public Health Bill. Another pilot could have been found to take it through its final stages. But the government had already decided to make further changes in the organisation of the social services. Mr de Valera had announced in January 1946 that two new departments would be set up, one for public health and one for social services.[94] On the fall of Dr Ward, the government evidently decided to put through this reform before proceeding further with health legislation. The bill enabling the two new departments to be set up passed through the Oireachtas at the end of 1946.[95] Its passage entailed the withdrawal of the Public Health Bill 1945, for the subject-matter of that bill was now divided between two departments. While most of its contents concerned the new Department of Health, some of the sections on sanitary law were still in the province of the Department of Local Government, and it therefore became necessary to draft two new bills in place of the previous one.[96] Thus it was not until May 1947 that a bill reforming the health services could be again introduced. By its own decisions, without any outside pressures being exerted, the government had held up its health legislation for almost a year. The delay was crucial for the course of Church-State relations in Ireland, because it gave the hierarchy

91. *Ibid.*
92. *Report of the Tribunal Appointed by the Taoiseach on the 7th Day of June, 1946, pursuant to resolution passed on the 5th day of June, 1946, by Dail Eireann and Seanad Eireann,* 5.
93. *Irish Times,* 13 July 1946.
94. *Dail Debates,* XCIX, 169, 171 (30 Jan. 1946).
95. Ministers and Secretaries (Amendment) Act 1946. The act is dated 24 Dec. 1946.
96. This was explained by Mr MacEntee: *Dail Debates,* CIII, 1027 (15 Nov. 1946).

time to move from an attitude of neutrality towards the government's plans to one of opposition.

The new Health Bill of 1947 was in the hands of the recently-appointed Minister for Health, Dr James Ryan. Dr Ryan was a very different personality from Dr Ward. He was a more senior member of the Fianna Fail party, having been a cabinet minister since the formation of Mr de Valera's government in 1932. He had hitherto been Minister for Agriculture, an office in which he bore the brunt of the economic war with Britain in the nineteen-thirties, and he had been popular and successful in that difficult post. So when in January 1947 Mr de Valera asked him to take over simultaneously the two new portfolios of Health and of Social Welfare,[97] the Taoiseach was transferring to these new departments one of his most experienced ministers. Dr Ryan was a deceptive politician to observe. In the Dail he tended to speak in a bumbling monotone, sometimes barely audible. A stranger hearing him speak for the first time might wonder if he was quite up to his job. But those who knew him well agree that he was an extremely shrewd politician, with a remarkable capacity for getting his way. He had a knack for lowering the temperature of political controversy, and the bumbling manner in the Dail, whether consciously assumed or not, suited this well. The transfer of health matters from Dr Ward to Dr Ryan meant almost certainly that health reform would be debated with less acrimony in future.

However, though the manner in which reforms were presented was likely to change, the substance of them was not. For Dr Ryan was supported by practically the same team as Dr Ward had been. The new Department of Health consisted almost entirely of officials from the old Department of Local Government and Public Health. The Chief Medical Adviser was still Dr James Deeny. The department remained—and still remains—in the same building as the Department of Local Government, the eighteenth-century Custom House on the north bank of the Liffey, and it is still possible to speak of a 'Custom House tradition' which embraces both departments. It is not surprising to find then that the new Health Bill 1947 was substantially the same measure as

97. He was appointed on 22 January 1947: *Irish Times*, 23 Jan. 1947.

the Public Health Bill 1945. The actual wording had in many places changed in the redrafting, but the meaning was much the same. The infectious diseases sections still conferred powers of compulsory detention.[98] The mother and child sections were described by Dr Ryan, as they had been by Dr Ward, as the most important part of the bill.[99] The proposed mother and child service was still to be free for mothers and children up to the age of sixteen, regardless of means.[100] It was still to be based on the dispensary doctor, and there still appears to have been no intention that a choice of doctor should be generally available.[101] The provision for compulsory inspection of schoolchildren remained.[102]

Yet, though the Health Bill 1947 was in essence the same measure as the Public Health Bill 1945, reactions to the two bills differed in a most interesting manner. Those quarters whose opposition had been strongest in 1945 were comparatively friendly in 1947. The *Standard,* which had condemned the 1945 bill, carried no criticism of its successor. The Fine Gael party, which had fought the 1945 bill tooth and nail, was—perhaps in response to Dr Ryan's conciliatory manner—quite cordial in its approach to the 1947 bill. On the second reading debate, Dr O'Higgins described it as 'on the whole non-controversial', while Mr Morrissey said 'we welcome this bill'.[103] In committee, the only real conflict took place on the proposal for compulsory inspection of schoolchildren, and here the most eloquent opposition came not so much from Fine Gael as from Mr James Dillon, who had previously belonged to Fine Gael and was to do so again, but who at that time sat as an independent. Mr Dillon argued that the proposal infringed the natural rights of the parents, who are primarily responsible for the welfare of the children.[104] Dr Ryan, however, insisted that compulsion must be maintained for use in exceptional cases.[105]

98. Section 34 of the bill as introduced.
99. *Dail Debates,* CV, 1950 (1 May 1947).
100. Sections 2, 18, 19 and 20 of the bill as introduced.
101. *Dail Debates,* CV, 1952 (1 May 1947: speech of Dr Ryan); Department of Health, *Outline of Proposals for the Improvement of the Health Services,* 20.
102. Section 21 of the bill as introduced.
103. *Dail Debates,* CV, 1963, 2003 (1 and 2 May 1947).
104. *Ibid.,* CVI, 1578, 1618 (11 June 1947).   105. *Ibid.,* 1626.

If Fine Gael was more indulgent to the government's plans in 1947 than it had been in 1945, the Irish Medical Association was inclined to move in the opposite direction. The first reaction of the Association's *Journal* to the new bill was friendly. It said: 'This newer measure . . . will, we think, meet with a fair degree of acceptance by the medical profession in nearly all its sections.'[106] But, as the months went by, the journal carried an increasing number of reports from branch meetings at which the government's proposals had been critically discussed, and its own editorial line became more unfavourable. One ground for complaint was the lack of provision for free choice of doctor.[107] Another objection was that the scheme, by increasing the work of dispensary doctors, would take work away from those doctors who lived by private practice alone.[108] Yet another complaint was that the free-for-all nature of the mother and child scheme meant that doctors would lose much of their income from paying patients.[109] By November 1947, the Central Council of the association was sufficiently aroused to pass resolutions stating that many provisions of the Health Act were 'unworkable', and objecting to the 'degree of State control and direction' which the government appeared to envisage.[110] It would be wrong, however, to portray the association as at this stage adamant against the government's plans. A report from the South-Eastern Branch, for instance, stated that the branch 'found it difficult to make up its mind [on the mother and child clauses], and was anxious to avoid panic conclusions based on insufficient knowledge'.[111] The Dispensary Doctors' Group objected to the mother and child proposals as they stood, but stated that 'certain solutions would be generally acceptable'.[112] Dr Ryan's conciliatory manner was appreciated by the association,[113] and seems to have had its effect in softening opposition.

106. *Journal of the Medical Association of Eire*, May 1947, 260.
107. *Ibid.*, July 1947, 2; Nov. 1947, 66.
108. *Ibid.*, July 1947, 2.
109. *Ibid.*, June 1947, 288; Aug. 1947, 17.
110. *Ibid.*, Dec. 1947, 103.
111. *Ibid.*, Aug. 1947, 30.
112. *Ibid.*, Dec. 1947, 103. The nature of these acceptable solutions was not stated in the report.
113. *Ibid.*, May 1947, 259.

The body whose objections to the 1947 act proved to be most marked was the Catholic hierarchy. This was not publicly known at the time: the facts were revealed only at the time of the mother and child scheme crisis in 1951. But it appears that the hierarchy, at its meeting of October 1947, sent a private protest to the government about the then newly-enacted Health Act. The most authoritative account of this protest that we possess is a summary given by the Archbishop of Dublin, Dr McQuaid, in a letter to the then Taoiseach, Mr John A. Costello, on 5 April 1951:

The Archbishops and Bishops wish . . . to point out that, on 7 October, 1947, they sent to the Head of the Government a letter in which they expressed grave disapproval of certain parts of the then recently enacted Health Act, 1947, especially those dealing with Mother and Child services. In Sections 21–28 the public authority was given the right and duty to provide for the health of all children, to treat their ailments, to educate them in regard to health, to educate women in regard to motherhood and to provide all women with gynaecological care. They pointed out that to claim such powers for the public authority, without qualification, is entirely and directly contrary to Catholic teaching on the rights of the family, the rights of the Church in education, the rights of the medical profession and of voluntary institutions.[114]

The confrontation had come. For the first time since the foundation of the State, so far as is known, an Irish government had received a formal protest from the hierarchy against a specific item of legislation.

Before we go on to discuss the government's reaction, however, one problem demands examination: why did the hierarchy act at this time? Why did it censure the act of 1947 when it had not censured the bill of 1945, even though Dr Ward had specifically raised the merits of the 1945 bill with Archbishop McQuaid? The case was a marginal one. Both bills, as we have seen, contained extraordinary features. The combination of compulsion, of bureaucratic centralisation, of lack of provision for choice of

114. Published in *Irish Independent,* 12 April 1951.

doctor meant that there was a real case for claiming that the State was making unnecessary inroads on individual liberty and that, therefore, Catholic social principles were being violated. On the other hand, there was a great deal of avoidable ill health in Ireland, and if the government claimed that these measures were essential for combating sickness, it was not easy for any other body to be confident that the government was wrong. The arguments for and against intervention by the hierarchy, then, were fairly evenly balanced. What has to be explained is why the balance, which appeared to be in favour of neutrality at the beginning of 1946, had swung in favour of intervention by the end of 1947.

Let me at once admit that I can give no certain answer to this question. The answer can only be given by the hierarchy, and the hierarchy's records are, quite naturally, not available to a researcher for a date so recent as this. Several bishops have been kind enough to give me interviews during the preparation of this book, but only two of these were members of the hierarchy as far back as 1947, and neither had any recollection of the episode. I am therefore obliged to rely on inferences from other sources. Nonetheless, I think that some of the factors affecting the bishops' decision can be suggested.

One possible explanation of the hierarchy's attitude might be that, although the differences between the 1945 and 1947 bills were not substantial, they were just sufficient to induce the hierarchy to take a stiffer line against the later measure than against the earlier one. The theory is worth investigating, because there is a tradition in the Custom House that apparently minor differences between the two measures were the cause of all the trouble. To test this theory, it will be necessary to take the reader on a rather tedious journey through the texts of the two measures in the successive stages. To make this journey as short as possible, attention will be confined to the sections on mother and child welfare.

The Public Health Bill 1945, as introduced, contained the following clauses:—

85—(1) A county authority may, with the consent of the Minister, make arrangements for attendance to the health of expectant mothers, nursing mothers and children and for the education of such mothers and children in matters relating to health . . .

87—(1) The parent of a child shall submit the child to any medical inspection provided for the child or at the child's school pursuant to the Public Health (Medical Treatment of Children) (Ireland) Act, 1919, or section 85 of this Act.

As the bill went through the Dail, Dr Ward made some concessions to opposition criticisms, but as far as the mother and child clauses were concerned, the changes he proposed actually strengthened the bill. In committee, the above clauses were deleted, and replaced by more elaborate ones which made the provision of the mother and child services mandatory and not merely permissive:—

40—(1) A county authority may, with the consent of the Minister, make arrangements for attendance to the health of expectant mothers and nursing mothers and for the education of such mothers in matters relating to health.

(2) The Minister may by order direct every county authority, every county authority of a particular class or a particular county authority as to the manner in which and the extent to which they are to exercise their powers under this section and a county authority to whom any such direction relates shall comply therewith.

41—(1) A county authority may, with the consent of the Minister, make arrangements for attendance to the health of children and for the education of children in matters relating to health.

(2) Arrangements under subsection (1) of this section may include arrangements for the holding of medical inspections of children at schools or other places.

(3) The Minister may by order direct every county authority, every county authority of a particular class or a particular county authority as to the manner in which and the extent to which they are to exercise their powers under this section and a county authority to whom any such direction relates shall comply therewith.[115]

115. *Public Health Bill 1945—as Amended in Committee.*

Only on the matter of compulsory school inspection did Dr Ward show some flexibility. Here he introduced sections authorising the minister to exempt from the regulations a school in which he was satisfied that adequate inspections were being carried out, and requiring school medical officers to exempt from inspection any child who could produce a certificate from a registered medical practitioner stating that he had examined the child within the previous seven days, and would be responsible for any treatment that the child might require.[116] But the principle of compulsory inspection was maintained.

Dr Ward had not yet finished amending his bill. He evidently felt that the duties of local authorities needed more precise definition, for among the amendments which he had down for discussion at report stage were two fresh clauses, which were to replace subsections (1) and (2) of section 41. The new sections read as follows:—

(1) A county authority, with the consent of the Minister, may do in the prescribed manner for children in their functional area who are not pupils of any schools the following things, that is to say:—

    (a) safeguard and improve their health and physical condition;

    (b) arrange for their medical inspection in schools or other places;

    (c) provide for their education in matters relating to health;

    (d) provide for treatment of their illnesses and defects;

    (e) ascertain cases of mental deficiency.

(1) A county authority shall do for the pupils of every school in their functional area to which this section applies, in the prescribed manner and subject to the prescribed conditions the following things, that is to say:—

[The same items follow here (a) to (e) as above.][117]

These clauses had not been discussed at the time of Dr Ward's departure from office, but they are worth noting as being at the

116. *Ibid.,* Sections 42 and 44.
117. *Public Health Bill 1945—Amendments for Report Stage.*

origin of the wording eventually enacted. They reappeared in almost the same form in the Health Bill 1947.

There is no need to go through the stages of the Health Bill 1947 in the same detail because changes made in its passage through the Dail were not substantial. We can move immediately to the text of the act as finally passed. The mother and child sections began as follows:—

21—A health authority shall, in accordance with regulations made under section 28 of this Act, make arrangements for safeguarding the health of women in respect of motherhood and for their education in that respect.

22—A health authority shall, in accordance with regulations made under section 28 of this Act, do, in respect of children in their functional area who are not pupils of any school, the following things:—

(a) safeguard and improve their health and physical condition;

(b) arrange for their medical inspection at schools or other places;

(c) provide for their education in matters relating to health;

(d) provide for treatment of their illnesses and defects;

(e) ascertain cases of mental deficiency.

23—A health authority shall, in accordance with regulations made under section 28 of this Act, do, in respect of the pupils of every school in their functional area to which this section applies, the following things:—

[The same items follow here (a) to (e) as in section 22.]

Sections 24, 25 and 26 laid down the procedure for medical inspections. These were to be compulsory, unless a certificate was presented from a registered medical practitioner stating that he had examined the child in question within a prescribed period.[118] Section 27 provided for the financing of the mother and child scheme, and Section 28 stated:

118. Section 25 (5).

The Minister may make regulations applicable to every health authority, every health authority of a particular class or a particular health
authority as to the manner in which and the extent to which they
are to exercise their powers under this Part of this Act.

The reader who has had the patience to follow the legislation
through its successive drafts will agree, I think, that there is no
substantial difference in the meaning between the different
versions. The particular phrase of the 1947 act which, according
to Custom House tradition, caused all the trouble was that in
section 21 requiring local authorities to 'make arrangements for
safeguarding the health of women in respect of motherhood
and for their education in that respect'. But though earlier
proposals do not contain these precise words, they contain ones
very similar to them. And in any case this was only one of the
points to which the bishops objected. The terms of their protest
were 'that the public authority was given the right and duty to
provide for the health of all children, to treat their ailments, to
educate them in regard to health, to educate women in regard
to motherhood and to provide all women with gynaecological
care'. These words would apply equally well to the 1945 bill.
So, if the hierarchy remained silent on the 1945 bill and condemned the 1947 act, its change in attitude can hardly have been
caused simply by changes in the texts of the measures. There
must have been other factors at work.

One factor that probably operated was the difficulty of getting
decisions on any issue from a body so unwieldy as the Irish
hierarchy. As one bishop has pointed out to me, it was difficult
for the hierarchy to offer an immediate reaction to anything. It
consisted of roughly twenty-eight bishops scattered all over
Ireland. Until very recently they met as a rule only twice a year,
in June and October. Problems were often remitted to committees, but the committees themselves consisted of bishops
living in different parts of the country, and it was not easy for
them to meet. When they reached a conclusion, they reported it
to the next meeting of the hierarchy, and, although it was
almost unknown for the hierarchy to turn down the committee's
recommendation, the decision-making process was nonetheless
a slow one. The hierarchy's silence on the 1945 bill, then, and

its subsequent readiness to speak on the 1947 act, might not necessarily mean a change of mind: it could have meant that it took the hierarchy eighteen months or so to reach any decision at all.

A second factor which may have had weight was that Dr Ryan did not cover his ecclesiastical flank in the way that Dr Ward had done. Dr Ward, as we have seen, consulted the Archbishop of Dublin when his bill came under fire for infringing Catholic social principles. Dr Ryan did not, in interview, recollect any consultation with bishops, and in the Dail in 1953 he specifically stated that the bishops did not intervene until after the bill had become law.[119] It is not surprising if Dr Ryan thought consultation unnecessary. He may have known of Dr Ward's previous demarche to the Archbishop of Dublin, and have thought that that settled the matter. Or if he did not know of Dr Ward's move—which is quite possible, because Dr Ward took his fall from office with bad grace, and may not have felt disposed to brief his successor on what he had been doing—Dr Ryan may have felt that, in view of the silence of the *Standard* and the muted attitude of Fine Gael, there was no longer any danger of his bill being attacked on grounds of Catholic social teaching. But however this may be, the fact that Dr Ryan made no effort to put his side of the case to the hierarchy could have helped to affect the outcome. Dr Ryan's talent for conciliation was formidable. He had already mollified Fine Gael and the Irish Medical Association. It would have been interesting to see what he could have done with the bishops, if he had believed the effort necessary.

A third factor worth considering is the possible influence of events in Northern Ireland. In August 1947 the Stormont government published a Health Services Bill providing for the extension to Northern Ireland of the British National Health Service.[120] Much of the measure was welcomed on all sides, but it included one highly controversial proposal. This was that all voluntary hospitals be taken over by a government-appointed Hospitals Authority. Among the institutions affected was the one Catholic

---

119. *Dail Debates*, CXXXVIII, 707 (23 April 1953).
120. *Irish News*, 27 Aug. 1947.

F

voluntary hospital in the north, the Mater Hospital in Belfast, and there were prompt protests from Archbishop D'Alton of Armagh and the diocesan chapter of Down and Connor at this confiscation of Catholic property.[121] But the northern government did not seem at first disposed to offer any concession, and it was not until November that it accepted an amendment permitting the Mater Hospital, at the cost of losing all aid from public funds, to opt out of the scheme.[122] This dispute, then, would have been much in the bishops' minds when they met in October, and it could have affected their attitude to health legislation even in the south. True, the immediate issues raised by the measures in the two parts of the country were different : in the north, the objection was that private property was being confiscated ; in the south, that family rights were being invaded. But the underlying objection in both cases was the same : that the State was encroaching beyond its proper sphere. If, then, the bishops seemed, even in the south, to be more sensitive to State control of health services in 1947 than they had been in 1946, part of the reason may be that events in the north had taught them how far this control could be pushed.

A fourth factor, however, may also have operated. The bishops, as already mentioned, are busy men, who cannot spare time to scrutinise every measure that is put before the Oireachtas on the chance that it might contravene Catholic social teaching. They therefore often depend on outsiders to draw their attention to possible dangers in legislation. So, if the hierarchy took a stronger line on the 1947 act than on the 1945 bill, one possible reason could be that they were lobbied more effectively on the later measure than on the earlier one.

There is evidence to show that such lobbying took place. Its source was the County Medical Officer of Health for Limerick, Dr James McPolin, and the Limerick branch of the Medical Association of Eire, of which he was chairman. Dr McPolin was an Ulsterman, who had been on the staff of the Mater Hospital in Belfast before crossing the border and taking up his post in Limerick. A man of voracious curiosity, he could fairly be described as an amateur theologian, and had a long-standing

121. *Ibid.*, 1 Sept., 20 Sept. 1947.
122. *Parliamentary Debates, House of Commons* [Northern Ireland], XXXI, 2783 (19 Nov. 1947).

interest in the Catholic social movement.[123] My informants agree that he was the moving spirit in causing the Limerick branch of the Medical Association to take up the ethical objections to the government's health policy.[124]

Dr McPolin and his branch of the association do not appear to have taken any special interest in Dr Ward's Public Health Bill in 1945–6. It was only some time after that measure had been dropped that their opposition to government policy crystallised, and that they began an open campaign against it. The first shot in this campaign appears to have been an article by Dr McPolin which appeared in a local paper, the *Limerick Leader*, at the end of 1946. In this article, which appeared under the headline 'The State is a Glutton for Power', Dr McPolin argued for the importance of a healthy family life, and for the necessity of vigilance against any threat to it from the State.[125] In January 1947, the Limerick branch of the Medical Association followed this up by issuing a strong statement condemning any legislation which might infringe the prior rights of the family.[126] In May, following on the publication of the Health Bill 1947, it convened a meeting of 'the entire medical profession of the county Limerick', which passed resolutions against the extension of State control, the provision of free aid to non-necessitous persons, and other features of the bill.[127] In July, Dr McPolin published an article in the new periodical of Catholic sociology, *Christus Rex*, in which he expounded at length his objections to the bill.[128] In December, Dr Ryan felt sufficiently concerned

123. e.g., in 1934 he spoke on the lay apostolate to the annual congress of the Catholic Truth Society of Ireland: *Irish Catholic Directory 1935*, 617 (26 June 1934). In 1935, he spoke on vocational organisation to a *Muintir na Tire* rural week-end: *Irish Weekly Independent*, 31 Aug. 1935.

124. I have gleaned information about Dr McPolin from interviews with civil servants, ecclesiastics, and other medical men, as well as from the obituary in the *Journal of the Irish Medical Association*, Dec. 1955, 395. I was particularly helped by Dr T. F. Macnamara, who was secretary of the Limerick branch of the Medical Association when Dr McPolin was its chairman. This does not mean that Dr Macnamara is responsible for all the views that I express about Dr McPolin.   125. *Limerick Leader*, 28 Dec. 1946.

126. Quoted by General Mulcahy from *Cork Examiner*, 28 Jan. 1947, in *Dail Debates*, CIV, 749–51 (11 Feb. 1947).

127. *Journal of the Medical Association of Eire*, Aug. 1947, 32.

128. J. McPolin, 'Public Health Bill', *Christus Rex* (1, 3) July 1947, 3–16. For further information about *Christus Rex*, see below, p. 161.

about the opposition in county Limerick to attend a special meeting of Limerick County Council and explain his measure.[129] Meanwhile, the minutes of the executive committee and central council of the Medical Association show that the Limerick branch was trying to prod the association as a whole into taking a stronger line against the bill.[130] In short, at a time when the association in general was still in the process of making up its mind, the Limerick branch had become known as the most outspoken centre of opposition to the government's plans.

So far, all this shows is that Dr McPolin and his friends were lobbying public opinion in general, and medical opinion in particular, against the Health Bill. It does not prove that they approached the hierarchy. But there is evidence to show that they did this as well. In December 1947 the following letter from the Bishop of Limerick, Dr Patrick O'Neill, to Dr McPolin appeared in the papers:

Dear Dr McPolin—Recently, on behalf of the Medical Association of Limerick and Clare, you inquired of me if section five of the Health Act, 1947, constitutes a menace to the rights and duties of doctors in connection with the professional secret, and if section 24 constitutes a threat to the fundamental rights of parents. I now answer both questions in the affirmative (for the diocese of Limerick).[131]

In this letter Dr O'Neill spoke only for himself, and made it clear that his ruling applied only to his own diocese; but there is excellent reason to suppose that he gave his ruling only after consulting his fellow-bishops. His letter, though not published until December 1947, was dated 16 October—in other words just nine days after the October meeting of the hierarchy, at which the bishops had despatched their joint protest to the government. So the chronology appears to have been: 1. The Limerick branch of the Medical Association asks Dr O'Neill for a ruling on the morality of the Health Act 1947; 2. Dr O'Neill defers a ruling until he can consult his fellow-bishops at the October meeting of the hier-

129. *Irish Weekly Independent*, 13 Dec. 1947.
130. *Journal of the Medical Association of Eire*, June 1947, 288; July 1947, 15; Aug. 1947, 28.
131. *Irish Independent*, 22 Dec. 1947.

archy; 3. At the October meeting the hierarchy decides that the bill is indeed objectionable. It is possible, of course, that other representations were put to the hierarchy at this meeting, and that the complaint from the Limerick doctors was only one of a number. But there is no evidence available of appeals from any other source, while the Limerick branch of the Medical Association had made itself well known for its opposition to the government's health plans.

The chain of circumstantial evidence to suggest that it was Dr McPolin and his allies in Limerick who moved the hierarchy to take up the question of health legislation is, then, quite strong. If I stop short of confidently asserting that this must have been the factor at work, it is because I have obtained the impression from interviews that Dr McPolin was widely considered an eccentric, and I am doubtful how far such a man would have been taken seriously by the hierarchy. But on the other hand, times were propitious to complaints of the kind that he was making. The trouble over the Vocational Organisation Report and the Dignan plan must have made many bishops receptive to suggestions that the State was arrogating too much power to itself.

It remains only to discuss the government's reaction to the hierarchy's unprecedented move in protesting against the Health Act 1947. The protest, as we have seen, was dated 7 October 1947. The government took its time about replying, and, by the time it did so, the path had been made easier for it by the independent action of another of its critics.

The main criticism of the Health Bill in the Dail had come, as we have seen, from Mr James Dillon. Mr Dillon, it will be remembered, had objected particularly to the powers of compulsion given to local authorities under the mother and child sections of the bill, and on 3 December 1947 he issued a summons against the Minister for Health seeking a declaration on whether the Health Act 1947, and particularly sections 21–28 thereof, was repugnant to the constitution and therefore invalid.[132] As counsel he briefed three prominent members of Fine Gael—Mr John A. Costello, Mr Cecil Lavery, and Mr Patrick McGilligan.[133] This action was taken quite independently of the hierarchy:

132. *Irish Times*, 8 Dec. 1947.   133. *Ibid.*

at that stage neither Mr Dillon nor his counsel knew that the hierarchy had already made its own protest privately to the government.[134]

The practice of Irish courts pronouncing on the unconstitutionality of bills was still in its infancy. It had become possible only after the coming into force of the 1937 constitution, and the number of precedents which had so far accumulated was too small to make it easy to predict how the courts would decide in any particular case. Nonetheless, there had already been three cases in which acts introduced by Mr de Valera's government had been struck down,[135] so Mr Dillon's venture was not a desperate one. And indeed the fundamental rights articles of the constitution provided some foundation for his case. Article 41, on the family, declares: 'The State recognises the Family as the natural primary and fundamental unit group of Society, and as a moral institution possessing inalienable and imprescriptible rights, antecedent and superior to all positive law.' Article 42, on education, declares: 'The State acknowledges that the primary and natural educator of the child is the Family and guarantees to respect the inalienable right and duty of parents to provide, according to their means, for the religious and moral, intellectual, physical and social education of their children.' Anyone who compares these clauses with sections 21-28 of the Health Act, quoted earlier in this chapter, will agree that a tenable case could be put up for a charge of unconstitutionality.

Mr Dillon, however, by initiating his court action, gave the government the chance of making a temporising reply to the hierarchy's letter. Mr de Valera, when he finally replied to the hierarchy on 16 February 1948, wrote simply to defer a fuller answer on the ground that the constitutionality of the act had been called in question.[136] At the time that Mr de Valera wrote,

134. Mr Costello later made this clear in the Dail: *Dail Debates*, CXXV, 735 (12 April 1951).

135. Offences against the State Act 1939; School Attendance Bill 1942; Trade Union Act 1941. See Loren P. Beth, *The Development of Judicial Review in Ireland, 1937–1966*, Table II.

136. See letter from Dr McQuaid to Mr Costello of 5 April 1951, published below, Appendix B, p. 426. The date of Mr de Valera's reply to the hierarchy was given as 16 February 1948 by Mr Costello in *Dail Debates*, CXXV, 735 (12 April 1951).

his continuance in office was in doubt. A general election had taken place and Fianna Fail had lost its overall majority. If all the opposition groups could unite, they would be able to vote Fianna Fail out of office. Two days later this happened, and, after sixteen years, Mr de Valera's government came to an end.

This episode ended, then, on an inconclusive note. The hierarchy had made its first protest against a government measure, but the government had not yet accepted, or rejected, or compromised on the hierarchy's representations. The problem was passed over to the new government.

CHAPTER VI

THE CLIMATE OF OPINION UNDER THE FIRST INTER-PARTY GOVERNMENT, 1948-51

The government which replaced Mr de Valera's on 18 February 1948 called itself the inter-party government, and was formed by a coalition of all parties in the legislature except for Fianna Fail. So many individuals in this government will be mentioned in the ensuing narrative that it might be helpful at the outset to give the composition of the cabinet in full. It was as follows:

Taoiseach	John A. Costello	Fine Gael
Minister for:		
Education	Gen. Richard Mulcahy	,,
Finance	Patrick McGilligan	,,
Justice	Gen. Sean MacEoin	,,
Defence	Dr T. F. O'Higgins	,,
Industry and Commerce	Daniel Morrissey	,,
Tanaiste and Minister for Social Welfare	William Norton	Labour
Minister for:		
Local Government	T. J. Murphy[1]	,,
External Affairs	Sean MacBride	Clann na Poblachta
Health	Dr Noel Browne	,,
Agriculture	James Dillon	Independent
Lands	Joseph Blowick	Clann na Talmhan
Posts and Telegraphs	James Everett	National Labour[2]

1. Mr Murphy died in May 1949 and was succeeded by another Labour deputy, Mr Michael Keyes.
2. Mr Everett rejoined the Labour party when National Labour reunited with Labour in 1950.

The government was at first sight an incongruous team. Fine Gael had hitherto been considered on the right of Fianna Fail; Clann na Poblachta, Labour, National Labour and possibly Clann na Talmhan had hitherto been considered on the left of it. Labour and National Labour had split apart as recently as 1944, and until the last moment it was touch and go whether National Labour would agree to serve in the coalition with its rival. Fine Gael was still largely led by those who had been on the Free State side in the Civil War of 1922-3, while Clann na Poblachta had been founded by extreme Republicans, men who had refused even to accept the regime *de facto* as Fianna Fail had done in 1927, and who waited until the nineteen-forties before adopting constitutional politics. Indeed Fine Gael, though the largest partner in the coalition, was unable to nominate its leader, General Mulcahy, to be Taoiseach because his prominence on the Free State side in the Civil War made him unacceptable to the Republicans in Clann na Poblachta.[3] However, a compromise candidate for the post of Taoiseach was found in Mr John A. Costello, a distinguished barrister who had been Attorney-General in the later years of Mr Cosgrave's government but who had not personally been involved in the Civil War, and the government was formed. Under Mr Costello's genial leadership, it held together better than many observers at the time of its formation would have thought likely.

As far as Church-State relations are concerned, the new government might have been expected to have a smoother passage than its predecessor. Nearly all the parties now in office had, when in opposition to Fianna Fail, expressed some degree of sympathy for the 'vocationalist' ideas of the Catholic social movement. Fine Gael had pressed for the implementation of the Vocational Organisation Report, and Labour had done the same for the Dignan plan.[4] A questionnaire sent to all parties by the Catholic Societies Vocational Organisation Conference, asking for their views on vocational organisation, had elicited favourable replies from Fine Gael and National Labour, and to some extent from Clann na Poblachta.[5] Not only that, but once in office the

3. Information from two members of the inter-party government.
4. See above, p. 118.
5. *Standard,* 30 Jan. 1948.

inter-party government seems to have gone out of its way to stress its Catholic allegiance. Almost its first action was to send, through the Taoiseach, a message of homage to the Pope, couched in terms even more emphatic than that sent by Mr de Valera in 1932. The message said: 'On the occasion of our assumption of office and of the first Cabinet meeting, my colleagues and myself desire to repose at the feet of your Holiness the assurance of our filial loyalty and of our devotion to your August Person, as well as our firm resolve to be guided in all our work by the teaching of Christ, and to strive for the attainment of a social order in Ireland based on Christian principles.'[6] The Minister for External Affairs, Mr MacBride, represented the government at the opening of the Holy Year of 1950 in Rome;[7] and Ireland was also officially represented at the proclamation of the dogma of the assumption of the Blessed Virgin Mary in November 1950.[8]

Yet despite these credentials, the inter-party government proved to have its difficulties in Church-State relations. Though the most celebrated crisis—that revolving round the mother and child scheme—was the problem of one minister rather than the government as a whole, it was not entirely a freak event. Important developments in the Irish climate of opinion at about this time were making such difficulties more likely. We shall now turn to examine these developments.

The most obvious feature of Irish catholicism in the late nineteen-forties was, to borrow a term from continental catholicism, a mood of increasing 'integralism'. All sorts of forces were at work to make Ireland a more totally Catholic State than it had yet become: more totally committed to Catholic social teaching as then understood, more totally committed to Catholic concepts of the moral law, more explicit in its recognition of the special position of the Catholic Church. There was nothing surprising

6. *Irish Catholic Directory, 1949,* 705 (24 Feb. 1948). For Mr de Valera's message of 1932 see above, p. 48.
7. *Irish Independent,* 26–28 Dec. 1949.
8. *Irish Weekly Independent,* 4 Nov. 1950.

in such a development: this had been the direction of thrust in Irish history ever since independence, and it was in these years that the process reached its culmination.

It is worth noting, however, that this was not the line of development among most continental Catholics in the post-war period. There the trend was the opposite of 'integralist': it was one of building bridges towards those of other traditions. In West Germany, this took the form above all of co-operation with Protestants. Most German Catholics abandoned the Centre party, the time-honoured vehicle of Catholic politics, and instead supported the new Christian Democratic party, which appealed to Christians of all denominations. In other parts of Europe, the openings which Catholics developed were more towards those in the socialist tradition. In Austria, the Catholic party, which had spent the inter-war years in constant conflict with the socialists, now entered into coalition with them. In the Netherlands, the Catholic party, which before the war had refused to ally with socialists, now preferred a socialist alliance to any other. In Italy, where the Christian Democrats won an absolute majority at the general election of 1948, their leader, Alcide de Gasperi, refused to form a single-party government and insisted on keeping other democratic parties, including Signor Saragat's section of the socialists, in the governing coalition. In France, a left-wing Catholic party, the M.R.P., made great gains, and down to 1951 maintained in the face of all vicissitudes an alliance with the socialists. In Belgium, the Catholic party found itself in conflict with the socialists more often than in partnership with them, but in the process moved so far to the left that on some issues it was hard to say which was the more radical.[8a]

The difference between Ireland and most continental countries is probably accounted for by their differing experience during the Second World War. All the countries mentioned in the last paragraph had been bombed and fought over; all had suffered the shock of enemy occupation by one side or the other. In the process

8a. For Catholic politics in post-war Europe see M. Einaudi and F. Goguel, *Christian Democracy in Italy and France;* M. P. Fogarty, *Christian Democracy in Western Europe;* M. Vaussard, *Histoire de la Démocratie Chrétienne: France—Belgique—Italie;* J. Rovan, *Le Catholicisme Politique en Allemagne;* W. Verkade, *Democratic Parties in the Low Countries and Germany.*

many community barriers were shaken, many established patterns of thought broken down. The resistance movements seem to have been particularly important in bringing people of different traditions together and accustoming them to co-operation. But in the countries which had remained neutral during the war, these catalysts of change had not operated. It is significant that it was not only in Ireland that Catholic politics continued along their traditional course. In Portugal, Spain and Switzerland—none of which had taken an active part in the war—the post-war ferment which affected Catholics in many parts of the continent seems also to have been non-existent or muted. But however natural it may have been, the fact remains that Irish catholicism, which during the thirties had appeared to be moving closer to continental patterns, was now drawing away again. Irish Catholics continued to talk about vocationalism at a time when it was becoming old-fashioned on the continent. Irish Catholics continued to emphasise their distinctive traditions, at a time when continental Catholics were increasingly concerned to find common ground with those of other traditions, and in particular with democratic socialists. The result was that Irish catholicism was coming to look increasingly right-wing when compared with continental catholicism.

The 'integralist' atmosphere of Ireland during these years can be illustrated in many different ways. In the first place, the Catholic social movement, dedicated to reconstructing Ireland according to the principles of *Quadragesimo Anno*, was more vigorous than ever. Associations and periodicals already active continued to thrive. *Muintir na Tire* was growing; *An Rioghacht* was still active. The Catholic Societies Vocational Organisation Conference sought to influence public opinion in favour of a vocational order. The *Standard* continued to provide a lively commentary on events from a Catholic social point of view. Alongside existing organs of opinion, new ones were springing up. In 1946 University College, Cork, under the aegis of Professor O'Rahilly, began a series of courses for trade unionists on Catholic social teaching.[9] In 1948 the Jesuits set up the Catholic Workers'

9. *Irish Weekly Independent,* 19 Oct. 1946. See also Con Murphy, 'Adult Education in U.C.C.', in *Rural Ireland,* 1951, 58-63.

College in Dublin, with a similar objective.[10] In 1950 the Dublin Institute of Catholic Sociology was founded with the object of running courses for all sections of the population.[11] In 1952 there began in Dublin the series of Social Study weeks, in which some large auditorium was hired and eminent speakers, often from overseas, expounded Catholic social teaching to audiences which were sometimes in the thousands.[12] In the following year another organisation, the Social Study Conference, held its first conference in Galway.[13]

The most important of the new foundations was the Christus Rex Society, which was approved by the Irish bishops in 1945, and held its first conference the following year.[14] Its objects were: 'to enlighten public opinion on social questions and help to form a public conscience sensitive to social abuses and ardent to "restore all things to Christ"; to promote the study of Catholic social teaching among the clergy and through them among the laity; to inspire co-ordinated effort by Irish priests for the reform of social evils and the realisation in public life of the principles of the Social Encyclicals.'[15] Membership was limited to secular priests, but its influence was not confined to them. The papers read at the society's annual conferences have always been well publicised in the press, and since 1947, the society has published the quarterly *Christus Rex*, the principal periodical in Ireland for the discussion of social questions.

The spread of Catholic social teaching was also aided by episcopal appointments in these years. Two names in particular may be mentioned. The first is that of the Most Reverend John D'Alton, Archbishop of Armagh from 1946 until his death in 1963 (and a cardinal from 1953). Dr D'Alton was a classical

10. D. Linehan, 'Courses for Workers—2. Catholic Workers' College', *Liberty* (IX, 2) Feb. 1954, 55–6. *Liberty* is the organ of the Irish Transport and General Workers' Union.

11. R. Burke-Savage, S.J., 'The Church in Dublin, 1940–65', *Studies* (LIV, no. 216) Winter 1965, 313.

12. *Irish Weekly Independent*, 12 July 1952. The estimate of audiences 'sometimes in the thousands' is derived from personal observation.

13. *Irish Times*, 3 Aug. 1953.

14. Rev. C. B. Daly, 'Christus Rex Society', *Christus Rex* (I, 1) Jan. 1947, 29–30.

15. From the notice on the cover of each issue of *Christus Rex* in 1949 and subsequent years.

scholar, but as archbishop he showed that his interests were by no means confined to the ancient past. Several of his lenten pastorals were on social questions: that for 1948 was a survey of 'the social teaching of the Church',[16] that for 1949 was an onslaught on 'the secular State',[17] and that for 1952 was on 'the Church and freedom'.[18] The other name to be noted is that of the Most Reverend Cornelius Lucey, who was consecrated coadjutor to the nonagenarian Bishop of Cork, Dr Cohalan, in January 1951, and who succeeded to the see in August 1952. Dr Lucey had been Professor of Ethics at Maynooth since 1929, and was one of the best-known writers and speakers in Ireland on social questions. He continued his interest in such matters after his consecration, and throughout the fifties and until well into the sixties he was, along with Dr Browne of Galway, one of the two bishops who spoke most frequently about public affairs. Like Dr Browne, his cast of mind was conservative, and the frequent pronouncements of these two prelates may have given the impression that the hierarchy as a whole was more conservative that it really was.

The question might here be raised: how much did all these organisations and individuals dedicated to the Catholic social movement really matter? Were they anything more than a vocal minority group? It is true that the number of people actively engaged must have been only a small proportion of the total population, and that the articulate exponents of the movement amounted to a mere handful. The same names kept cropping up in different contexts, as speakers at *Muintir na Tire* rural weeks or at the Dublin Institute of Catholic Sociology, as contributors to the *Standard*, as office-holders in the C.S.V.O.C. or *An Rioghacht*. One is reminded of a stage army, in which the same actors come round again and again, wearing different uniforms. But though only a handful of Irishmen may have been actively involved in the exposition of Catholic social teaching, it seems reasonable to suppose that in so overwhelmingly Catholic a country they would have had a responsive audience. Facts such as the steady growth of *Muintir na Tire*, the packed audiences at the Dublin Social

16. Printed in *Christus Rex* (II, 2) April 1948, 3–16.
17. *Irish Independent*, 28 Feb. 1949.
18. Published as a pamphlet by the Catholic Truth Society of Ireland.

Study weeks, the coverage given in the press to the conferences of the various Catholic social organisations, all support this supposition. It must also be remembered that there was no alternative body of teaching seriously competing for the attention of Irishmen. The communist movement in Ireland was tiny. There were hardly any exponents even of the democratic socialist tradition. For want of competitors, as well as on its own merits, the Catholic social movement was a force in Ireland. It was conditioning the language of public discourse, and concepts such as vocationalism, the principle of subsidiarity, and the danger of excessive State control were current to an increasing degree.

On the edge of the Catholic social movement was an organisation known as *Maria Duce* ('under Mary's leadership'). Maria Duce developed, sometime in the years 1945–7,[19] from among the members of a study-circle conducted by Father Denis Fahey, C.S.Sp., whose views were described in chapter III.[20] The organisation had a six-point programme, listing a range of objectives from the maintenance of the indissolubility of marriage to the development of vocational organisation. But the point which came first on its list, and which was its distinctive feature, was the claim that the State should formally recognise the Catholic Church as the one true Church.[21] The State already

19. The years 1945–7 have been given to me by one ex-member as the foundation period. J. Blanchard, *The Church in Contemporary Ireland*, 76, states, without giving his source, that the organisation was founded in 1945.

20. See above, pp. 72–3.

21. The text of *Maria Duce's* six-point programme is as follows:
   1. The Catholic Church is the One True Church and ought to be acknowledged as such by States and Nations. The Non-Catholics ought always to be treated in accordance with the teaching of the Church and the principles of Christian Charity, so that the rights of all human persons be respected.
   2. The State must recognise the Catholic Church as divinely appointed to teach man what favours or hinders his supernatural destiny.
   3. The Unity and Indissolubility of Christian Marriage ought to be most carefully maintained, as symbolising the union of Christ and His Mystical Body.
   4. The Education of Youth ought always to envisage youth as members of the Mystical Body.
   5. The Social Doctrine contained in the Papal Encyclicals ought to be reduced to practice in such wise as to promote the virtuous life of individual members of the Mystical Body of Christ organised in families, Vocational Associations and States. Property, therefore, ought to be widely diffused.

acknowledged, under Article 44 of the constitution, 'the special position of the Holy Catholic Apostolic and Roman Church as the guardian of the Faith professed by the great majority of the citizens'. But this, in the eyes of *Maria Duce,* was not nearly good enough. Article 44, it complained, 'merely recognises the Catholic Church as the Church of the majority of Irishmen, not as the One True Church founded by Our Divine Lord'.[22] About the end of 1949 it proceeded to organise a petition for the amendment of this article.[23]

This petition received limited support. The most notable success occurred when Westmeath County Council was reported to have passed unanimously a resolution stating: 'That we call on the Government of the Republic of Ireland to amend drastically Article 44 of the Constitution, thereby putting the One True Church (Founded by Our Divine Redeemer) on a plane above man-made religions of the world.'[24] From subsequent statements, however, it appeared that only about half-a-dozen members of the council had still been present at the meeting when the resolution was passed,[25] and the seconder admitted that he did not know the contents of the resolution when he supported it.[26]

Moreover this Social Doctrine insists that Society thus organised on a Vocational basis avoids the pitfalls inherent both in the unbridled individualism favoured by Capitalism and in the excessive state-control sponsored by Communism.

6. As money governs the supply of the lifeblood to the entire economic body, the Catholic Plan for Social Order demands that the monetary system ought to be so arranged as to facilitate the production, distribution, and exchange of material goods and services in view of the virtuous life of members of the Mystical Body of Christ in contented families.

I take this text from a *Maria Duce* associate-membership card which has come into my possession.

22. *Maria Duce. Memorandum to Hierarchy, Public Bodies, T.D.s and Senators,* 1.

23. A petition form was enclosed in issue no. 20 of *Fiat.* Issues of *Fiat* were not dated, but this one carried a letter of 12 Sept. 1949, which establishes the earliest possible date of publication.

24. Cited by Mr M. J. Kennedy at the next meeting of the council: *Westmeath Independent,* 18 Feb. 1950.

25. Mr Kennedy said there were six present when it was passed: *ibid.,* 18 Feb. 1950. Mr J. Grenham said there were five or six present: *ibid.,* 1 April 1950.

26. *Ibid.,* 18 Feb. 1950. The lack of significance attached to the resolution at the time it was passed is shown by the fact that none of the local papers mentioned it in the lengthy accounts they published of the council meeting: *Westmeath Independent,* 4 Feb. 1950; *Midland Herald,* 2 Feb. 1950; *Westmeath Examiner,* 4 Feb. 1950.

The rump of the council who had passed the resolution were wrathfully denounced by other councillors at subsequent meetings,[27] and an attempt by *Maria Duce* to follow up its temporary success in Westmeath by circularising all deputies, senators and local authorities produced no result, for no other local authority appears to have adopted any similar resolution, and certainly neither the Dail nor the Senate discussed its memorandum.[28]

Nonetheless, *Maria Duce* cannot be dismissed as of trivial importance. Its core of full members numbered only about a hundred, but it had a much larger number of associate members — perhaps five or six thousand.[29] Its associated periodical *Fiat* had a circulation which, I am told, went well into five figures, and its rallies in Dublin sometimes attracted attendances of thousands. Its support perhaps came most from the lower middle classes, from people not doing well in the world who were resentful and bewildered—the kind of person who voted *Poujadiste* in France—but there was a sprinkling of doctors, barristers and retired army officers in the movement. It was never fostered by the Archbishop of Dublin, and about 1954 it appears to have been required by him to change its title to one less associated with sacred persons. But under its new name, *Firinne* ('truth'), it survived until the beginning of the nineteen-sixties, as did the periodical *Fiat*. Perhaps it was only a lunatic fringe, but it was still of interest as a symptom. One can learn something of the tendencies in a society by observing on which particular fringe of it the lunatics break out.

While *Maria Duce* was working to exalt the juridical status of the Catholic Church, other Catholics were working, on a more mundane level, to improve the material status of individual Catholics. The Knights of St Columbanus had been formed to counter discrimination against Catholics and had over the years, rightly or wrongly, gained a reputation of being so energetic in their counter-measures that they were suspected of discriminating in favour of their own members. It was about this time that the Knights—or rather, I am informed, one particular circle of the

27. *Westmeath Independent,* 18 Feb., 1 April 1950.
28. *Maria Duce. Memorandum to Hierarchy, Public Bodies, T.D.s and Senators.*
29. I am indebted for this and other points in this paragraph to conversations with two former members of *Maria Duce.*

Knights—pulled off their most celebrated *coup*. The Meath Hospital in Dublin, though formally non-denominational, was largely run by Protestants, and was reputed to discriminate against Catholics and graduates of the National University when making appointments.[30] Taking advantage of lax rules of admission to the governing body, a number of Knights and their friends joined in a group and at the next annual meeting, voted most of the existing members of the Joint Committee (which ran the hospital) out of office, and replaced them with their own nominees.[31] On this occasion, however, the Knights overreached themselves. Many Catholics disliked such a manner of proceeding, and in the Dail, a group of deputies from all parties united to undo the *coup*.[32] They carried a private member's bill which reconstructed the Joint Committee and had the effect of dislodging the intruders.[33]

Not only were many Catholics concerned with building a more Catholic social order at home; they were also concerned to show solidarity with their fellow-Catholics abroad. These were the years when the Cold War reached its height. In eastern Europe, the Church was suffering systematic harassment from communist regimes. In some western European countries, communism was presenting a dangerous electoral threat. Irish Catholics were quick to show their sympathy. During the Italian general election of 1948, the Archbishop of Dublin, Dr McQuaid, appealed over Radio Eireann for funds with which to fight the communists, and within four weeks nearly £20,000 were collected[34]—the largest collection among Irish Catholics for the aid of their brethren abroad to be taken up since the one for Spanish

30. *Seanad Debates*, XXXIX, 484–5 (28 Feb. 1951: speech of Senator Michael Colgan). Senator Colgan was one of those who took part in the *coup*.

31. *Irish Times*, 16 April 1949. Further details came out in the case of Buckley and Others v The Governors of the Meath Hospital and Others, 14–24 Nov. 1950: *Irish Law Times Reports* (LXXV) 1951, 143–9.

32. The sponsors of the private member's bill included three ex-Lord-Mayors, one from Fianna Fail, one from Fine Gael, and one from Labour: *Seanad Debates*, XXXIX, 481 (28 Feb. 1951: speech of Senator Michael Hayes).

33. Meath Hospital Act 1951. That the act really did dislodge the newcomers is shown by the angry complaints made on their behalf by an article in *Standard*, 15 June 1951.

34. See the report of Dr McQuaid's broadcast expressing his thanks: *Irish Independent*, 12 April 1948.

Catholics in 1936. The show trials of Catholic prelates in eastern Europe made a particular impression. Already in 1946, the Dail had passed a unanimous resolution of protest at the imprisonment of Archbishop Stepinac of Zagreb,[35] and in 1949 it passed a similar resolution on the imprisonment of Cardinal Mindszenty, Primate of Hungary.[36] A rally in Dublin to protest against Cardinal Mindszenty's conviction is said to have attracted the enormous attendance of 150,000.[37] This Irish anti-communism was not just a bourgeois phenomenon. In July 1950, two women collecting signatures in Cabra, a working-class area of Dublin, for a peace petition, were taken for communists, pursued by a crowd, and had to be rescued by the police.[38]

So far we have been discussing the efforts of groups of Catholics to make Ireland a more integrally Catholic State. It might be appropriate now to move to the work of a single individual who, because of his position, was able to exert an important influence in the same direction. Mr Justice George Gavan Duffy was a member of the High Court from 1936 to 1946 and President of that court from 1946 until his death in 1951. His judgments were noted for their trenchancy and originality, and he was one of the most important judicial innovators that Ireland has had. Where religious issues arose, his policy was to use the provisions of the constitution to override precedents built up by English and Protestant judges, and thus to give Irish law a more distinctly Catholic cast. This policy had already become evident before the period covered by this chapter began. In 1943, a case came up in which Judge Gavan Duffy had to consider whether a bequest for a contemplative religious order was legally a charitable bequest.[39] The relevant precedent, an English case of 1871, showed clearly that such bequests were not charitable bequests within the legal meaning of that term.[40] Judge Gavan Duffy, however, had no hesitation in thrusting that precedent aside. 'The England of 1871', he said, 'was not edified by sequestered piety, unaccompanied by

---

35. *Dail Debates*, CIII, 1401 (21 Nov. 1946).
36. *Ibid.*, CXIV, 39 (16 Feb. 1949).
37. *Irish Weekly Independent*, 7 May 1949.
38. Mentioned by 'Aknefton' in *Irish Times*, 29 July 1950.
39. Thomas A. Maguire v Attorney-General and Very Rev. Canon Maguire, P.P., 13 May 1943: *Irish Law Times Reports* (LXXVII) 1943, 139–48.
40. *Ibid.*, 144.

civic works of mercy', but, he went on, 'there is not now, and never has been the flimsiest warrant for attributing the same outlook to public opinion here.'[41] He continued: 'In my judgment, a testamentary gift to found a convent for the perpetual adoration of the Blessed Sacrament is, beyond all doubt, a gift charitable at common law, because it is a gift to God, a gift directly intended to perpetuate the worship of God. And that conclusion is in harmony with the Constitution enacted by the Irish people "In the Name of the Most Holy Trinity . . . to Whom as our final end, all actions both of men and States must be referred." '[42] Two years later, Judge Gavan Duffy had to consider a case in which a priest had claimed privilege when required to reveal confidential information in an inferior court, and had been fined for contempt.[43] On the precedents, the inferior court had been right in so fining the priest, for there was a definite ruling from an English judge that communications made to a priest, even in the confessional, were not privileged.[44] Judge Gavan Duffy declared, however, that the constitution had created a new situation and that the precedent no longer applied:

While common law in Ireland and England may generally coincide, it is now recognised that they are not necessarily the same; in particular, the customs and public opinion of the two countries diverge on matters touching religion, and the common law in force must harmonise with the Constitution. . . . That Constitution in express terms recognises the special position among us of the Holy Catholic Apostolic and Roman Church as the guardian of the Faith professed by the great majority of the citizens; and that special recognition is solemn and deliberate. The same Constitution affirms the indefeasible right of the Irish people to develop its life in accordance with its own genius and traditions. In a State where nine out of every ten citizens today are Catholics and on a matter closely touching the religious outlook of the people, it would be intolerable that the common law, as expounded after the Reformation in a Protestant land, should be taken to bind a nation which persistently repudiated the Reformation as heresy.[45]

---

41. *Ibid.*, 145.   42. *Ibid.*, 148.
43. Annie Cook v. Thomas Carroll, 31 July 1945: *ibid.* (LXXIX) 1945, 116–21.
44. *Ibid.*, 117.
45. *Ibid.*, 117–18.

He ruled, accordingly, that the priest had been entitled to claim privilege and that, accordingly, no contempt of court had been committed.[46]

So far, Judge Gavan Duffy's judgments in the religious field had aroused little controversy. Despite their challenging tone and despite their apparent assumption that to be Irish and to be Catholic were almost synonymous, their substance was reasonable enough and he could fairly claim to have done no more than redress the anti-Catholic bias of previous English judgments. In 1950, however, he was involved in a much more contentious affair, the celebrated Tilson case.[47] Ernest Tilson was a Protestant who had married a Catholic in a Catholic church in 1941, and had then signed the undertaking, required by the Catholic Church in a mixed marriage, that the children of the marriage be brought up as Catholics.[48] But in 1950, following differences with his wife, he lodged his three eldest children in a Protestant children's home, and said that he wished them to be brought up as Protestants.[49] The mother applied to the High Court for their return, and the case largely depended on whether the undertaking given by the father at the time of the marriage should be considered as binding. The precedents in such a case were clear: under common law the father is the head of the family, he has the right to decide in what religion the children should be brought up, and it had been explicitly laid down that he cannot be bound by an ante-nuptial agreement.[50] When the case came before him, however, Judge Gavan Duffy held, on this as on previous occasions, that the constitution enabled the precedents to be overthrown. At one point in his judgment he even suggested that 'possibly the constitutional recognition of the special position of the Catholic Church would authorise our Courts to take judicial notice of Canon Law',[51] and, although he did not pursue that line of thought, he did hold that the general principles of Article 41, 42 and 44, on the family, education and religion, 'present the ante-nuptial agreement of the parties upon the creed to be imparted to their future children in a new setting'.[52] He continued:

46. *Ibid.*, 121.   47. Tilson v. Tilson: *ibid.* (LXXXVI) 1952, 49–73.
48. *Ibid.*, 50, 53.   49. *Ibid.*, 51–2.
50. Well summarised by Judge Gavan Duffy in *ibid.*, 54–5.
51. *Ibid.*, 58.   52. *Ibid.*

'In my opinion, an order of the Court designed to secure the fulfilment of an agreement, peremptorily required before a "mixed-marriage" by the Church whose special position in Ireland is officially recognised as the guardian of the faith of the Catholic spouse, cannot be withheld on any ground of public policy by the very State which pays that homage to that Church.'[53] He concluded by ruling that the boys be returned to their Catholic mother.[54]

By this judgment, Judge Gavan Duffy invaded one of the most sensitive areas of inter-denominational relations in Ireland. The Catholic Church's regulations for mixed marriages have aroused strong feelings. On the one side, many Catholics would argue that this is the kind of regulation that the Church has a right to lay down for its own members, that if Protestants do not like it they do not have to marry Catholics, but that if a Protestant does sign the undertaking, thereby inducing a Catholic to marry him who might not otherwise have done so, it is wrong for him to go back on the undertaking afterwards. On the other side, many Protestants would argue that the regulation puts an unfair burden on the conscience of the Protestant partner in such a marriage, and they would also argue that in the particular circumstances of Ireland, where Protestants are a small and scattered minority, it is not so easy for them to find marriage partners of their own faith, and that the regulation therefore acts as an instrument for the erosion of the Protestant community. Hitherto the Irish courts had managed to avoid taking sides in this issue, and the rule that the father's will should prevail had, whatever its other shortcomings, at least the merit of impartiality between denominations, for sometimes the father would be the Protestant partner in a mixed marriage, and sometimes he would be the Catholic partner. Judge Gavan Duffy, however, by his ruling had come down squarely in favour of the Catholic Church's point of view.

The case at once went on appeal to the Supreme Court, where it probably caused the judges much embarrassment. The majority of the court (four judges out of five) sought to resolve the issue by coming to the same conclusion as Judge Gavan Duffy, but on different grounds. In their judgment they stated that there was no

53. *Ibid.*, 59.   54. *Ibid.*, 61.

need to discuss Articles 41 and 44, and added that 'the Court, in arriving at its decision, is not now holding that these last-mentioned Articles confer any privileged position before the law upon members of the Roman Catholic Church'.[55] Instead, they rested their decision on Article 42, which states that it is the duty of the parents, in the plural, to provide for the education of the children. They argued from this that the duty is exercised jointly by both parents, and that 'if they together make a decision and put it into practice it is not in the power of the father—nor is it in the power of the mother—to revoke such decision against the will of the other party'.[56] If they hoped, however, to avoid controversy by deciding the matter on this narrow ground, they were soon disillusioned. The only Protestant in the Supreme Court, Judge Black, delivered a dissenting judgment in which he argued that Article 42 was intended only to recognise the existing right of parents to educate their children, and not to alter the balance of rights between father and mother.[57] The judgment was followed by a crop of angry letters in the *Irish Times*,[58] and has ever since remained a prime example for those who wish to argue that Ireland is a clerically-dominated State.[59] Without necessarily endorsing this judgment, one can at least say that the deliverance of such a ruling at such a time was symptomatic of the 'integralist' atmosphere of these years.

Another trend which is detectable during these years is a readiness on the part of the bishops to give their flocks advice on how to apply Catholic principles in particular circumstances, even on matters where they had not hitherto been accustomed to speak. One such episode occurred just a few weeks before the inter-party government was formed. In the autumn of 1947 the Galway Blazers, one of the best-known hunts in Ireland, elected as its joint master a Protestant lady who had been divorced and had remarried. Protests ensued, and many Catholic farmers refused to allow the hunt to pass any longer over their lands.[60] A joint statement from the bishops of the area concerned—Arch-

55. *Ibid.*, 67.　　　56. *Ibid.*, 66.　　　57. *Ibid.*, 69–71.
58. *Irish Times*, 31 July–12 Sept. 1950, *passim*.
59. See, e.g. the tendentious account in P. Blanshard, *The Irish and Catholic Power*, 171–2.
60. *Irish Times*, 22 and 23 Dec. 1947.

bishop Walsh of Tuam, Bishop Dignan of Clonfert, and Bishop Browne of Galway—endorsed the attitude of their people:

... It has been contended on the other side that divorce and remarriage are entirely the private affair of the individuals concerned; that no one has a right to show disapproval of such conduct and that Catholic farmers ought to admit over their lands whatever person the hunt committee may select as Master. Such a contention shows gross ignorance or contempt for the religious convictions and feelings of a Catholic people.

The sanctity and permanence of the marriage bond are not a matter of indifference to Catholics. They are fundamental truths of their religion. They are sacred principles of Christian morality necessary for the moral health of the family and the nation. To remarry while a former spouse is living is, in Catholic eyes, contrary to the Natural Law, and, in the case of baptised persons, contrary to the Sacrament instituted by Christ. A person who publicly acts counter to Catholic principles in this matter cannot expect to be received by a Catholic people with the same favour, and to be given the same honour and privileges as those who respect Catholic moral standards.[61]

This statement was not completely without precedent, because as far back as 1938 one of the bishops concerned, Dr Walsh (then Auxiliary Bishop of Tuam) had advised Catholics not to keep up relations with divorced persons.[62] But the admonition then had been in general terms; now it was directed at a particular individual. The joint master concerned tried at first to ride out the storm, arguing that she did not believe she was breaking any rule of her own Church;[63] but she soon found it impracticable to withstand the pressure, and resigned.[64]

An example of specific advice from a bishop in a quite different field could be found only a few weeks later. Archbishop D'Alton of Armagh devoted his lenten pastoral for 1948 to 'the social teaching of the Church', and in the course of it suggested that the Irish trade union movement should affiliate to the International Federation of Christian Trade Unions, a body consisting mainly

61. *Ibid.*, 22 Dec. 1947.
62. *Irish Weekly Independent*, 5 Feb. 1938.
63. *Irish Times*, 23 Dec. 1947.
64. *Irish Weekly Independent*, 3 Jan. 1948.

of Catholic trade unions on the continent of Europe.[65] It was a favourable moment to press such a proposal, for the whole problem of international affiliation was in the melting pot for the trade unions. The Irish trade union movement had split in 1945, following the split in the Labour party of 1944. The larger fragment, the Irish Trade Union Congress, was affiliated to the World Federation of Trade Unions, but that body itself was about to break up into its communist and non-communist elements. The smaller fragment, the Congress of Irish Unions, had as yet no international affiliation.

Dr D'Alton's suggestion obtained different reactions from the two Irish bodies. The C.I.U. approved his proposal, and at its 1949 conference voted for affiliation to the International Confederation of Christian Trade Unions.[66] The I.T.U.C. proved less amenable. It included many Northern Ireland Protestants among its members, and had therefore to be careful about how enthusiastically it followed the lead of Catholic prelates. The comment of its general secretary, Mr Ruaidhri Roberts, on Dr D'Alton's pastoral was that 'trade unions in Ireland are not organised on sectarian lines'.[67] At its 1949 conference it rejected, by 110 votes to 14, a motion to affiliate to the Christian international, adopting instead a proposal to affiliate to the newly-formed and non-confessional International Confederation of Free Trade Unions.[68] The issue, however, soon ceased to have any practical significance. Both Irish bodies opened negotiations with the international of their choice, but both were so shattered when they discovered the affiliation fee expected of them—£600 in each case[69]—that they proceeded no further.[70] On this occasion, then, episcopal advice bore no fruit, even with the body which was initially well disposed to it.

It was not only individual bishops who were ready to give precise advice on particular issues; the hierarchy as a whole

65. *Christus Rex* (II, 2) April 1948, 8.
66. *Congress of Irish Unions. Fifth Annual Meeting . . . 1949*, 114.
67. *Standard*, 13 Feb. 1948.
68. *Irish Trade Union Congress. Fifty-fifth Annual Report . . . 1948–9*, 128.
69. *Congress of Irish Unions. Sixth Annual Meeting . . . 1950*, 97; *Irish Trade Union Congress. Fifty-sixth Annual Report, 1949–50*, 35.
70. *Congress of Irish Unions. Seventh Annual Meeting . . . 1951*, 17; *Irish Trade Union Congress. Fifty-seventh Annual Report, 1950–1*, 55, 142.

appeared more ready to do so. This is best illustrated by telling the story of the agitation for extended Sunday opening of public houses, which flared up briefly in the years 1947–50. Two different Sunday opening codes were in operation at that time— one for the county boroughs of Dublin, Cork, Limerick and Waterford, and one for the rest of the country. In the four county boroughs, public houses were allowed to open on Sundays between 1 and 3 p.m. (1.30 and 3 p.m. in Dublin) and 5 and 7 p.m. These were much shorter hours than those permitted on weekdays, but during them the pubs were freely open, and allowed to serve drink on the same conditions as on weekdays. In the rest of the country, pubs were allowed to serve drink on Sundays for a longer period—from 1 to 7 p.m. (8 p.m. in summer)—but might do so only under severe restrictions.[71] They were not open to all comers, but might serve only *bona fide* travellers, which meant people who came from more than three miles away. A writer in the publicans' trade journal explained how the law was supposed to operate:

Behind the closed door and the drawn blind of the publichouse, between the hours of 1 p.m. to 7 p.m. in Winter, and between the hours of 1 p.m. to 8 p.m. in Summer, drink can legally be consumed. It is true that the traveller has to perform certain antics, suggestive of membership of a secret society, to get in. He must knock, but not with loud determination, on the door, then be looked upon by the searching eye of the doorkeeper. He must then repeat the password 'traveller' and be prepared to answer, if asked, where he spent the night before. Having done all the law says should be done, he may then enter the sombre and mysterious depths of the darkened bar and have his drink.[72]

Such a law would clearly be hard to enforce. If the public houses could allow in travellers on a Sunday, it would be difficult to stop them allowing in local people as well. The same writer gave a picture of what happened in practice:

Commonsense, however, dictates a very different course. Commonsense holds the law to be an ass, and while the stranger performs the

71. This summary is taken from *The Pioneer* (I, 10) Oct. 1948, 10.
72. M. A. Cole, 'To open, or not to open: that is the question', *Licensed Vintner and Grocer* (XIV, 6) Christmas 1948, 45.

prescribed rites at the front door, the local inhabitant slips in by the back. Few people feel any sense of guilt about this, although, in general, a person doing wrong usually knows it without too much trouble. It is quite obvious that breaking this law, which says that the local man must not drink in his local 'pub' on Sunday but must walk three miles to another one, does not offend the traditional code of Irishmen.[73]

Relying on arguments such as these, rural publicans began in 1947 an agitation to bring the law about Sunday opening in rural areas more into line with what happened in practice.[74] In January 1948, a special convention of the leading publicans' trade organisation, the Licensed Grocers' and Vintners' Association, decided to press for general Sunday opening between the hours of 1 and 3 p.m., and 5 and 7 p.m., or in other words to bring the whole of the country into line with the county boroughs.[75] In April, a deputation met the new Minister for Justice, General Sean MacEoin, who appeared to be sympathetic.[76] In May, a Fianna Fail backbencher, Mr Martin Corry, announced his intention of introducing a private member's bill to permit the general opening of public houses between certain hours on Sundays.[77]

Before anything further could be done, however, an unexpected intervention occurred. The Irish hierarchy at its June meeting issued a statement on the matter:

We desire to express our grave concern at the proposal to have legislation enacted for the removal of restrictions on the sale of intoxicating drink on Sundays.

We view any legislation on such lines as a most lamentable and retrograde step calculated to lead to a grave increase in intemperance and to other moral evils which follow in its train.

We protest most emphatically against the violation of the precept of Sunday observance which such legislation would involve, and we

73. *Ibid.*
74. For the origins of the agitation see M. A. Cole, 'A Retrospect', *Licensed Vintner and Grocer* (XIV, 12) May 1949, 19.
75. *Licensed Vintner and Grocer* (XIII, 9) Feb. 1948, 2.
76. *Ibid.*, (XIV, 6) Christmas 1948, 44.
77. *Ibid.*, (XIV, 1) June 1948, 6.

feel sure that all who have at heart the moral and material interests of our people, especially of the poor, will offer to the proposal their most resolute opposition.[78]

The hierarchy was at once backed by the temperance organisations. The Pioneer Total Abstinence Association, which was one of the largest organisations of any kind in Ireland, claiming 360,000 members in July 1948,[79] arranged for deputies to be deluged with messages from their local Pioneer branches, urging them to vote against Mr Corry's bill.[80] Meanwhile a clerical temperance organisation, the Father Mathew Union of Total Abstaining Priests, tackled the publicans direct. It called a conference with the Licensed Grocers' and Vintners' Association, and at the conference it took the most intransigent line. According to a report published later:

The representatives of the Fr. Mathew Union refused to discuss the rights or wrongs of Sunday Opening. That was a matter which had been decided by the Hierarchy. The only question at issue was whether the Trade would accept the direction of the Bishops by withdrawing all support of the Bill and submitting to the ruling of the Bishops in the matter. Eventually, to the credit of the Trade representatives, they accepted the position that, as Catholics, they must recognise their obligations to fulfil the wishes of the Bishops in a matter which concerned closely the morals of the people.[81]

The publicans' representatives accordingly agreed to withdraw their proposals for general Sunday opening.[82]

After this, it is not surprising to find that Mr Corry's bill was defeated when it came up for second reading. It is quite possible that opinion in the Dail was not prepared for it and that it would

78. *Irish Catholic Directory, 1949*, 721 (22 June 1948).
79. *The Pioneer* (I, 7) July 1948, 1.
80. It was claimed that practically every centre of the association had registered a protest: *The Pioneer* (I, 10) Oct. 1948, 10. One deputy said later that he had been 'drowned' by resolutions from various Pioneer societies asking him to vote against the bill: *Dail Debates*, CXIV, 233 (17 Feb. 1949: speech of Dr Maguire).
81. Rev. S. McCarron, S.J., 'Sunday opening', *The Pioneer* (III, 6) June 1950, 6.
82. *Irish Independent*, 3 Nov. 1948.

have been defeated anyway, even without external pressure. When the question had last been discussed in the Dail in 1942, a motion proposing the general opening of public houses on Sundays had been defeated by 61 votes to 25, although on that occasion there had been no intervention by the hierarchy or the temperance organisations.[83] But as things were, the debacle was crushing. Mr Corry's bill was rejected by 103 votes to 26.[84]

The publicans were not yet entirely resigned to abandoning the struggle. At intervals during 1949, their trade journal contained hints that the committee of the Licensed Grocers' and Vintners' Association was reformulating its proposals.[85] Finally, in February 1950, the chairman of the association, Mr J. O'Connell, announced that the committee had decided that 'a formula can be found which would meet the reasonable needs of the trade, while not conflicting with the wishes of the Hierarchy'.[86] It would be interesting to know the terms of the formula which, it was hoped, would combine such incompatible objectives, but the public never found out, because before the proposals were published, a further and still more decisive statement was issued by the hierarchy.

This statement, issued by the Irish bishops after their meeting of June 1950, is of so formidable a nature that it is worth quoting at some length:

At our general meeting in June 1948, we protested strongly against a private member's bill then before the Dail, which would permit the opening of public houses on Sundays for the sale of intoxicating drink. Largely in deference to our wishes the Bill was decisively rejected, and we were under the impression that our guidance in this matter, so intimately connected with the observance of Sunday and with public morals, was accepted, and we expected that no further attempt would be made to modify the existing civil law forbidding the sale of intoxicating drink on the Lord's Day.

We regret, however, to have to state that our hopes have been disappointed, that there is still amongst a certain class an agitation for

83. *Dail Debates*, LXXXVIII, 1843 (4 Nov. 1942).
84. *Ibid.*, CXIII, 123 (17 Nov. 1948).
85. *Licensed Vintner and Grocer* (XIV, 9) Feb. 1949, 3; *ibid.* (XIV, 10) March 1949, 3; *ibid.* (XV, 5) Oct. 1949, 2.
86. *Ibid.* (XV, 10) March 1950, 4.

new legislation, and that pressure is being brought to bear on the responsible authorities to introduce in the Dail a Bill which would permit the opening of public houses at least for some hours on Sunday.

It has, therefore, become necessary for us to set forth our views on this matter once more . . .

From the earliest times the Church has prohibited on Sunday public trading, markets and other forms of public buying and selling. The Code of Canon Law has renewed this law and stated it in the most explicit terms: canon 1248 forbids, unless lawful custom or special indult direct otherwise, public trading, markets and other forms of public buying and selling. There is no doubt whatever that the opening of public houses for the sale of intoxicating drink comes under this prohibition; and to introduce the practice would be a grave violation of the law of the Church. In fact, the opening of public houses, by reason of the drunkenness and other sins and temporal evils to which it is calculated to lead, would be particularly repugnant to the sanctity of the Lord's Day.

Accordingly, where there has been no existing and longstanding custom, to open public houses on Sundays even for a few hours would be a serious violation of this ecclesiastical law. So long as this ecclesiastical law remains it would be sinful to agitate for their opening . . . [87]

In other words, not only was the proposed legislation wrong, but even to make a case for it was wrong. This statement was issued only a few months before the mother and child scheme crisis, and it has been overshadowed by the later and more sensational event. All the same, it was a remarkable document, and it would be hard to find an episcopal statement couched in more peremptory tones for the whole period covered by this book. It was, for the time being, completely effective in its purpose: the agitation for a change in the Sunday opening laws was stopped in its tracks, and several years elapsed before anyone broached the matter in public again. The masterful handling of the Sunday opening question by the hierarchy provides one more example of the atmosphere in this period, and helps to

87. *Irish Catholic Directory, 1951*, 744–5 (20 June 1950).

make intelligible the hierarchy's readiness to intervene in the mother and child scheme case as well.

So far in this chapter the growth of integralist forces in Ireland has been discussed without reference to its effect on government policy; but such a development was bound to have an influence here as well. Apart from the mother and child question, which will be discussed in the next chapter, there were two fields in which the prevailing climate of ideas in Irish catholicism had a visible effect on ministerial plans. These fields were social insurance and legal adoption.

Social insurance fell within the sphere of the Minister for Social Welfare, Mr William Norton, and at the time Mr Norton took office, it was a subject ripe for reform. There existed three distinct social insurance schemes—unemployment; sickness; and widows' and orphans' pensions—covering different but overlapping groups of workers.[88] Benefits under all three schemes were low, and the existence of three different schemes led to administrative complications. Mr Norton accordingly proposed, in a white paper published at the end of 1949, to unify the schemes, simplify the regulations, extend the benefits, and add further benefits such as a contributory old age pension.[89]

These proposals evoked a barrage of criticism from exponents of Catholic social teaching. The president of *An Rioghacht* opposed them.[90] *The Standard* and *Christus Rex* published unfavourable leading articles.[91] The Catholic Societies Vocational Organisation Conference produced an alternative scheme of its own.[92] A particularly violent article was published in *Christus Rex* by a Cork priest, Rev. E. J. Hegarty,[93] which was afterwards published as a pamphlet and used as ammunition by opponents of the scheme.[94] Father Hegarty marked the extreme

---

88. For an excellently-presented account of these schemes, see *First Report of the Department of Social Welfare, 1947–1949*.
89. Department of Social Welfare, *Social Security*.
90. *Irish Weekly Independent*, 3 Dec. 1949.
91. *Standard*, 4 Nov. 1949; 'Vigilans' in *Christus Rex* (IV) Jan. 1950, 78–80, April 1950, 168–70, Oct. 1950, 369–70.
92. *Standard*, 10 Nov. 1950.
93. 'The principles against State welfare schemes', *Christus Rex* (IV, 4) Oct. 1950, 315–33.
94. *Dail Debates*, CXXV, 251 (5 April 1951: speech of Captain Cowan).

wing of the opposition, but many of the best-known spokesmen of the Catholic social movement went on record as criticising the proposals—Father E. J. Coyne, S.J.,[95] Father Felim O Briain, O.F.M.,[96] Dr Cornelius Lucey (then not yet a bishop),[97] and Dr Peter McKevitt.[98] Dr Dignan, Bishop of Clonfert, who as author of the famous Dignan plan of 1944 could be considered an authority on such matters, was mildly critical.[99] *Christus Rex* was able to claim with some justification that 'from those pre-occupied with social principle' the proposals had evoked 'more criticism than has any contemplated legislation in recent years'.[100] Indeed anyone reading the papers during 1950 might have expected that it was here, if anywhere, that a Church-State clash would come. Dr Browne's mother and child scheme was at that stage known to be facing opposition from the doctors, but it was not otherwise arousing much public interest. It was not until February 1951, within weeks of the final crisis, that the spotlight of publicity shifted, and it began to appear that Dr Browne's scheme rather than Mr Norton's might be the centre of contention.

The criticism of Mr Norton's proposals came on various grounds. Some writers questioned the whole direction of government policy: they argued that true security would come, not from social insurance schemes, but from the wide distribution of property, and they blamed the government for not working in that direction.[101] Other writers deplored the increase in State control which the scheme entailed.[102] They were particularly concerned at the abolition of the National Health Insurance

95. *Standard,* 9 Dec. 1949, reporting a speech to the Statistical and Social Inquiry Society of Ireland.

96. *Standard,* 16 Dec. 1949; 'Social security for farmers', *Rural Ireland,* 1950, 100–7.

97. *Irish Weekly Independent,* 22 July 1950.

98. *Ibid.,* 28 Oct. 1950.

99. 'The government proposals for social security', *Christus Rex* (IV, 2) April 1950, 103–12.

100. 'Vigilans' in *Christus Rex* (IV, 4) Oct. 1950, 369.

101. e.g. Dr Lucey in *Irish Weekly Independent,* 22 July 1950; Rev. E. J. Hegarty in *Christus Rex* (IV, 4) Oct. 1950, 333.

102. e.g. Mr W. A. Phillips, President of *An Rioghacht,* in *Standard,* 2 Dec. 1949; 'Vigilans' in *Christus Rex* (IV, 1) Jan. 1950, 80; Most Rev. Dr Dignan in *Christus Rex* (IV, 2) April 1950, 112.

Society, the autonomous body which had hitherto run one of the social insurance schemes, and its merger with a government department.[103] They urged instead that the recommendations of the Vocational Organisation Report should not be forgotten, and that social security should as far as possible be run by vocational groups.[104] A particularly insistent criticism was that the scheme violated distributive justice, by not giving help where it was most needed. The scheme did nothing for small farmers and other self-employed people, who were often just as badly off as many wage-earners, and yet they, through taxation, would help to finance the State's contribution to the insurance funds.[105]

Mr Norton did not take this criticism lying down. He ensured, first of all, that he had the support of his ministerial colleagues. Mr Costello, the Taoiseach, spoke publicly in favour of his scheme[106]—which is more than he ever did for Dr Browne's mother and child scheme. A comment in the *Irish Times* just a few days before the latter scheme met its crisis, brings out an important difference between the two measures. The writer said: 'Unlike Mr Norton's Social Welfare Bill, Dr. Browne's scheme has not been a matter of Cabinet policy.'[107] Equally important, Mr Norton made sure that he was not without friends in ecclesiastical quarters. One member of his party, Deputy Thomas Kyne, specifically claimed that 'irrespective of any public statement by any high-ranking Church authorities or lay philosophers, we have the consent and the blessing of the hierarchy of the country to the Social Welfare Scheme'.[108] If by this he meant that Mr Norton had formally asked the hierarchy for a ruling, in the way that Dr Noel Browne was later to do with his health scheme, he appears to be incorrect. The recollection of my informants, on both the ministerial and the

---

103. This was accomplished by a separate measure, the Social Welfare Act 1950.

104. e.g. Mr W. A. Phillips in *Standard*, 2 Dec. 1949; the Catholic Societies Vocational Organisation Conference in *ibid.*, 10 Nov. 1950.

105. e.g. Rev. E. J. Coyne, S.J. in *Standard*, 9 Dec. 1949; Rev. F. Ó Briain, O.F.M. in *ibid.*, 16 Dec. 1949, and in *Rural Ireland*, 1950, 100–7; Most Rev. Dr Dignan, *op. cit.*, 107; Rev. E. J. Hegarty, *op. cit.*, 318–19.

106. *Irish Weekly Independent*, 18 Feb. 1950, 9 Dec. 1950, 10 Feb. 1951.

107. 'Aknefton' in *Irish Times*, 7 April 1951.

108. *Irish Times*, 9 April 1951.

G

episcopal side, is that no such ruling was sought or given. But Mr Norton does seem to have been feeling his ground informally. One prominent figure in the Catholic social movement remembers discussing the question with Mr Norton at length. One of his cabinet colleagues remembers being informed that Archbishop McQuaid was not opposed to the scheme. The report of the Administrative Council of the Labour party records an unnamed ecclesiastical authority as stating that the scheme was 'reasonably adequate, earned and no deterrent to thrift'[109]— tepid approval, it must be admitted, but at least not a condemnation.

Mr Norton also hit back publicly at the criticisms of his scheme. To the 'distributive justice' argument, that nothing was being done for the small farmers, he replied that the small farmers received State help in many other ways.[110] To the argument that the scheme was not vocational he replied that 'we are dealing with an urgent practical problem, not with one that can wait until all ancillary problems of vocationalism have been solved.'[111] In general, he argued that his scheme did no more than apply religious principles: 'As a Christian nation we must give practical expression to our Christianity. Surely it would not be suggested that it is a Christian attitude to allow unemployed men or women, or widows and orphans, to beg from door to door, nor would it be the Christian attitude to pay such low rates of benefit as bear no relation to the requirements of the time.'[112] He showed that he too could cite encyclicals, by quoting a passage from Pope Pius XI's encyclical *Divini Redemptoris* of 1937 in support of his scheme: 'Social justice cannot be said to have been satisfied as long as working men . . . cannot make suitable provision through public or private insurance for old age, for periods of illness and unemployment.'[113]

As events turned out, Mr Norton's measure never became

109. *The Labour Party. Report of the Administrative Council for the years 1950–51 and 1951–52,* 21.
110. *Irish Weekly Independent,* 4 March 1950; *Irish Times,* 5 Feb. 1951.
111. *Dail Debates,* CXXIV, 1070 (2 March 1951).
112. *Ibid.,* 1088.
113. *Ibid.,* CXXV, 621 (11 April 1951).

law. Although his white paper was issued in October 1949, the Social Welfare Bill based on it did not receive its second reading until April 1951,[114] and before it could go any further the inter-party government had fallen. Nonetheless, the episode lasted long enough to illustrate the climate of opinion in which ministers had to operate: a climate in which even the most well-meaning proposals were narrowly scrutinised to see whether they violated Catholic social teaching as then interpreted. It will be noted that, on this issue, the hierarchy was more cautious than some of the lay and clerical exponents of Catholic social teaching, for it made no pronouncement against Mr Norton's plan. The fact should be borne in mind when we come on to the mother and child scheme crisis. If, to many observers, the hierarchy seemed to be taking an extreme step in pronouncing against that scheme, it must be recalled that, to other observers, it was showing almost excessive moderation in not pronouncing against Mr Norton's proposals as well. The climate in which argument took place about public affairs in the Ireland of these years was such that the hierarchy was by no means on the extreme edge of vocal Irish opinion.

While Mr Norton was grappling with social insurance, his colleague General MacEoin, the Minister for Justice, was facing the question of legal adoption. The main difference in their positions was that Mr Norton was the initiator of the controversial policy, while General MacEoin confronted a problem which had been raised by an external pressure group. It is perhaps surprising that the question was still unsettled in Ireland, for in most countries provision for legal adoption had been made well before this period.[115] The world-wide growth of the practice has been traced to the First World War. In the words of one authority: 'The 1914–18 war gave the first great fillip to adoption by creating a vast number of orphans and illegitimate children. In other ages, perhaps, people would have been content simply to take the children into their homes. But modern life consists largely of social insurances, passports,

---

114. *Ibid.,* 637.
115. M. Kornitzer, *Legal Adoption in the Modern World,* 317, lists the following Christian countries as having no legal adoption in 1952: Netherlands, Portugal, Ireland, Salvador, Haiti, Honduras, Nicaragua, Paraguay.

identity cards, a thousand and one compulsions which require an unambiguous civil status. A legal form giving recognition to adoption had, therefore, to be created or re-created in every country.'[116] In England and Wales, legal adoption was introduced in 1926, in Northern Ireland in 1929, in Scotland in 1930.[117] In the main part of Ireland, however, agitation did not even begin until the late nineteen-thirties. The earliest example that I have come across is a resolution of the Dublin Board of Public Assistance in 1937.[118] One important welfare association, the Joint Committee of Women's Societies and Social Workers, took up the question in 1938,[119] and the first question in the Dail was asked in 1939.[120] Further questions were asked in the Dail during the middle forties,[121] but it was not until about the time of the change of government that the issue became urgent.

It is hard to say why the demand for legal adoption should have become acute at this time. Possibly the rise in the illegitimacy rate during the war meant that the need was growing.[122] Possibly the societies interested in children's welfare were coming to prefer placing children in adoption to putting them in institutions. This was certainly true of one important organisation, the Catholic Protection and Rescue Society, which began in 1945 a policy of energetically seeking to place children in adoption.[123] The immediate catalyst of the agitation appears to have been a correspondence in the *Dublin Evening Mail* at the end of 1947,[124] during which one adopting parent after another wrote to deplore their unsatisfactory legal position. As a result of this correspondence an organisation was founded at the

116. *Ibid.*, 318.
117. *Ibid.*, 9.
118. *Irish Times*, 10 June 1937. I owe this and many subsequent newspaper references to scrapbooks kindly lent me by Mrs V. Penney, formerly Hon. Secretary of the Adoption Society (Ireland).
119. According to a statement from this organisation published in *Dublin Evening Mail*, 3 Dec. 1949.
120. *Dail Debates*, LXXV, 329 (30 March 1939).
121. *Ibid.*, XCII, 529 (2 Dec. 1943); XCVIII, 168 (11 Oct. 1945); CI, 2584 (27 June 1946); CVI, 2163 (19 June 1947); CVII, 311 (26 June 1947); CVIII, 366 (15 Oct. 1947).
122. See above, p. 31.
123. Information from an officer of the society.
124. *Dublin Evening Mail*, 17 Nov. 1947 ff.

beginning of 1948 to campaign for the legalisation of adoption in Ireland.[125]

The Adoption Society (Ireland), as the new organisation was called, was a body of amateurs. Few of its members had any experience of politics, and most of them were unknown to each other before. It included people from many walks of life, of all political views, and of all denominations, although Catholics, as was natural in a mainly Catholic country, predominated. Yet despite its scratch nature, it proved an uncommonly effective pressure group. Its officers seem to have worked together remarkably well, and it is still possible, twenty years afterwards, to recapture from them in conversation something of the enthusiasm with which they set about their work. The very fact that they were amateurs making their first venture into politics may have helped them: it meant that people could see that they were not cranks or compulsive interferers, but ordinary decent citizens who sincerely felt a grievance.[126]

The Adoption Society succeeded in winning a considerable amount of sympathy. Though its main strength lay in Dublin, branches were formed in Cork,[127] Limerick[128] and Waterford.[129] The annual conference of the Labour party and the executive of the Irish Trade Union Congress passed resolutions of support.[130] A circular to local authorities appealing for support was particularly successful, perhaps because the society stressed the practical point that an increase in adoption would mean fewer children being maintained by local authorities at public expense.[131] Dublin Corporation, the largest local authority in the country, responded promptly with a favourable resolution,[132] and by May 1951 the society was able to report that favourable resolutions had been passed by 46 out of 48 public bodies.[133] In the Dail, energetic lobbying by officers of the society built up a body of friends in all parties—Maurice and Percy Dockrell in Fine

125. *Ibid.*, 3 Jan. 1948.
126. This account of the society is derived from conversations with three of its former officers.
127. *Irish Times*, 8 and 13 Nov. 1948.
128. *Ibid.*, 1 Feb. 1949.   129. *Ibid.*, 8 March 1949.
130. *Dublin Evening Mail*, 11 Oct. 1949; *Irish Times*, 29 Oct. 1949.
131. The text of the circular is published in *Galway Observer*, 6 Aug. 1949.
132. *Irish Times*, 21 Sept. 1949.   133. *Dublin Evening Mail*, 26 May 1951.

Gael, James Larkin junior in Labour, Alfred Byrne and Peadar Cowan among the independents, Pa McGrath in Fianna Fail. Above all, officers of the society are agreed, they received invaluable help and guidance from Jack Lynch, then a newly-elected Fianna Fail deputy and now, of course, Taoiseach. These friends in the Dail were important because they could ask parliamentary questions and approach the minister informally on the society's behalf.

When these friends approached the Minister for Justice, however, they found it extraordinarily difficult to extract a decision. The first parliamentary questions came from two Fine Gael deputies in April 1948. The minister, who was then only a few weeks in office, reasonably replied that the matter was being considered, and that an early decision would be given.[134] Nothing was then heard until December 1948, when General MacEoin told Mr Byrne that examination of the problem was taking longer than he expected, but that a decision would be taken as soon as possible.[135] In March 1949 he told the same deputy: 'There are certain difficulties, which I regret it has not yet been found possible to overcome.'[136] In April 1949 Mr McGrath asked the minister to state 'the precise nature of the difficulties', but General MacEoin replied that he did not think 'anything would be gained at the present stage' by his making a statement on the matter.[137] He gave an equally indefinite reply to a deputation of T.D.s who saw him the following month on behalf of the Adoption Society.[138] A further meeting with deputies in December 1949,[139] and parliamentary questions in November 1949 and February, April, June, July and October 1950, made absolutely no advance, the minister refusing either to give a decision or to make any further statement about the difficulties in his way.[140]

134. *Dail Debates*, CX, 641 (14 April 1948).
135. *Ibid.*, CXIII, 1171 (9 Dec. 1948).
136. *Ibid.*, CXIV, 683 (2 March 1949).
137. *Ibid.*, CXIV, 2224 (5 April 1949).
138. Adoption Society (Ireland): Hon. Secretary's typescript report for year ended 22 March 1950.
139. *Ibid.*
140. *Dail Debates*, CXVIII, 872 (16 Nov. 1949); CXIX, 313 (21 Feb. 1950); CXX, 1120 (26 April 1950); CXXI, 2075 (21 June 1950); CXXII, 1498 (12 July 1950); CXXIII, 32 (25 Oct. 1950).

It was not until 29 November 1950, twenty months after he had taken office, that General MacEoin finally gave his answer. Mr Byrne and Captain Cowan had put down questions on the matter. General MacEoin was not in the Dail that day, but the Minister for Defence, Dr O'Higgins, read the reply on his behalf. It was: 'After very careful consideration of this matter, I have decided not to introduce proposals for any legislation which would provide for the irrevocable transfer of a parent's rights and duties in respect of a child to any other person.'[141]

An attempt must now be made to investigate the difficulties which so mysteriously stayed the minister's hand. First there was an instinctive, almost subconscious, objection to be taken into account. It was the strong feeling, especially in the Irish countryside, that property should go to someone of one's own blood. If a couple were childless, there would almost certainly be relatives with large families anxious for the land, and to bring in an outsider by adoption to inherit the property could build up fierce resentment. It is a fact that the demand for legal adoption came almost entirely from the towns, and that, when legal adoption was finally introduced, adoptions in the early years were much more numerous in proportion to population in the towns than in the countryside.[142] One officer of the Adoption Society can remember a rural deputy saying to him that to interfere with the line of succession was 'like interfering with a stud-book'. General MacEoin was himself a rural deputy, representing Longford-Westmeath, and he must have been aware of this kind of objection—indeed he may have shared it himself.

This, however, was not the difficulty raised by General Mac-Eoin when at last, over two months after he had announced his refusal to legislate, he gave some explanation in public of his reasons. In February 1951 he was challenged on the matter at the Ard-Fheis (i.e. annual conference) of his party, Fine Gael, and in reply he mentioned two arguments against legislation. The first was that he felt the insecurity of adopting parents under the existing law was exaggerated. In his own words: 'As the law

141. *Ibid.*, CXXIII, 1401.
142. In the first five years there were 1,593 adoptions in Dublin County Borough, 514 in Cork County Borough, and 1,265 in the rest of the country: see the *Reports of An Bord Uchtála* for 1953 to 1957.

stood it gave ample protection to the person who had an adopted child, because that child could not be taken back by the parent unless they had as good a home as the adopted child had got, and they had to go into court to prove it.'[143]

His second argument was more fundamental. It was that to deprive a natural mother irrevocably of all rights over her child was unjust and unchristian. As he put it: 'No law could be framed that would compel a mother to waive for all time her rights to her child. Such a law would be against charity and against the common law of justice.'[144] In support of General MacEoin's point it can be said that in a number of countries the adoption law does not provide for the totally irrevocable surrender of rights by the natural parent.[145]

A more exhaustive defence of the decision not to legislate was given, however, only a few days later by the Attorney-General, Mr Charles Casey. Mr Casey's words carried authority, for he was responsible for the legal advice which the minister received. He added two points to the list of arguments used against legislation. The first was to raise doubts about the constitutionality of an adoption law. He said:

Article 42 [of the constitution] provides that: 'The State acknowledges that the primary and natural educator of the child is the Family and guarantees to respect the inalienable right and duty of parents to provide, according to their means, for the religious and moral, intellectual, physical and social education of their children.'

This article requires very careful consideration. It is clearly binding on both parents in the ordinary family, and in my opinion, equally binding on the mother of an illegitimate child. In other words, if she cannot allow her child to be irrevocably adopted, can the State pass legislation to enable her to do so?[146]

As it happens, this fear of Mr Casey's has since been proved groundless. In Nicolau's case, 1966, the courts considered the constitutionality of the Adoption Act which was passed in 1952,

---

143. *Irish Times*, 8 Feb. 1951.   144. *Ibid.*
145. The comparative table in M.-H. Mathieu et al., *Perspectives Chrétiennes sur l'Adoption*, 203–23, indicates that, in most of the seventeen countries covered, adoption is in certain circumstances revocable.
146. *Irish Times*, 14 Feb. 1951.

and ruled that the words 'family' and 'parents' which appear in Article 42 of the constitution apply only to a family and parenthood based on marriage, so that the rights of a natural parent are not guaranteed by it.[147] But this was by no means an inevitable judgment. Professor J. M. Kelly, the leading authority on Irish constitutional law, expresses some surprise at it,[148] and I have been told by one of those concerned with Nicolau's case that it was considered absolutely touch and go whether the courts would invalidate the Adoption Act or not. So Mr Casey, in raising the question of constitutionality, was not just being obstructive but drawing attention to a serious difficulty.

Mr Casey's second point was more specifically religious, and deserves extended quotation. He said:

This country is predominantly a Catholic country. That does not mean that Parliament should penalise any other creed, but it does mean this, that Parliament cannot surely be asked to introduce legislation contrary to the teaching of that great Church.

It follows that we must examine the position of that Church in relation to Child Adoption. The Church claims to be the one true Church, founded by Christ, and that all other Christian Churches not in communion with Rome are in heresy. The Catholic Church has to-day a membership of 400,000,000 in the world of those who acknowledge in full its teaching. Every member of that Church is bound to practise his Faith and to bring up his or her children in the same true Faith.

The Catholic Church has never taught that those outside its communion cannot be saved, but it does teach that those in the Church who have reached the use of reason must remain in it for salvation and that membership of the Church is the best means of saving one's soul. Bearing these matters in mind, how can any Catholic logically demand or permit any legislation which would endanger the soul of a single child?

147. J. M. Kelly, *Fundamental Rights in the Irish Law and Constitution*, 244. This case arose as follows. Nicolau was a Greek Cypriot living in London who had an illegitimate child by an Irish girl. He was willing to marry the mother and make a home for the child, but the mother refused and arranged for the child to be adopted in Ireland. Nicolau sought to have the adoption order quashed on the ground, *inter alia*, that the Adoption Act abrogated the rights which Article 42 of the constitution guaranteed to him as the natural father. See J. M. Kelly, *op. cit.*, 240–5.   148. *Ibid.*, 245.

. . . Everyone knows that each year there are illegitimate children born. Those who have prosecuted or defended know that death has often been inflicted on the child by the anguished mother. No one knows the mental anguish of the unmarried mother in her terrible suffering. Her mind and judgment are unbalanced. Her world is indeed black. If in her anguish some kindly people, who believe they are doing a Christian act, offer her a home and sanctuary for her child, who can blame her if she consents?

If you have legal adoption, her child is gone for ever from her control. Let me take a case of a Catholic girl who takes this step and hands her child over to kindly people not of her faith. When that mother has rehabilitated herself and become more normal, she will know that she has done wrong according to the belief of her faith, yet she is powerless to bring her child up in what she knows is the true faith. The adopters may have acted *bona fide*, yet legislation has denied her the opportunity to discharge the rights and duties of the natural mother imposed on her by the law of God.[149]

This argument is remarkable on two main grounds. The first is its detailed recital of the Catholic Church's teaching on the conditions for salvation, and its explicit statement that the State should harmonise its legislation with this teaching. Ever since the State was founded it had in fact been harmonising its legislation with Catholic teaching—as witness its policy on divorce, contraception and the control of pornographic literature—and in a country so overwhelmingly Catholic it would be surprising if it were otherwise. But I have not come across anywhere else quite so emphatic a proclamation of the policy by a high officer of the State. It was one more example of the integralist atmosphere of these years.

The other main feature of this argument was the implication that the Catholic Church was opposed to legal adoption, and that the ground for opposition was a fear that, if adoption were legalised, Protestants who had got control of the illegitimate children of Catholics could not be forced to surrender them. To a non-Irish reader, or indeed, to an Irish reader unacquainted with the background, such a fear might seem far-fetched. But a number of Protestant institutions did exist which catered for unmarried mothers of all denominations and would undertake

149. *Irish Independent,* 14 Feb. 1951.

to look after their children. Opinions can differ about the merits of these institutions. Their defenders could argue that they were performing a work of Christian charity which was not adequately performed by anyone else in Ireland; otherwise why would they have clients? Their critics accused them of taking unfair advantage of the plight of a Catholic mother to separate her and her child from her religion.[150] Fortunately we need not go into the rights and wrongs of these institutions. It is enough to know that they existed, and that they aroused deep and sincere dislike in many Catholics. A special organisation, the Catholic Protection and Rescue Society, had been in existence since 1913 to combat their activities. A study of its annual reports shows that by the nineteen-forties the problem was felt to be growing less acute, but even as late as 1950 it was still possible for it to make a statement such as the following:

In presenting this report the Committee wish to emphasise that there are still some proselytising agencies quite active in our country. Many of the children taken over by this Society during the last year were in grave danger of being handed over to Protestants. Parish Priests from various parts of the country in seeking our help were quite satisfied that there was a real threat to the Faith of the child. We actually removed six children from Protestant institutions and assisted a Catholic mother in recovering the custody of her three children from a Bird's Nest.[151]

The fear that it would facilitate proselytism, then, was probably the strongest objection to legal adoption. Even before the change of government, the previous Minister for Justice, Mr Gerald Boland, had mentioned this as the biggest obstacle to legislation. As he explained in reply to a parliamentary question: 'It has not been found possible to devise any scheme which would afford satisfactory safeguards against the danger that the question of the child's religion might become involved in a controversial

150. See, e.g., the reports of the Catholic Protection and Rescue Society, *passim*, especially 1933 and 1938. I have to thank the officers of this society for allowing me to consult their file of annual reports.

151. *Catholic Protection and Rescue Society of Ireland. Report and Statement of Accounts for . . . 1950*, 1. The Bird's Nest was the name of one of the best-known of these Protestant children's homes, and is sometimes used as a generic name for them all.

and undesirable manner.'[152] In General MacEoin's time as minister, there was some public opposition on this ground to legal adoption. An article appeared in several provincial papers stating that Catholic social workers were against it, and adding that the real objection to legislation was that it would be abused by proselytising groups.[153] And at one meeting attended by representatives of the Adoption Society at the High School of Commerce, Rathmines, it was reported that 'as one entered the hall, pamphlets were being handed out by some unknown persons, more or less accusing the members of the Adoption Society of being engaged in the work of the "soupers" or proselytisers'.[154] The existence of this fear of proselytism helps to explain why Catholics should have been more suspicious of legal adoption in Ireland than in many other countries. In most countries the Catholic Church appears to have accepted legal adoption without difficulty; but then in most countries proselytism has not been such a factor.

This raises the question of how far ecclesiastical authority applied direct influence in Ireland. I am in a position to state that the Archbishop of Dublin, Dr McQuaid, was consulted about the adoption issue by both General MacEoin and his predecessor in the Department of Justice, Mr Gerald Boland, and, when consulted, advised against legislation. This issue, however, is one which I have had the advantage of discussing in interview with the Archbishop of Dublin, and I can also say that his viewpoint was a good deal more *nuancé* than the bald statement that he advised against legislation might suggest. Dr McQuaid was not opposed in principle to legal adoption. He was aware that the Catholic Church accepted it in other countries, and for that matter, that it is recognised in canon law. It was with his approval that the Catholic Protection and Rescue Society had been pursuing since 1945 the policy of arranging *de facto* adoptions for the children in its care. But he did feel that the advocates of legal adoption, in their zeal to safeguard the rights of the adopting parents, tended to overlook the fact that the natural mother and child had rights too, which must equally be safeguarded in any

152. *Dail Debates*, XCVIII, 168 (11 Oct. 1945).
153. The article appeared in *New Ross Standard*, 8 Dec. 1950, *Wicklow People*, 9 Dec. 1950, and doubtless elsewhere.   154. *Dublin Evening Mail*, 13 Mar. 1951.

legislation. He did not feel, in 1950, that a solution which reconciled all these rights had yet been found. He also considered that public opinion required more preparation.

The objections to legal adoption, then, turn out on investigation to be intelligible and not unreasonable. There seems no good reason why the subject should not have been frankly discussed in the Dail, and the difficulties ventilated. This, however, was prevented by General MacEoin's refusal to give deputies any information whatever on the difficulties in his way. The most likely explanation of his attitude is that he was a pious Catholic of an old-fashioned kind who found it repugnant to bring the Church in any way into public controversy. But by cloaking his difficulties in secrecy, he brought about the very thing that he wished to avoid. For suspicions arose that there must be occult pressures at work; and, Ireland being the country it is, the immediate suspicion was that these pressures came from the Church. The impression was reinforced when, a few months later, Dr Noel Browne blew the gaff in the mother and child controversy and showed that, in his case at least, there had been behind-the-scenes pressures from the hierarchy. The legal adoption issue was important, then, for the atmosphere of mystery which it engendered. It helped to build up the impression that Ireland was some kind of theocratic State, in which a government formally answerable to the Dail and the people could in some way be manipulated by the Church behind the scenes.

So far, the period of the inter-party government has been discussed as one of increasing 'integralism'—a period in which various groups and individuals were working to make Ireland more totally Catholic, each according to their own conception of what being totally Catholic entailed. And this was undoubtedly, so far as the subject-matter of this book is concerned, the most important feature of these years. But at the same time counter-currents were detectable as well. Almost every episode which has been used to illustrate the strength of 'integralist' forces could also be used to illustrate the opposition which those forces aroused. *Maria Duce* was an active and vocal pressure group, but the amount of committed support which it secured from the general public was extremely limited. The Knights of St Columbanus were strong enough to carry out a *coup* in the Meath Hospital, but the result was that their *coup* was reversed by act of parliament. Judge Gavan Duffy's decisions looked as if they were opening a new era in the judicial interpretation of the Church's legal position, but he died in 1951, and no other judge has shown any interest in extending the line of development which he initiated. The Galway Blazers were forced to discard a joint master who was unacceptable to local ecclesiastical opinion, but the interesting point perhaps is that they should have seriously attempted to oppose this opinion. Archbishop D'Alton's advice to the trade unions on which international union they should join was rejected out of hand by the larger of the two Irish trade union congresses, and in the end not acted on even by the smaller one. Mr Norton did not abandon his social insurance plan because it was opposed by the pundits of the Catholic social movement, and the Adoption Society—as we shall see in a later chapter—did not abandon its campaign for legal adoption because ecclesiastical pressure was thought to be acting against it. Even the agitation for general Sunday opening of public houses, which was so peremptorily condemned by the hierarchy, came to a halt only temporarily, and was revived a few years later. The impression remains that the more insistent 'integralist' forces became, the more resistance they provoked.

The conflict may have been to some extent one between generations. Puritanical, conformist pressures had been increasing in Ireland for several decades. The older generation, it could be argued, had grown to maturity along with the growth of these pressures, and had had time to adjust to them as they developed, while the younger generation was growing up into an atmosphere in which these pressures were fully formed, and was therefore more likely to find them oppressive. Certainly there are exceptions to this hypothesis—*Maria Duce,* for instance, appears to have won much of its support from among the young, and it would be hard to prove that those who, say, opposed Mr Norton's social welfare scheme, or who deluged their deputies with protests against the Sunday opening proposal, belonged to an older generation than those who favoured these measures. Nonetheless, there are some stray indications of a generational conflict in the Ireland of this time. The only sociologist to have done field work during this period—Father Alexander Humphreys, who was working in Dublin in 1949–50—found some contrast in attitude between the older and younger generation among Dublin artisans, the younger generation being more ready to criticise the clergy.[155] And those whom we find spearheading the opposition to attitudes which we have described as 'integralist' do seem often to have been younger men. The leaders of the Adoption Society were mostly in their thirties at this time. The leaders of the Irish Association of Civil Liberties, an organisation which became involved in controversy with *Maria Duce,* were also for the most part youngish men. The secretary of the Licensed Grocers' and Vintners' Association, Mr Christopher Reddin, who appears to have been the key figure in the Sunday opening agitation, was thirty-nine in 1948.[156] The central figure in the biggest rumpus of all in these years, Dr Noel Browne of the mother and child scheme, was thirty-five in 1951 and the youngest member of the inter-party government. On the other hand, one can detect, as might be expected, a greater readiness to accept the *status quo* from among those of an older generation. Dr Noel Browne's colleagues, who were not prepared to follow him into conflict with the hierarchy, were on average about twenty years older than he was. And the most obvious example of conservatism among older leaders would be the bench of bishops.

In the last two chapters we saw developing a conflict between two philosophies of government, the 'vocational' and the 'bureaucratic'. It now appears that, underlying this conflict, was a deeper tension between forces that can be labelled 'integralist' and those opposing them. The consensus about moral and social questions which, to outward appearance at least, had been so overwhelming in Ireland for the first two decades after independence was breaking down. It is not surprising that this should have been an unusually disturbed period in Church-State relations.

155. A. Humphreys, *New Dubliners,* 158.
156. For biographical details, see *Licensed Vintner and Grocer* (XXII, 5) Oct. 1956, 5, and the obituary in *ibid.* (XXIV, 7) Dec. 1958, 1.

CHAPTER VII

THE MOTHER AND CHILD SCHEME, 1951:
THE CRISIS

Of all the issues which ruffled the course of Church-State relations during the first inter-party government, the most serious was the crisis over mother and child health services. The member of the government responsible in this area was the Minister for Health, Dr Noel Browne, and, as Dr Browne was to have such an explosive effect on Church-State relations in Ireland, a word about his career and personality would be in order. His father was a member of the Royal Irish Constabulary who resigned during the Anglo-Irish War. Young Noel Browne himself was, thanks to wealthy friends, given an expensive education at Beaumont College, the English Jesuit public school, and at Trinity College, Dublin. But his family background was one of hardship and, in particular, was overshadowed by the scourge of tuberculosis. His father and mother died of that disease when he was still young and later his elder sister, who had brought up the family, died of it too. He himself suffered from it for a time when a student at Trinity. It is not surprising then, that on qualifying as a doctor, he became a tuberculosis specialist. When Clann na Poblachta was formed as a radical, crusading party, Dr Browne joined it. He became its candidate for Dublin South-East in the general election of 1948, fought his campaign largely on the need for improved tuberculosis facilities, and was one of the ten Clann na Poblachta candidates elected.[1]

1. This account is taken from Michael McInerney, 'Dr Noel Browne: a political portrait—1', *Irish Times,* 9 Oct. 1967, and from Michael McInerney, 'Noel Browne: Church and State', *University Review* (V, 2) Summer 1968, 174–5. These are two different versions of a long interview by Mr McInerney, political correspondent of the *Irish Times,* with Dr Browne. Both versions of the interview need to be consulted, because each contains points which the other omits.

Almost immediately afterwards, negotiations began for the formation of the inter-party government. The leader of Clann na Poblachta, Mr Sean MacBride, found himself allocated two seats in the proposed administration. He had little basis to go on in assessing the parliamentary capacity of his followers: one deputy had, like himself, secured return at a by-election a few weeks before the general election; the remaining eight Clann na Poblachta deputies were in Parliament for the first time. Mr MacBride decided, in this field of dark horses, to pick Dr Browne. Dr Browne was known chiefly for his work in the field of tuberculosis, and the intensification of the campaign against that disease had been a plank in the Clann na Poblachta election platform. Another point in his favour was that, being young, he had no controversial political past, and one of the objects of Clann na Poblachta was to break away from past political dissensions. Mr MacBride, therefore, asked the Taoiseach for the portfolios of External Affairs for himself and Health for Dr Browne, and received them. He had more difficulty with the National Executive of his own party, some of whose older members were none too pleased at the promotion of Dr Browne over their heads, but eventually obtained acquiescence there as well. Thus, at the age of thirty-two and at the outset of his parliamentary career, Dr Browne found himself a member of the government.[2]

For his first two years or so in office, Dr Browne's ministerial career was generally applauded. The most immediate problem facing him was the one about which he himself felt most concern —the fight against tuberculosis—and in tackling it he showed a restless, tearing energy. The most serious inadequacy was the shortage of hospital beds, which the Fianna Fail government had planned to remedy by building three large regional sanatoria, in Dublin, Cork and Galway,[3] but at the time the new government took over, the building of these had not even begun,[4] and

2. This account of the process whereby Dr Browne was selected is derived from interview with Mr MacBride.

3. Authorised by the Tuberculosis (Establishment of Sanatoria) Act 1945.

4. As late as 1949, site works had not yet been completed at Galway, and had not even begun at Dublin and Cork: *Dail Debates*, CXVI, 1805 (1 July 1949: speech of Dr Browne).

in the meantime hundreds of lives were likely to be lost through lack of proper treatment. What was needed was temporary bed accommodation to tide over the gap until the three regional sanatoria were ready.[5] Dr Browne found the beds he needed by extending the existing T.B. institutions, by turning over other kinds of hospitals to T.B. work, by taking over other buildings such as a teacher-training college in Dublin.[6] He found the money he needed by using the capital as well as the interest of the Irish hospitals sweepstake fund.[7] He worked his officials hard, but he worked himself hard too, and I have found in the course of interviewing for this book that he won a generally respectful opinion for himself among the officials with whom he had to deal. The following reminiscence from the former County Manager for Roscommon, Mr J. G. Browne, will give an idea of his administrative methods:

Early in 1948 (I think it was the month of March), I received a telephone message from the department saying that Dr. Browne would like me to call to the Custom House the following Monday morning to discuss the question of the Roscommon Co. Council taking over the mental hospital [at Castlerea] and opening it as a temporary regional sanatorium, the first in the country, pending the erection of the permanent regional sanatorium in Galway. The appointment was for 9 a.m.! Naturally I was there in good time and was ushered into the Ministerial office promptly at 9 o'c. Dr. Browne was already there and I can never forget my first impressions.

He sprang up from his desk and hurried across the room, shaking my hand warmly, and thanked me for attending so early, explaining that he had to leave for Cork at 10 o'c. (By the way, in those early days he frequently drove his own open sports car which he drove at incredible speeds.) The discussions started; in the course of them I referred to the fact that Ballinasloe Mental Hospital Committee would have to agree to the proposal and there was a Fianna Fail majority on the Board Committee.

5. *Ibid*, 1803-5.
6. For details, see Dr Browne's speeches on the Department of Health estimates: *ibid.*, CXI, 2282 (6 July 1948), CXVI, 1804 (1 July 1949).
7. M. McInerney, *op. cit., Irish Times*, 9 Oct. 1967. The idea of using the fund's capital for hospital-building appears not to have originated with Dr Browne. Mr MacBride has informed me that it was one of the conditions on which he insisted when he agreed to join the inter-party government.

I can never forget his response. He said: 'That is one of my troubles, Mr. Browne; I don't know a lot about politics.' In justice to the committee, they readily agreed to the proposal. He then set me a dead-line; June 30th. It was tough going. At that time the personnel for dealing with T.B. in Ireland were few, and, accompanied by selection boards, I had to visit England and Wales (London, Liverpool, Manchester and Cardiff) to recruit staff. I lost half a stone weight in the process, but it was a labour of love, because (I met him regularly at that time) he was so enthusiastic and appreciative and was obviously working so hard himself.[8]

Dr Browne's energetic measures paid off. By July 1950 he was able to announce that his emergency bed programme was almost complete. Two thousand extra beds had been provided for T.B. patients in a little over two years, bringing the total up to 5,500.[9] Meanwhile—partly as a result of the improved hospital facilities, partly through the use of new drugs, which Dr Browne also encouraged—the tuberculosis death rate came tumbling down, from 124 per 100,000 of the population in 1947 to 73 per 100,000 in 1951.[10] These were spectacular achievements. Of all the members of the inter-party government, Dr Browne seemed to produce most in the way of definite results, and this fact helps to explain the sensation when his ministerial career came to an abrupt end in April 1951. For it was no routine member of a ministerial team who was falling from office, but an outstandingly successful administrator.

However, though from the point of view of his record as Minister for Health it was Dr Browne's tuberculosis work that mattered most, from the point of view of Church-State relations, it is on his mother and child welfare proposals that attention must be concentrated. At the time that Dr Browne took office it was not realised how sensitive this issue might be. The new ministers were not aware at first that the mother and child sections of the Health Act 1947 had provoked a protest from the hierarchy to Mr de Valera. Mr Costello said in 1951 that he became aware of this protest 'some time after we assumed

8. Letter in *Irish Times*, 13 Oct. 1967.
9. *Dail Debates*, CXXII, 1212 (11 July 1950).
10. *Statistical Abstract of Ireland, 1954*, 36.

office', but was unable to say on what date.[11] Dr Browne appears to have known nothing about it until October or November 1950.[12] A passage in the Labour party's annual report implies that the government as a whole did not know of the hierarchy's protest of 1947 until later still.[13] This was unfortunate, for it meant that the hierarchy's interest in the subject was not appreciated until the minister's preparations were far advanced. In its early stages, the implementation of the mother and child sections of the 1947 act must have seemed to the new government a comparatively uncomplicated piece of administrative business.

At the outset, Dr Browne obtained the government's decision on two points of principle. The first was whether the provision for compulsory inspection of schoolchildren in the 1947 act should be maintained. Here, it will be remembered, there was a strong body of opposition within the government itself. Mr Dillon, now Minister for Agriculture, had opposed this provision when the bill was passing through the Dail, and, after its passage, had initiated a court action to test its constitutionality.[14] In that action his counsel included Mr McGilligan, now Minister for Finance, and Mr Costello, now Taoiseach. Dr Browne appears to have been fully in sympathy with them, for in July 1948 he stated in the Dail: 'I have always considered compulsion of any kind as being a degradation of the intelligence of the average civilised member of any community, and I deprecate the use of compulsion as I did on a former occasion when a highly controversial Health Bill was introduced into the Dail. I was not in the Dail at that time but I opposed it as much as I

---

11. *Dail Debates*, CXXV, 734 (12 April 1951). This speech of Mr Costello's, made in the debate on Dr Browne's resignation, is a major source for the events of 1948–51.

12. This seems clear from Dr Browne's own account of events: *ibid.*, 669. Mr Costello believed that he gave Dr Browne a copy of the hierarchy's 1947 letter in November 1950: *ibid.*, 744.

13. 'On the change of Government in February 1948, the Health Act was not adverted to and the Government were unaware of the Hierarchy's objections until the memorandum, drawn up by the Minister for Health and referred to above, was submitted to them.': *The Labour Party. Report of the Administrative Council for the years 1950–51 and 1951–52*, 15. The memorandum referred to was one drafted by Dr Browne in March 1951.

14. See above, pp. 141, 153.

could outside.'[15] It is not surprising therefore that the government seems to have taken a decision early on this point. On 19 March 1948 Dr Browne announced that sections 25 and 26 of the act would be repealed or amended, and that sections 22, 23 and 24 would be amended to ensure that regulations made under those sections would not infringe parental rights.[16] Mr Dillon had already withdrawn his court action,[17] which was rendered superfluous by the decision to amend the sections to which he objected, and the amending bill was in due course introduced into the Dail,[18] although it had not yet received its second reading at the time the inter-party government fell in June 1951.

The other question was whether the mother and child service should be planned as a free-for-all scheme, as Fianna Fail had intended, or whether a means test should be introduced. This issue was raised by Dr Browne at a government meeting on 25 June 1948.[19] He pointed out that to introduce a means test might mollify the medical profession, whose opposition to the Health Act was hardening.[20] At this stage he does not himself appear to have felt strongly about the issue;[21] but the government decided not to deviate from the intentions of its Fianna Fail predecessor. As Mr Costello later explained: 'we were young as a Government at that time, and we thought we could not put the provision he suggested through the House.'[22] Dr Browne accordingly wrote to the Medical Association informing it that its objections to a free-of-charge mother and child scheme had been fully considered and that the government had decided against making any change in the act.[23]

The decisions of principle had now been taken, and Dr Browne

15. *Dail Debates*, CXI, 2582 (8 July 1948).
16. *Irish Times*, 20 March 1948.   17. *Standard*, 5 March 1948.
18. *Dail Debates*, CXXIII, 568 (9 Nov. 1950: first reading of Health Bill 1950).
19. *Ibid.*, CXXV, 736 (12 April 1951: speech of Mr Costello).
20. *Ibid.*, 737. The *Journal of the Medical Association of Eire*, Dec. 1947 to July 1948 *passim*, carries many reports of protests against the proposed health services passed by various branches of the association.
21. On this point there is no great difference between Mr Costello's account in *Dail Debates*, CXXV, 737 and Dr Browne's in *ibid.*, 947 (17 April 1951).
22. *Ibid.*, 737.
23. *Journal of the Medical Association of Eire*, Oct. 1948, 63.

was free to plan the mother and child service which the 1947 act authorised. The framing of this scheme took longer than Dr Browne had hoped,[24] but at length, in June 1950, the draft proposals were completed.[25] It is worth dwelling for a moment on the contents of this scheme, for it is a curious fact that, despite all the controversy which it provoked at the time and since, it has never been published. It will be printed in full in Appendix A, and some of its salient points will be mentioned here.

In its general lines the scheme followed the pattern which the framers of the 1947 act had envisaged. It provided, as the act had laid down, for 'safeguarding the health of women in respect of motherhood and for attendance to the health of children up to 16 years of age'.[26] It was to be based on the dispensary doctors, whose numbers were to be increased to cope with the increased volume of work,[27] although in the country districts, as an interim measure, private practitioners were to be allowed to participate in the scheme.[28] It provided that doctors taking part in the scheme should keep records of the illnesses of their patients, on record cards 'designed to facilitate the extraction by modern methods of statistical data'.[29] It was to be free of charge for the entire population, and to be administered without a means test.[30] On this point, Dr Browne's view had hardened since he raised the matter in cabinet in 1948, and he came to take the position that it was the one point in the scheme that was not open to negotiation. As he stated in the Dail on 11 July 1950: 'In relation to these services—I might as well make this point clear as it is the one point on which I propose to stand irrevocably—I will not concede in any way in relation to the means test. I believe that a means test in relation to health is an unforgivable degradation and an interference with the privacy of the individual.'[31]

The scheme was by no means proof against criticism. One might question whether Dr Browne was wise in insisting so strongly on having no means test. This only meant that the

24. *Dail Debates*, CXXII, 1217 (11 July 1950).
25. June 1950 is the date which the scheme carries on its face.
26. Department of Health, *Proposals for a Mother and Child Health Service under Part III of the Health Act, 1947*, para. 5. I have to thank the Secretary of the Irish Medical Association for allowing me to see a copy of this document.
27. *Ibid.*, paras. 10, 38.   28. *Ibid.*, para. 36.   29. *Ibid.*, para. 33.
30. *Ibid.*, paras. 5, 66.   31. *Dail Debates*, CXXII, 1298.

resources available were spread more thinly. A scheme limited to the less-well-off sections of the community would have had the merit of concentrating the State's resources on those who needed help most. Again, it could be questioned whether the facilities existed as yet to service so ambitious a scheme. In Dublin, for instance, the maternity hospitals were already over-stretched, and the scheme appeared likely to increase the pressure on them.[32] Finally, the decision to base the scheme on dispensary doctors, even in augmented numbers, was open to objection. It meant deliberately forgoing the services of other doctors who might be well qualified. It was quite out of line with the practice in most advanced countries, which is that any doctor who wishes may contract to participate in the State-supervised schemes.

These, however, were administrative objections. As far as ethical principles were concerned, there were several character-istics of Dr Browne's scheme which champions of Catholic social teaching might have been expected to applaud. To begin with, one might point to the manner in which the scheme was drawn up. Dr Browne did not leave it to his civil servants to work out the scheme; at the outset he set up a Consultative Child Health Council to advise him on how it should be framed, and made clear that he would not implement the mother and child sections of the 1947 act until he heard the council's views.[33] The council held twenty-two meetings between May 1948 and June 1949,[34] and the scheme eventually produced was based on its recommendations.[35] This council contained representatives of the various interests concerned—paediatricians, obstetricians, local authorities and the departments of Health, Education and Social Welfare.[36] It was in fact an example of the use of con-sultative councils of the kind recommended by the Vocational

32. A point made by Professor John F. Cunningham in 'Mother and Child Service: the medical problem', *Studies* (XL, no. 158) June 1951, 150-3.

33. *Dail Debates*, CXI, 2572 (8 July 1948).

34. *Ibid.*, CXXIII, 1771 (6 Dec. 1950: reply by Dr Browne to a question by Mr P. McGrath.)

35. *Ibid.*, CXVIII, 1722 (1 Dec. 1949: reply by Dr Browne to a question by Mr Childers.)

36. I have to thank the Department of Health for providing me with a list of the council's members.

Organisation Commission.[37] The mother and child scheme was planned in a much less 'bureaucratic' way than was usual in Irish government at that time.

Further points which might have gratified proponents of Catholic social teaching could be found in the text of the scheme itself. It was framed in terms which showed distinctly more concern for the freedom of the individual than the parent act had done. At the outset the document stressed that 'no portion of the scheme is compulsory and facilities under the scheme will be provided by health authorities only with the consent of the persons concerned or, in the case of children, the consent of parents or guardians'.[38] It went on to state that people who did not use the general practitioner facilities offered under the scheme would still be free to use other facilities, such as hospital services.[39] It also provided a measure of freedom of choice of doctor. In the cities, dispensary doctors were to be grouped in Mother and Child Health Service Districts, and a child living in one of these districts might be registered with any of the dispensary doctors within it, thus providing a choice of between five and ten doctors.[40] In the countryside the scheme was less precisely worked out, but there too a choice of doctors was promised wherever possible.[41] This was an important innovation, for freedom of choice was not mandatory under the 1947 act, and it seems, from the statements of Fianna Fail spokesmen, that such a choice had not been envisaged by them.[42]

In including these features in his scheme, Dr Browne was not consciously arming himself against attacks on the ground of Catholic social principle. He was not yet aware that such attacks were likely, and he included these provisions presumably because they seemed reasonable in themselves. In the event, as we shall see, they proved insufficient to protect the scheme against condemnation by the hierarchy on the ground of Catholic social teaching.

37. *Commission on Vocational Organisation. Report,* 311–450 *passim.*
38. Department of Health, *op. cit.,* para. 5.
39. *Ibid.,* para. 7.   40. *Ibid.,* paras. 12 and 13.
41. *Ibid.,* paras. 36, 38–9.
42. *Dail Debates,* CXI, 2287 (6 July 1948: speech of Dr Ryan); *ibid.,* CXVI, 1827 (1 July 1949: speech of Mr Derrig). See also Department of Health, *Outline of Proposals for the Improvement of Health Services* [1947], 20.

Before we examine Dr Browne's relations with the hierarchy, however, some other episodes that occurred about this time should be discussed. For it is an important fact in explaining the development of Dr Browne's trouble with the bishops that it was only one of the conflicts in which he became involved, and, until a very late stage, not the most important one. Simultaneously, he was fighting on three other fronts. He was engaged in a fierce struggle with the Irish Medical Association, he aroused the antagonism of several of his cabinet colleagues, and he became involved in conflict with his own party leader, Mr Sean Mac-Bride. It will clarify matters if these three disputes are outlined first.

The trouble with the Irish Medical Association was slow to develop. Doctors generally admired Dr Browne's work against tuberculosis, and in July 1949 the then president of the association, Dr Patrick Moran, said that 'most cordial relations now exist between the Department and the Medical Association'.[43] It was not until about the end of 1949 that relations began to worsen. The association was angered by an order from the Minister for Health directing local authorities to report to him personally within twenty-four hours any complaint made against medical officers in the performance of their duties.[44] The minister was irritated at the opposition shown by the association to a proposal for departmental control of the then newly-introduced drug, streptomycin.[45] The association in its turn was affronted by an angry speech from the minister, in which he spoke of the 'uncompromising hostility of a section of the profession', and added that 'it would be unfortunate if that section drove a wedge between those responsible for giving effect to the will of the people . . . and the family doctor'.[46]

It was the mother and child scheme, however, which brought the hostility between the minister and the association to a head. The scheme was sent to the association for comment about the beginning of July 1950.[47] The Central Council of the association

43. *Journal of the Medical Association of Eire*, Aug. 1949, 17.
44. *Ibid.*, Nov. 1949, 67.   45. *Ibid.*, Feb. 1950, 17.
46. *Ibid.*, 1–2.
47. Dr Browne stated, on 11 July, that the scheme would 'soon be considered by the Irish Medical Association': *Dail Debates*, CXXII, 1217.

acted with alacrity, collected comments from the branches, and was in a position to put its views to the minister by the time a delegation met Dr Browne on 24 October. At this meeting the means test proved the crux. The minister said that there was nothing else immutable in the proposals, but he 'was adamant that there would be no means test'.[48] To the association, on the other hand, one of its principal objections was that the scheme provided a free service to those who were in a position to pay.[49] The Central Council of the association decided to hold a referendum of its members on the issue.[50] The result of the referendum, which was announced on 23 November, showed that on the crucial question—'Do you agree to work a mother and child scheme which includes free treatment for those who could pay for themselves?'—779 doctors, or 78 per cent of those replying, answered 'no', while only 215, or 22 per cent of those replying, answered 'yes'.[51]

The referendum, however, only embittered the dispute. On the one hand, the association's leaders felt they had received enough support to persevere in their opposition. But on the other hand, the figures could be interpreted to show that only a minority of the profession was intransigent. Out of 1,886 ballots sent out, only 1,011, or 54 per cent had been returned,[52] and on top of that there were several hundred doctors who did not belong to the Irish Medical Association and who had not, therefore, been consulted. If these facts were taken into consideration, it appeared as if the proportion of the total profession who had voted 'no' was only about 30 per cent.[53] Dr Browne was accordingly fortified in his belief that, if he stood firm, he could beat the leaders of the association.

48. Irish Medical Association, 'Report of conference held at the Department of Health on the 24th October, 1950, between the Minister for Health and a deputation appointed by the Association to discuss Proposals in connection with a Mother and Child Scheme under Part III of the Health Act 1947.' I have to thank the Secretary of the Irish Medical Association for allowing me to see this cyclostyled document.   49. *Ibid.*

50. *Journal of the Medical Association of Eire*, Nov. 1950, 73.

51. *Ibid.*, Dec. 1950, 111. I have corrected the percentages, which are inaccurate in the original.

52. *Ibid.*

53. Dr Browne used this argument in a speech reported in *Irish Times*, 12 Jan. 1951.

Dr Browne appears to have become very bitter against the Irish Medical Association at this time. One of his cabinet colleagues has told me that he appeared to develop a 'pathological hatred' of the doctors. Further evidence of his state of mind can be found in a cyclostyled document, headed *The Mother and Child Scheme. Is it Needed?*, which was circulating in Clann na Poblachta branches about the end of 1950.[54] The document was unsigned, but it would hardly have circulated in Clann na Poblachta without Dr Browne's approval, and indeed its vigorous style, and the occasional use in an authoritative manner of the first person singular, leads to the suspicion that it was actually written by Dr Browne. The suspicion is increased almost to certainty by the fact that a private detective employed by the Irish Medical Association discovered the original stencils of the document in the dustbins of the Custom House.[55] This document was a sustained attack on the medical profession in general and the specialists in particular. It poured scorn on the *bona fides* of their objections to the mother and child scheme, and insinuated that their real objection was that they might lose money. A brief quotation will give the flavour:

The Tuberculosis Services were made 'free without a means test' about three years ago. They were 99 per cent State-organised and there was no 'howl' when they became quite free. You might ask why there was no howl. The reasons are not far to seek. Generally speaking tuberculosis is largely a poor man's disease. Remember there is little money in tuberculosis and that is why the State Service and organisation, free and so on, was good enough—there was no objection. But there's plenty of money in the mothers and their children; even if they die the 30 per cent who voted against the scheme will insist that they must have their 'pound of flesh'.[56]

This particular allegation was not even accurate. The Irish Medical Association had in fact protested against the tuberculosis

54. The I.M.A. stated in February that it had obtained a copy of this document some weeks previously: *Irish Times*, 13 Feb. 1951. It cannot have been compiled earlier than 23 November, because it contains an analysis of the I.M.A.'s referendum results which were announced on that day.

55. Information from a doctor formerly prominent in the I.M.A.

56. I am indebted to a doctor formerly prominent in the I.M.A. for letting me see a copy of this document.

services being made free to those who could afford to pay for them.[57]

If this was Dr Browne's attitude, it is not surprising to find that he did not persevere in his negotiations with the Irish Medical Association. Consultations continued through January and February 1951,[58] but suddenly, on 5 March, Dr Browne announced that the I.M.A. was indulging in delaying tactics, and that he could countenance no further delay in the introduction of the scheme.[59] An outline of the scheme was issued to the press the following day, and appeared in the newspapers of 7 March.

Meanwhile, and as a result of his conflict with the I.M.A., Dr Browne was facing trouble on another front—in his relations with his colleagues. Several of these were uneasy at his handling of the negotiations with the doctors. The uneasiness was most acute among Fine Gael ministers, some of whom were professional men themselves, and not disposed to accept Dr Browne's hostile assessment of the medical profession. Mr Costello, for instance, was shocked at Dr Browne's attitude to the doctors. As he later put it: 'They acted the part which you would expect a noble profession to act in regard to this matter and the only thanks they have got is vilification.'[60] The Minister for Defence, Dr O'Higgins, was in a particularly difficult position, because he was a medical man himself and on good terms with leaders of the I.M.A. Even among the more left-wing members of the coalition, however, there was uneasiness at Dr Browne's handling of the situation: to antagonise the principal interest group concerned did not seem the best way of securing results. As the leader of the Labour party, Mr Norton, remarked later: 'the goodwill of the doctors . . . must be relied on to implement a scheme of this kind.'[61] At various stages several members of the government—Mr Costello, Mr Norton, Mr Dillon and Dr

---

57. *Journal of the Medical Association of Eire,* June 1950, 96.
58. *Journal of the Irish Medical Association,* Feb. 1951, 40; March 1951, 56. Further details in a speech by Dr T. F. O'Higgins, Minister for Defence: *Irish Times,* 12 Feb. 1951.
59. *Irish Times,* 6 March 1951.
60. *Dail Debates,* CXXV, 750 (12 April 1951).
61. *Ibid.,* 953 (17 April 1951).

O'Higgins—attempted to mediate between the association and their colleague, but without success.[62]

Dr Browne's relations with his fellow-ministers were seriously worsened by his abrupt decision, at the beginning of March, to go ahead with his scheme. This decision, taken apparently without consulting his colleagues, naturally angered those ministers who already had reservations about his handling of the question. Indeed there is evidence that his career as a minister almost came to an end at this point. According to the newspapers, on the night of 6 March several ministers met and discussed the whole history of the scheme. The *Irish Times* reported that some ministers regarded the position with dissatisfaction.[63] The *Irish Independent* mentioned the possibility of Dr Browne resigning, and pointed out that the Government Information Bureau, when announcing Dr Browne's intention to introduce the scheme, made clear that it was doing so 'at the request of the Department of Health'. This form of words, the newspaper reported, was intended to show that the government did not fully approve of Dr Browne's statements.[64]

In the event, Dr Browne stayed on in the government for the moment. He himself stated when he did eventually resign from the government a month later—and this was one of the few statements in his resignation speech that was not rebutted by other ministers—that, about this time, the Taoiseach and several other ministers expressed concern about the growing opposition of the I.M.A. and suggested that there should be a means test in the scheme after all. Dr Browne, in his own words, challenged them 'that they should consider this matter not as individuals but as a Cabinet and if they so wished reverse their decision of 1948 to exclude a means test', and added that he would take whatever action he thought fit about his own position. 'But', he stated, 'they all refused to take this course.'[65] Apparently they still hoped that the issue could be resolved without a crisis. But Dr Browne, by defying his colleagues to push him out of

62. *Ibid.*, 747 (speech of Mr Costello).
63. *Irish Times,* 7 March 1951. According to this report, the ministers who met were Messrs Costello, Norton, Mulcahy, McGilligan, MacBride and Dillon.
64. *Irish Independent,* 7 March 1951.
65. *Dáil Debates,* CXXV, 673 (12 April 1951).

the government, was treading on dangerous ground. He was ensuring that if trouble subsequently arose from another quarter, his colleagues would be all the less inclined to help him.

Simultaneously, but for different reasons, Dr Browne was engaged in an even more serious conflict with another cabinet colleague—his own party leader, Mr Sean MacBride. This dispute, unlike the one between Dr Browne and the I.M.A., is little documented, and I have had to rely primarily on the recollections which the two principals have kindly given to me. Naturally their memories have different emphases, but I find that they dovetail into each other well enough and that it is possible to construct a reasonably coherent picture of what happened. Both men agree that the estrangement began quite late—Mr MacBride suggests about the beginning of 1950. Both agree also that an important part was played by the late Noel Hartnett. Mr Hartnett had been director of elections for Clann na Poblachta in 1948 and was a leading member of the party. He was Dr Browne's intimate friend and had indeed introduced him to Clann na Poblachta and to Mr MacBride. So long as Mr Hartnett remained close to Mr MacBride as well as to Dr Browne, all was well; but at some stage he became estranged from Mr MacBride, and the estrangement between the latter and Dr Browne followed. By November 1950, Mr MacBride felt so markedly the change in Dr Browne's attitude that he decided to have the matter out with him, and invited him to discuss things over dinner at the Russell Hotel. The atmosphere at this eerie dinner comes through sharply in Mr MacBride's recollection: he remembers Dr Browne telling him, in a calm tone as if they were discussing the weather, that he (Mr MacBride) had completely failed as leader of the party, that the Clann was stagnant, and that he (Dr Browne) intended to bring down the government and break up the Clann.[66] Dr Browne remembers the dinner but is sure that he never made such threats. However that may be, Mr MacBride felt from then on

---

66. On this point I do not have to rely only on Mr MacBride's recollections of many years later. Mr MacBride was so startled by this conversation that he wrote a memorandum of it the same night, of which he has kindly provided me with a copy.

that he was walking round with Dr Browne's knife poised at his back.

The point at issue between Dr Browne and Mr MacBride appears to have been the future course of Clann na Poblachta. When the party was founded in 1946, by a group of ex-I.R.A. men disenchanted at the lack of results from a policy of violence, it quickly attracted many idealistic young Irishmen who felt that all other Irish parties were complacent and stale. Then came the general election of 1948 and the formation of the inter-party government. As Dr Browne recalls it, Clann na Poblachta agreed to join the government only to show that it could administer, and intended soon to leave. He recalls Mr MacBride telling him at the time to build hospitals, and saying that when they were 'that high' (pointing about three feet off the ground) they would get out. But, he adds, when the hospitals *were* 'that high', Mr MacBride did not wish to get out. Mr MacBride, however, did not feel that they were in the government simply to give proof that they could administer; he believed that the continuance of the inter-party government had a positive merit, as showing that Irishmen of many different traditions could work together.[67]

About the middle of February, relations between Mr MacBride and Dr Browne seemed near breaking-point. The immediate point at issue was an embarrassment in which the Minister for Posts and Telegraphs, Mr James Everett, had landed the government. Mr Everett, by appointing one of his own political friends to the postmastership of Baltinglass, county Wicklow, over the head of a well-qualified and popular local candidate, had provoked a wave of protest against political jobbery, not only in Baltinglass itself, but over the whole country.[68] Mr MacBride, while not approving of Mr Everett's action, did not think it

---

67. This account of the issues between Mr MacBride and Dr Browne, based primarily on their recollections, receives some corroboration from a contemporary newspaper account. In the *Irish Times* of 21 February 1951 its political correspondent reported that there was a cleavage in Clann na Poblachta between those, such as Mr MacBride, who believed that the existing government should be maintained, and those who, like Dr Browne and Mr Hartnett, argued that the party was in danger of losing its soul, and must cleave to its principles at the expense of quarrelling with the other parties in the government.

68. For an account of this episode see Lawrence Earl, *The Battle of Baltinglass*.

was the sort of issue on which to bring down the government. Dr Browne and Mr Hartnett, on the other hand, felt that this was the sort of issue on which Clann na Poblachta should fight or else lose its radical soul. Mr Hartnett resigned from the party altogether;[69] Dr Browne, while remaining a member of the party and of its National Executive, resigned from its inner circle, the Standing Committee.[70] For the time being, however, things went no further. Mr MacBride spent much of March on a visit to France and the United States, and the conflict between him and Dr Browne was still unresolved when, during March, it suddenly became clear that Dr Browne's relations with the hierarchy were to be of crucial importance.

For the origins of Dr Browne's encounters with the hierarchy we must go back to the middle of 1950. The bishops, or some of them, must have received copies of Dr Browne's draft mother and child scheme soon after it was issued in June of that year. The problem of where these copies came from is a mystery which I have not been able to clear up. Dr Browne, in April 1951, indicated that he had sent copies to the Medical Association and, for information, to his colleagues in the government;[71] but he did not mention sending copies to anyone else, and as he did not yet know about the hierarchy's protest against the Health Act in October 1947, he was not likely to have sent copies to the bishops because he had no reason to suppose that they would be interested. The Irish Medical Association does not seem to have been the channel either. I have interviewed three doctors prominent in the association at that time and all are positive that the association as such had no contacts with the hierarchy. But though the association as a body seems to have made no demarche, there was nothing to stop individual doctors from doing so. Some doctors may have known of the private protest which the hierarchy made to Mr de Valera against the Health Act in October 1947. This is suggested by a remark made in the Medical Association's journal at the beginning of 1948.

69. *Irish Times*, 14 Feb. 1951. Mr Hartnett's letter of resignation, stating his reasons, was later published: *Irish Independent*, 16 April 1951.
70. *Irish Times*, 15 Feb. 1951.
71. *Dail Debates*, CXXV, 668.

It stated: 'High ecclesiastical authorities are apparently not satisfied that certain sections of the Health Act of 1947 do not mean too great an intrusion of the State into the rights of the individual. We cannot say more than has appeared in the public Press, but obviously this matter is not going to be allowed to rest.'[72] If some doctors knew that the hierarchy was already concerned about the trend of health legislation, it may have occurred to them to mobilise the support of the hierarchy in their struggle against the mother and child scheme. It would not have been difficult for them to provide the bishops with copies: though the draft scheme was classified as a confidential document, apparently every member of the I.M.A. was issued with a copy,[73] so there were plenty in existence.

Be that as it may, the hierarchy, at its usual autumn meeting which was held that year on 10 October 1950, had the mother and child scheme on its agenda. The bishops felt that many of the features to which they took exception in the 1947 act were still visible in the new scheme, and they took two decisions. One was to draw up a letter of protest to the Taoiseach. The other was to set up a committee, consisting of the Archbishop of Dublin, Dr McQuaid, the Bishop of Galway, Dr Browne, and the Bishop of Ferns, Dr Staunton, to see the Minister for Health and, as a matter of courtesy, inform him of the protest before it was transmitted to the Taoiseach.[74]

The letter to the Taoiseach informs us of what features in the scheme the hierarchy found objectionable. It is printed in full in Appendix B,[75] but its main points can be summarised under five headings:

1. The right to provide for the health of children belongs to parents, not to the State. The State 'may help indigent or neglectful parents: it may not deprive 90 per cent of parents

---

72. *Journal of the Medical Association of Eire*, Jan. 1948, 2. The mention of what has appeared in the press is presumably a reference to the public condemnation of the Health Act by Bishop O'Neill of Limerick: see above, p. 152.
73. This is mentioned in the I.M.A.'s report of the meeting between its deputation and Dr Browne on 24 October 1950: cited above, footnote 48.
74. Information kindly provided by the Bishop of Galway.
75. See below, pp. 404–5.

H

of their rights because of 10 per cent necessitous or negligent parents'.

2. The scheme contained provision for the physical education of children and for the education of mothers. These were matters in which the State had no competence. Furthermore they could cover topics, such as birth control and abortion, on which the Catholic Church has definite teaching. There was no guarantee in the scheme that this teaching would be respected.

3. The scheme regarded illness as a matter for public record and research, without regard to the individual's right to privacy.

4. The elimination of private practitioners which the scheme would produce had not been shown to be advantageous to the patient, the public or the medical profession.

5. Rather than providing a costly bureaucratic service, the State might provide more maternity hospitals, and give adequate maternity benefits and taxation relief for large families.

Before this letter reached the Taoiseach, the committee of the hierarchy appointed for the purpose had interviewed Dr Browne at Archbishop's House, Dublin. Of this crucial interview, which took place on 11 October, widely differing reports have been given. One account was provided in the Dail, the following April, by Mr Costello, relying on his memory of what Dr McQuaid had told him immediately after the interview had taken place:

I was told by His Grace the Archbishop of Dublin, on the 12th October, that he had just had, the day before, an incredible interview with the then Minister for Health. . . . He told me that, at that interview, the Minister for Health brushed aside all suggestions about the invalidity of the means test and the free-for-all scheme, and would consider nothing but the question of education, on which he said 'you have a point there' and that he would consider it. The Minister himself terminated the interview and walked out.[76]

76. *Dail Debates*, CXXV, 739–40.

A contrasting account was provided, on the same occasion, by Dr Browne himself:

On the 10th October 1950, I was informed that His Grace the Archbishop of Dublin, wished to see me in connection with the proposed scheme. I attended at the Archbishop's House on the following day where I met His Grace and Their Lordships, the Bishops of Ferns and Galway. I was informed that at a meeting of the hierarchy on the previous day at Maynooth, His Grace and Their Lordships had been appointed to put before the Government certain objections which the Hierarchy saw in the scheme; that I was being informed of these objections as a matter of courtesy before transmission to the Taoiseach as head of the government.

His Grace read to me from a letter which had been prepared for transmission to the Taoiseach. A general discussion followed. At the conclusion of this interview I was under the impression, erroneously as it now appears, that His Grace and Their Lordships were satisfied with my explanation of the scheme and with my answers and undertakings given in regard to the objections made by them.[77]

Dr Browne has since amplified this account in interview with Mr Michael McInerney of the *Irish Times*. According to Mr McInerney, Dr Browne's 'recollection of the meeting was that it was most friendly, that it ended with a cup of tea and that the Archbishop graciously saw him to the door inquiring about his own wife and family.'[78]

A further account of this meeting, which to some degree reconciles these reports, has been kindly given to me by the Bishop of Galway, who remembers that the minister was truculent at first, and that they did not get anywhere until the bishop challenged him on paragraphs 56 and 57 of the scheme, which provided for gynaecological care.[79] He pointed out that this could involve ante-natal clinics which taught birth control or abortion. The minister said that he did not intend that. The bishop replied 'But you don't show that'. The minister assured

---

77. *Ibid.*, 669.
78. M. McInerney, 'Noel Browne: Church and State', *University Review* (V, 2) Summer 1968, 182.
79. For the contents of these paragraphs, see below, Appendix A, p. 392.

the bishops that he would make rectifications, and the interview ended amicably.

If recollections of this interview are conflicting, they are also conflicting about what happened afterwards. Dr Browne claimed that he was allowed to remain under the impression that he had satisfied the bishops. As he put it in April 1951: 'On the following day [13 October] the Taoiseach spoke to me of his interview with His Grace the Archbishop of Dublin, and he informed me he had been told by His Grace that he and Their Lordships were satisfied following their interview with me. The Taoiseach has since denied that he made this statement. What is certain, however, is that he did not give me to understand that His Grace and Their Lordships remained unsatisfied.'[80] He was not deterred from this conclusion when, in mid-November, the Taoiseach gave him a copy of the hierarchy's letter. Dr Browne noted that the letter was dated 10 October—i.e. before the interview at which he believed he had satisfied the bishops—and he presumed that he had been given it simply for the purposes of record.[81] He prepared a reply, also for the purposes of record, which he handed to the Taoiseach for transmission to the hierarchy, and as he explained in April 1951: 'As I heard nothing further about the matter from either the hierarchy or the Taoiseach until a couple of weeks ago I had no reason to believe that the hierarchy were not fully satisfied, and the work of preparing for the introduction of the mother and child scheme continued.'[82]

Mr Costello's recollections were quite different. He recalled that, after the meeting between Dr Browne and the bishops, he asked both Dr Browne and Dr McQuaid to allow him to adjust the matter, and informed both sides that in the meantime he would not send a formal reply to the hierarchy's letter of 10 October.[83] He recalled saying to Dr Browne twice since Christmas 1950: 'I have not yet replied to the bishops' letter.'[84] Mr Costello's memories fitted in with those of Dr Browne's party leader, Mr MacBride, who recalled that in December 1950,

---

80. *Dail Debates*, CXXV, 669. See also the letter from Dr Browne to Mr Costello, 19 March 1951: printed below, Appendix B, pp. 409–10.
81. *Dail Debates*, CXXV, 669–70.
82. *Ibid.*, 670.
83. *Ibid.*, 742–4.   84. *Ibid.*, 752.

and on numerous occasions subsequently, he had urged Dr Browne to settle his differences with the hierarchy.[85]

It seems hard to believe that ministers can have been at cross-purposes on so serious a matter for so long. But it must be remembered that all during these months, October 1950 to March 1951, the most urgent business appeared to be Dr Browne's dispute with the Irish Medical Association. The difficulties with the bishops were, with the bishops' own consent, set aside for later consideration. As Mr Costello explained: 'I was in close touch with His Grace the Archbishop, the representative of the hierarchy, during all that time . . . and gave him an account of the efforts we were making to try and adjust this unfortunate and very disedifying dispute between the Minister for Health and the medical profession. His Grace quite approved and agreed that it was better to try and do everything possible to have the matter adjusted.'[86]

It was not until Dr Browne broke with the I.M.A. and published details of the mother and child scheme, on 6 March 1951, that his dispute with the hierarchy came suddenly to the forefront. Dr Browne sent copies of the brochure outlining his scheme to all members of the hierarchy.[87] From several of the bishops he received acknowledgements containing no expression of disapproval.[88] But from the Archbishop of Dublin, on 8 March, he received a freezing reply.[89] The letter began by thanking Dr Browne for sending the pamphlet, and remarking that the archbishop welcomed 'any legitimate improvement of medical services for those whose basic family wage or income does not readily assure the necessary facilities'. But it went on: 'I regret, however, that as I stated on the occasion when on behalf of the hierarchy, I asked you to meet me with Their

85. *Ibid.*, 792. Mr MacBride did not give the date of his first conversation on the subject with Dr Browne, but stated that it occurred shortly after the Taoiseach had had an interview with the I.M.A. As this interview appears to have occurred on 29 November (see *Journal of Medical Association of Eire*, Dec. 1950, 95; *Journal of the Irish Medical Association*, Jan. 1951, 19), the conversation between Mr MacBride and Dr Browne can be confidently dated to early December.

86. *Ibid.*, 747.

87. This is stated in the letter from Dr Browne to Mr Costello of 19 March 1951: see below, Appendix B, p. 410.

88. *Ibid.*

89. Printed below, Appendix B, p. 406.

Lordships of Ferns and Galway, I may not approve of the Mother and Child Service, as it is proposed by you to implement the Scheme. Now, as Archbishop of Dublin, I regret that I must reiterate each and every objection made by me on that occasion, and unresolved, either then or later, by the Minister for Health.' The archbishop went on to say that he was sending a copy of his letter to the Taoiseach.[90]

Dr Browne's reaction to this letter was surprising. He appears to have sought to brush it off as of no importance. According to the Taoiseach, he sent no reply or even acknowledgement to the archbishop.[91] Mr Costello, meanwhile, had shown the letter to colleagues in the government and on 12 March, or thereabouts, the Tanaiste, Mr Norton, asked Dr Browne what he was going to do about it. His reply, as reported by Mr Norton to Mr Costello, was: 'I am not going to do anything about that letter; there is nothing in it; it does not require an answer; the whole thing is all nonsense; there is nothing in the Archbishop's allegation.'[92] On 14 March Mr Costello himself asked Dr Browne about the matter, and received the reply: 'There's nothing in that; there is nothing in those letters; I am assured on the advice of theologians that there is nothing in that letter.'[93] The following day, 15 March, Mr Costello tried again to bring home to Dr Browne the seriousness of the situation, and wrote him a formal letter, telling him that he must satisfy the objections of the hierarchy as stated in their letter of 10 October 1950 and in Dr McQuaid's letter of 8 March 1951.[94] Dr Browne's reply was to deny that the hierarchy opposed his scheme. He said that he had met the hierarchy's objections in his interview of 11 October 1950, that only the Archbishop of Dublin had protested on this occasion, and that since the receipt of Mr Costello's letter he had been in communication with a member

---

90. One small point can be cleared up here. That evening, 8 March, Dr Browne broadcast an explanation of the mother-and-child scheme. Mr Costello commented on this: 'Over the air he, in effect, defied the Archbishop.' *Dail Debates*, CXXV, 760. Dr Browne has since explained that he did not receive the archbishop's letter until he returned to his office after the broadcast: M. McInerney, 'Noel Browne: Church and State', *University Review* (V, 2) Summer 1968, 187.

91. *Dail Debates*, CXXV, 756.   92. *Ibid.*   93. *Ibid.*, 758.

94. Printed below, Appendix B, pp. 408–9.

of the hierarchy 'who further assures me that, so far as he is aware, the hierarchy as such have expressed no objection to the Mother and Child Scheme whatsoever on the grounds of faith and morals'.[95] The most likely explanation of Dr Browne's attitude during these days is that he was so intent on his combat with the doctors that he had no attention to spare for anything else. Mr Costello remembered Dr Browne coming to see him on 14 March and asking for an immediate meeting of the cabinet to authorise the expenditure of a further £30,000 on the mother and child scheme. According to Mr Costello, Dr Browne said: 'If I get the £30,000 I will have the doctors killed on Sunday; I will finish the controversy on Sunday; it will be finished for all time, if I get the £30,000; the private medical practitioners are meeting on Sunday and I believe that if I get the £30,000 the controversy will be at an end.'[96] If Dr Browne really thought that, with one more heave, he could beat the I.M.A., it is less surprising that he left the Archbishop of Dublin on one side for the moment.

It was not until 22 March that Dr Browne finally decided—following, Mr Costello believed, a conversation with Mr Norton—that the bishops ought not to be ignored any longer.[97] He sought, and obtained, an immediate interview with Dr Mc-Quaid.[98] Our only account of this interview comes from Mr Costello, to whom the Archbishop of Dublin described it later in the same day:

Dr Browne arrived at the Archbishop's residence and made the case that he had already satisfied Their Lordships. Dr McQuaid went through the details of the interview of 11th October 1950, which seemed to shock the then Minister, who had no recollection, good, bad or indifferent, of those details. He was then persuaded that his recollection was utterly and absolutely inaccurate and unreliable. He now accepts that position . . . Dr Browne asked for a decision. He requested an authoritative decision from the entire hierarchy. He

95. Printed below, Appendix B, pp. 409–10. The member of the hierarchy who gave Dr Browne this assurance seems to have been Dr Dignan of Clonfert. Dr Browne does not now clearly recall this in interview, but one of Dr Browne's cabinet colleagues gave me a circumstantial account of how Dr Browne met Dr Dignan and received this assurance.

96. *Dail Debates*, CXXV, 757.   97. *Ibid.*, 765.   98. *Ibid.*

first put to His Grace the Archbishop of Dublin the question: 'What is Your Grace's view? Is this mother and child scheme contrary to Catholic social teaching?' And His Grace said to him: 'Most definitely, yes, in my opinion.' Dr Browne then said: 'That is an end of it. If that is so, it is a very serious matter for me, as it will involve my leaving the Cabinet.' Then he said: 'As it is so important, I would like and ask [sic] Your Grace to get a decision from the entire hierarchy.'[99]

Dr Browne in a telephone conversation the same day told Mr Costello what he had agreed with the archbishop.

He said he had agreed with His Grace that the matters arising out of the mother and child scheme should be adjudicated upon by the hierarchy; that his case should be transmitted by me as head of the Government to Dr Staunton [bishop of Ferns and secretary of the hierarchy]; and that the question should then be decided as a matter of faith and morals by the hierarchy. He said he would have no alternative but to accept the decision and he gave an undertaking to His Grace to that effect. He said he had requested His Grace to have the matter put on the agenda for the meeting of the hierarchy in Low Week, so as to have an early decision.[100]

In accordance with this arrangement, Dr Browne despatched a memorandum to the Taoiseach on 24 March.[101] The Taoiseach forwarded it to Dr Staunton on 27 March.[102] A special meeting of the hierarchy was convened for 4 April,[103] and Dr Browne used the interval to lobby for support among the bishops. He certainly visited Archbishop D'Alton of Armagh, Bishop Browne of Galway and Bishop Staunton of Ferns at this time;[104] he also, either at this time or a little earlier, saw Bishop Dignan of Clonfert.[105]

99. *Ibid.*, 766–7.   100. *Ibid.*, 766.
101. Letter printed below, Appendix B, p. 416.
102. Letter printed below, Appendix B, pp. 417–18.
103. Mr Costello's references to this meeting (*Dail Debates*, CXXV, 766–8) give the impression that it had already been arranged, and that Dr Browne's case had to be added to the agenda; but I am informed by the Bishop of Galway that the meeting was specially called to consider Dr Browne's case.
104. M. McInerney, 'Noel Browne: a political portrait—3', *Irish Times*, 11 Oct. 1967.
105. Information from Dr Browne and from a cabinet colleague of his.

Dr Browne's memorandum went carefully through the points in the hierarchy's letter of 10 October 1950. It is a long document, and its full text will be found in Appendix B,[106] but its arguments can be summarised as follows:

1. Dr Browne agreed that the right to provide for the health of children belonged to parents, not the State. But the State was not taking away parents' rights; it was merely providing a scheme whereby parents could exercise that right more effectively. There was no obligation on parents to use the scheme. A parallel could be found in primary education, where the right to educate rested with parents, but the State provided schools which parents were free to avail themselves of or not, as they chose.

While on this point, Dr Browne challenged the implication in the hierarchy's letter that only about ten per cent of the population were necessitous. He observed that the Public Assistance services (which are provided for 'poor persons unable by their own industry or other lawful means' to meet their own medical needs) covered over thirty per cent of the population, and claimed that 'there is a considerable section of the community outside that category which is unable to afford proper medical care for their children, or can provide for that care for an ailing child only by inordinate sacrifices on the part of other members of the family'.

2. Although the education of children and mothers could raise moral issues, it also included such matters as training in habits of personal cleanliness, care of teeth, correct deportment, and correct diet during pregnancy. It was only the latter type of education that was to be provided under the scheme, and care would be taken to include nothing of an objectionable nature. However, to ensure that there would be nothing objectionable, the minister was ready to submit to the hierarchy for their approval the regulations he made on these matters, or 'to consider any other course in regard to them which the Hierarchy might suggest'.

106. See below, pp. 418–25.

3. There was nothing new in illness being treated as a matter of public record. Local authorities already provided services such as the venereal disease and infectious disease services, and the dispensary medical service. All these necessitated the keeping of records. The mother and child scheme would introduce no new principle.

4. The scheme would not result in the elimination of private practitioners. The minister agreed that the scheme as drafted was based on the dispensary doctors, but this was only tentative. He had already stated his willingness to allow private practitioners to come in, and if enough wished to do so the scheme would be amended to include them.

5. The alternative courses suggested by the hierarchy were already being followed. The government was building more maternity hospitals, and increasing social insurance benefits. Taxation was already arranged so as to give relief to large families. As an addendum to this point the minister observed that other social services were provided without a means test, and without, so far as he was aware, any objection being taken. He instanced children's allowances and the infectious diseases service.

The memorandum ended with the minister respectfully asking whether, in view of these observations, 'the Hierarchy considers the Mother and Child Scheme is contrary to Catholic moral teaching'. It was an able document. On points 2 and 4 he was offering, or was stating that he had already made, concessions. On the other points he was arguing that the proposed scheme contained nothing that was not already found in other government services, and was in effect asking the hierarchy why these features should be condemned in the mother and child scheme when they were not condemned elsewhere.

Dr Browne's memorandum was considered by the Standing Committee of the hierarchy on 3 April 1951, and by the hierarchy as a whole on 4 April.[107] The hierarchy's decision, which was unanimous, was delivered by Dr McQuaid to Mr Costello

107. See letter from Dr McQuaid to Mr Costello, 5 April 1951: printed below, Appendix B, p. 426.

at Government Buildings on 5 April.[108] It was that 'the Hierarchy must regard the Scheme proposed by the Minister for Health as opposed to Catholic social teaching'.

The hierarchy's reply, the text of which will be found in Appendix B,[109] began by pointing out that the hierarchy had already disapproved of the Health Act 1947, on which the mother and child scheme was based. It went on to state that the hierarchy would approve of a 'sane and legitimate' health service, but not one which fostered undue control by the State in a sphere so delicate, nor one which must result in the undue lessening of the proper initiative of individuals and associations. The letter then touched on Dr Browne's memorandum in these terms: 'The Bishops do not consider it their duty to enter into an examination of the detailed considerations put forward by the Minister for Health in his memorandum, save in so far as they wish to point out the fallacy of treating the proposed Mother and Child Health Scheme on a basis of parity with the provision by the State of minimum primary education, or the prevention of infectious disease or a scheme of children's allowances.' Having thus dismissed the closely-reasoned argument of Dr Browne's submission, the bishops returned to their objections to the scheme, listing them under seven heads. The heads can be summarised as follows:—

1. and 3. The State arrogates to itself a control in respect of education in very intimate matters. The minister has stated that he is willing to amend the scheme, but it is the principle that must be amended, and by an act of the Oireachtas.

2. The State arrogates to itself a function which the vast majority of citizens can fulfil by individual initiative and lawful associations.

4. and 5. The scheme will involve such heavy taxation as morally to compel citizens to use the services provided.

6. It must damage the self-reliance of parents whose income would enable them to provide medical treatment for their dependents.

108. *Dail Debates,* CXXV, 771.   109. See below, pp. 426–8.

7. Finally, the scheme must be implemented by ministerial regulations rather than by legislative enactments.

Dr McQuaid told Mr Costello, when he delivered this document, 'that he, during his period of ten years as Archbishop, had never seen such detailed and close and long consideration given to any document as was given to the submission by Dr Browne'.[110] Perhaps the very length of the discussion, and the number of people concerned in it, affected the clarity with which the decision was formulated, for this is the most disappointing contribution to the series of exchanges between the government and the hierarchy. It bears all the marks of a document in which many hands have been involved—some points are made twice over, objections of a disparate nature are thrown together, and at the same time important points made by Dr Browne are not answered. It may be noted too that some of the points made—those numbered 4 to 7—were fresh, and that the Minister for Health could certainly have put up some kind of a rebuttal to them, if he had had the chance. But the bishops, perhaps, did not feel it necessary to take as much trouble over this document as they could have done. For it was clear that Dr Browne was not backed by a united government. The press had already carried reports that some ministers were dissatisfied with the mother and child scheme.[111] Mr Costello, in forwarding Dr Browne's memorandum to the hierarchy, refrained from adding any word of support for it.[112] The point was taken by the bishops, who stated in their reply to Dr Browne's submission that they were 'pleased to note that no evidence had been supplied in the letter of the Taoiseach that the proposed Mother and Child Health Scheme advocated by the Minister for Health enjoys the support of the Government'.[113] They had evidently not bargained for Dr Browne releasing the correspondence to the public. Had they done so, they might have framed their reply to his memorandum with the greater cogency that was undoubtedly possible.

110. *Dail Debates*, CXXV, 771.
111. *Irish Independent*, 7 March 1951; *Irish Times*, 7 March 1951: see above, p. 209.
112. Letter from Mr Costello to Dr Staunton, 27 March 1951: printed below, Appendix B, pp. 417–18.　　113. See below, p. 427.

Dr Browne was not yet prepared to admit defeat. He had, it is true, asked the hierarchy for a ruling and had promised to abide by it. But he had asked the hierarchy to decide whether his scheme was contrary to Catholic moral teaching; it had decided that the scheme was contrary to Catholic social teaching. Dr Browne seized on this distinction and, when the matter was raised in cabinet the following day, 6 April, argued that the difference was vital. In the words of an interviewer to whom he has since told the story:—

He made a last effort to convince the Ministers that the hierarchy had not answered his request for a ruling on whether the scheme was contrary to moral teaching. They had replied that it was contrary merely to social teaching. He explained naturally to the Cabinet that to act contrary to moral teaching was a mortal sin, but that it would not be a mortal sin to act against social teaching! Social teaching changed from country to country and in Ireland, indeed, from city to city. There was a State Health Service in Belfast and indeed in Armagh, to which the Church had not objected.[114]

But the other members of the government were not prepared to consider the distinction significant. To them, a condemnation was a condemnation, whether it came on the ground of moral teaching or of social teaching. Dr Browne asked each of his colleagues one by one round the table if they would still support the scheme, and each of them in turn refused.[115] Dr Browne then left the meeting, asking for time to consider his position.[116]

The government, relieved of Dr Browne's presence, quickly agreed that his scheme should be abandoned and a less controversial alternative prepared. As Mr Costello reported them to the Dail, the decisions were:

1. that the scheme referred to should not be further pursued;
2. that in the light of the Government's conviction that mothers and children should not be deprived of the best available health care by reason of insufficient means, a scheme or schemes for a mother and

114. M. McInerney, 'Noel Browne: a political portrait—2', *Irish Times*, 10 Oct. 1967.
115. *Ibid.*
116. *Dail Debates*, CXXV, 776 (speech of Mr Costello).

child health service should, as soon as possible, be prepared and undertaken which would (a) provide the best modern facilities for those whose family wage or income does not permit them to obtain, of themselves, the health care that is necessary for mothers and children and (b) be in conformity with Catholic social teaching, and

3. that consideration should be given to the question whether any amendments of the Health Act, 1947, additional to those proposed in the Health Bill, 1950, are necessary or desirable and, if so, that proposals for such amendments should be submitted to the Government.[117]

Mr Costello informed the Archbishop of Dublin of these decisions in a letter of 9 April,[118] and received a gracious reply the following day, expressing the archbishop's 'deep appreciation of the generous loyalty shown by you and by your colleagues', and repeating that it was the bishops' 'urgent desire' that 'due provision should be made by the Government for the health of those mothers and children whose insufficient means would not allow them to avail themselves of the best modern facilities'.[119]

Meanwhile, things had gone badly for Dr Browne on another front. Mr MacBride had returned from his American trip towards the end of March, evidently feeling that his quarrel with Dr Browne had dragged on unresolved for long enough. It was brought to a head in two long and stormy meetings of the National Executive of Clann na Poblachta, held on 31 March and 8 April.[120] Dr Browne has described these meetings as skilfully orchestrated performances in which charges were made with the design of separating him from every section of the party. 'He had slandered old Republicans and I.R.A. men; it was suggested he was pro-Communist and anti-Catholic and anti-Bishops. He had been seen talking to Dr Owen Sheehy Skeffington of Trinity and to Leftists, and was photographed shaking hands with the Protestant Archbishop of Dublin. . . . It was charged that he wanted to form a new political party and to supersede the present leader.'[121] Mr MacBride has commented

117. *Ibid.*, 780.   118. For text see *ibid.*, 780–1   119. For text see *ibid.*, 782.
120. *Irish Times*, 10 April 1951, for meeting of 8 April; *ibid.*, 13 April 1951 for Clann na Poblachta statement giving details of the meeting of 31 March.
121. M. McInerney, 'Noel Browne: a political portrait—3', *Irish Times*, 11 Oct. 1967.

on this to me that his National Executive, which consisted of forty-eight people drawn from all over the country, was not composed of 'yes-men', and that in any case there was no need to stage-manage the proceedings, for Dr Browne, by his behaviour, had already lost the confidence of the great majority of the members. But whether stage-managed or not, the result of these meetings was gratifying to Mr MacBride. Dr Browne was censured by an overwhelming majority for disloyalty to his party leader, and for mishandling the mother and child negotiations. One resolution specifically recorded that 'if the leader of the Party deems it necessary to call for the resignation or removal of Dr Browne from the government', he would have the 'loyal support' of the National Executive.[122] Mr MacBride now knew that if he wished to force the issue with Dr Browne, he would have the backing of the great majority of his party executive.

As it happened, the opportunity to force the issue occurred almost at once. It was innocently provided by the National Executive of the Irish Trade Union Congress, which had been concerned at the possible watering down of Dr Browne's scheme and which had already, on 30 March, passed a resolution urging its early implementation.[123] When reports began to circulate that the scheme might be withdrawn altogether and that Dr Browne might resign, the National Executive of the I.T.U.C. sent a deputation to Dr Browne asking him to postpone his resignation and to consider the possibility of introducing, as a compromise, a scheme based on insurance.[124] Dr Browne was prepared to explore this possibility,[125] and he allowed the fact that he was reconsidering his resignation at the request of the

122. Text as quoted in *Statement by Mr. Sean MacBride, S.C., T.D., at the Fifth Ard Fheis of Clann na Poblachta held in Dublin on 30th June and 1st July 1951,* 10. I am indebted to Mr MacBride for letting me have a copy of this cyclostyled document.

123. *Irish Times,* 31 March 1951.

124. *Irish Trade Union Congress. Fifty-Seventh Annual Report . . . for 1950–51,* 36–7.

125. *Ibid.* Dr Browne has expressed the belief, in interview both with Mr McInerney (*op. cit., Irish Times,* 11 Oct. 1967) and with myself, that this proposal from the I.T.U.C. could have provided a solution. But there is no proof that the government would have accepted it and the hierarchy—I am informed by one of the trade union officials involved—was not even approached.

I.T.U.C. to be reported in the press.[126] The effect, however, was only to anger his cabinet colleagues still further. Mr Costello indignantly remarked: 'I do not suppose that in the history of Cabinet Government any such thing has happened as that a Minister who was considering his position, whose colleagues had treated him as we had treated him, proceeded to tell the Press what he was doing at the instance of the Trade Union Congress and did not discuss matters in private with his colleagues.'[127] Mr MacBride also decided that his action was insupportable.[128] Thus the I.T.U.C., by its well-meant attempt at compromise, had brought about the circumstances in which Dr Browne's colleagues finally decided to break with him.

On 10 April, Mr MacBride wrote to Dr Browne, requiring him to send his resignation to the Taoiseach.[129] On the following day, 11 April 1951, Dr Browne complied.[130] Mr Costello gave Mr MacBride's action his full support, and stated that if Mr MacBride had not called for Dr Browne's resignation he himself would have done so.[131]

The astonishing events of October 1950 to April 1951 provide endless scope for controversy. Of the many possible aspects that could be picked out for discussion, I should like to confine myself to two. The first is—what assessment is to be made of the conduct of Dr Browne? He was at the centre of every storm. He took on simultaneously four different opponents—the bishops, the Irish Medical Association, most of his cabinet colleagues, and his own party leader. Any of these could have been mollified by appropriate concessions, but Dr Browne showed little desire to conciliate. The comment of the *Journal of the Irish Medical Association* on his fall, though it comes from

126. *Irish Times*, 9 April 1951.　　　127. *Dail Debates*, CXXV, 777.

128. 'The position became completely impossible when he began to issue bulletins to the press concerning his resignation from the Government.'— Statement by Mr. Sean MacBride, S.C., T.D., at the Fifth Ard Fheis of Clann na Poblachta . . . *1951*. 10.

129. Letter printed below, Appendix B, pp. 399–401.

130. His letter of resignation was read by Mr Costello to the Dail: *Dail Debates*, CXXV, 779. His vitriolic reply to Mr MacBride is printed below: Appendix B, pp. 402–3.

131. *Dail Debates*, CXXV, 777.

an antagonist, is not unfair: 'Having flown in the face of advice from his colleagues, and having refused to treat with the Medical Association on any but terms of capitulation, it yet became necessary for the hierarchy of the Catholic Church in Ireland to voice their objection before his remarkable intransigence yielded to the practical difficulties of the situation.'[132] But the question remains: why did he behave in this way?

Some of his colleagues had no doubt about the answer. He acted like this, they considered, because he was temperamentally incapable of coping with the problems that he had to face. Mr Costello's indictment was formidable: 'Deputy Dr Browne was not competent or capable to fulfil the duties of the Department of Health. He was incapable of negotiation; he was obstinate at times and vacillating at other times. He was quite incapable of knowing what his decision would be to-day or, if he made a decision to-day, [whether] it would remain until to-morrow.'[133] Mr MacBride said that 'for the last year, in my view, the Minister for Health has not been normal.'[134] Mr Norton recorded that he and other ministers 'did everything we could to endeavour to induce Dr. Browne to handle this matter calmly, to handle this matter with sagacity, not to push matters to a crisis and . . . to avoid having a head-on collision', and added that 'if this matter had been handled with tact, with understanding and with forbearance by the Minister responsible, I believe we would not have had the situation which has been brought about to-day'.[135] From outside the cabinet a Clann na Poblachta deputy, Mr Con Lehane, added his impressions of Dr Browne: 'My experience of the ex-Minister for Health has been that he is constitutionally incapable of listening to criticism . . . I have had the experience of seeing him walk out over a fairly long period, a period of a year or more, from five, if not six, different committee meetings.'[136]

One can accept a great deal of this criticism. Dr Browne must have been a most difficult colleague. It is an observable fact that he ended by exasperating his cabinet colleagues, alienating his party executive, antagonising the principal interest group in his

132. *Journal of the Irish Medical Association*, May 1951, 75.
133. *Dail Debates*, CXXV, 777.
134. *Ibid.*, 798.   135. *Ibid.*, 953–4.   136. *Ibid.*, 933.

field and bringing about a hostile ruling from the Catholic hierarchy. And yet—one's final verdict must depend on what one supposes Dr Browne was trying to do. The unspoken assumption behind his critics' complaints is that he was, like themselves, a pragmatic politician with short-term practical aims. On that assumption, he could certainly be condemned. If his principal object was to get as much of his mother and child scheme into operation as practicable, he was going the worst possible way about it.

But was Dr Browne just a practical politician trying to force a way through to an immediate objective? Tense and highly-strung though he undoubtedly is, he had shown in his management of the campaign against tuberculosis that when he wanted immediate results he knew how to obtain them. The very fact that his behaviour over the mother and child scheme was so ill-adapted to such an aim makes one wonder if his basic aim was not something else. His conduct suggests that—perhaps instinctively, more than as a fully-thought-out strategy—he courted a showdown: that he wished to bring about a collision between the Irish State and a powerful vested interest. He might not win the immediate battle, but even by fighting it he would crack the mould of Irish society, and make easier that social change to which as a radical he was committed.

If this was Dr Browne's real objective, then one must have more respect for his achievement. His only miscalculation was that he collided with the wrong opponents. The quarry he clearly had in mind was the Irish Medical Association, and when the hierarchy intervened his first reaction was to brush it aside as a tiresome irrelevancy. As things turned out, however, it was with the hierarchy that the showdown came.

The result was that his actions had an even more extensive effect than he perhaps anticipated. Before this episode, Church-State relations were little discussed in Ireland, and there was a widespread feeling that it was somehow disedifying for the role of the Church to be examined in public. Mr Costello's speech in the debate on Dr Browne's resignation provides a good illustration of this attitude. The Taoiseach was clearly shocked at Dr Browne's action in exposing all that had happened to the public gaze. He said near the outset of his speech: 'All this matter was intended to be private and to be adjusted behind closed doors and was never intended to be the subject of public controversy, as it has been made by the former Minister for Health now, and it would have been dealt with in that way had there been any reasonable person, other than the former Minister for Health, engaged in the negotiations at that time.'[137] In his peroration he returned to the point: 'All these matters could have been, and ought to have been, dealt with calmly, in quiet and in council, without the public becoming aware of the matter. The public never ought to have become aware of the matter.'[138] Nearly twenty years later, Mr Costello's words may in their turn seem rather shocking to a younger generation of Irishmen, in their avowed anxiety to hush up a matter of great public importance. But the fact that Mr Costello could unselfconsciously utter such words in 1951 is a sign of his confidence that Irish public opinion would generally agree with him. If Church-State relations are now a topic of rational discussion in Ireland, this is in part due to Dr Browne's courage, or rashness, in bringing them into the open nearly two decades ago. This may not have been quite the consequence that he envisaged when he embarked on the mother and child controversy, but it is an important consequence nevertheless. Dr Browne has enlarged the area of political discourse in Ireland.

The other topic which I should like to discuss is— what does this episode prove about the extent and limits of the power of the Catholic hierarchy in Ireland?

Two opposing theories on this matter can be found. One is that the episode proves Ireland to be a theocratic State, where the power of the Catholic hierarchy is decisive in any matter in which it chooses to intervene. The point was made immediately by the *Irish Times*, in an angry leading article which it published on the morning after Dr Browne's resignation. 'The most serious revelation, however,' it wrote, 'is that the Roman Catholic Church would seem to be the effective Government of this country.'[139] The argument was taken up by Ulster Unionist spokesmen, as a justification for their opposition to a united

137. *Ibid.*, 739.   138. *Ibid.*, 784.   139. *Irish Times*, 12 April 1951.

Ireland. As one pamphlet published by the Ulster Unionist Council put it, the episode made clear that 'in any matter where the Roman Catholic Church decides to intervene the Eire Government must accept the Church's policy and decision irrespective of all other considerations'.[140]

Such an argument can be buttressed from the words of politicians involved at the time. They readily proclaimed their acceptance of the Catholic hierarchy's authority in this matter. Mr Costello, in his letter to the Archbishop of Dublin on 9 April informing him of the government's decision to withdraw Dr Browne's scheme, specifically stated that 'that decision expresses the complete willingness of the Government to defer to the judgment so given by the hierarchy that the particular scheme in question is opposed to Catholic social teaching'.[141] In the Dail debate following Dr Browne's resignation he reasserted this attitude. 'I, as a Catholic,' he said, 'obey my Church authorities and will continue to do so, in spite of the *Irish Times* or anything else.'[142] He was echoed by other ministers. Mr Norton in the same debate said: 'If this question is raised as one in which the Bishops are to be on one side and the Government on the other side, I say, on behalf of the Government, that issue is not going to arise in this country. This Government will not travel that road. . . . There will be no flouting of the authority of the Bishops in the matter of Catholic social or Catholic moral teaching.'[143] Specially interesting were the words of Mr Mac-Bride, who as a former member of the much-condemned I.R.A. had a record of defiance of episcopal rulings. He said: 'Those of us in this House who are Catholics, and all of us in the Government who are Catholics are, as such of course, bound to give obedience to the rulings of our Church and of our hierarchy.'[144] Some of the Fine Gael ministers were almost truculent in their defence of what had happened. Mr McGilligan, the Minister for Finance, stated at a Fine Gael meeting that he would not break the moral law, and if he was not sure what the moral law was he would resort to the bishops. 'We are quite proud of what happened', he said.[145] General MacEoin, the Minister for Justice,

140. *Southern Ireland—Church or State?*, 2.   141. *Dail Debates*, CXXV, 781.
142. *Ibid.*, 784.   143. *Ibid.*, 951–2.   144. *Ibid.*, 789.
145. *Irish Times*, 1 May 1951.

said a little later that they had been attacked for accepting advice on spiritual matters from those with authority to give that advice, but no government worthy of the name would reject such advice.[146]

It was not only Dr Browne's opponents in the government, however, who proclaimed their acceptance of the bishops' authority. Dr Browne himself was equally explicit. Indeed it was he who raised the question in the first place, by asking the hierarchy for a ruling. He went through, it seems, a brief period of hesitation when, after the bishops' decision of 5 April, he tried to argue that because it was based on social teaching and not on moral teaching it was therefore not binding. But he soon abandoned this line of argument. In his resignation speech he stated that 'I as a Catholic accept unequivocally and unreservedly the views of the hierarchy on this matter',[147] and reserved his complaints for the way in which he had been treated by his colleagues in the government. During the subsequent general election campaign he pursued the same line, repeatedly criticising his erstwhile cabinet colleagues, but never criticising the bishops, and on one occasion describing the allegation that he had opposed the hierarchy as 'malicious'.[148] The same attitude was generally adopted by his supporters. Mr Jack McQuillan, for instance, a deputy from Roscommon who followed him out of Clann na Poblachta, stated in his letter of resignation that he accepted the ruling of the hierarchy, and reserved his complaints for the way in which Mr MacBride had, as he claimed, kept the party in the dark about what was happening.[149] Even if one assumes that Dr Browne and his friends took this line from policy rather than from inner conviction, it is still significant. It shows that in their belief it was not electorally profitable for an Irish politician to appear to be in conflict with the Church.[150]

146. *Ibid.,* 14 May 1951.   147. *Dail Debates,* CXXV, 668.
148. *Irish Times,* 23 May 1951.   149. *Irish Independent,* 14 April 1951.
150. One interviewer has come away with the impression that Dr Browne 'can hardly be called an orthodox Catholic': T. P. Coogan, *Ireland since the Rising,* 101. Yet Dr Browne has revealed that he 'during the whole crisis consulted regularly an eminent Catholic theologian on doctrinal matters and on moral and social teaching.': M. McInerney, 'Noel Browne: Church and State', *University Review* (V, 2) Summer 1968, 204. The two statements are not incompatible, of course.

There was, it is true, one ministerial colleague of Dr Browne's who felt sufficiently uneasy at the bishops' ruling to take some action about it. This was the Minister for Agriculture, Mr James Dillon. Mr Dillon's appearance at this juncture in such a role may seem surprising. It was he who had been the most eloquent opponent of the mother and child sections of the Health Bill 1947—on which Dr Browne's scheme was based—at the time that it was passing through the Dail, and he had felt so strongly on the subject that he had begun a court action to test their constitutionality.[151] But Mr Dillon's objection to these sections had been different from the bishops'. He had objected to the compulsory element in them, and his point had been met by the Health Bill 1950 which Dr Browne had introduced in the Dail.[152] The bishops, on the other hand, based their objection partly on the fact that the scheme was free for all. Mr Dillon had no objection to this aspect of the scheme and had indeed defended its free-for-all nature.[153] He felt sufficiently strongly about this to write formally to the Pope, asking for a ruling on whether it was contrary to Catholic social teaching to introduce a health scheme in which no charge was exacted from those who were able to pay. Mr Dillon's memory is that for a considerable time—possibly because of an interregnum in the papal nunciature at this period—he heard nothing. Eventually, he received a request to call at the papal nunciature in Phoenix Park. There a secretary informed him that the Vatican was reluctant to give rulings in general terms, and asked him to state a particular case. By that time the inter-party government had fallen, the incoming Fianna Fail administration had announced its own health plans, and Mr Dillon felt that the particular case no longer existed; so he took the matter no further.[154]

Yet this little-known intervention by Mr Dillon is one further proof that the authority of the hierarchy was accepted by all concerned. Even a minister who did not consider that the hierarchy's ruling was in this instance wise did not feel entitled to ignore it. To him, the legitimate way of questioning it was to

151. See above, p. 153. 152. See above, p. 201 and note.
153. Speech of 12 Nov. 1950, quoted by Dr James Ryan in *Dail Debates*, CXXXIX, 1026 (17 June 1953).
154. Information from Mr Dillon.

appeal to the one authority which by Church law was entitled to overrule the local hierarchy.

Nonetheless, before drawing the conclusion that when the Irish hierarchy makes a pronouncement, Irish politicians will unhesitatingly obey, certain considerations must be borne in mind. As far as Dr Browne is concerned, he had thrown away his freedom of action by promising beforehand to accept whatever decision was reached. As far as most of his cabinet colleagues are concerned, the hierarchy's decision suited them well. Some of them disliked the mother and child scheme in itself. Mr Costello clearly viewed it with distaste, and he has confirmed to me in interview that he agreed with the bishops' condemnation of it. Some of the other Fine Gael ministers probably agreed with him here—after all, Fine Gael when in opposition had criticised the trend of Irish health legislation. The Minister for Defence, Dr O'Higgins, must have found the situation which the scheme created particularly trying. A medical man himself, he was constantly torn between his political commitment to his ministerial colleague and his professional loyalties. Other ministers may have felt that even if they themselves had no objection to the scheme, it was folly to try and force it through in the teeth of the medical profession, and that Dr Browne ought to have been more conciliatory. Mr Norton expressed this opinion in the Dail.[155] Other ministers again, though they may have had no strong feelings about the scheme, developed strong feelings about Dr Browne. The obvious instance is Mr MacBride, who believed that Dr Browne was conspiring to depose him from the party leadership. In normal circumstances one would expect that, in a coalition government, the strongest ally of a minister would be his party leader. Dr Browne, by his own actions, had ensured that his party leader was his bitterest opponent. The hierarchy's decision in the mother and child episode, then, was one which it cost most ministers nothing to accept. It provides us with no evidence of how the government would have reacted if the hierarchy had produced some ruling with which they strongly disagreed.

Indeed some people have been so impressed with such con-

---

155. *Dail Debates*, CXXV, 953.

siderations that they have come up with an opposite theory of what the mother and child scheme episode really proves. Far from accepting that the bishops are the real rulers of Ireland, they suggest that they were the stooges of lay politicians who used them to get rid of Dr Browne. This theory was distinctly implied by Dr Browne himself, in his resignation speech in the Dail.[156] In my experience it frequently comes up in conversation when the episode is discussed, and it is still from time to time met in print. A recent and temperate expression of it can be found in an interview with Mr Sean Lemass, who remarked: 'The whole situation was mishandled. I am not so sure that it was not allowed to develop in this way because the coalition leaders were anxious to get an excuse to drop Noel Browne, who must have been a very difficult colleague in the Government at the time.'[157]

There is some circumstantial evidence to support this view. As we have already seen, Dr Browne had aroused the anxieties of his cabinet colleagues as early as 6 March, when he suddenly announced his intention to go ahead with the mother and child scheme, and one might well wonder why they did not insist on his resignation at that point. It was not, however, a propitious moment to get rid of Dr Browne. Two independent deputies had recently announced the withdrawal of their support from the government,[158] and its slim parliamentary majority had become even slimmer. In the country, its position was shaken by the Baltinglass affair. Dr Browne himself was one of the best-known and most highly-regarded ministers in the eyes of the general public. Yet little more than a month later, he was out of office. The only new factor was that in the meantime, the hierarchy had come out against his scheme and thereby added the weight of its authority to the forces arrayed against Dr Browne. The 'stooge' theory at least has the merit of fitting the chronology.

Whether it fits the psychology of those concerned, however, is another matter. The calculation may have been at the back of

156. *Ibid.,* 673–5.
157. Michael Mills, 'Sean Lemass looks back—7', *Irish Press,* 17 Jan. 1969.
158. Mr W. Sheldon: *Irish Times,* 2 Dec. 1950; Mr P. D. Lehane: *ibid.,* 13 Dec. 1950.

some ministers' minds that, if they sat back and waited, Dr
Browne would embroil himself with the hierarchy and their
problem would be solved, but I have absolutely no evidence
that any of them thought like this. It certainly would not have
been in character for Mr Costello, who is a kindly and straight-
forward person, to have indulged in such a manoeuvre. If Dr
Browne's colleagues put up with him from 6 March to 10
April, there is a simpler explanation than that they were waiting
for the hierarchy to pull their chestnuts out of the fire. It is that
Irish political culture is in some ways surprisingly gentle—
gentler than that of Washington, Westminster or Stormont.
Ministers are rarely sacked in Ireland: however difficult or
incompetent they may be, they are generally endured by their
colleagues. Indeed until the dramatic dismissal of Mr Neil
Blaney and Mr Charles Haughey in May 1970, on suspicion of
complicity in a plot to run guns to Northern Ireland, Dr Browne
himself was the only minister ever to have been asked to resign.[159]

There is, moreover, another limitation to the 'stooge' theory
of the hierarchy's role. Let us suppose, for the sake of argument,
that Dr Browne's ministerial colleagues really were just waiting
for the bishops to provide an opportunity for demanding Dr
Browne's resignation. Such a calculation would make sense
only if the bishops had independent authority of their own.
The assumption would be that the country was more likely to
acquiesce in the dropping of the mother and child scheme if
both bishops and ministers demanded it than if ministers demanded it alone. Those who adopt the 'stooge' theory are un-
consciously paying a greater tribute to the bishops' power than
they intend.

The truth seems to lie somewhere in between the two theories
we have discussed. On the one hand, we can concede that the
hierarchy's intervention was, in the immediate sense, decisive.
Until the hierarchy spoke, Dr Browne was still strong enough
to persevere; immediately it had spoken, his scheme was
abandoned and very shortly afterwards he himself was asked to

---

159. The nearest parallel occurred in 1924, when, following a mutiny in the
army, some ministers pressed for the dismissal of the Minister for Defence,
General Mulcahy. But General Mulcahy resigned of his own accord: T. de V.
White, *Kevin O'Higgins*, 161.

resign. On the other hand, we can agree that the hierarchy's opposition was only one of the forces which Dr Browne had raised up against himself. He had also aroused the opposition of the I.M.A., the hostility of his party leader, and the irritation and anxiety of most of his cabinet colleagues. Whether the hierarchy's ruling would have been so decisive without these other factors—whether indeed a ruling would have been made in such confident terms—seems uncertain. The mother and child scheme crisis shows that the Catholic hierarchy wielded great influence in Ireland; but the exact nature and extent of that influence cannot fairly be deduced from a single episode such as this.

CHAPTER VIII

THE MOTHER AND CHILD SCHEME, 1951:
THE SUBSEQUENT CONTROVERSY

The resignation of Dr Browne on 11 April 1951 sparked off an animated debate on Church-State relations. Dr Browne himself provided much of the data for discussion by sending to the newspapers, on the day of his resignation, the text of the three-cornered correspondence that had passed between himself, the Taoiseach and the hierarchy. He also forearmed himself against the possibility that the Irish tradition of not involving the Church in public controversy might inhibit the press from printing the dossier which he had sent them. A few days before his resignation he saw Mr Robert Smyllie, editor of the *Irish Times*—which, being Protestant-owned, was less likely to be affected by this inhibition than the other Dublin morning papers, the *Irish Independent* and the *Irish Press*—and secured a promise from him that he would publish the letters.[1] This disposed of any hesitations that the other papers might have had, and the full documentation appeared in all three of them on the morning of 12 April.[2]

Much information was also provided during the Dail debate on Dr Browne's resignation. On 12 April Dr Browne made a statement, in which, while accepting the decision of the hierarchy, he charged his colleagues with misleading him about their own attitude and the attitude of the hierarchy to his scheme. That evening Mr Costello replied, in a long and indignant speech which provided a great deal more information about the course of events, and Mr MacBride gave details of his own difficulties with Dr Browne. The debate was continued the

1. M. McInerney, 'Noel Browne: Church and State', *University Review* (V, 2) Summer 1968, 193.
2. It is published in Appendix B.

following week, on 17 April, with contributions from two independent deputies, Captain Peadar Cowan and Mr Oliver Flanagan, who sympathised with Dr Browne, from a Clann na Poblachta deputy, Mr Con Lehane, who attacked Dr Browne's conduct within Clann na Poblachta, and from a Fine Gael deputy, Mr T. F. O'Higgins, who defended the government. The debate was concluded by the Tanaiste, Mr Norton, who gave further details of the dealings between Dr Browne and his ministerial colleagues.[3] For a country which was little accustomed to the public discussion of Church-State relations, the flood of information was unprecedented, and it is not surprising that it aroused intense interest.

Comment quickly began to appear in the press. The *Irish Times* was first off the mark, with a leading article on 12 April sharply attacking the hierarchy's interference and the government's cowardice. Further criticisms of government or hierarchy appeared in the *Bell* and in the Irish-language publication *Comhar*.[4] On the other side the lead was taken, as might be expected, by the *Standard,* which in its issues of 20 and 27 April published two vigorous apologies for the hierarchy by Professor Alfred O'Rahilly. I have been told by a member of the *Standard's* staff that these articles raised its circulation to the highest figure it has ever reached—83,000, a remarkable figure for a serious weekly in a country so small as Ireland. It was soon followed by defences of the hierarchy in *Studies* and *Christus Rex*.[5] Meanwhile the two Irish dailies which habitually printed many readers' letters—the *Irish Times* and the *Dublin Evening Mail*—printed a flood of correspondence on the subject, in which the balance of opinion was critical of the hierarchy and government. A discussion also appeared in the English Catholic weekly the *Tablet,*[6] which was worth noting partly because the *Tablet* has a considerable circulation in Ireland, and partly because of the high level of argument on both sides.

3. *Dail Debates,* CXXV, 667–77, 732–804, 894–954.
4. *The Bell* (XVII, 2) May 1951, 5–7, June 1951, 5–13; *Comhar* (X, 5) May 1951, 12–13, (X, 7) July 1951, 12–13.
5. Rev. E. J. Coyne, S.J., 'Mother and Child Service', *Studies* (XL, no. 158) June 1951, 129–49; Vigilans, 'As I see it', *Christus Rex* (V, 3) July 1951, 297–303.
6. *Tablet,* 21 April–12 May 1951 *passim.*

Finally, the bishops themselves began to publish justifications of their stand. Statements, of varying degrees of effectiveness, were published by Bishop Farren of Derry,[7] Archbishop D'Alton of Armagh,[8] Archbishop Kinane of Cashel,[9] Bishop Staunton of Ferns,[10] Bishop O'Neill of Limerick,[11] and the Coadjutor-Bishop of Cork, Dr Lucey.[12] The most active, and on the whole the most cogent of the episcopal apologists was Bishop Browne of Galway.[13] It was months before the controversy died away, and some important contributions were not published until well into 1952.[14]

The controversy was, in fact, the most extended debate on Church-State relations that has ever taken place in independent Ireland, and it deserves a detailed analysis. Three different issues can be distinguished in the literature. First, were the bishops entitled to intervene at all over the mother and child scheme? Second, supposing they were entitled to intervene, were they right to do so in private, or should they not have spoken in public, so that Dail and people could know what was going on? Third, supposing they were entitled to intervene, and to intervene in the way they did, did they apply Catholic social teaching correctly in this particular case? We shall examine the arguments used on each of these issues in turn.

The charge that the hierarchy should not have intervened at all can be found only twice in the whole literature of the controversy. It is contained, by implication, in the *Irish Times'* leading article of 12 April:

A Mother and Child scheme, embodying a means test, is in accordance with Christian social principles; a Mother and Child scheme without a means test is opposed to them! So much, if we read them correctly, emerges from the documents which the hierarchy con-

7. *Irish Press*, 18 April 1951.
8. *Irish Catholic Directory, 1952*, 681 (under date 18 June 1951).
9. *Ibid.*, 675–7 (17 June 1951).   10. *Ibid.*, 686 (1 July 1951).
11. *Ibid.*, 655 (22 April 1951).   12. *Ibid.*, 714–16 (12 Nov. 1951).
13. *Ibid.*, 657–9 (30 April 1951), 660–1 (6 May 1951).
14. W. Conway, 'The Church and State control', *Christus Rex* (VI, 2) April 1952, 111–31; Most Rev. C. Lucey, 'The moral aspects of means tests', *Irish Theological Quarterly* (XIX) 1952, 205–22.

tributes to the discussion. For ourselves we cannot pretend to follow the reasoning, and we doubt if it will be followed by the puzzled and disappointed people of this country. . . . There are obvious reasons why the doctors—though certainly not all of them—should object to the absence of a means test, but the plain man, unversed in subtleties, will be at a loss to determine why the Church should take sides in the matter at all. This newspaper has not been uncritical of the ex-Minister's proposals, and holds no brief for his particular scheme. Our sorrow is that he has not been permitted to fight it out on its own merits.

The point was put more directly by Captain Cowan, in his speech to the Dail on 17 April:

The outstanding objections of the hierarchy may be taken as an objection to the provision of a free for all mother and child scheme. In setting down their objections, the bishops trespass on the domain and seek to usurp the powers of the legitimate civil authority. In so doing, they act contrary to the provisions of the Constitution of this country . . . The bishops deal with State taxation, which is a matter for this House and this House alone. They give views on facts, express prophetic opinions and seek to determine the meaning of, or the inferences to be drawn from, a statute. These are matters, as any student of moral theology knows, that are not within the definition of Catholic doctrine on which the bishops may speak with authority to Catholics.[15]

In short, the argument of both the *Irish Times* and of Captain Cowan was that the bishops had stepped outside their legitimate sphere.

For expressing these views, the newspaper and the deputy were subjected to an avalanche of polemic. The champions of the hierarchy, sensing perhaps that this was where they were on their strongest ground, concentrated their arguments on this point. Not all the controversialists handled the topic felicitously. Dr Staunton, the Bishop of Ferns, in a sermon on 1 July referred to communist persecution of the Church in eastern Europe and compared it with the Cromwellian persecution in their own country. He went on: 'Those who carry on the Crom-

15. *Dail Debates*, CXXV, 900-1.

wellian tradition in our country cannot use these methods, but they have the same aim as their predecessors, the aim which is the Communist aim, to drive the Catholic Church out of the life of this country. Their leading newspaper has told us of this aim, and, considering the forces still at their disposal even here, we should be foolish not to take careful note of it. In our country Cromwellians and Communists can unite in their hatred of the Catholic Church.'[16] For Dr Staunton to deduce, from what the *Irish Times* had said, that it hated the Catholic Church and hoped to drive it out of Irish life, was somewhat extravagant. However, the bishops' position was defended more temperately and more cogently by a fellow-prelate, Archbishop D'Alton of Armagh. Speaking at Maynooth on 18 June, Dr D'Alton said:

The bishops have recently been criticised for intervening in connection with a proposed Health Scheme, which some professed to regard as a purely political question outside their competence. I may say at once that the bishops have neither the desire nor the intention of intervening in any question that is purely political.

While leaving to Caesar the things that are Caesar's, they must, however, concern themselves with the things that are God's. From the nature of their office they have the right and the duty to intervene when religious or moral issues are involved. They are commissioned to expound the teaching of the Church established by Christ in all matters of faith and morals, and they must strive to safeguard their flocks from error.

To all who are unbiased it should be clear by now that serious moral issues were raised by the proposed Health Scheme, and that the bishops would be failing in their duty if they did not point out the dangers inherent in it.

We have evidently still amongst us relics of the old Liberalism, which considered that the State is not bound by the ordinary Moral Law, and that there should be no challenge to its authority.[17]

This topic was handled with particular verve by Dr O'Rahilly in the *Standard*. He stressed the absurdity of the *Irish Times*

---

16. *Irish Catholic Directory, 1952,* 686.   17. *Ibid.,* 681.

asserting the right to criticise the government whenever it wished while denying that right to the Catholic bishops:

The issue raised by the *Irish Times* is quite general. It is not specifically Catholic at all. In the external forum, on the juridical plane, our bishops are not claiming any special privilege at all. Naturally, owing to the statistical fact that Catholics are in a large majority, the Catholic bishops, in matters of faith and morals, have a decisive influence. But their claim to record ethical criticisms, in public or in private, concerning government measures, is one which is equally applicable to religious minorities; and indeed it is even a more vital liberty for them.

The issue involved is the right of citizens, through their religious associations, to pass moral judgments on the State.

It is not only childishly futile, it is actually suicidal, for a Protestant organ such as the *Irish Times* to launch an attack on this right. For its denial is plain totalitarianism. . . .

In any country in which the Catholic Church loses its freedom, the State makes short work of the 'counterparts' of the *Irish Times,* not to mention other Churches, trade unions and so on.

It is simply playing with fire to keep urging the State to ignore and to muzzle Churches and great professional bodies, such as that of medicine.[18]

The contention that the Catholic bishops, alone among the citizens in a democratic State, should be limited in what topics they were permitted to raise with the government, was indeed a difficult one to sustain. The *Irish Times'* attitude was virtually repudiated by another Protestant-owned journal, *The Church of Ireland Gazette.* In an editorial on Dr Browne's resignation the latter observed:

It is said that the Roman Catholic hierarchy is the villain of the piece, and that Northern Ireland has one more illustration, if such were needed, that the real power in the Republic of Ireland is the Church of Rome.

18. *Standard,* 20 April 1951.

But some of the doctors who rejoiced over the defeat of Dr Browne's proposal were Protestants. They sympathise with him in the manner of his defeat, but they don't consider that the opinions expressed by the Roman Catholic hierarchy were unwarranted or tyrannical . . .

When the bishops of the Church of Ireland expressed their opinions on an Education Bill to the Government of Northern Ireland, nobody found fault with this procedure. Why should there be an outcry when the bishops of the Church of Rome in Ireland expressed their views in a dignified letter to the Taoiseach?[19]

In an effort to meet the difficulties, the periodical *Comhar* produced a variant of the *Irish Times*/Captain Cowan argument. It argued that, though the bishops were entitled to speak, the government should not have obeyed them. In defence of this complicated position, it resurrected the distinction which Dr Browne himself had at one stage relied on but had quickly abandoned—the distinction between the social and the moral teaching of the Church. *Comhar* believed that the government would have been justified in rejecting a ruling made only on the ground of social teaching.[20] But to judge by its correspondence columns, the readers of *Comhar* were not unanimous in support of its editorial line.[21]

The second great issue in the debate was whether the bishops should have spoken in public or in private. This was the theme of a number of letters in the *Irish Times*. Mr W. J. White, for instance, the novelist and broadcaster, contrasted the secrecy of the Catholic bishops in Ireland with the openness with which the Anglican bishops in England had recently mobilised opposition to a private member's divorce bill. The latter, he argued, was the right way for bishops to act in a democratic country.[22] The point was taken up in the *Bell* by another well-known writer, Mr Peadar O'Donnell, who thought that Mr Costello had been ill-advised to co-operate with the bishops in seeking to have the matter adjusted behind closed doors. He argued

19. Quoted in *Irish Times*, 23 April 1951.
20. *Comhar* (X, 5) May 1951, 12-13.
21. *Ibid.* (X, 6) June 1951, 11. I have to thank my wife for reading these items for me.
22. *Irish Times*, 22 May 1951.

I

that there had been far too much of a conspiratorial tradition in Irish history, so that there were special reasons in Ireland for insisting that decisions be taken publicly.[23] But the most forthright expression of the view that the bishops had been wrong to approach the government privately came, on this point again, from Captain Cowan:

> The most disquieting feature of this sorry business is the revelation that the real government of the country may not, in fact, be exercised by the elected representatives of the people as we believed it was . . . but by the bishops, meeting secretly and enforcing their rule by means of private interviews with Ministers and by documents of a secret and confidential nature sent by them to Ministers and to the head of the alleged government of the State. As a Catholic I object to the usurpation of authority of the government by the bishops. As a Catholic, I protest against this secretive, occult and objectionable practice. As a Dail Deputy, I am entitled to know all the factors that enter into the consideration of legislation, the enactment of which is part of my duty. The people I represent, the majority of them Catholics, are entitled to be similarly informed. It is wrong, morally wrong, for the bishops to keep them and me in the dark and to exercise control in civil affairs behind their and my back in regard to matters to which they as citizens and I as their representative have express authority under the Constitution of this country to deal with . . .

> The majority of the people in this State are Catholics; the majority of the elected representatives of the people are Catholics. The Catholic hierarchy are entitled to express their views on all matters of public welfare, as are the clergy of all denominations. Such views do and must command respect, but they ought to be and they must be expressed in public so that they may be known to every citizen of the State. As a Parliament, we would be failing in our duty if we did not insist on this. If we do not, our democracy is a fraud, our Constitution a sham, and our general elections humbug, pretence and swindle. I may be the only Deputy who will speak thus openly but, let no one deceive himself, the sentiments I express are shared by the majority of intelligent deputies.[24]

Defenders of the hierarchy, however, were ready with answers to such arguments as these. There were good reasons, they could

23. 'The principle at issue', *The Bell* (XVII, 2) May 1951, 6.
24. *Dail Debates*, CXXV, 898–900.

claim, why it was better for the bishops to approach the government direct than to protest against its policies publicly. Archbishop D'Alton mildly pointed out in his Maynooth speech of 18 June:

The bishops have been criticised also for the manner of their intervention. It is their custom, when the need arises, to convey their views privately to the head of the government in office. They could make their views known in a more public and spectacular fashion, but that would have the effect, which they wish to avoid, of drawing them into the stream of party politics.

Since a native government was established, the bishops have intervened very rarely, and then only in fulfilment of some clear duty of their office. To say, as has been said, that they are endeavouring to usurp the government of the country may furnish a headline for lurid oratory on the twelfth of July, but it is wholly at variance with the truth.[25]

Dr Browne, the Bishop of Galway, in a speech at Salthill on 30 April declared:

There was nothing secret or underhand in the way the bishops had acted. The letters in which they sent their views to the government were not secret; the government were free to publish them if they wished, and, when the occasion required it, they did publish them. The bishops followed the universal usage of sending their letters direct, not through the Press, for no person, not even governments, like to see letters addressed to them appear first in the public newspapers.[26]

Finally on this point, one can cite a retired civil servant, Mr W. D. Carey, who replied in the *Irish Times* to the contention of Mr W. J. White that it would have been more in accord with democratic practice if the bishops had acted publicly. Mr Carey pointed out that in fact this would be the reverse of democratic

---

25. *Irish Catholic Directory, 1952,* 681. The reference to 12 July may require elucidation for some non-Irish readers. This is the day when the Orange Order, a Protestant organisation centred in the north of Ireland, holds its annual meetings, at which speeches critical of catholicism are sometimes made.
26. *Irish Times,* 1 May 1951.

practice. His experience as a civil servant was that the bishop's method of approach was 'in all respects the normal and recognised method'. He added that 'the practice of receiving and considering such private representations is most helpful to the Minister, facilitates the working of the parliamentary machine, and is definitely in the public interest'. He did not see why religious denominations alone should be excluded from a method used by the Irish Medical Association, the Institute of Journalists, trade unions, and many other interest groups.[27]

So far, the defenders of the hierarchy would seem to have had the best of the argument. On grounds of prudence, good manners and accepted democratic practice, it was better for the hierarchy to act as it had done, by approaching the government in private. The controversy, however, was given an interesting fresh twist by Mr Sean O'Faolain in the June issue of the *Bell*. He started by bringing out, more clearly than most controversialists on either side, the essential difference between the Catholic hierarchy and any other interest group in Ireland:

Nobody, so far as I have observed, has denied the right of the Catholic bishops to 'comment'; or to give 'advice' on proposed legislation; or to enunciate the official attitude of the Roman Catholic Church to proposed legislation. That principle is fully and wholeheartedly admitted. I believe that not even the most ashen-jawed, beetle-browed, black-bowler-hatted Orangeman in Portadown could reasonably object to that principle. I doubt if anybody, north or south, could even object to the hierarchy publicly condemning any proposed piece of legislation, provided that, in the end, it is the parliament which freely decides. . . . In practice, the hierarchy does much more than 'comment' or 'advise'. It commands.

There has been a lot of talk about the rights of institutions to advise, comment and consult and so on. If we accept this principle, and I do not see why not, should we not also give the same rights to, say, the Protestant hierarchy; or to the Presbyterian Synod; or to the Worshipful Company of Masons; or to the Trades Union Congress; or to any other representative institution?

But how can we? Nobody *can* give those other institutions the same

27. *Ibid.*, 24 May 1951.

rights for the simple reason that nobody can give them the same power.

> The Maynooth Parliament [i.e. the hierarchy] holds a weapon which none of the other institutions mentioned holds: the weapon of the sacraments. The Church of England cannot wield the power of the Catholic Church because it does not hold this weapon. If a Prime Minister in England were informed by the Archbishop of Canterbury that a proposed law would be condemned by the Church of England, he would deplore it, but he would not be afraid of any effects other than political effects. If our Taoiseach were informed thus by the Protestant Archbishop of Dublin he would measure the effects in the same way. And likewise with most other institutions, religious or secular. But when the Catholic Church, through its representatives, speaks, he realises, and the Roman Catholic public realises, that if they disobey they may draw on themselves this weapon whose touch means death.[28]

Mr O'Faolain's language was highly coloured. He appeared to imply that Catholic bishops, if they find that their advice in political matters is not followed, habitually excommunicate the recalcitrant members of their flock. A glance at the historical record will show that this is not true. However, refusal of the sacraments has happened—as republicans discovered during the civil war of 1922–3. And even if no spiritual penalty is in question, advice from the hierarchy will be considered by many Catholics as binding on their consciences in a way that would be true of suggestions from no other quarter. Mr O'Faolain had a point, even if he overstated it: the Catholic hierarchy is not on a par with other interest groups.

The next question which Mr O'Faolain raised was: what should be done about this? He did not expect the Church to remain silent on issues where it believed it had a duty to speak; but he did expect the State to try to restrain its power. And in doing this, an essential weapon was publicity:

> Mr Costello faced by this clerical opposition to a piece of legislation which he and his cabinet, on behalf of the government, on behalf of the people, were proposing, should have strongly and stubbornly

28. S. O'Faolain, 'The Dail and the bishops', *The Bell* (XVII, 3) June 1951, 6–7.

resisted the bishops to the limit. He should have been scrupulously careful to avoid all 'secret diplomacy', behind the back of the Parliament. (It is, really, this whispering behind curtains which has done most to upset the people.) He should have kept the Parliament fully informed. He should have asked the hierarchy to come out in the open. Mr de Valera, who had earlier met the same opposition, should have done likewise. . . . Had these men told the bishops that the Dail would have to thrash out the whole matter in public, and that they would not accept the decision of the hierarchy unless that decision was publicly conveyed to the Dail as a command then, at least, the minimal principle of our special democratic ideology would have been preserved. More than that, I believe that the hierarchy would have acted far more prudently if they had been met in this sturdy way.[29]

Mr O'Faolain was answered in the *Standard* by the indefatigable Alfred O'Rahilly. Dr O'Rahilly scored some felicitous points. He noted that Mr O'Faolain seemed quite uninterested in the content of the bishops' decision. His own interest, he claimed, was primarily in that content. Even if 'I became an agnostic, I should still, in the interests of liberty especially of the less well-off, strongly uphold the bishops' defence of conjugal and parental rights against invasion by the State'. Again, Mr O'Faolain had argued that the members of Mr Costello's government should have automatically opposed the hierarchy. 'It seems never to occur to the writer that nearly all these persons might heartily agree with the bishops.' On the question of whether the Irish bishops had too much power, Dr O'Rahilly welcomed such power as they did have: 'It is better to have power dispersed and to have it dissociated from physical force. Most competent observers of to-day think that the chief menace to liberty comes from the all-powerful State with its police, guns and increasing monopolies.' He dismissed the argument that the hierarchy wielded a special weapon, the weapon of the sacraments. They had issued no appeals or threats, and laymen could disobey them with impunity.[30]

In this controversy, the honours seemed fairly even. Dr O'Rahilly could reasonably urge that the threat to liberty in

29. *Ibid.*, 8–9.   30. *Standard*, 22 June 1951.

Ireland at that time came from the State, not the Church, and that Irishmen should be thankful for the survival of the Church as an autonomous source of authority which could check the State's encroachments. But he dismissed too airily Mr O'Faolain's contention that the Church was *sui generis*, with powers possessed by no other interest group in the State, and that, therefore, procedures appropriate for dealing with other interest groups might not be appropriate in the case of the Church.

The third issue raised in controversy was—granted that the bishops had the right to intervene as they did, was their interpretation of Catholic social teaching on this matter convincing? Many defenders of the hierarchy at this point enunciated a general principle: they said that in current conditions the growing power of the State, both in Ireland and elsewhere, should cause serious concern, that the examples of Hitler's Germany and Stalin's Russia showed the risks of allowing State power to grow unchecked, and that the Irish bishops were rightly vigilant lest in Ireland its power should extend beyond the danger point. The argument was put by different spokesmen with varying degrees of cogency. One of the most extravagant expressions of it came from Bishop Farren of Derry, who, in the course of a denunciation of the mother and child scheme in the Republic and the welfare State in Northern Ireland, declared: 'The power and the spirit behind practically all social legislation at the present time is taken from the worst principles of both Nazi and Russian materialism.'[31] A more temperate and reasoned expression of this point of view came in an article by Dr William Conway, then Professor of Moral Theology at Maynooth and now Cardinal Archbishop of Armagh. Dr Conway examined the reasons for the rapid growth of State power in modern times. He showed that this growth was a response to genuine needs and was in general accepted by Catholic social theorists. But he did suggest that the process was an accelerating one, and that the final changeover to a totalitarian State could happen quickly and unexpectedly. 'There comes a point when the State has advanced so far into the closely-woven economy that free enterprise is paralysed; at that stage the State must either retreat

31. *Irish Press*, 18 April 1951.

or take over complete control at once. That point was reached in Germany in 1935; the vessel had been sinking slowly for some time but the end came very quickly.' The existence of periodic elections was no safeguard: experience elsewhere showed that an all-powerful State could mould public opinion to its own liking. In these circumstances the Church was right to be watchful, and 'when a particular measure manifestly involves an unwarranted extension of State-control' she would express an opinion.[32]

The most eloquent vindication of the Irish hierarchy's stand, however, came from across the Irish Sea. In England, a number of right-wing Catholics had been campaigning against the welfare legislation of the Labour government. They used against it much the same arguments as were used against the Irish mother and child scheme—that it violated the principle of subsidiary function, that it sapped individual responsibility, that it involved an undue encroachment by the State on individual liberties, and so on. In this crusade they had received little comfort from the English Catholic hierarchy, which had refrained from commenting on the merits or demerits of the welfare State. They therefore welcomed the statement of the Irish hierarchy, which provided them with the kind of support for their point of view that they had not obtained from their own bishops.

Foremost among these right-wing English Catholics was the editor of the *Tablet,* Mr Douglas Woodruff. His leading article on the Irish hierarchy's statement is worth quoting from at length, for it was one of the ablest vindications of it to be published. He said:

. . . With clarity and vigour they [the Irish bishops] have set out several important truths which in many parts of the world Catholics, in the years since the war, have either become confused about or have judged it prudent to soft pedal; and, for our part, we are profoundly grateful to the Irish hierarchy for this plain speaking at a time when it is the fashion of the hour to present as 'social justice' a succession of State policies which are, in fact, repugnant to justice. Thus the Irish bishops have done us all a great service in insisting that there

32. W. Conway, 'The Church and State control', *Christus Rex* (VI, 2) April 1952, 111–31.

must be evidence of real need before it can be right for State officials to take one man's property and give it to another. They make no concessions to the fallacy so widespread in the ranks of British Socialism, and criticised so insufficiently by Catholic supporters of that movement, of equality for equality's sake—the claim that it can be right for the government to take away from one man and give to another for the sake of symmetry, and not because the poor man is in such urgent and demonstrable need that his necessities give him a valid claim to be helped . . .

Mr Woodruff, who holds a first-class honours degree in history, went on to draw an interesting historical parallel between the situation in contemporary Europe and that in the period of absolute monarchy:

In the substance of their objections, the Irish hierarchy show a penetration, a perception of what is implied, which makes their action, entirely domestic in intention, a notable contribution to the debate going on today among Catholics all over Europe, and particularly in Germany, France, Italy and Spain. All four are countries where Catholic moral teaching ought to mould legislation, but in each there is a great temptation to Catholics, seeking mass proletarian support, to compromise themselves with Socialist ideas. The whole process is parallel to that which took place in the long political debate of the sixteenth and seventeenth centuries which ended in the enthronement of royal absolutism, the forerunner of the doctrine of absolute majority-rights under which the world suffers today. The Catholics of the sixteenth and seventeenth centuries had a much better political tradition than their new adversaries, one richly constitutional, resting on the division of powers, but they failed to maintain their principles, because the tide was running so very strongly in favour of absolutism. There was a strong, simple case for absolutism, which any man could make by pointing to the evils of anarchy and civil war, and by saying that, where men were divided on religion, the danger of civil war was always present, and the need for the sovereign absolute ruler the more imperative. The whole cause of religion suffered grievously, both directly and by association, from the failure of the Catholics to counter-balance the dominant political tendency of that age, which was quickly carried to excess. So will it be in the twentieth century, the great age of collectivism, of the closely controlled economies, of the excessive claims of rulers claiming to rule by right of majority.[33]

33. *Tablet,* 21 April 1951.

The sweep of Mr Woodruff's vision was magnificent. He pictured the Irish bishops in the twentieth century, like Bellarmine and Suarez in the seventeenth, standing as a beacon to warn Catholics of the dangers they incurred by drifting with the superficially attractive, but ultimately disastrous, intellectual currents of the day.

On looking back, we can see one point which all these apologists for the hierarchy ignored. They all assumed that the power of the State was an indefinitely expanding force, with nothing but the vigilance of the Church opposing it. But if the model of society which Catholic social theorists extolled—with power diffused among governments, subordinate associations and families—was really, as they claimed, the one which harmonised best with man's nature, then one might expect countervailing forces to State power to develop naturally, and a state of equilibrium to be reached. This seems in fact to be what has since happened. State power has not expanded indefinitely anywhere. In Britain, the welfare State has not become all-encompassing, and, by the nineteen-seventies, debate has shifted from whether the social services should be expanded to whether they should be made more selective. Even in Soviet Russia there is less tyranny, not more, than in Stalin's day. It is easier, however, to believe today that there are inherent limitations to the growth of State power than it was in the early nineteen-fifties. The point was not made at the time even by opponents of the hierarchy's ruling.

Critics of the hierarchy reserved their fire for a different point. While tacitly conceding that the growth of State power could be a danger, what they in effect asked was: why did the hierarchy draw the line where they did? What was so heinous about the mother and child scheme that it provoked a condemnation from the hierarchy, while other services which also involved extensive State intervention were not condemned? Two analogies in particular were frequently raised: with primary education, and with the British National Health Service.[34] The State ensured that free primary education was available without means test to the entire population, and had never been condemned for doing

34. See e.g. the correspondence in the *Irish Times* in April and May 1951.

so. If it was all right to do this for education, why was it not all right to do the same for a medical service? Again, the British National Health Service provided a free universal service which covered maternity and child welfare along with other medical needs. Yet it had never been condemned by the hierarchies of England and Wales or of Scotland. Nor had it been condemned by the Irish hierarchy when it was introduced in Northern Ireland. Why should such a scheme be all right in the United Kingdom and not in the Republic of Ireland?

Defenders of the hierarchy did not leave these points unanswered. The difference between primary education and medical services was elucidated by Father James Kavanagh, a priest of the Dublin diocese who specialised in social questions, in the course of a letter to *The Irish Times*:

Dr. Browne says in his memorandum that the State, in his health scheme, is providing facilities for parents just as the State provides facilities for primary education. A little reflection will help us to see that there is little parity between the two. In primary education the State rightly assists parents, but it does not *control* education. It gives grants, and very generous grants, towards the building of schools; it provides the money for the payment of teachers, but the ownership of the schools is not vested in the State. So anxious has been the Irish State always in regard to parental responsibility in the domain of education that it does not give the full cost of the erection of a school —the people have contributed throughout the various parishes of the land some portion of the cost, so that they know the schools are not State schools, but theirs.[35]

Dr O'Rahilly in the *Standard* took the point further. He argued that the analogy with education would lead to a structure of health services quite different from that proposed by Dr Browne:

If the State wishes to give medical help to families, it should proceed as it does in education, where it does not establish State schools or appoint teachers over the heads of the parents. Just as the State subsidises family schools, mostly through the respective religious bodies, so let it subsidise mother and child, not by a State medical service (which inevitably involves sex education), but—by coupons or

35. *Irish Times*, 24 April 1951.

otherwise, and by subsidising professional and voluntary institutions —through some scheme which will allow the families to become patients of their own doctors who are not amenable to bureaucratic interference.

The primary objection to the proposed scheme is not to its being 'free', but to the substitution of the State for institutions, existing or capable of being created, ultimately responsible to the families concerned.[36]

The picture painted of the Irish education system by Father Kavanagh and Dr O'Rahilly was somewhat *couleur de rose*. Despite Father Kavanagh's point that there was always a local contribution towards the cost of each school, and despite Dr O'Rahilly's description of the schools as 'family schools', Irish parents had remarkably little say in the running of primary schools. Parent-teacher associations were rare and in any case had no powers; there were no school boards elected by the people of a locality to share in the administration of the schools; the county and urban councils had no say in primary education. Responsibility for each school was shared between the local clerical manager and a tightly centralised Department of Education in Dublin. However, the existence of these clerical managers did mean that primary education was not simply a State service in Ireland, and so the parallel between it and the mother and child service could be challenged.

It was the analogy with the National Health Service which gave defenders of the hierarchy most trouble. So much so in fact that they generally ignored it, and I have not anywhere come across a clear explanation of why the hierarchies of these islands accepted the British health scheme and yet condemned the Irish. The argument might have been used that it was pointless for the bishops to speak out in the United Kingdom, where Catholics are so small a minority that they can have little influence on policy. But if they feel that a principle is at stake, Catholic bishops do often speak out, even when they have little chance of influencing the outcome, and the hierarchy of England and Wales has on occasion made statements on issues of public policy. By a coincidence there was an example in the very week

36. *Standard,* 20 April 1951.

that the mother and child scheme crisis broke. The English hierarchy issued a statement deploring a recommendation in the recently-published report of the Royal Commission on Population, which proposed the promotion of birth-control as public policy.[37]

The nearest to an explanation of the difference between the Irish and the British cases that I have come across is to be found in the speech by Bishop Browne of Galway at Salthill, from which quotation has already been made. He said:

It was with great concern that the Irish bishops saw the Health Act of 1947 give to public authority the right and duty to educate women in respect to motherhood and to educate all children in matters relating to health, for education in regard to motherhood and in regard to health means instructions in regard to the sacred and delicate subjects of sex, chastity, marriage, child birth and family life.

This is moral teaching which belongs to the Church established by Christ. The State had no authority to interfere in this sphere. It has no right to tell girls or women how they shall act or behave in regard to the most important and sacred matters of conscience and of spiritual salvation.

. . . The same Act gave the State the right and duty to provide for the treatment of the illnesses and defects of all children, but the rights of the parents were ignored.

The Act was based on the Socialistic principle that the children belonged to the State, was contrary to the Constitution and reminded one of the claims put forward by Hitler and Stalin.

Surely the world had learned so much of the horrors of such claims that any country which respected Christian rights and liberties should be anxious not to give the State such dangerous powers.

The bishops in 1947 had asked and expected that this un-Christian and totalitarian legislation should be amended. Instead, in 1950, they found the country presented with a Mother and Child scheme which entrusted to public officials the treatment of all mothers before, at, and after childbirth, and their education in regard to motherhood

37. *Irish Times*, 13 April 1951.

and all matters concerning their bodily health. No guarantee was given that these officials would respect Catholic moral teaching, and the women of the country were to be enticed to submit to treatment by these 'district medical officers' with the promise that it would be free. These officials would be employed and dismissed by the State and would be bound to obey the instructions of superior officials.

The establishment of this scheme would soon eliminate the free medical practitioner and create a monopoly of socialised medical services under complete State control—a terrible weapon to put into the hands of men who might not have received instruction in Catholic principles, or who might repudiate such principles. The scheme also struck at the Catholic doctrine that parents had the right and responsibility of rearing and providing for their children.[38]

Nowhere in this speech did the bishop specifically refer to the parallel with the British National Health Service, but it may have been in his mind. For the defects of the Irish proposals which he singled out for criticism were on the whole not present in the British scheme. British legislation makes no mention of 'educating women in respect to motherhood', nor does it give the State the duty 'to provide for the illnesses and defects of all children'; it speaks rather of providing services for those who require them.[39] In Britain, doctors under the National Health Service are not employed directly by the State but by area executive committees, on which doctors themselves are strongly represented.[40] In scope, it is true, the British National Health Service Act is even more wide-ranging than the Irish Health Act of 1947, since it provides a free-for-all service which extends to all, and not just to certain kinds of, medical needs; but its terminology sounds a good deal less totalitarian than the Irish legislation.

Nonetheless, even if the distinction be accepted between the mother and child scheme on the one hand and primary education or the National Health Service on the other, the difficulty remained of explaining why the hierarchy should have drawn the line against the growth of State control at exactly

38. *Ibid.*, 1 May 1951.
39. e.g. National Health Service Act 1946, section 33.
40. A. Lindsey, *Socialized Medicine in England and Wales*, 85, 156, 164.

the point it did. The principles used by the hierarchy in condemning the mother and child scheme could easily be applied to other services which the hierarchy itself had not condemned. This is best illustrated by quoting, not the hierarchy's critics, but its supporters. One opponent of Mr Norton's social welfare scheme wrote triumphantly to the press to say that the arguments used by the hierarchy against Dr Browne's proposals were equally valid against Mr Norton's.[41] Father E. J. Coyne, S.J., in his defence of the hierarchy in *Studies,* took the opportunity of defending means tests in principle and appeared to deprecate, for instance, the granting of food subsidies and housing subsidies without a means test.[42] Members of the Irish Medical Association had already used arguments similar to the hierarchy's to condemn not just the mother and child service but the infectious diseases service, which under the Health Act 1947 was also to be available free for all.[43]

The difficulties of applying the Irish hierarchy's principles can best be seen by following the correspondence provoked in the *Tablet* by Mr Woodruff's eloquent defence of the Irish bishops. The week after Mr Woodruff's leading article, an objection was raised by Mr Andrew Phelan, who wrote that it was not at all easy to base the objections of the hierarchy upon a principle. It was said that the scheme was unjust because the burden of taxation would oblige many citizens to use the State services who would otherwise cater for their needs upon their own initiative and at their own cost. But, he went on, 'if this be an unwarranted encroachment of the State upon individual rights the State has thus encroached for a very long time. Universal taxation is used to provide universal education services. Where lies the difference between education and medical services?'[44]

Mr Phelan's objection was answered the following week by Mr V. Foy Feery. Mr Feery argued that education was not on the same footing as a health service:

---

41. Letter from Thomas A. O'Connor in *Dublin Evening Mail,* 14 April 1951.
42. E. J. Coyne, S.J., 'Mother and Child Service', *Studies* (XL, no. 158) June 1951, 146.
43. *Journal of the Irish Medical Association,* June 1950, 96, and discussion in subsequent issues.
44. *Tablet,* 28 April 1951.

Education entails a constant, heavy expenditure during the whole of the school age, which cannot be undertaken by the majority of parents, however carefully they save. Consequently the State is justified in providing financial and other help, through the medium of universal taxation.

On the other hand, medical attention is not normally required over long periods without cease. There is sufficient time between the periods of ill-health for the parents to save money for the next medical bill, and this they must do, as far as lies within their power. Where expense is incurred on a scale so large that it is not possible for the parents to meet it, e.g. due to a major operation, then the State may step in and assist the parents to pay the bill.

A compulsory, national health scheme provides for the State to invade the rights and usurp the duties of parents and others without the essential grave reasons for doing so.[45]

Mr Feery, then, in defending the Irish bishops against Mr Phelan's criticism, had condemned all universal health schemes—which was further than the bishops themselves had gone. But at least Mr Feery accepted the principle of free universal education. The following week another correspondent, Mr Dryden Gilling Smith, threw that overboard as well. 'The principle of "universal taxation for universal education"', he wrote, 'is not necessarily a right one, because it is seldom questioned.' He explained that it made the individual unnecessarily dependent on the government, and urged that for education, and for other social services, there should be a right of contracting out.[46] This correspondence in the *Tablet* showed how even those who most heartily sympathised with the Irish bishops found difficulty in agreeing on how the bishops' principles should be applied.

The Irish hierarchy has been subjected to much ill-informed criticism as a result of its ruling on the mother and child scheme. This and previous chapters should have shown that there was substantial ground for its decision. The growth of State power was a genuine problem in Ireland, especially in view of the centralising tendencies and the impatience with interest groups

45. *Ibid.*, 5 May 1951.   46. *Ibid.*, 12 May 1951.

that were so noticeable in Irish administration. The Health Act 1947, on which the mother and child scheme was based, undoubtedly had objectionable features. The mother and child scheme itself, while avoiding some of the objections to the parent act, had other undesirable features of its own. Nor can the bishops be fairly accused of hostility to social reform. The issue in their eyes was not whether there should be social services, but what was the most humane form for these social services to take. And yet, when all this is said, it is doubtful whether the decision to condemn the mother and child scheme in such peremptory terms was prudent. The ensuing controversy revealed the weakness of the bishops' position, with the statements of their allies proving, if anything, more damaging than those of their opponents. The discussion showed that it was impossible to explain satisfactorily why the mother and child scheme should be the subject of a solemn condemnation when other and similar public services were not.

At this point it might be interesting to glance at how these matters were handled in other countries where Catholic influence was strong. True, it is not possible to find any precisely parallel case. There appears to be no example elsewhere of a health measure, or any other item of social legislation, being specifically condemned by the hierarchy of the country concerned.[47] This in itself is not surprising; it merely serves to underline the extraordinary nature of the Irish proposals.

What can be done is to look at the framework of ideas within which Catholics discussed these issues in one or two other countries. France is a good example to take, because French social services were radically recast in the post-war years, at a time when the M.R.P., the left-wing Catholic party, was an important partner in every government coalition and therefore had substantial influence over the shape which the social services assumed. The specific contributions of the M.R.P. to the pattern of those services were two. First, it insisted on the principle of

47. This generalisation is based on a consultation of the books listed in the Bibliography under the heading 'comparative material on other countries'. I have also been through the periodical *Documentation Catholique* for the years 1946–55.

plurality of insurance funds—in other words, that instead of there being a single insurance fund embracing the entire country, there should be separate funds for various occupations and professions.[48] Second, it insisted that the boards of management of these funds be directly elected by the contributors.[49]

One can see here the application of Catholic social principles. The division of the social insurance scheme into separate funds, each with a directly elected board, was administratively untidy and was regretted by the government department concerned.[50] But it brought the administration closer to the people affected, ensured a diffusion of power and a multiplication of subordinate associations. The terms in which these principles were defended would be familiar to an Irish student of Catholic social teaching. In 1946, for instance, a spokesman of the C.F.T.C. (the Catholic trades unions) attacked the idea of a unified insurance scheme as leading to *une étatisation généralisée*—a sweeping extension of State power.[51] And yet, though there was a community of ideas between French and Irish exponents of Catholic social thinking, there was also a difference of emphasis. One feature of the French social security plan was its progressive extension to the entire population. This feature was not just acquiesced in by the M.R.P. as a concession to their Socialist and Communist partners in government: it was welcomed for its own sake. The M.R.P. spokesman in one debate on social security stated that 'his party aimed at the implementation of a social security plan which would guarantee a minimum standard of living not only to every worker but to every Frenchman.'[52] There is no implication here that social services are necessary evils whose expansion should be closely watched, lest they be extended to those who could do without them. Nor does the M.R.P. appear to have been worried by the argument that too much social security might 'sap the moral fibre' of the people. Indeed it urged that one social service, namely family allowances, should be raised to such a level as to 'guarantee an identical standard of life for all workers rendering the same services, account being

48. H. Galant, *Histoire Politique de la Sécurité Sociale Française*, 63, 109.
49. *Ibid.*, 63, 95.   50. *Ibid.*, 37–8, 43, 115.
51. *Ibid.*, 128.   52. *Ibid.*, 91.

taken of their family expenses'[53]—a claim which seems to have been considered excessive even by its left-wing partners in government.

In Italy, thanks to the extensive social legislation of the Fascist regime, there was much less need to recast social services after the war. But even there, discussion arose about what changes, if any, might be required, and the Catholic Social Week for 1949 was devoted to the theme of 'social security'. The conclusions published by this congress were, like the statements of French social Catholics, phrased in language which would be familiar to an Irish student of Catholic social teaching.[54] For instance, Conclusion IX was couched in terms which might almost be taken from the Irish bishops' judgment on the mother and child scheme. It was headed 'responsibility and initiative of the family' and it stated: 'Social security . . . ought to be organised in a way which will guarantee to the family its integrity, its vitality, its capacity for initiative, and the power to fulfil completely its educative tasks; and all this not by minimising the parental sense of responsibility, but rather by putting it in a position to develop. . . .' Other conclusions emphasised the importance of intermediate groups, of personal initiative and liberty of choice.[55] Yet at the same time these conclusions stressed some points which were soft-pedalled or even ignored in the Irish controversy. Conclusion X emphasised that 'all citizens should be considered equal in respect to the problem of health', called for an organisation adequate to put this ideal into practice, and pointed out that this could be done only by the intervention of the public authorities. Conclusion I welcomed the 'vast reforms' in social welfare which had occurred in all civilised countries since the war, and acknowledged them as an expression of human solidarity and a satisfaction of the legitimate aspirations

53. *Ibid.,* 66. The fact that all footnotes in this and the preceding paragraph refer to one book does not mean that I have relied uncritically on a single source for information about French Catholics and social services. For other works consulted, see the works by Bosworth, Einaudi and Goguel, Fogarty, Friedlander and Williams cited in the Bibliography under the heading 'comparative material on other countries', and also the report of the 1951 *Semaine sociale* listed under the same heading.
54. *La Sicurezza Sociale: XXIII Settimana Sociale dei Cattolici d'Italia,* 247–53.
55. *Ibid.,* Conclusions IV, IX, X.

of the less well-off. Conclusion III made the point, which I have not seen made by anyone in Ireland at this time, that social security can for many people mean an increase, not a decrease, in their liberty, by enabling them to satisfy their needs and to extend their activities.

The most notable contribution to this Italian Catholic Social Week was a paper by Father Agostino Gemelli, O.F.M., Rector of the Catholic university in Milan, on 'the defence of health in a system of social security'. Father Gemelli was an extremely well-qualified speaker. He was a leading figure of the Catholic social movement in Italy, and at the same time a distinguished doctor, with research interests in psychology.[56] Father Gemelli stressed a point which was hardly mentioned in Ireland: the transformation of medicine in recent years. Increasing specialisation, increasingly elaborate means of treatment, and the increasing collectivisation of life as a whole, meant that medicine was no longer a liberal profession carried on by individuals: it had become the exercise of a social function.[57] In these circumstances doctors could not maintain their nineteenth-century freedoms, and, while he agreed that State medicine should be avoided, there was another danger—commercial medicine—which was equally to be avoided.[58] As a model to be emulated he selected the British National Health Service, singling out for commendation the fact that it applied to the entire population, and describing the extra taxation which it entailed as an example of Christian solidarity.[59] He closed with the peroration: 'All men are equal in the face of illness; all have, as a matter of urgency and in the same degree, the right to medical care and to means of prevention.'[60]

Father Gemelli's paper was known in Ireland, and was used as ammunition in the mother and child controversy. It was quoted by Captain Cowan in the Dail debate following Dr Browne's resignation as proof that the attitude of the Irish hierarchy to the extension of health services was not that adopted by all Catholic

---

56. 'Padre Gemelli, dieci anni dopo', *Presenza* (I, 2) July 1969, 7–21. A measure of Fr. Gemelli's stature is that his funeral sermon was preached by Cardinal G. B. Montini, then Archbishop of Milan, and now, of course, Pope Paul VI: *ibid.*, 16–17.

57. *La Sicurezza Sociale*, 180–4.   58. *Ibid.*, 188.
59. *Ibid.*, 166–8, 202.   60. *Ibid.*, 205.

authorities on the subject.[61] The inference was not watertight: the fact that Father Gemelli admired the British National Health Service was no proof that he would have admired Dr Browne's mother and child scheme, because as we have seen, there were significant differences between the two measures. But there can be no doubt, from the general tone of his lecture, that Father Gemelli was more indulgent towards the extension of public medical services than were the exponents of Catholic social teaching in Ireland.

Two impressions are left by this brief look at Catholic thought on social services in France and Italy. The first is that Catholics in these countries and in Ireland were all speaking within a common tradition. They argued from shared premises: the very phrases, 'subsidiary function', 'intermediate associations', 'parental responsibility', crop up in one country as in another. But the other impression is that, within this common tradition, there was a difference of emphasis. Catholic social thought has always been based on a tension: it stresses the rights of individuals and intermediate associations as against the State; but it also stresses the right of individuals to receive aid from larger bodies, including the State. In Ireland, the first of these principles had come to be stressed so strongly that the second was in danger of being underemphasised; on the continent, the balance was more carefully maintained. The impression suggested in Chapter VI is strengthened here: that Catholic social thought in Ireland had slipped towards the right. It was no longer in the main stream

From this brief glance at developments abroad we may move on to the question: what was the effect of the mother and child scheme controversy on public opinion in Ireland? It must be said at once that the evidence for answering this question will be fragmentary. It could only have been answered satisfactorily by a series of opinion polls, and opinion polls did not then exist in Ireland. Indeed they were only beginning to become established, as an instrument of political research, in the later nineteen-sixties So we must do the best we can with such partial indications as are available.

61. *Dail Debates*, CXXV, 901–3.

One possible quarry of information might be found in election returns. As it happened, a general election occurred only a few weeks after the mother and child scheme crisis broke. That crisis had lost the government the vote of Dr Browne and of one or two deputies sympathetic to him; when, at the beginning of May, three rural deputies decided to oppose the government because of its refusal to increase the price of milk, its majority disappeared altogether, and Mr Costello dissolved the Dail.[62] The general election on 30 May produced the following shifts in party strengths:

	1948	1951
Fianna Fail	68	69
Fine Gael	31	40
Labour	14	
National Labour	5	16
Clann na Poblachta	10	2
Clann na Talmhan	7	6
Others	12	14

These results, however, are confusing for anyone trying to find in them a popular verdict on the mother and child scheme. On the one hand, the greatest gains were made by Fine Gael, which as principal partner in the coalition had the largest share in the responsibility for abandoning the scheme. On the other hand, the greatest losses were suffered by Clann na Poblachta, which also had a share in the responsibility for dropping the scheme. The truth is that even though the mother and child crisis had occurred only shortly before, in most constituencies it was not an issue in the general election. The opposition party, Fianna Fail, which had remained silent when the debate on Dr Browne's resignation took place, did not now make the mother and child scheme an issue. Indeed it was difficult to say what the issues were in the election. The parties supporting the inter-party government fought the campaign as a team, and as they consisted of some groups to the left of Fianna Fail and others to the right, they had to compromise by coming down in the centre —that is, in just the same position as their opponents. In these

62. *Irish Times,* 5 May 1951.

circumstances, the contest descended into an argument about who would make the better administrators, and the *Irish Times* summed up the theme of the election in words taken from the then recent musical, *Annie Get Your Gun*—'Anything you can do I can do better.'[63] In this situation, the increased vote for Fine Gael can be explained as an acknowledgement that it had once again become credible as a governing party. Fine Gael had undergone a long decline in the thirties and forties,[64] but there was evidently a reservoir of latent support for it. Once it had shown, by its prominence in the inter-party government, that it was not so moribund as it had seemed, sympathisers came flocking back to it. Clann na Poblachta, on the other hand, had attracted support in 1946–8 as a radical party. Once it entered a coalition whose centre of gravity was, inevitably, well to the right of it, its supporters were likely to become disillusioned.

There was just a handful of constituencies where the results might have some bearing on public attitudes to Dr Browne's scheme. These were the constituencies in which Dr Browne himself and his immediate allies were standing. Dr Browne stood again in Dublin South-East. His friend Mr Jack McQuillan, who had followed him out of Clann na Poblachta, stood again in Roscommon. Captain Cowan stood again in Dublin North-East, and a new candidate, Dr Michael ffrench-O'Carroll, standing specifically as a supporter of Dr Browne, challenged Mr Mac-Bride in Dublin South-West. Now all these candidates did well. Dr Browne was particularly successful; he increased his first-preference vote in Dublin South-East from 4,917 in 1948 to 8,473. Mr McQuillan in Roscommon more than held his own with 3,666 first-preference votes as against 3,025 in 1948. Captain Cowan in Dublin North-East fell from 4,692 first-preference votes in 1948 to 3,606 in 1951, but he retained his seat, which was a significant fact, for he is said to have undertaken no campaign during the election.[65] It might be said, in partial explanation of the success of these three candidates, that, whereas they were all newcomers in 1948, they were all sitting deputies in 1951, and that a sitting deputy has an advantage because he is

63. *Ibid.*, 29 May 1951.   64. See above, p. 113.
65. M. McInerney, 'Dr. Noel Browne: a political portrait—3', *Irish Times*, 11 Oct. 1967.

better known. However that may be, it does not apply to Dr
ffrench-O'Carroll. He, standing for the first time, was easily
elected with 5,842 first-preference votes, while Mr Sean Mac-
Bride, the sitting deputy whom he was particularly challenging,
scraped home for the last seat with only 2,853 first-preference
votes—a startling contrast to his poll of 8,648 first-preference
votes in 1948.[66] Too much must not be made of these polling
figures. It would be unwise to treat them as a vote of censure on
the hierarchy—especially as Dr Browne himself, during the
election campaign, disclaimed any intention of defying the
hierarchy's ruling. But they do show a public sympathy for
those connected with Dr Browne's scheme, the scheme which
had received the hierarchy's disapproval.

There is another source of evidence for public attitudes to the
mother and child scheme. This is provided by the comments of
those who supported the hierarchy's line, a number of whom
complained of the difficulty of getting the public to see their
point of view. Dr D'Alton, Archbishop of Armagh, speaking in
Dublin on 10 October, said:

A recent controversy left one with the uneasy feeling that we are
more deeply infected than we think with the virus of secularism and
materialism. In the course of the controversy it became evident that
for many the chief consideration was the fact that the State was
offering something for nothing. They did not pause to reflect on how
the miracle was to be achieved, or on the burdens it would entail.

Others sought to evade the moral issues involved by distinguishing
between the moral and social teaching of the Church. We heard
echoes, too, of the old Liberal idea about the overriding power of
parliament and its consequent immunity from criticism. We should
expect, at least from our Catholic representatives in the Dail, a clear
grasp of the moral problems involved in such a controversy, so that
they may not be swayed by the clamours of ignorant or hostile
critics.[67]

66. Polling figures from: Dail Eireann, *Copies of the Public Notices of the Results
of the Elections and of the Transfers of Votes in respect of:* (a) *General Election, 1948,*
(b) *General Election, 1951,* (c) *By-elections, 1944 to 1952 (inclusive).*
67. *Irish Catholic Directory,* 1952, 709.

A similar point was made by 'Vigilans', the commentator of *Christus Rex*:

As the Bishop of Galway said the other day, they [the Irish people] do not seem to understand our language. That was very clearly illustrated during the present year when a great many well-disposed Catholics just could not understand what was the central objection to the Mother and Child Scheme. We have still a long way to go to make the people as a whole see for themselves the validity of much of Catholic social teaching.[68]

The same complaint can be found, stated in more extreme terms, in the report of a speech by the Supreme Knight of the Knights of St Columbanus, Mr Stephen Mackenzie:

Referring to the recent controversy over the proposed Mother and Child Scheme, the Supreme Knight said it was lamentable to see the large number of Catholics who disagreed with the teaching of the Hierarchy and the number of highly-educated people who did not appear to know the rudiments of the Catholic religion.

The organ of the Protestant minority, he said, missed few occasions to discredit the doctrines and leaders of the Catholic Church, and this year it had openly attacked the religious leaders of the people . . .

One aspect of the attack by the *Irish Times* was the confidence with which those who represented the Cromwellian traditions in Ireland were attempting to continue that tradition of endeavouring to drive the Catholic Church out of the life of the country.

'We must ask ourselves have they good reason for that confidence', he added. Another aspect of the attack was the number of Catholics in the upper and lower strata of Irish life who accepted the judgment of a Protestant paper against that of their own bishops.[69]

Mr Mackenzie went on to advert to a circumstance that others, for instance Dr O'Rahilly,[70] had also noted—that, while the Protestant-owned daily in Dublin, the *Irish Times*, criticised

68. Vigilans, 'As I see it', *Christus Rex* (V, 4) Oct. 1951, 388.
69. *Irish Catholic Directory, 1952*, 687–8 (2 July 1951).
70. *Standard*, 27 April 1951.

the bishops, the two Catholic-owned dailies, the *Irish Independent* and the *Irish Press,* did nothing to defend them:

> Mr. Mackenzie said that, while the *Irish Times* continued its campaign, our two national papers remained silent, and neither by editorial nor otherwise showed that the bishops were defending the essential rights of parents and children. The whole episode showed that there was at present greater need than ever before for a body of laymen who understood the essential fact that the Church had the right to teach with authority on matters of faith and morals and who were prepared to defend its teaching.[71]

The consensus among the bishops' defenders, then, appeared to be that there was widespread confusion, if not opposition, among Catholics in regard to the bishops' ruling. This agrees with the recollections of the many people, clerical and lay, with whom I have discussed the episode. Almost without exception they remember a feeling of puzzlement, a difficulty in seeing clearly just what the bishops' objection was. Some go further and remember feeling that the bishops were definitely wrong. I have not, I think, met anyone, outside the hierarchy itself, who remembers feeling with equal conviction that the bishops were right.

One last question remains to be raised: how did the spokesmen of the Catholic social movement react to their evident failure to convince Catholic opinion on the mother and child issue? It might have been expected to lead to a reappraisal, a period of self-questioning in which Catholic social theorists asked themselves whether their failure to win wider public acceptance might be due to weaknesses in their own thinking. This, however, was not what happened. Their reaction, rather, was to reiterate their current teaching with increased emphasis. There were never so many denunciations of State power as in the year or two after the mother and child scheme crisis. Canon Hayes told a *Muintir na Tire* gathering that the logical conclusion to increasing State power was to be found in the Kremlin.[72] Bishop

---

71. *Irish Catholic Directory, 1952,* 688.
72. *Irish Weekly Independent,* 18 Aug. 1951.

Staunton of Ferns deplored the current desire to seek all help from the State.[73] Bishop O'Callaghan of Clogher denounced the wrong tendency of the State to interfere increasingly.[74] Archbishop D'Alton of Armagh, in a lenten pastoral, defined the welfare State as 'a milder form of totalitarianism'.[75] Quotations could be multiplied, but perhaps a better way of conveying the flavour of what Catholic social theorists were saying in these years would be to give one quotation, from a well-qualified source, at greater length. The following passage comes from a sermon by Dr Cornelius Lucey, then Coadjutor-Bishop of Cork, given at Limerick on 12 November 1951:

This is the age of the State, the age of the eclipse of the individual person and the family by the government departments and civil servants. . . . In some countries the eclipse is complete, the government exercising absolute control over all its citizens. . . . Things have not come to this pass here in Ireland, thank God. But they have come a certain distance and the tendency is to go further. There is no weakening in the principle we profess; there is no claim by the State to do what it likes with us, or no admission by the citizens that they cannot look after themselves; the government is, in theory, still the servant of the people. But what do we find in practice? The servant doing so much for us that we are fast losing the will and the way to do things for ourselves. But in the main the drive for more and more State services comes from the State itself.

For instance, what demand was there from the public for a free-for-all mother and child health service until the scheme was suggested and proposed, and pushed by propaganda paid for out of public funds by the department itself? And it is not the political parties, it is not the Ministers who are always to blame. Often, too, the drive comes from the officials of the department, men in executive and administrative posts with an itch for planning; experts, convinced that they know better than ourselves what is good for us.

The Welfare State is almost upon us. Now, under one pretext, now under another, the various departments of State are becoming father and mother to us all. Now it is on Socialist reasoning thinly disguised —because mothers and children are the hope of the future and so of

73. *Ibid.*   74. *Ibid.,* 1 Dec. 1951.
75. John Cardinal D'Alton, *The Church and Freedom,* 16.

the nation and the State, because all in the land are equal and so should receive the same treatment, etc.; now it is on humanitarian grounds—because parents cannot afford to look after their children as well as the State can, or cannot be expected to know how to look after them as well as the department experts can, and hence the constant references to examples of bad or careless parents. . . .[76]

To be fair, not all exponents of Catholic social teaching were so one-sided as this. Speakers could be found, such as Monsignor Arthur Ryan of Belfast or Dr William Philbin of Maynooth, who acknowledged the wide scope for legitimate State intervention.[77] But these were very much minority voices. It does seem true to say that the characteristic weaknesses of the Catholic social movement in Ireland were accentuated in the aftermath of the mother and child scheme crisis. The dangers of State power were so much stressed that opposite dangers—such as that the State might not intervene enough to protect its weaker citizens —were almost forgotten. The correct balance of power between the State and other bodies was so much discussed that more pressing problems—such as high emigration or low productivity —were almost overlooked. The handicap which the Catholic social movement in Ireland suffered as a result of its late start was being exposed. Its intellectual tradition was still weak and lacked rigour.

It was in this atmosphere, then, of repeated and often ill-balanced denunciations of State power, that Irish governments in the early nineteen-fifties had to conduct their business. In the next chapter we shall see how the incoming Fianna Fail administration, formed after the general election of 1951, faced this situation.

76. *Irish Catholic Directory, 1952*, 714–15.
77. See the report of a lecture by Mgr Ryan in *Irish Times*, 31 March 1952: and Very Rev. W. J. Canon Philbin, 'The individual and the State', *Irish Ecclesiastical Record* (5th series, LXXIX) Jan. 1953, 1–19.

CHAPTER IX

FIANNA FAIL RESOLVES THE ISSUES, 1951–3

Mr de Valera's second government, formed after the general election of 1951, included few changes in the team with which he had left office three years before. Dr James Ryan, for instance, once again became Minister for Health and Minister for Social Welfare, and Mr Gerald Boland again became Minister for Justice. Mr de Valera may not have been altogether wise in passing over the opportunity to bring fresh faces onto his front bench. But his stress on continuity meant that at least his government consisted of men who were used to working together. The personal feuds which had done so much damage to the inter-party government were not apparent in the new administration.

The incoming administration was left with much unfinished business to settle. As far as the theme of this book is concerned, three items in particular are of interest. First there was social welfare, where Mr Norton's proposed legislation, which had aroused so much criticism from Catholic social theorists, had been cut short in mid-passage by the general election. Second there was legal adoption, where the government had to face persistent demands for legislation on the one hand, and the opposition, real or supposed, of the Church on the other. Third and most important, there was the question of health services, where the situation caused by the hierarchy's protests against the Health Act 1947 and the mother and child scheme of 1950–1 had still to be resolved. We shall discuss these three topics in turn.

Social welfare was disposed of with relative ease. It will be remembered that the main criticism which Catholic social theorists had levelled against Mr Norton's scheme was that it

273

catered only for insured workers, and violated distributive justice by doing nothing for self-employed people, such as small farmers, who often needed help just as much.[1] Soon after returning to office, the Fianna Fail government introduced a measure which, while retaining most of the benefits for insured workers which Mr Norton had proposed, also increased the social assistance benefits on which the self-employed depended when in need.[2] It is hard to assess how far Fianna Fail, in taking this line, was influenced by the hope that it would pacify exponents of Catholic social teaching. The party's own strength among the small farmers of Ireland would be sufficient to explain its concern for the small farmers' interests. But, whether calculated or not, Fianna Fail policy did have the effect of making Catholic social theorists look more favourably on its measure than on Mr Norton's,[3] and it passed into law, without serious controversy, as the Social Welfare Act 1952.

The legal adoption issue was also fairly quickly settled. This was largely due to the persistence of the Adoption Society (Ireland), which declined to accept as settling the question General MacEoin's refusal, in October 1950, to introduce legislation. The society's next move was to arrange for the preparation of a private member's bill. The measure was ready by the following autumn and, on 8 November 1951, was placed on the Dail's order paper in the names of Mr Pa McGrath of Fianna Fail and Mr Percy Dockrell of Fine Gael.[4] The bill was likely to be backed by the society's many friends in the Dail. The Minister for Justice, Mr Boland, was personally much better disposed to adoption legislation than General MacEoin had been, and though he was not prepared at this stage to introduce legislation himself, he encouraged the introduction of the private member's bill.[5] The forces favouring legislation were

1. See above, p. 181.

2. For an outline of the proposals see *Dail Debates,* CXXX, 616–46 (27 March 1952: speech of Dr Ryan on second reading of the bill).

3. A point which was noted with irritation by supporters of Mr Norton's scheme: see *ibid.,* 680 (speech of General Mulcahy), 808–9 (speech of Mr James Larkin junior).

4. Adoption Society (Ireland): Hon. Secretary's report for year ending 31 March 1952.

5. Information from Mr Boland.

gathering momentum, and the principal remaining question-mark was the attitude of the Church.

The Adoption Society, however, had been tackling the difficulties in that quarter as well. Its officers had realised under the previous government that, unless they secured some kind of clearance from the Catholic hierarchy, it was unlikely that they would obtain legislation, and they had decided to approach the bishops themselves. The first problem they had to settle was which member of the hierarchy to approach. The society consisted largely of Dubliners, and so the Archbishop of Dublin, Dr McQuaid, might have seemed the appropriate person. But Dr McQuaid was believed (perhaps not quite justly) to be unfavourable, and so it was decided to approach the chairman of the hierarchy, Archbishop D'Alton of Armagh. Indeed one reason why the society was so anxious to open branches outside Dublin was that it could then claim to be a national society and so not within the exclusive jurisdiction of the Archbishop of Dublin.[6] A letter was sent to Archbishop D'Alton on 8 February 1950.[7] Dr D'Alton replied asking the society for a written statement of its case, which the society sent to him, and he in his turn put it to the general meeting of the bishops in June 1950.[8] The hierarchy remitted the question to a committee, whose membership was later reported as consisting of Archbishop McQuaid as chairman, and Archbishop Kinane of Cashel, Bishop Browne of Galway, Bishop Farren of Derry, and the Coadjutor-Bishop of Cork, Dr Lucey, as members.[9]

The committee took a long time to reach a conclusion. Indeed it was not until 10 January 1952 that it issued a statement. However, the statement, when it came, was favourable in principle to legal adoption. It made clear that, provided certain safeguards were included, the hierarchy would not oppose such a measure. The text was as follows:—

1. Legal Adoption, if it be restricted within certain limits and protected by certain safeguards, is consonant with Catholic teaching.

---

6. Information from officers of the Adoption Society.
7. Adoption Society (Ireland): Hon. Secretary's report for year ending 29 March 1951.
8. *Ibid.*   9. *Irish Catholic Directory, 1953,* 630.

(a) *Limits:*
Parents have a natural right and obligation to provide for their children in regard to religious and moral training, physical well-being and preparation for civil life.

Only for the gravest reasons may parents permanently relinquish this right or consider themselves excused from this obligation.

(b) *Safeguards:*
The safeguards must be such as the Church considers sufficient to protect Faith and morals.

A child's right in respect of Faith and morals must be protected by such safeguards as will assure his adoption by persons who profess and practise the religion of the child and who are of good moral character.

An Adoption Bill should contain such reasonable safeguards as will minimise the moral dangers that may arise as a result of adoption.

It is imperative that there should be supervision and control of all institutions holding children for adoption.

2. The Church regards the natural family as the ideal unit of family life and, therefore, must oppose any measure in an Adoption Bill that would tend to substitute an artificial for a natural family.[10]

The last remaining difficulty was cleared away by this statement, and Mr Boland now decided to introduce legislation himself.[11] During the drafting his department kept in close touch with the authorities of all denominations,[12] and in particular with those of the Catholic Church. The Archbishop of Dublin and his delegate, Father (now Monsignor) Cecil Barrett, went over every clause,[13] and the text of the bill bore out the closeness

10. *Ibid.*
11. He informed the Adoption Society of his intention on 28 January 1952. See Adoption Society (Ireland): Hon. Secretary's report for year ending 31 March 1952.
12. Consultation with minority denominations is shown by several references in Mr Boland's Dail speeches: *Dail Debates*, CXXXII, 1106 (11 June 1952). 1752 (26 June 1952); *ibid.*, CXXXIII, 826 (15 July 1952).
13. Information from the Archbishop of Dublin.

of the consultation, for regard was had to all the limits and safe-guards for which the committee of the hierarchy had asked. Adoption was restricted to illegitimate and orphan children between the ages of six months and seven years.[14] The adopting parents were to be 'of the same religion as the child and his parents or, if the child is illegitimate, his mother'.[15] The adminis-tering authority was, before authorising an adoption, to satisfy itself that 'the applicant is of good moral character, has sufficient means to support the child and is a suitable person to have parental rights and duties in respect of the child'.[16] Provision was made for the registration and supervision of adoption societies.[17] Perhaps the provision that adopting parents were to be of the same religion as the natural parents was the most important, because, in one stroke, it removed the bogey of proselytism. There could be no question of Protestant parents adopting Catholic children (or vice versa) and, since legal adoption has been established, proselytism has practically ceased to be an issue in Ireland.

Opinions can differ about the significance of this episode in Irish Church-State relations. On the one hand, it could be argued that it showed how an energetic pressure group could stimulate bishops as well as ministers into re-examining questions which they had hitherto been reluctant to handle. But on the other hand, there was no question of the hierarchy being obliged to accept a measure which it did not want. It was not opposed to legislation in principle, but was anxious only that certain safe-guards be included. The minister, for his part, did not even take the decision to legislate until the committee of the hierarchy had spoken, and closely consulted the Archbishop of Dublin during the drafting. The episode seems better evidence of the strength than of the limits of episcopal authority in Ireland.

The reader who has followed this chapter so far might, indeed, feel that the second de Valera government was remarkably cautious in handling matters of mixed concern to Church and State. In the social welfare and legal adoption questions, it seemed

14. Adoption Act 1952, sections 9 and 10.   15. *Ibid.*, section 12 (2).
16. *Ibid.*, section 13 (1).   17. *Ibid.*, sections 34–8.

K

anxious to remove any ground for complaint whether from the hierarchy or from other exponents of Catholic social teaching. However, it would not have been in line with party tradition if a Fianna Fail government had decided to settle all Church-State questions by simply conceding everything that was asked of it. And an account of developments in the field of health legislation will show that the government, though cautious, was not entirely complaisant.

The question of reshaping the health services was a complicated one. Indeed the incoming Minister for Health, Dr Ryan, had to face not so much one question as a series of interrelated ones. He had to decide what to do with the mother and child sections of the 1947 act, which had been the subject of protests from the hierarchy in 1947 and again in 1951, but which still remained on the statute book. He had to decide what to do with the Health Bill 1950, the measure which Dr Browne had introduced in order to remove the compulsory provisions from the mother and child sections of the Health Act 1947, but which had not yet reached its second reading. Finally, he had to decide whether to clear up the mother and child question alone, or whether, while he was about it, to legislate for other health problems as well.

Silence reigned for a considerable time about Dr Ryan's intentions. The planning that went on was purely departmental, and, unlike Dr Browne, Dr Ryan made no use of consultative councils in drafting his proposals. But at last, in July 1952, he issued a white paper outlining his intentions,[18] and in February 1953 he published the text of a health bill which gave those intentions a precise form.[19] As the white paper and the bill did not vary greatly from each other, it will be convenient to discuss their contents together.

These documents revealed that Dr Ryan had decided to tackle his problems on a broad front. They subsumed the provisions of the Health Bill 1950, included other provisions about mother and child welfare, and then went beyond to tackle a range of

18. Department of Health, *Proposals for Improved and Extended Health Services, July 1952.*
19. *Irish Times,* 9 Feb. 1953. The bill, though not printed till 1953, was known as the Health Bill 1952 because it had been formally introduced in 1952.

other health problems as well. Among a number of important provisions, two may be singled out as the most significant.

The first was a great increase in financial provision for hospital treatment. At this date two groups of hospital patients were entitled to free treatment. Those eligible for the medical assistance service, in other words the poorest thirty per cent or so of the population, received such treatment under legislation going back to the nineteenth century; and those suffering from tuberculosis and certain other infectious diseases received it under the Health Act 1947. All other hospital patients were liable to meet their full hospital bills from their own resources. But, with the introduction of much more efficient but also much more expensive methods of diagnosis and treatment, hospital costs were rising rapidly in the post-war years. Dr Ryan mentioned in 1953 that the cost to local authorities of paying for a hospital patient had risen since 1947 from £2.2.0 a week to £5.12.0 a week,[20] and the charges to paying patients had doubtless risen in proportion. The result was that more and more people who needed hospital treatment were finding difficulty in meeting the cost. There was probably no area of medical care where greater State aid was so urgently needed, and Dr Ryan accordingly proposed that large fresh groups of the population be entitled to receive hospital treatment either free or at much reduced rates. The effect of his proposals was to provide financial assistance towards the hospital bills of about eighty-five per cent of the Irish population.[21]

The other important feature of Dr Ryan's scheme was his revised proposals for mother and child welfare. His bill repealed the mother and child clauses (sections 21 to 28) of the Health Act 1947, and replaced them with sections that showed much more solicitude for individual rights. There was no longer any suggestion that local authorities were responsible for the health of mothers and children. The new measure said simply that local authorities would 'make available' the services required.[22] The white paper made clear that mothers would have a free

20. *Seanad Debates*, XLII, 600 (5 Aug. 1953).
21. B. Hensey, *The Health Services of Ireland*, 24.
22. Health Bill 1952, as introduced, sections 13-20.

choice of doctor, and that all qualified doctors would be eligible to participate in the service.[23] As a further guarantee, the bill stated that people were free to use the mother and child service (and all other services provided under the bill) or not to use them, as they wished. Section 4 of the bill laid down: 'Nothing in this Act or any instrument thereunder shall be construed as imposing an obligation on any person to avail himself of any service provided under this Act or to submit himself or any person for whom he is responsible to health examination or treatment.' There was only one important respect in which the provisions of the 1952 white paper resembled those of the 1947 act. This was that the mother and child service was to apply, free for all, to the entire population.[24] Dr Ryan justified this provision by referring to the frequent and recurring expenses of young married couples, even those who appeared to be well off. He mentioned that he had considered a means test at the level of £1,000 per annum, but had then reflected that so few couples would be above that level that he had decided to have no means test at all.[25]

Dr Ryan's proposals received an unfriendly reception from more than one quarter. Exponents of Catholic social teaching were almost unanimously critical. They saw in his plans an unwarrantable encroachment by the State beyond its proper sphere. The Catholic Societies Vocational Organisation Conference complained that the white paper disclosed a 'further intended encroachment by the State on functions which should be performed by subsidiary bodies'.[26] *An Rioghacht* declared that 'State Assistance where necessary should be of a supplemental nature and must never usurp the God given rights and responsibilities of parents', and warned that 'wholesale extension of State supplied (so called "free") Social and Medical Services is calculated to produce an insidious social anaemia which in time will destroy the will to practise the natural virtues'.[27] A contributor to the *Standard* argued that the white paper was 'based on the socialistic principles that it is better to provide for people's

---

23. Department of Health, *op. cit.*, 13.   24. *Ibid.*
25. See the report of a discussion between Dr Ryan and a deputation from the I.M.A., in *Journal of the Irish Medical Association*, Nov. 1952, 332.
26. *Standard*, 24 Oct. 1952.   27. *Ibid.*, 19 Dec. 1952.

needs than to make it possible for them to provide for themselves, and that the State has a primary right to "improve"
your health'.[28] The solutions preferred by these critics were a
resurrection of the Dignan plan, the provision of health services
by vocational organisations, or a voluntary health insurance
scheme.

The proposals also provoked fierce opposition from the Irish
Medical Association. The association objected to the extension of
State control, to the provision of free medical services for those
who could afford to pay, and to the absence of a statutory health
council which doctors and other interest groups could use as a
platform from which to give advice on the running of the health
services.[29] In support of its objections, the association now openly
sought ecclesiastical help. In 1950–1 it had been individual
doctors, not the association as such, who had approached the
bishops: in 1952–3 it was the association as a body which acted.
Sometime during this period a deputation from the I.M.A. met
the Archbishop of Dublin, Dr McQuaid;[30] and in March 1953,
after the publication of the bill, the association sent a formal
protest against it to the heads of all the Churches, drawn up in
language which closely followed the wording of the Catholic
bishops' protest against the mother and child scheme in 1951:

We, the members of the Irish Medical Association, desire to inform
the heads of all Churches that we unanimously reject the proposals
contained in the Health Bill, 1952, and refuse to co-operate should
the Bill become law, on the following grounds:

(i) This Bill signifies in its essence the State control of the medical
profession;

(ii) Under this scheme the State must enter unduly and very intimately into the life of patients and doctors;

(iii) In order to implement this Bill, the State must levy a heavy tax,
by direct or indirect methods, on the whole community, independently
of the desire or necessity of the citizens who will make use of the
facilities that may be provided;

28. 'A barrister' in *ibid.*, 14 Nov. 1952.
29. *Journal of the Irish Medical Association,* Nov. 1952, 328, 332.
30. Information from a member of the I.M.A. who was himself on the
deputation.

(iv) In implementing this Bill by taxation, direct or indirect, the State will in practice morally compel its citizens to avail of its services;

(v) In implementing this particular scheme the State must have recourse, in great part, to Ministerial Regulations, as distinct from enactments of the Oireachtas.[31]

The alternative which the association put forward was a voluntary health insurance scheme.[32]

The most formidable of Dr Ryan's critics, however, was the Catholic hierarchy. A word should be said here about the evidence for relations between hierarchy and government on this topic. Documentation, apart from what can be gleaned from Dail debates, is meagre. A rich oral folklore has grown up around what happened, but as a source it is quite unreliable. For a truthful account of this episode one is particularly dependent on interviews with participants. Fortunately, several of those most closely concerned have been kind enough to discuss these events with me, and in what follows I shall be relying, except where otherwise stated, on interviews with Dr James Ryan, the then Minister for Health, with the Most Reverend Dr Browne, Bishop of Galway, and with the Most Reverend Dr Lucey, Bishop of Cork.

The first move came at the end of July 1952, when Dr Ryan sent copies of his white paper to the heads of all religious denominations, including all the Catholic bishops.[33] Dr Ryan later stated that he saw one head of a Christian Church other than the Catholic,[34] but apart from this the minority denominations sent him only acknowledgements, and it was with the Catholic hierarchy that all consultations were conducted.

The hierarchy, at its October meeting, decided that the white paper was not satisfactory, and set up a committee to pursue the matter with the government. The committee, as first established, had Archbishop McQuaid of Dublin as its chairman, with Bishop Browne of Galway, Bishop Lucey of Cork, and Bishop Staunton of Ferns as members. At a later stage, when the Arch-

---

31. *Journal of the Irish Medical Association*, April 1953, 127.
32. Text in *ibid.*, Dec. 1951, 129 ff.
33. See Dr Ryan's statement in *Dail Debates*, CXXXVIII, 707 (23 April 1953).
34. *Ibid.*, 708. I believe this to have been Dr Barton, Church of Ireland Archbishop of Dublin.

bishop of Dublin was away in Australia, the chair was taken by Archbishop Kinane of Cashel. This committee had several meetings with representatives of the government. Dr Ryan later told the Dail: 'At one of these meetings with the Catholic hierarchy the Taoiseach was present; at another, the Tanaiste was present; and at some others, I was alone, that is, as far as members of the government are concerned.'[45]

The committee of the hierarchy secured one concession from the government. When the Health Bill was published in February 1953, it incorporated one significant change from the proposals of the white paper: the mother and child service was no longer to be provided free of charge to all sections of the community. Women in the higher income group (that is, roughly the richest fifteen per cent of the population) were to be entitled to use it only if they paid a small voluntary insurance contribution.[36] Dr Ryan later told the Dail that the Church had been one of the critics of his original proposal: 'It was opposed by the ecclesiastical authorities as giving a free service to people who could well afford to pay for it.'[37] The change was only a small one, and it could be argued that Dr Ryan had made it to meet the letter rather than the spirit of the bishops' objections. The charge was made by Fine Gael speakers. Mr Costello described Dr Ryan's concession as 'merely a fraudulent subterfuge to get over a moral objection'.[38] Mr Dillon (now once again a member of Fine Gael) asked, in his flamboyant way: 'Is this the Fianna Fail formula for external relations with Catholic morality? Is this the Fianna Fail method of purchasing orthodoxy with 20 pieces of silver?'[39] But whatever the taunts of the opposition, the hierarchy appears to have acquiesced in Dr Ryan's proposal, for it remained substantially unaltered through all the vicissitudes that the bill endured.[40]

---

35. *Ibid.*   36. Health Bill 1952, section 15 as introduced.
37. *Dail Debates*, CXXXIX, 1606 (18 June 1953).
38. *Ibid.*, CXXXVIII, 47 (15 April 1953).
39. *Ibid.*, CXXXVII, 1270 (25 March 1953).
40. Dr Ryan's original proposal was that the contribution from the members of the higher income group should be £1 per annum. He later moved amendments permitting him to fix the contribution at any figure not exceeding £2 per annum, so as to give himself more flexibility if the cost of the scheme proved greater than anticipated: *ibid.*, CXXXIX, 1226 (11 June 1953); CXLI, 1054 (30 July 1953).

However, though this was the only concession which the bishops appear to have secured between the publication of the white paper and the publication of the bill, it was not the only matter on which they felt concern. The committee of the hierarchy was anxious about the increase in State control which the measure appeared to bring with it. One point in particular which aroused its anxiety was the future of voluntary hospitals. The proposal to make local authorities pay the bills of a much larger proportion of hospital patients had, as a by-product, the effect of giving local authorities much more power over the hospitals. They could use their bargaining power to force changes in the running of such hospitals; they might even, by refusing to send patients, force a particular hospital to close down. As many voluntary hospitals were run by religious orders, the bishops naturally felt a concern for their welfare. Another point which alarmed them was a provision authorising local authorities to set up medical schools in hospitals under their care.[41] Dr Ryan later explained that the intention was only to allow post-graduate courses to be run in such hospitals,[42] but, as it stood, the measure appeared to authorise the invasion by the State of the field of medical education, which had hitherto been left to the universities.

On none of these points, however, did Dr Ryan appear ready to make definite concessions. After their last meeting with him, on 23 March 1953, the committee of the hierarchy felt that an impasse had been reached. A formal letter was written to the government stating that the matter was to be remitted to the general body of the bishops. This letter was intended as a warning that the committee of the hierarchy was not satisfied. Dr Ryan, however, did not realise that it was so intended. He believed at this stage that he had satisfied the bishops, and was surprised when it later appeared that he had not. And so both government and hierarchy moved forward on a collision course, each believing that its signals had been correctly interpreted by the other. The episode showed a curious inability to communicate with each other on the part of both ministers and bishops.

41. Health Bill 1952, section 57 as introduced.
42. *Dail Debates*, CXL, 1423 (16 July 1953).

Dr Noel Browne was not the only minister with whom this difficulty of communication arose.

The hierarchy discussed the issue at a special meeting held on 13 April 1953. The bishops now decided to issue a public letter, informing the faithful of their objections to the bill. It is sometimes surmised that the bishops on this occasion appealed to the public because in 1950–1 they had been criticised for acting in secret, and they wished to avoid being criticised on this ground again. I am informed, however, that this hypothesis is incorrect; the bishops had, after all, been negotiating in confidence up to this point, and if they now decided to publish their criticisms it was only because the negotiations had failed to produce satisfactory results. A letter was sent to the press on 17 April, over the signatures of the chairman and secretaries of the hierarchy. The recipient papers, according to a well-informed Fine Gael deputy, were the *Irish Independent,* the *Irish Press,* the *Standard,* and the *Irish Catholic.*[43] The *Irish Times,* it will be noticed, was not on the list: that paper was, after its attitude in 1951, in disgrace with the Catholic bishops.

The full text of the letter is too long to be quoted here, and will be found in Appendix C. However, its main points can be given at once. The letter started by saying that the bishops favoured the best possible health services, 'without unduly interfering with the rights of individuals, families, the medical profession, and voluntary institutions, and without unduly lessening personal responsibility and initiative'. It went on to acknowledge that the bill contained some improvements over the Health Act 1947. It repealed the mother and child sections to which the bishops had already objected, and the provisions for compulsory examination. Nonetheless, the hierarchy considered that, on three counts, the bill was contrary to Catholic teaching.

First, 'according to Catholic teaching each individual has the primary responsibility to provide for his own health and the father has the responsibility to provide for the health of his family'. The bill, on the other hand, 'proceeds on the assumption that the Public Authority is responsible for the treatment of all mothers in child-birth and for the institutional and specialist

43. *Ibid.,* CXXXIX, 889 (9 June 1953: statement by Mr P. McGilligan).

services for seven-eighths of the population'. This transfer of power to the State must lower the people's sense of responsibility and seriously weaken their moral fibre.

Second, 'it is a principle of Catholic teaching that the State should not assume immediate control in social and economic spheres except when it is clearly demanded by the common good'. The bill, however, extends considerably the already wide field of State-controlled medical services. Local administration is to be in the hands not of an independent local authority but of an official subordinate to the minister (by which the bishops meant, presumably, the county manager). The minister is given extremely wide regulation-making powers by which he could in time alter doctor-patient relationships, medical practice and hospital administration. The bill does not even guarantee the choice of doctor in the maternity service which was promised by the white paper. It tends towards the elimination of voluntary hospitals, and, by giving local authorities the right to maintain medical schools, it brings the State into medical education.

Third, 'the bill contains no safeguard that patients will not be obliged to accept treatment in obstetrics, gynaecology, psychiatry, from men who are imbued with materialistic principles or advocate practices contrary to the natural law'.

The bishops' letter contained points of very varying merit. Of their three main points, the second was the one which had most substance. The bill did indeed extend the scope of State-controlled medical services, and it was not self-evident that all the extensions were desirable. The degree of control left in the hands of the county manager was probably inevitable, given the structure of Irish local government, but it did mean that there would be less local autonomy in the running of the services than existed, for instance, under the British National Health Service. The regulation-making powers given to the minister were indeed extensive. It was difficult to see why the bill did not guarantee mothers a free choice of doctor when the white paper said that such a choice was intended. The lack of safeguards for voluntary hospitals, or the sweeping powers given to local authorities in the field of medical education, left the door open for abuse. In short, the health bill showed that the Department of Health, although chastened by its encounters with the hierarchy in 1947 and 1951, had by no means abandoned its 'bureaucratic' traditions. It still appeared to assume when drafting legislation that its officials knew best, that local authorities, voluntary institutions and the medical profession all needed careful watching, and that in the public interest, its hands should be tied as little as possible. It had still not grasped that, to many Irishmen, the greatest menace was not the selfishness of sectional interests but the power of a centralising government department, and that in their eyes, departmental powers needed to be defined just as strictly as those of any subordinate group.

The bishops' other points, however, seemed much more dubious. To take their third point next, it was not true that the bill contained no safeguard against patients being obliged to accept treatment from men 'who are imbued with materialistic principles or advocate practices contrary to the natural law.' Section 4 specifically provided that no one was to be obliged to avail himself of any service offered under the bill. It was difficult to see what more the bishops could want, unless they wished the State not to employ doctors at all without first screening them to make sure that their views coincided with those of the Church.

The first of their three points seemed equally hard to sustain. It was not true that the bill proceeded on the assumption that 'the Public Authority is responsible for the treatment of all mothers in child-birth and for the institutional and specialist services for seven-eighths of the population'. This would have been a valid criticism of the Health Act 1947, but it was not true of the Health Bill 1952 which was carefully worded so as to avoid such a criticism. All it did was to make available services which individuals could then accept or reject as they wished. Perhaps the bishops really meant something different. Perhaps they did not want these services to be offered at all; or perhaps they wanted them to be offered to some but not all of the classes that were being covered by the bill; or perhaps they wanted them to be offered on a different basis, such as in return for insurance contributions.[44] It is unfortunate that the bishops'

---

44. If their preference was for an insurance basis—and the comments of other exponents of Catholic social teaching might suggest that it was—then there were serious administrative objections to its adoption. For an analysis of such

letter was not worded so as to indicate more precisely where their objection lay.

If the hierarchy's letter had reached the public, it is unlikely, then, that it would have had such a telling effect as its authors evidently expected. Though it contained some valid criticisms, there were so many ambiguities and so many statements open to contradiction that the government would probably have had the better of any public controversy. From all this, however, the hierarchy was spared by the reaction of Mr de Valera. He was sent a copy of the bishops' letter twelve hours before the newspapers received theirs. His prompt reaction was that publication of the letter must be stopped. He discovered that the chairman of the hierarchy, Cardinal D'Alton, was administering confirmation at the southern end of his diocese, near Drogheda in county Louth. The President of Ireland, Mr Sean T. O'Kelly, acting as intermediary, telephoned the cardinal and asked him to accept a visit from Mr de Valera and Dr Ryan. On receiving his agreement, the Taoiseach and the Minister for Health drove up to Drogheda to ask Cardinal D'Alton to agree at least to a delay in the publication of the letter.

The question that arises here is: why was Mr de Valera so anxious that publication should be stopped? It may have been that, on a quick perusal of the bishops' letter, he decided that, in the event of a public controversy, the government's case would not be so overwhelming as to ensure a clear-cut victory. I have no evidence, however, that this calculation crossed his mind. The truth seems to have been that Mr de Valera was an old-fashioned Irish Catholic who found the idea of a public wrangle between politicians and the Church profoundly distasteful. Even during the Civil War of 1922–3, when he disagreed totally with the hierarchy's attitude, he had refrained from public controversy, and much more recently, after the mother and child scheme crisis of 1951, he had considered that Dr Browne

---

objections see the letter from the Secretary of the Department of Health to the Medical Secretary of the I.M.A., published in *Journal of the Irish Medical Association*, Sept. 1952, 274. This letter is immediately concerned with the I.M.A.s' voluntary insurance scheme, but many of its points would apply equally to any insurance scheme.

was wrong to publish his correspondence with the hierarchy.[45] Now the same outlook displayed itself again.

At the actual meeting with Cardinal D'Alton, two main arguments appear to have been used in support of the request that publication be suspended. One was that the bishops' letter contained incorrect statements which, if it were published, would have to be contradicted by the government. The other was that Mr de Valera had been away in Utrecht having eye treatment until only shortly before, and therefore needed time to become *au fait* with the points at issue. The first of these arguments was in effect a threat, and the second in effect a plea. It would be interesting, and it would shed light on the respective power of Church and State in Ireland, if we could say which of these two arguments was pressed more strongly in the conversation. This, unfortunately, is not a point on which my sources are agreed.

The sudden appearance of the two ministers, with their request that publication of the letter be delayed, put Cardinal D'Alton in a difficult position. The cardinal was only *primus inter pares* in the hierarchy. He had no authority to countermand a decision taken by the hierarchy as a whole. He managed, however, with some difficulty, to get through on the telephone to Archbishop Kinane of Cashel, the acting chairman of the committee which had been dealing with the matter, and after consulting him he decided that he could take it on himself to authorise the withdrawal of the hierarchy's letter. It was collected back from the newspaper offices on 19 April. In return for securing the withdrawal of the letter, the ministers promised further consultation with the episcopal committee.[46]

The further consultations took place, by courtesy of President O'Kelly, at Arus an Uachtarain (the presidential residence in Phoenix Park, Dublin) on 21 April. Mr de Valera and Dr Ryan were present for the government, and the members of the

45. So he told Dr Browne: M. McInerney, 'Dr. Noel Browne: a political portrait—5', *Irish Times*, 13 Oct. 1967.
46. In view of the Archbishop of Dublin's reputation for intransigence, it is worth pointing out that the crisis occurred while he was out of the country. In fact he has told me that, when he left, he believed discussions to be progressing satisfactorily, and that he learnt about the breakdown only after it had occurred. He has also pointed out to me that he personally has never broken with any minister or government.

episcopal committee for the hierarchy. My informants on both sides remember that agreement was quite quickly and easily reached. According to a note kept by one of the participants, six points were agreed on as follows:

1. The service should be decentralised and humanised, by more use of advisory councils.
2. Free choice of doctor.
3. Free choice of hospital.
4. Free choice of consulting specialist.
5. Medical 'courses' instead of medical 'schools'.
   [This was a reference to the power given to local authorities under the bill to set up medical schools.]
6. No one to be obliged to accept any teaching contrary to his faith.

The actual drafting of amendments to meet these points remained in the hands of the government, and no further meeting between ministers and the episcopal committee appears to have taken place.

Meanwhile, Ireland was agog with rumours. Even though the bishops' letter had been withdrawn, the fact that it had been issued could not be kept secret. Indeed it had been in the newspaper offices for long enough for copies to be made, and there were probably hundreds of people in Dublin who had seen it. The *Irish Independent* reported that rumour was circulating by the evening of 17 April[47]—that is, the day that the letter was sent to the press. When the Dail met again the following week, opposition deputies made determined efforts to extract from the government just what had happened. Mr McGilligan taunted the government with suppression, but Mr de Valera—who has always known how to give away nothing when he wishes—was at his most enigmatic:

Mr McGilligan: I want to know if the Taoiseach has caused to be delayed and attempted to have suppressed the document referred to?

47. *Irish Independent,* 22 April 1953.

The Taoiseach: The Taoiseach and the Government are conducting their business in the best public interest.

Mr McGilligan: I asked a simple question.

The Taoiseach: You will not get the answer from me.[48]

Dr Ryan was a little more explicit. In a characteristically low-key contribution, he described his encounters with the bishops in such a way as to rob the proceedings of drama and tension, and to imply that nothing more had happened than routine consultations with an interested body:

When the White Paper was issued in connection with this Bill I sent a copy of it to the heads of all Churches, including all bishops, both Catholic and Protestant. Subsequently, I met representatives of the Catholic hierarchy and a representative of one other Christian Church. At one of these meetings with the Catholic hierarchy the Taoiseach was present; at another, the Tanaiste was present; and at some others, I was alone, that is, as far as members of the government are concerned. I need hardly add that I would have been very pleased to meet representatives of other Churches if they so desired. I do not want to give the impression that I refused to meet any of them. As a result of those meetings, I am endeavouring to meet the wishes of the Catholic hierarchy in some of the amendments which I have already outlined. They have asked for the greatest possible freedom for the person availing of the provisions of the Bill, that is, a choice of doctor, a choice of hospital, and they are naturally solicitous lest any person would be obliged to accept treatment contrary to his religious beliefs. To cover this point, I shall propose an amendment by way of addendum to Section 4, that is, the point that no person will be obliged to accept treatment contrary to his religious teaching.

They also place great importance on the provision of consultative councils, both centrally and locally. Whatever our religious beliefs may be, whatever Party we belong to, I feel we can all subscribe to their advice on these matters.[49]

Further progress on the bill was delayed while the necessary amendments were prepared, but eventually, in June and July

48. *Dail Debates,* CXXXVIII, 577 (23 April 1953).
49. *Ibid.,* 707–8 (23 April 1953).

1953, committee stage was taken and the amendments passed. The bishops were not the only interest group whom the minister conciliated at this stage: other amendments were designed to meet points raised by the I.M.A.,[50] by the headmasters of secondary boarding schools,[51] and by critics in the Dail.[52] However, the amendments which were included wholly or partly in response to the wishes of the bishops can be easily isolated. They were as follows:

1. An addition was made to section 4 stating that no one using the services under the act need submit himself to any teaching which was 'contrary to the teaching of his religion'.[53] Dr Ryan, in moving the amendment, said that majority legal opinion considered it unnecessary, for the point was already covered by the existing wording of section 4, which provided that no one was obliged to submit to any treatment against his wishes; but 'on the other hand, we had certain people who were, if you like, nervous about the Bill from the religious point of view and as they were satisfied that this particular addendum would improve the sub-section, I saw no objection to adopting it'.[54]

2. An amendment was added to make clear that there would be a choice of doctor under the mother and child scheme.[55] This could be considered a drafting amendment, for, as the white paper had made clear, the intention all along had been that such a choice would be available. Nonetheless, it was a useful safeguard to have this intention clearly written into the act.

3. A section was added ensuring that people who made use of institutional services under the bill should have a choice of hospital.[56] As originally introduced, the bill envisaged that a patient would go to whichever hospital the local authority provided. To provide a choice for the patient marked a real

50. e.g. *ibid.*, CXXXIX, 1115 (11 June 1953: safeguarding payments to staff of voluntary hospitals); CXL, 1422 (16 June 1953: safeguarding doctors' right to use radio-active substances).

51. *Ibid.*, CXXXIX, 1652 (18 June 1953: exempting secondary schools from the medical examination service).

52. *Ibid.*, 1226 (11 June 1953: see above, note 40).

53. *Ibid.*, 780 (9 June 1953).   54. *Ibid.*, 788.

55. *Ibid.*, 1511 (17 June 1953).   56. *Ibid.*, 1693 (18 June 1953).

safeguard for liberty (and one which, incidentally, is not provided under the British National Health Service). This can be considered the most important of the amendments which the bishops' intervention secured.

4. The provision for a consultative National Health Council, which already existed under the Health Act 1947, was modified. Under the 1947 act, this council consisted entirely of members appointed by the minister. A section was now inserted in the Health Bill 1952 under which at least half the members of the council were to be nominated by the professional associations of the medical and ancillary professions.[57] The change, probably, was more apparent than real. The minister was in any case likely to consult professional associations in making his nominations. He still possessed the right to withdraw recognition from a professional association,[58] so control of who was nominated to represent the professions did not entirely pass from his hands.

The new section also laid down that the National Health Council was to meet at least once a quarter. This was perhaps the more important innovation, because it had hitherto met at the discretion of the minister and there had been long periods when it had not met at all.[59]

5. A new section was introduced to provide for consultative health committees to be attached to each local authority.[60] These consultative committees were to be local equivalents of the National Health Council, with power to advise on the local authority's operation of health services. They were not, however, to have any executive powers.

6. A new section was added affecting the compulsory detention provisions of the Health Act 1947. That act had allowed the Chief Medical Officer in a county or county borough to order the detention of someone whom he considered to be a source of infectious disease.[61] This could be criticised on the ground that it left drastic powers in the hands of a single official, and a provision was now introduced whereby such an order had to be counter-

57. *Ibid.*, 2057 (25 June 1953).   58. *Ibid.*
59. According to the *Journal of the Irish Medical Association*, April 1953, 120, the council had just had its third meeting in six years.
60. *Dail Debates*, CXXXIX, 2169 (25 June 1953).
61. Health Act 1947, section 38.

signed by another medical practitioner.[62] Dr Ryan, in introducing this section, did not say on whose suggestion he was acting; but I am informed that the suggestion came from the bishops.

This change has been of slight importance in practice, because the power of compulsory detention has hardly ever been used. In 1957 Dr Noel Browne asked the then Minister for Health how many people had been detained under the provisions of the Health Acts 1947 and 1953. The answer was—one.[63]

7. The section authorising local authorities to establish medical schools was amended so as to permit them to provide 'courses of instruction'. Dr Ryan, in moving this amendment, treated it as a matter of drafting, designed to allay a fear expressed by the Irish Medical Association that the preserve of the medical schools was about to be invaded.[64] But it is clear from what has already been said that the objection was also raised by the bishops.

Fortified by these amendments, the bill received no further opposition from the hierarchy. It passed through its remaining stages without serious trouble, and became law in October 1953.

So much for the course of events in 1953: now for their interpretation. What do they prove about the influence of the Catholic hierarchy in Ireland? This is a question which has received widely differing answers. On the one hand, some critics have accused Fianna Fail of in effect surrendering to the hierarchy. The charge was made by Mr Paul Blanshard in his book, *The Irish and Catholic Power*.[65] It was also made by Dr Noel Browne, in his interview of 1967 with Mr Michael McInerney of the *Irish Times*. Dr Browne, it should be explained before quoting from this interview, was in 1953 an independent deputy supporting the Fianna Fail government:

His first experience of Fianna Fail as an independent observer was pleasant and hopeful. It seemed that Fianna Fail was determined to implement its 1947 decision on the Mother and Child Scheme. The first proposals put before the Parliamentary Party on the scheme were

62. *Dail Debates*, CXXXIX, 2003 (24 June 1953).
63. *Ibid.*, CLXIV, 695 (20 Nov. 1957).
64. *Ibid.*, CXL, 1423 (16 July 1953).
65. P. Blanshard, *The Irish and Catholic Power*, 83.

radical. But when the Bill came up for its Committee Stage the amendments had completely garrotted the original proposals. It was clear that the compromise sought with the Bishops had little of the dialogue but much of the veto again. A means test was included 'secretly and behind closed doors' to use an Opposition description. It would seem that the Bishops had greater staying power than the politicians. There was no protest from the rank-and-file of the Party. . . .

Dr Browne has a bitter comment to make on the ultimate Mother and Child scheme: '. . . I understood that the original Ryan proposals were valuable and represented considerable advances on the existing services. As time went on I gathered that there was a repeat of the hierarchical opposition which I had myself experienced and to which Mr de Valera made substantial concessions. It would seem that Fianna Fail were quite prepared to stand up to the hierarchy on that peculiarly indefinable abstraction "The Republic" but that the lives of mothers and children in Ireland were not worth quarrelling with their Lordships about. Even a united Cabinet would not take on the bishops.'[66]

This interpretation, however, goes well beyond the evidence. To argue that the modifications to which the government agreed 'completely garrotted the original proposals' can hardly be sustained. Of the seven amendments just listed, numbers 1, 2 and 7 could be considered drafting amendments, which merely made explicit what had in any case been the government's intentions. Numbers 4, 5 and 6—those dealing with consultative bodies and with the countersigning of detention orders—made modifications in the structure of the services which could only be called minor. The most important was number 3, providing for a choice of hospital, but even that made no alteration to the basic principles of the act. The intention to give free maternity services, and free or heavily subsidised hospital services, to eighty-five per cent of the population remained unchanged.

Certainly the comments made by other critics of the bill showed that in their eyes the bishops had not made much improvement to it. The Irish Medical Association was particularly bitter. Its

66. M. McInerney, 'Dr. Noel Browne: a political portrait—4', *Irish Times*, 12 Oct. 1967.

published statements proclaimed its unaltered opposition to the measure,[67] and in private its leaders felt that, having been encouraged by the bishops in their opposition, they had now been let down.[68] Some of the exponents of Catholic social teaching also showed dissatisfaction. In July 1953, *Christus Rex* feared that the bill would pass with token amendments, sufficient to avert a condemnation but inadequate to meet the real objections to it.[69] In August, Father Felim O Briain, preaching in Galway cathedral to members of the Social Study Conference, said that the bill 'by no means conformed to Catholic morality, and our politicians, by ignoring many fundamental Catholic social principles, had prepared and supported a thoroughly immoral piece of social legislation'.[70] In the Dail, a specially persistent critic was Mr Patrick McGilligan of Fine Gael. He had acquired a copy of the hierarchy's letter of April 1953, and—more solicitous for the bishops than the bishops were themselves—tried repeatedly to show that the government's amendments did not adequately meet the hierarchy's objections.[71] There seems indeed to have been some resentment in Fine Gael at how lightly the bishops had let off the government. One prominent member of Fine Gael has remarked to me that the bishops appeared to accept from Fianna Fail things which they had refused to accept from the inter-party government.

It is not surprising, then, that many observers, far from seeing in the episode a victory for the bishops over Fianna Fail, have seen in it a victory for Fianna Fail over the bishops. This is the view which generally appears in the folklore: I have heard a number of versions of it in conversation, all of them inaccurate on some important point of fact. It has already found its way into print on at least one occasion, in the autobiography of Mr Brian Inglis, a journalist who at this period was working on the *Irish Times*. Mr Inglis writes:

67. e.g. *Journal of the Irish Medical Association*, June 1953, 190; *ibid.*, Aug. 1953, 27; *Irish Independent*, 3 Aug., 12 Oct. 1953.
68. Information from a doctor formerly prominent in the I.M.A.
69. Vigilans, 'As I see it', *Christus Rex* (VII, 3) July 1953, 626.
70. *Irish Independent*, 3 Aug. 1953.
71. *Dail Debates*, CXXXIX, 865 (9 June 1953), 1040 (10 June 1953), 1454, 1546 (17 June 1953).

The dispute arose when the Fianna Fail Government brought in its own Mother and Child Bill; not so obviously modelled on Bevan's as Browne's had been, but still Left enough to alarm the hierarchy. This time, the bishops drew up a formal statement of their disapproval, and issued it to the newspapers. Just before they went to press, the document was suddenly withdrawn. The reasons were not made public, but it was assumed that de Valera had issued an ultimatum: either the document must be withdrawn, in which case he would allow consultations with the hierarchy and try to meet their objections; or, he would treat it as a declaration of war. The bishops had apparently taken de Valera's refusal to try to make political capital out of the Browne affair as a sign that he was weakening; this intimation that he was ready to fight scared them off, for the chances were that on this issue he would win—and win or lose, the struggle would certainly promote the revival of anti-clericalism in Fianna Fail, many of whose leaders had memories of defying the hierarchy in the Troubles. Eventually a few amendments were made to the original Bill, designed to satisfy the hierarchy that Catholic social teaching was not being ignored or flouted. On examination they proved to be largely verbiage, making no serious alteration to the substance of the Bill; but the bishops allowed themselves to be convinced that their objections had been met.[72]

Mr Inglis's account illustrates how folklore has crept in. It does not seem that in reality Mr de Valera's conversation with Cardinal D'Alton at Drogheda contained anything so crude as an ultimatum. Nor does it seem fair to say that the bishops were scared off. And the amendments which they secured seemed more than mere verbiage to them: those members of the episcopal committee with whom I have discussed the matter are positive that they considered that the settlement was satisfactory and that their objections had been met. Nonetheless, despite its exaggerations, Mr Inglis's account seems a good deal closer to the truth than Dr Noel Browne's. To say that the agreed amendments made 'no serious alteration to the substance of the Bill' is much more accurate than to claim that they had 'completely garrotted the original proposals'. In the short run, at least, one can say that the government had the better of the contest.

Before making a final judgment, however, it is worth seeing

72. B. Inglis, *West Briton,* 204.

what happened in the longer run, and glancing at the development of Irish health services since 1953. Most of the services authorised by the Health Act 1953 were brought into force by ministerial regulation in March 1956,[73] and the act remained the basis of the Irish health services until the passage of the recent Health Act 1970. In one interesting area, however, the Health Act 1953 was never put into force. This was in the provision of mother and child services to the higher income group. Fianna Fail, it will be remembered, had originally proposed that the higher income group should receive these services free, on the same basis as the remaining eighty-five per cent of the population. Under pressure from the bishops, Dr Ryan had modified this proposal, and had agreed that members of the higher income group should be included within the scope of the mother and child service only on payment of a small insurance contribution.[74] But on the principle that they should be included he had not been prepared to yield. Yet, as things turned out, this provision, in defence of which Dr Ryan had shown such determination, was quietly abandoned; and, under the Health Act 1970, it has now been formally repealed.[75] It is worth examining how this has happened.

In the first place, responsibility rested with Dr Ryan's successor, Mr T. F. O'Higgins of Fine Gael, who was Minister for Health in the second inter-party government of 1954–7. Mr O'Higgins was interested in the possibilities of voluntary health insurance as a means of meeting the health needs of the higher-income group, and at the beginning of 1955 he set up an advisory body to go into the matter. Among the points which the advisory body was to investigate was the feasibility of including maternity benefit in a scheme of voluntary health insurance. If it did prove practicable to include such benefit, there would then be no necessity to implement the provisions of the Health Act 1953 on this matter.[76] As things turned out, the report of the advisory body showed that to include maternity benefit in a voluntary health insurance scheme would mean raising the premiums to unacceptable

73. *Report of the Department of Health, 1955–1956*, 20, 32.
74. See above, p. 283.
75. Sections 62 and 63.
76. *Dail Debates*, CLVI, 35–6 (10 April 1956: statement by Mr O'Higgins).

heights,[77] and so Mr O'Higgins was reluctantly obliged to exclude maternity from the scope of the scheme. But all this took time. The advisory body did not report until May 1956, and the minister did not announce his decision until November 1956.[78] A few weeks later the second inter-party government fell, and Fianna Fail returned to office.

The decision now rested with the new Minister for Health, Mr Sean MacEntee, whom we last met as Minister for Local Government and Public Health at the time of the Dignan plan. The country was now undergoing an economic crisis, and the government, far from being able to spare money for extended health services, had to retrench on those services which already existed.[79] In any case, Mr MacEntee's instincts were conservative, and during his first estimates speech, in reply to a plea by Dr Browne for the extension of no-means-test services, he defended means tests on principle. 'In the case of those who can afford to contribute something', he said, 'I think it is only right, just, fair and equitable that they should contribute. In the case of those who can afford to pay the whole cost of treatment, I think it is also only just, fair and equitable that they should pay the whole cost, so as to lighten the burden on the community and make those services more readily available to those who are in dire need of them.'[80] As Mr MacEntee held the portfolio of health from 1957 to 1965, this meant that a long period ensued in which there was no likelihood of health services being extended to the higher income group.

By the time Mr MacEntee retired, what had once been a financial expedient had become a matter of departmental principle. The next Minister for Health, Mr Donogh O'Malley, said that 'such a health service as existed in Britain would not be suitable in this country in toto. He believed the vast majority of the people were against completely socialised medicine. Those who could

77. A majority of the advisory body actually advised in favour of including maternity benefit: see *Advisory Body on Voluntary Health Insurance Scheme. Report*, 10–11. But their calculations were effectively controverted in a minority report: *ibid.*, 27–8.
78. *Dail Debates*, CLX, 663 (7 Nov. 1956).
79. *Report of the Department of Health, 1957–1958*, 68.
80. *Dail Debates*, CLXIII, 131 (26 June 1957).

pay should pay'.[81] His successor, Mr Sean Flanagan, was even more definite. He was against large extensions of the health services, 'not because we are afraid to raise the money, but because we see no justification for such an extension'. He explained that he saw no reason why it should be accepted that it was the duty of the State to organise the provision of all health services for all the people—any more than it had a duty to organise free transport or free bread for all. 'Our health policy has been, is, and will be based on a different philosophy and one, I think, which is more in accord with our national tradition.'[82]

One might question the antiquity of the national tradition to which Mr Flanagan referred. It had not apparently been discovered by Fianna Fail in the period 1947–53. But this is what makes his statement interesting. Mr Flanagan's language was closer to that of the bishops of fifteen years earlier than it was to that of Fianna Fail ministers of fifteen years earlier. In face-to-face negotiations with the government of 1953 the bishops had suffered something approaching a defeat, but over a longer period their warnings seem to have made more impression. When seen over a perspective of two decades, the bishops' intervention looks less ineffective than it appeared at the time.

This brings to an end our account of the long-drawn-out controversy between the hierarchy and successive governments over the shaping of health services in Ireland. This controversy, which originated with the hierarchy's protest against the Health Act 1947, marks the most important encounter between Church and State to have occurred in independent Ireland, and some general comments on it would be in order.

One obvious remark is that it is surprising to find a Catholic hierarchy concerning itself with such an issue. Questions of this nature are not generally considered to be within the province of Catholic bishops, either by the world in general or by Catholic bishops themselves. I have not come across any other instance in which a Catholic hierarchy has sought to influence the precise provisions of a country's social services. That it should have happened in Ireland in the years after 1947 can be explained only

81. *Irish Press*, 25 Feb. 1966.
82. *Irish Times*, 18 April 1967.

by reference to the special circumstances of the country and period. The Catholic social movement had come late to Ireland, and it had got under way at a time when its most characteristic idea was the principle of vocational organisation, advocated in the papal encyclical *Quadragesimo Anno* of 1931. This idea—put forward with the circumstances of countries very different from Ireland in mind—was taken up by the Irish pioneers of social catholicism, and applied with more enthusiasm than discretion to the circumstances of their own country. The fruit of their enthusiasm was found in two documents published in 1944, the Vocational Organisation Report and the Dignan plan. But, as soon as their ideas had been worked out in detail, they began to arouse resistance among ministers and civil servants, who felt their established 'bureaucratic' patterns of work to be under threat. To the enthusiasts for Catholic social teaching this seemed like sinning against the light. They saw Catholic officials in a Catholic country refusing to accept what they believed to be the implications of Catholic teaching. The result was that they redoubled their efforts to secure acceptance of their point of view. Although on any objective view there were much more serious social evils in Ireland—such as the inability of many thousands of Irishmen to gain a living in their own country—the Catholic social movement in Ireland during the late forties and early fifties became almost exclusively preoccupied with the problem of State power.

Yet, when all this is said, there is another and equally surprising feature about these events. This was that the concessions which the Catholic hierarchy extracted from the Department of Health had not been granted long before. For anyone who examines the concessions secured by the hierarchy will, I think, agree that they were moderate and generally beneficial. The most controversial was the exclusion of the richest fifteen per cent of the population from the scope of the free mother and child service, which may have been unpalatable to some who dislike means tests on principle. But it did at least mean that State aid was more closely directed to those who needed it most, and it has been accepted without protest by the excluded fifteen per cent. Other points secured by the hierarchy would seem wholly unexceptionable. No one could object to free choice of doctor being written into the act, or to free choice of hospital being conceded, or to the machinery for consultation with interested groups being strengthened. Yet the centralising, bureaucratic tradition of the Department of Health was so strong that successive ministers proved reluctant to accept even a slight decentralisation of power. Pleas from other quarters—doctors, publicists, other politicians—were brushed aside, and it needed the intervention of the most prestigious body in Irish society—the Catholic hierarchy—to secure such changes. If, on the one hand, it is surprising that the hierarchy intervened on a subject such as health services, it is on the other hand surprising that it had such occasion to intervene.

The hierarchy's action is more open to criticism in detail than in principle. For there can be no doubt that the bishops failed to make the best of their case. Their objections to Dr Browne's mother and child scheme could not wholly stand up to scrutiny, as the course of subsequent controversy showed. Their objections to the health bill in 1953 contained ambiguities and errors, and would probably have carried as little conviction with the general public had not Mr de Valera, by securing the suppression of their letter, spared them the humiliation of its public dissection. The Catholic social movement in Ireland was still at an adolescent stage. First principles were still being applied too enthusiastically to particular situations without rigorous examination of the logic. The result was that, when the bishops started pronouncing on questions of social ethics, their arguments too often lacked cogency.

CHAPTER X

OLD ATTITUDES FACE INCREASING RESISTANCE,
1953–9

The half-dozen years following the Health Act of 1953 provide a considerable amount of material for the study of Church-State relations. Public interest in the subject had been aroused by the dramatic clash of 1951 and the more smothered crisis of 1953, and any episode which might illustrate the hierarchy's attitude to public affairs was likely to be well reported. The difficulty in discussing these years is not dearth of material but the lack of an obvious linking theme. Issues came up of a sharply disparate nature, ranging from licensing laws through higher education to the ethics of boycotting. Another factor making for incoherence was the unusual instability of government which occurred in these years. The Fianna Fail government which took office in 1951 lasted only until 1954, when it was replaced by the second inter-party government under Mr John A. Costello. That in its turn lasted only until 1957, when Fianna Fail returned to office. After a further two years, Fianna Fail changed leaders: Mr de Valera became President of Ireland, and Mr Sean Lemass took over as Taoiseach. Nonetheless, despite the variety of issues that arose, and the number of different governments which had to deal with them, one or two common themes in this period can be detected.

One feature of the years 1953–9 is the continuity with previous periods shown in the subject-matter of episcopal pronouncements. To judge by their public statements, most of the bishops were still preoccupied with the same kind of topic as had concerned them in previous years, and their attitudes on these topics had not changed. Indeed, the choice of subject sometimes showed a harking back, not just to the immediate past, but to the Ireland of pre-war days. The dance-hall evil, for instance, which had been

303

so often denounced by the bishops in the nineteen-twenties and thirties, reappeared as a subject for episcopal warnings in the early fifties. In August 1953, Archbishop Walsh of Tuam instructed his people that, as from 1 October 1953, all dance-halls in his diocese, whether or not in the control of the clergy, should close not later than midnight in winter and 1 a.m. in summer.[1] Similar regulations were issued in other dioceses.[2] It was natural that the subject should have come to the fore again at this period: the end of petrol-rationing, and the increasing number of cars on the road, made possible a revival in the dance-hall industry. What is interesting is that the bishops should have dealt with the question exactly as they had done two or three decades before—by direct instruction to their people, laying down precise hours for dancing—and that they should have been confident that such instructions would be obeyed.

Another feature of the nineteen-fifties that must have reminded Irishmen of pre-war days was the reappearance of controversial statements by bishops on foreign affairs. During the 1939-45 war rigorous censorship had prevented everyone, bishops included, from making controversial statements, and during the cold-war period that followed Irishmen were so united on the iniquity of the communist persecution of the Church in eastern Europe that there was little scope for disagreement. But as the fifties wore on, and issues became less clear-cut, so there was more room for difference of opinion, and some of the Irish bishops distinguished themselves, as had their predecessors at the time of the Spanish Civil War, for a somewhat simplistically anti-communist point of view. Bishop Browne of Galway, returning from a visit to the United States in 1953, expressed the opinion that Senator Joe McCarthy, whose techniques for exposing communists were then arousing so much controversy, was not a mere witch-hunter and had been unjustly criticised.[3] Bishop Lucey of Cork, the following

---

1. *Irish Catholic Directory, 1954,* 727 (under date 30 Aug. 1953).
2. An instruction for the diocese of Galway laid down similar hours for that diocese, and stated that this brought it into line not only with the diocese of Tuam, but also with Achonry, Elphin and Killala: *Irish Weekly Independent,* 10 Sept. 1953. The following Lent, the pastoral of the Coadjutor-Bishop of Killaloe referred to a law concerning hours of dancing being recently introduced in that diocese: *ibid.,* 4 March 1954.
3. *Ibid.,* 27 Aug. 1953.

year, expressed a similar opinion.[4] In 1958, the action of the Irish delegation at the United Nations in voting for consideration of Communist China's entry into the organisation drew a rebuke from Cardinal D'Alton, who declared that Catholic Ireland was strongly opposed to the recognition of Red China.[5]

On one or two issues the outlook of the hierarchy seemed even to harden during these years. An example can be found in its attitude to Trinity College, Dublin. The Irish hierarchy, as explained in a previous chapter, had a long-standing, and historically well-founded, distrust of Trinity as a university which was by tradition a bulwark of Protestant ascendancy in Ireland, and the bishops had, in the statutes of successive National Councils, discouraged Catholics from attending it.[6] The National Council of 1927, for instance, passed the following statute:

Non-Catholic Colleges, inasmuch as they are intrinsically dangerous to faith and morals, remain under the ban of the Church. Since there are within the Irish Free State three University Colleges sufficiently safe in regard to faith and morals, we, therefore, strictly inhibit, and under pain of grave sin, we forbid priests and all clerics by advice or otherwise, to recommend parents or others having charge of youth to send the young persons in their charge to Trinity College. Likewise, we forbid priests and clerics to recommend young people themselves to attend Trinity College.[7]

It will be noted, however, that though this statute implied the strongest disapproval of Trinity College, and though it expressly forbade clerics to encourage the attendance there of Catholic students, it stopped just short of explicitly forbidding Catholic students to attend, and in fact a number of lay Catholics continued to enter Trinity as students.

The first tightening of the screw occurred in 1944, when Dr McQuaid, Archbishop of Dublin, included the following section in the diocesan regulations which he issued at the beginning of each Lent:

4. *Ibid.,* 1 April 1954.   5. *Ibid.,* 2 Oct. 1958.
6. See above, p. 18. See also Statute no. 335 of the National Council of 1875, and Statute no. 491 of the National Council of 1900.
7. Statute no. 404. English translation from the lenten pastoral of Archbishop Byrne of Dublin, 1930, as quoted in *Catholic Bulletin* (XX, 4) April 1930, 359.

Parents have a most serious duty to secure a fully Catholic upbringing for their children, in all that concerns the instruction of their minds, the training of their wills to virtue, their bodily welfare and the preparation for their life as citizens.

Only the Church is competent to declare what is a fully Catholic upbringing: for, to the Church alone which He established, Our Divine Lord, Jesus Christ, has given the mission to teach mankind to observe all things whatsoever He has commanded (St. Matthew, xxviii, 20). Accordingly, in the education of Catholics, every branch of human training is subject to the guidance of the Church, and those schools alone which the Church approves are capable of providing a fully Catholic education.

Therefore the Church forbids parents and guardians to send a child to any non-Catholic school, whether primary or secondary or continuation or university. Deliberately to disobey this law is a mortal sin, and they who persist in disobedience are unworthy to receive the Sacraments.

Any priest subject to our jurisdiction, who in any way assists in sending a Catholic to be educated in a non-Catholic educational establishment in this diocese is, by the fact, visited with grave penalties.

No Catholic may enter the Protestant University of Trinity College without the previous permission of the Ordinary of the Diocese. Any Catholic who disobeys this law is guilty of mortal sin and while he persists in disobedience is unworthy to receive the Sacraments. In this Diocese, it is reserved to the Archbishop to grant permission to attend Trinity College. Permission is given only for grave and valid reasons and with the addition of definite measures, by which it is sought adequately to safeguard the Faith and practice of a Catholic student.[8]

For the first time, a Catholic bishop had expressly forbidden Catholic laymen to enter Trinity without his permission. The fact that the diocese concerned was the largest in the country, and that its geographical location made it the principal reservoir of potential students for Trinity, made the prohibition doubly important.

However, the prohibition still applied only to one diocese. It was possible for Catholics from other dioceses to argue that

8. *Irish Catholic Directory, 1945,* 674 (20 Feb. 1944).

Dr McQuaid did not reflect the thinking of the hierarchy as a whole, and that they were still free to enrol in Trinity if they wished. It was not until 1956 that this comforting argument was undermined. The National Council of that year passed the following statute on the subject of Trinity College:

We forbid under pain of mortal sin:

1. Catholic youths to frequent that College;

2. Catholic parents or guardians to send to that College Catholic youths committed to their care;

3. Clerics and religious to recommend in any manner parents or guardians to send Catholic youths to that College or to lend counsel or help to such youths to frequent that College.

Only the Archbishop of Dublin is competent to decide, in accordance with the norms of the instructions of the Holy See, in what circumstances and with what guarantees against the danger of perversion, attendance at that College may be tolerated.[9]

Henceforward the ban was explicit for all dioceses, and the fact that the Archbishop of Dublin was appointed to deal with requests for permission to enter Trinity from all over the country meant that uniformity in enforcing the regulations was ensured. In practice, dispensations have been quite frequently given, and the law is less draconian in operation than it appears in print; but the point remains true that it was in the nineteen-fifties that the Catholic hierarchy's legislation concerning Trinity took on its severest form.

Another familiar theme in episcopal statements during these years was the suspicion of increasing State control, which had been so obvious during the preceding period as well. Cardinal D'Alton told a congress at Sligo in 1954 that it was wrong for a man to depend on the State for his needs if he could avoid it.[10]

---

9. Statute no. 287. English translation from an article by Archbishop McQuaid in *Sunday Independent*, 12 Feb. 1967. The statutes of 1956 came into force in 1960: *Irish Catholic Directory 1961*, 694 (15 Aug. 1960).

10. *Irish Weekly Independent*, 15 July 1954.

Bishop Browne of Galway spoke in 1955 of the Church being the principal bulwark against totalitarianism.[11] Bishop Lucey of Cork told a Glasgow audience in 1956 that socialism was the real enemy to be watched.[12] Archbishop McQuaid of Dublin in the same year criticised those who 'have given themselves the vocation to manage us like children'.[13]

This episcopal suspicion of encroachments by the State was best illustrated by a controversy that arose during 1955. In the summer of that year Mr James Dillon, Minister for Agriculture in the second inter-party government, announced plans for the reorganisation of higher agricultural education in Ireland. The trend in Ireland until that time had been towards a proliferation of agricultural faculties. University College Dublin had a large faculty of agriculture; Trinity College Dublin had a small one; University College Cork had a faculty of dairy science; and University College Galway, which still had nothing, was agitating for a faculty of its own.[14] Mr Dillon proposed to reverse this process of dispersion. His plan provided that agricultural students should go first to the university college of their choice, for two years of 'fundamental scientific education', but that for the remaining two years of their course they should all come together at a single Agricultural Institute. Mr Dillon argued that this was the best way of ensuring quality. 'It was manifest', he said, 'that we had not available the trained personnel to man four faculties of agricultural science adequately, and that the only consequence of attempting to do this would be to leave us with four inadequate faculties of agricultural science instead of one good centre of agricultural education and research.'[14a] The new institute was to have as much autonomy as the universities,[15] and the universities and the farming organisations were to nominate a majority of its governing body.[16] Mr Dillon has told me in interview that the model which he had in mind was the Dutch

---

11. *Ibid.*, 26 May 1955.   12. *Standard*, 23 Nov. 1956.
13. *Irish Weekly Independent*, 24 May 1956.
14. See report of a meeting at University College Galway to appeal for the establishment of an agricultural faculty: *Irish Times*, 19 July 1955.
14a. Interview in *Irish Independent*, 20 July 1955.
15. Speech by Mr Costello at *Muintir na Tire* rural week: *Irish Times*, 15 Aug. 1955.
16. *Irish Times*, 16 Aug. 1955.

agricultural university at Wageningen, which has done so much to make Dutch agriculture the most efficient in the world. Mr Dillon's proposals, however, met with a great deal of opposition. The principal critics were the universities, and organisations representing the farmers such as the newly-founded and rapidly-growing National Farmers' Association. Their grounds for objection were numerous. The scheme would be unnecessarily expensive.[17] The students would be removed from the cultural atmosphere of the universities, and given a purely technical training.[18] The concentration of students in a single centre took no account of regional variations in Irish agriculture.[19] There had been insufficient consultation with the interests affected.[20] The government's financial control was too close, and would be used to strangle initiative.[21]

So far, there would seem to have been nothing specifically religious about the opposition to Mr Dillon's plan. It represented the reaction of interest groups in almost any country when they find a government moving into what they consider their territory. It is an interesting coincidence that the Agricultural Institute controversy in Ireland came only a year after the Crichel Down episode in England, where it was the British Ministry of Agriculture that was in the dock, and where the basic issue—the claim that a government department was going beyond its legitimate sphere—was somewhat similar. But what differentiated the two countries was the kind of argument which opponents of the two government departments invoked in their support. In England critics of the Ministry of Agriculture in the Crichel Down affair appealed to constitutional theory, and the argument was conducted in terms of concepts such as ministerial responsibility.[22] In Ireland, critics of the equivalent department appealed to Catholic social teaching, and the argument revolved round concepts such as subsidiary function.

17. *Irish Farmers' Journal*, 23 July 1955.
18. Letters from Dr Alfred O'Rahilly in *Irish Independent*, 26 July and 7 Sept. 1955.
19. *Ibid.*, 26 July 1955.
20. *Ibid.*, 26 July 1955; statements by Mr P. I. Meagher and Mr H. Meredith in *Irish Times*, 28 and 30 July 1955.
21. *Irish Farmers' Journal*, 20 Aug. 1955.
22. R. D. Brown, *The Battle of Crichel Down, passim.*

L

An advantage of the use of such language was that opponents of the government's plans could mobilise bishops to speak on their behalf. Archbishop Walsh of Tuam said at a meeting in Galway that he had 'no confidence in any institute established in Dublin to direct agricultural activities in Ireland'.[23] Bishop Browne of Galway argued that the institute would not be autonomous and added that 'it was entirely wrong that the State should take over education at university level'.[24] Bishop Lucey of Cork was particularly eloquent, and, since his remarks show well how the terminology of Catholic social teaching could be applied to the question, he is worth quoting in some detail. At a meeting in Cork he said:

The accepted principle is that in agriculture as in industry, commerce and professions, etc., the proper function of the State is to help the private citizen and his organisations rather than to edge them out with its own agencies. If, then, an institution like a University can cater for agricultural education and research with State aid, or if an independent Institute can do so, the State should use these instead of taking control itself.

The people of this country would vote down a government that openly committed itself to a policy of Socialisation. But Socialisation can be a gradual, hidden and undeclared process. One Department after another can nibble more and more from the field of private enterprise until finally little worthwhile remains outside civil service control. That is why it is so necessary to examine the proposed Institute and see if it be part of the larger trend or movement towards out-and-out Statism.

The State has made no frontal attack on the autonomy of the Universities. But it has begun to supersede them a little by the creation of the higher Institutes. There are two already,[25] and now there is to be a third. But we are assured that the proposed Institute of Agriculture will not be a State-run body. The basis for this assurance is that the Governing Body of the Institute will have only ten out of its 35 members nominated by the government. But what are the facts?

23. *Irish Times*, 19 July 1955.
24. *Irish Independent*, 7 Sept. 1955.
25. Dr Lucey was presumably referring to the Dublin Institute for Advanced Studies and the Institute for Industrial Research and Standards.

The Governing Body is scheduled to meet only three times a year. It will have no funds at its disposal save what the Government decides to give it. It will neither appoint nor control the Director. He will be a Government nominee who will administer the Institute and preside at its every meeting. In a word, the Governing Body, so called, will not be the real governing authority in the Institute at all. Significantly enough, in the draft Bill the section dealing with the Director is put before that dealing with the Governing Body. There is no doubt in the minds of the drafters as to who is the more important—Director or Governing Body. . . .

I suggest that the Institute be made a really autonomous body; that it should have control of the advisory services now operated by the department; that it should stand in the same relationship to the universities for the theory and practice of agriculture as the General Medical Council does for medicine; and that each of the university colleges have a faculty of agriculture—each faculty, however, being 'slanted' towards, and specialising in, the branch of agriculture proper to the province.[26]

Faced with opposition on such a scale, Mr Dillon had no alternative but to withdraw his proposals and put forward a more modest scheme.[27] It was this scheme which, with few modifications, was passed into law by the ensuing Fianna Fail administration in 1958.[28] Under the revised proposals, all suggestion that the Agricultural Institute should be a teaching body was dropped. It has become a body for the co-ordination of research, on the lines of the Agricultural Research Council in Britain, and agricultural education in Ireland continues to be the task of the universities.

The Agricultural Institute affair was not directly a clash between Church and State. The scheme could not operate without the good will of the universities and the organised farmers, so the opposition of these two interests was by itself enough to defeat Mr Dillon's plans. But the fact that bishops were prepared to speak out on such a matter illustrated their continuity in attitude: it showed that they maintained the 'high' view of their role in

26. *Irish Times*, 17 Sept. 1955.
27. For the clearest account of these events see *Seanad Debates*, XLVIII, 1257–61 (12 Dec. 1957: speech of Mr de Valera on second reading of Agricultural Institute Bill).
28. Agriculture (An Foras Talúntais) Act 1958.

Irish society which had been illustrated by their opposition to various health schemes in the years 1947–53.

The most uncompromising expression of this 'high' view of the bishops' role can be found in a speech made by Bishop Lucey of Cork to the Christus Rex congress in 1955. He was reported as saying:

The Church was not just one group among the many groups making up the State, but had a firmer and broader basis than any of them. Thus it was that when the bishops in this country took a stand not so long ago on the Health Bill, they were not acting as a mere pressure group: they were not exercising the democratic right they undoubtedly had as citizens to make representations directly to the Government. They intervened on the higher ground that the Church is the divinely appointed guardian and interpreter of the moral law, and that the proposed Bill was in certain essential respects at variance with that law, so that it was their duty as bishops and officers of the Church to oppose the Bill.

In a word their position was that they were the final arbiters of right and wrong even in political matters. In other spheres the State might for its own good reasons ignore the advice of the experts, but in faith and morals it might not.[29]

The crucial sentence here was the statement that the bishops were 'the final arbiters of right and wrong even in political matters', which, if left without qualification, might be taken as a claim to far-reaching rights of interference in the whole field of public affairs. Dr Lucey's speech drew an angry rejoinder from one member of the Dail, who wrote to the *Irish Times*:

As a member of Dail Eireann, I was absolutely horrified at the Most Reverend Dr Lucey's speech in Killarney, wherein he stated that 'the Bishops were the final arbiters of right and wrong *even in political matters*'.

I am a Catholic, and perhaps not an outstanding one either, but I certainly deny the Bishop of Cork's right to make this statement. I do not accept it, and there are many more like me throughout the country.

29. *Irish Times*, 13 April 1955.

If his Lordship had stated that where, in the opinion of the bishops, a question of faith and morals was involved, they had every right to express themselves, I would agree, but otherwise they have no right whatever to interfere in matters of a political nature. . . .

I, as a member of the Dail, neither now or at any other time in the future will accept dictation from the bishops, or from a bishop, on matters of a political nature; and, even if it meant retiring from public life as a result of making a stand on this question, I would gladly do so.

Unfortunately these fighting words were belied by the end of the letter. He concluded: 'I am not signing my name to this letter, because I do not want to finish my political career before it starts. . . . I hate but one thing, hypocrisy! Yours, etc. "Quo Vadis".'[30]

One might well conclude that, if the only politician to protest against Dr Lucey's statement felt obliged to hide behind a *nom-de-plume*, the bishop's claim was acquiesced in by the majority of Irish politicians. It was left to Dr Lucey himself, at a later date, to make the necessary qualifications. In his lenten pastoral of 1957 he wrote:

The power of the Pope, the bishops and the clergy, though great, is limited. In the first place they do not so much lay down the law as interpret the law that God has laid down; thus their power really amounts to little more than pointing out to people the obligations that are already theirs. Secondly, they have no sanctions at their disposal other than those of a religious or moral nature to enforce their ruling—the Church has no physical means of coercing governments, the professions or anyone else. Thirdly, their power extends only to the religious and moral implications of what goes on—the Church has no competence to control public affairs itself or indicate the practical ways and means of dealing with current public problems. Finally, the Church no more supersedes the individual conscience in public life than it does in private life.[31]

From the anthology of episcopal statements so far given, one might draw the conclusion that the atmosphere in Ireland during the period covered by this chapter was the same as in preceding

30. *Ibid.*, 16 April 1955.   31. *Ibid.*, 4 March 1957.

years, and that bishops could stress the same themes with the same degree of acquiescence from public opinion as they had previously secured. This, however, would not be entirely accurate. For another feature of these years was a mounting criticism of, and resistance to, hitherto accepted attitudes.

To a small extent the change can be seen even within the hierarchy itself. One new recruit to the hierarchy during these years attracted attention for the fresh ground that he broke. This was the Most Reverend William Philbin, Bishop of Clonfert from 1954 to 1962 and Bishop of Down and Connor since 1962. Things have been changing so rapidly in Ireland in the past few years that, by the time of writing, Dr Philbin has come to be regarded as a conservative; but in the nineteen-fifties his speeches and articles on social questions attracted interest because of their originality of theme. One example may be given by way of illustration. Speaking in 1956 at a meeting to commemorate the encyclicals *Rerum Novarum* and *Quadragesimo Anno,* Dr Philbin stated that he did not propose to contribute a further discussion of those encyclicals' content. There was another way, he said, of honouring them: it was to ask 'whether there are not aspects of economics, other than those dealt with magisterially in the encyclicals, about which religion and morality should also have something to say'. He went on: 'The social encyclicals presuppose that the machinery of production is efficient and that its output is being disposed of advantageously. They set out the principles governing the just division of the accruing profit as between employers and employed.' But, he pointed out, other difficulties too can beset economies, and in Ireland at that stage the most important problems were low productivity, high emigration, and an adverse balance of trade. The contribution which religion might make, he suggested, was to inculcate the virtues of hard work and forethought, on which the country depended for economic progress.[32]

---

32. Most Rev. William Philbin, 'The religious incentive in economics', *Rural Ireland,* 1957, 17–22. For other papers by Dr Philbin on social questions, see: 'Government by the people', *Studies* (XLVII, no. 187) Autumn 1958, 233–46; Patriotism and the faith: landmarks and horizons', *Christus Rex* (XIII, 4) Oct. 959, 231–43; and the following pamphlets: *Patriotism* (1958); *Neighbourliness* 1958); *The Irish and the New Europe* (1962).

This might not seem an earth-shaking conclusion to reach, but it had its novelty at the time. For a bishop to read an entire paper on a social topic without once denouncing the excessive power of the State was at that date unusual. For him to suggest that all the answers to economic problems might not be found in *Rerum Novarum* or *Quadragesimo Anno* was unusual also. Ireland would have been spared a great deal of unnecessary controversy, and a great deal of energy expended on minor issues might have been devoted to more important ones, if such reflections had been commoner over the preceding ten years.

It is outside the hierarchy, however, rather than inside it, that evidence for new attitudes during these years is most easily found. One excellent illustration of the clash between old attitudes and new is provided by the history of the Censorship of Publications Board. The board, as was explained in an earlier chapter, was established under an act of 1929 and empowered to ban books and periodicals which it considered indecent or obscene.[33] An amending act in 1946 introduced some modifications in the law, including the establishment of an Appeal Board;[34] but this was only a minor landmark in the censorship's history. The major turning-points are marked not by legal changes but by changes in the tides of opinion, both among the general public and within the board itself. Thanks to a recent excellent book by Dr Michael Adams, these tides of opinion can now readily be charted. In the nineteen-thirties, according to Dr Adams, the censorship aroused no great controversy, and such criticism as there was came as much from those who considered it too lax as from those who considered it too severe.[35] It was during the nineteen-forties that criticism of the board for excessive severity began to mount.[36] As if in reaction, the Censorship Board became even stricter, and the number of books banned, which had averaged a little over a hundred a year during the thirties, reached a peak during the years 1950–55, when it averaged over six hundred a year.[37] Among the authors who had titles banned were some of the most celebrated figures in modern literature: André Gide, Jean-Paul Sartre, Ernest Hemingway, John Steinbeck, Tennessee

33. See above, p. 37.   34. Censorship of Publications Act 1946.
35. M. Adams, *Censorship*, 71–80.   36. *Ibid.*, 81–98, 146, 249–50.
37. Figures calculated from *ibid.*, 119, 243.

Williams, Graham Greene, to name only a few.[38] The increased severity of the Censorship Board in its turn provoked an intensified reaction. Individual bannings were taken up and criticised with increasing frequency in the *Irish Times* and elsewhere.[39] The Irish Association of Civil Liberties, an organisation set up in 1948 to act as a watchdog on bureaucracy,[40] took up the question of censorship and in 1956 organised a petition for an enquiry into the working of the Censorship Board.[41] The Minister for Justice (Mr James Everett of the Labour party—the second inter-party government was then in office) did not grant the petition, but what he did do was to appoint two relatively liberal-minded men to vacancies on the board.[42] Their attitude so exasperated the three conservative members of the board that the latter ultimately resigned,[43] and the next Minister for Justice (Mr Oscar Traynor of Fianna Fail, which had in the meantime returned to office) appointed three liberals to succeed them.[44] Thus, in the space of a few months, and without any legislative changes being required, the board was completely reconstructed, and its conduct since 1957 has aroused much less controversy. Though the total number of bannings remained quite high, averaging practically four hundred a year in the period 1958–64,[45] most of the books banned seem to have been mere pornography, and there have been far fewer complaints of the board suppressing works of real literary merit.[46]

The controversy over the censorship in the nineteen-fifties did not directly involve the hierarchy. Individual bishops during the fifties continued to warn their flocks against the dangers of reading evil literature,[47] but I have not come across any instance of a bishop taking up a position publicly on the question of whether the Censorship Board had been performing its functions wisely. Nonetheless, the controversy has some relevance to a discussion

38. *Ibid.*, 247–50.
39. *Ibid.*, 147–55, 250–1.
40. *Irish Times*, 23 March 1948.
41. M. Adams, *op. cit.*, 148.
42. *Ibid.*, 120.
43. *Ibid.*, 121–2.
44. *Ibid.*, 122.
45. Figures calculated from *ibid.*, 119. Nineteen sixty-four is the last year or which Dr Adams provides figures.
46. *Ibid.*, 251–3.
47. e.g. Archbishop Walsh of Tuam, speaking at Croagh Patrick: *Irish Weekly Independent*, 1 Aug. 1957; Bishop Lucey of Cork, speaking at St Patrick's Church, Cork: *ibid.*, 28 May 1953.

of Church-State relations. The censorship had been originally introduced as one of a number of measures to meet the concern of the Church at the declining standards of morality in Ireland.[48] There was, until 1956, always a Catholic priest among its members.[49] The growing restiveness at its operations, and the government's response to this restiveness by reconstructing the board, suggests a change of atmosphere, a feeling that structures once acquiesced in to maintain the Catholic values of the Irish people were coming to be felt as oppressive.

If the hierarchy was only indirectly concerned in the censorship controversy, several other episodes occurred about this time in which acts of individual bishops or even of the hierarchy as a whole aroused what had for many years been a rare phenomenon in Ireland—public opposition to the wishes of a bishop.

The first of these, chronologically, was the curious incident of the Yugoslav football match. A match between Ireland and Yugoslavia was arranged to take place in Dublin on Wednesday 19 October 1955. On the preceding Friday, the executive of the Irish Football Association received a telephone call from the chancellor of the archdiocese of Dublin, in which he expressed regret that the association had not had the courtesy to consult the archbishop before arranging such a match, and asked if even at that late hour it could not be cancelled.[50] The objection to the match was, of course, that Yugoslavia was a country under a communist government which had persecuted the Catholic Church. It emerged that in 1952 the Football Association had consulted the archbishop about the desirability of arranging a match with Yugoslavia, and, on his advice, had decided not to arrange the fixture.[51] But by 1955 the cold war was in a state of thaw, the imprisonment of Archbishop Stepinac and other ecclesiastics by the Yugoslav government was three years further in the past, and many Irish Catholics saw less reason for maintaining their previous reserve towards everything connected with eastern Europe. The archbishop's attitude, then, no longer received such general support from Catholics as it might have done a few years earlier. Reactions to his protest varied. The

48. See above, pp. 35–7.
49. M. Adams, *op. cit.*, 245–6.
50. *Irish Times*, 17 Oct. 1955.
51. *Ibid.*

inter-party government then in office appears to have agreed with his attitude. The Department of Defence withdrew the army band that had been booked to play at the match,[52] Radio Eireann declined to broadcast a commentary,[53] and the President of Ireland, Mr Sean T. O'Kelly, acting presumably on the advice of the government, cancelled his acceptance of an invitation to attend.[54] But the Football Association's executive decided, with only one dissentient, to carry on with the match,[55] and it took place before an audience of 21,000, which was considered quite a good attendance for a week-day evening.[56] The welcoming ceremony was performed by the President of the Football Association, Mr Oscar Traynor, who was a front-bench member of Fianna Fail.[57] This episode has been used by one critic of Irish catholicism as an example of the hidden power wielded by the Archbishop of Dublin;[58] but it would seem rather to illustrate the limits of that power than the extent of it. One experienced observer wrote at the time that the episode showed that 'far from being subject to clerical domination, the great majority of our people reacts sharply against unfair pressure'.[59] His judgment seems to fit more closely with the facts.

The following year, 1956, saw the beginning of a dispute between the Bishop of Killala, Dr O'Boyle, and the Irish National Teachers' Organisation. The cause of the dispute was the bishop's decision to hand over control of a seven-teacher primary school at Ballina, county Mayo, which had hitherto been staffed entirely by laymen, to a religious order. The I.N.T.O. opposed this change on two grounds. It objected to what it described as the 'discourteous and furtive' manner in which the bishop carried out the change, keeping his decision secret until the last moment, and then presenting the lay staff of the school with a *fait accompli*.[60] But it objected still more to the change itself. Most primary schools in Ireland with lay headmasters were small schools, of three teachers or less; most of the larger schools were in the hands

52. *Ibid.*
53. *Ibid.*, 18 Oct. 1955.
54. *Ibid.*, 17 Oct., 1955.
55. *Ibid.*
56. *Ibid.*, 20 Oct. 1955.
57. *Ibid.*
58. Peter Lennon, 'Grey eminence', *Guardian*, 11 Jan. 1964.
59. John J. Horgan in *Round Table* (XLVI, no. 182) March 1956, 171.
60. *Irish Independent*, 12 May 1956.

of religious orders.[61] The few headmasterships of large schools which were in lay hands were, then, specially important to the I.N.T.O., for they provided the 'plums' of the teaching profession, and any reduction in their number diminished the opportunities for promotion available to lay teachers. The heads of the I.N.T.O. had for long been concerned at what they considered a tendency for the larger schools in lay hands to be transferred to religious orders, and had complained to the hierarchy about it in 1943.[62] They had then been assured that the bishops did not favour, as a rule, the transfer to religious orders of schools hitherto staffed by lay teachers;[63] but the Ballina decision revived all their fears.

A long-drawn-out dispute ensued. The I.N.T.O.'s first reaction was to call the teachers in the Ballina school out on strike.[64] At the request of the Archbishop of Dublin—who had shown himself a good friend of the teachers during their strike against the government in 1946[65]—the organisation revoked this decision and instead appealed to Rome.[66] Rome remitted the case to the Papal Nuncio in Ireland, who asked the Archbishop of Dublin to mediate.[67] The Archbishop worked out a settlement which would have been acceptable to the I.N.T.O., but the Bishop of Killala in effect rejected it, and the I.N.T.O. responded by calling the long-threatened strike.[68] The dispute was finally settled by the mediation of the then Minister for Education, Dr Patrick Hillery, in 1962. Under its terms the headmaster from a religious order remained at Ballina, and the bishop agreed to pay a substantial additional salary to one of the lay teachers on the staff.[69] The result was not a brilliant one for the I.N.T.O. but, in the view of the historian of the organisation, its acceptance of the settlement has been justified. For there has been no subsequent case of a lay school being transferred to a religious order, and indeed a

---

61. T. J. O'Connell, *History of the I.N.T.O.*, 98, gives the following figures for 1953: of 4,117 Catholic primary schools with three teachers or less, 4,017 were staffed completely by lay teachers. Of 613 schools with more than three teachers, 447 were controlled by religious.

62. *Ibid.*, 97.   63. *Ibid.*   64. *Ibid.*, 102.

65. See above, p. 121.

66. T. J. O'Connell, *op. cit.*, 104. The text of the I.N.T.O.'s statement to Rome is published in P. Duffy, *The Lay Teacher*, 125–54.

67. *Ibid.*, 112.   68. *Ibid.*, 113–16.   69. *Ibid.*, 118.

number of newly-built schools which might have gone to religious are now staffed entirely by lay teachers.[70]

The point at issue in the Ballina case was not new: the I.N.T.O. had been concerned for years at the loss of large primary schools to religious orders. But the organisation's decision to bring the matter to a head at this time, the sharp language which it used in public about the Bishop of Killala, and its readiness to use strike action against him, were indications of how the atmosphere was changing in the Ireland of the nineteen-fifties.

The revival of physical-force nationalism in the nineteen-fifties can perhaps also be fitted into this pattern. Between 1954 and 1961 the Irish Republican Army and other armed groups carried out a number of attacks on the army and police in Northern Ireland.[71] These attacks were condemned by both government and opposition;[72] they were also condemned by the Church. In January 1956 the following statement was issued by the hierarchy:

We, the Archbishops and Bishops of Ireland, feel it our duty to warn all Catholics against erroneous ideas and claims which are advanced in regard to the raising of military forces and the waging of war.

Catholic moral teaching lays down precise conditions in order that war be at all lawful. War is the cause of very grave evils, physical, moral and social. It is not lawful, unless it be declared and waged by the supreme authority of the State. No private citizen or group or organisation of citizens has the right to bear arms or to use them against another state, its soldiers or citizens. Just as no private citizen has the right to inflict capital punishment, so he has not the right to wage war. Sacred Scripture gives the right to bear the sword and to use it against evil-doers to the supreme authority and to it alone. If individuals could arrogate to themselves the right to use military force there would be disorder and chaos leading inevitably to tyranny and oppression.

70. *Ibid.*, 120.

71. A useful account of these events is contained in T. P. Coogan, *The I.R.A.*, 273–344.

72. See the strong declaration by Mr Costello, then Taoiseach, and the statement by Mr de Valera, then Leader of the Opposition, that he was in entire agreement, in *Irish Times*, 7 Jan. 1957.

The second condition for a lawful war is that there be a just cause. It must be certain that all peaceful means have been tried and found unavailing, that the matter at issue far outweighs the havoc that war brings and that it is reasonably certain that war will not make things worse. No private individual has authority to judge these issues, or to involve the people from whom he has received no mandate, in the serious losses inevitable in hostilities.

But of all wars, a civil war between the people of one nation causes greatest injury and is most to be avoided.

Acting then in virtue of the authority conferred on us by our sacred office, we declare that it is a mortal sin for a Catholic to become or remain a member of an organisation or society, which arrogates to itself the right to bear arms or to use them against its own or another state; that it is also sinful for a Catholic to co-operate with, express approval of, or otherwise assist any such organisation or society, and that, if the co-operation or assistance be notable, the sin committed is mortal.

With paternal insistence we warn young men to be on their guard against any such organisation or society and not to be induced by false notions of patriotism to become members of it.

We appeal also to the general body of our people to avoid violence, cherish peace, and, as a Christian nation, give an example to the world of order, forbearance, concord and goodwill.[73]

These strong words, however, were not sufficient to eliminate support for the physical-force movement. On New Year's Day 1957 two young men, Sean South and Fergal O'Hanlon, were killed in an attack on Brookeborough police barracks in Northern Ireland.[74] Sean South was an ardent Catholic, a former member of the Legion of Mary and of *Maria Duce*.[75] The journey of his funeral cortège from the border to his home town of Limerick called forth demonstrations of sympathy. Large crowds, including many priests, turned out as it passed through the various towns on the way.[76] Many local authorities passed resolutions of

73. *Irish Independent,* 19 Jan. 1956.   74. *Irish Times,* 2 and 3 Jan. 1957.
75. M. Seoighe, *Maraíodh Seán Sabhat aréir,* 49, 63.
76. *Irish Times,* 4 and 5 Jan. 1957.

sympathy with his relatives and those of Fergal O'Hanlon.[77] Too much, it is true, can easily be read into these manifestations. Those who saluted Sean South were perhaps only recognising his courage and idealism, and did not necessarily endorse his physical-force policy. Nor did they necessarily oppose the hierarchy's condemnation of physical-force organisations. But even if they did not actually disagree with the hierarchy, they were coming fairly close to it. The bishops had declared it sinful, not just to belong to such an organisation, but to 'express approval of, or otherwise assist' it. Between expressing approval of such an organisation, and expressing sympathy with a man who had lost his life in the service of such an organisation, the distinction was fairly fine.

The problem of physical-force nationalism was not a new one for the Irish hierarchy. As was pointed out in a previous chapter, the hierarchy had always found it difficult to secure the compliance of its flock in its opposition to such movements.[78] Nonetheless, the fact that the problem re-emerged at this moment at least does nothing to contradict the picture which we have been building up of the middle and later fifties. These years do seem to have been a period in which the bishops had increasing difficulty in securing acceptance of their point of view.

None of the episodes so far mentioned involved a dispute between ministers and bishops. On the Yugoslav football match, and again on the physical-force movement, the government held the same opinion as the bishops concerned. In the Ballina dispute the government was not involved until the final stage, when the Minister for Education acted as mediator. Other episodes occurred, however, during these years in which ministers and bishops did not see eye to eye.

One such instance was provided by the Fethard-on-Sea boycott of 1957. Fethard-on-Sea is a tiny village in county Wexford where, on 13 May 1957, a boycott was begun by Catholics of their Protestant neighbours.[79] Two Protestant shopkeepers lost their Catholic customers;[80] a Protestant music teacher lost eleven out of her twelve pupils;[81] and the Catholic school-teacher at the

77. *Ibid.*, Jan. 1957 *passim.* 78. See above, pp. 9–11.
79. *Irish Times*, 27 May 1957. 80. *Ibid.*, 3 June 1957.
81. *Ibid.*, 22 June 1957.

local Protestant primary school resigned.[82] The cause of the trouble was the break-up of a mixed marriage. A Catholic farmer of the neighbourhood had married in 1949 a Protestant woman, who had then given the promise, required by the Catholic authorities in a mixed marriage, that the children would be brought up as Catholics. But she had since changed her mind and in April 1957 she suddenly disappeared, taking her two children with her, and, from the safety of Belfast, informed her husband that she would agree to a reunion only if he would agree to the children being brought up as Protestants. Catholics in Fethard-on-Sea believed that some of the local Protestants had aided her departure (though this was strongly denied by the Protestants) and the boycott was their form of retaliation.[83]

The boycotters received substantial clerical support. The local priests promised to stand by them.[84] The bishop, Dr Staunton of Ferns, refused, despite an appeal from the Church of Ireland bishop, Dr Phair, to express any disapproval.[85] Another bishop, Dr Browne of Galway, preaching at a congress in Wexford to a congregation including Cardinal D'Alton and six other bishops,[86] described the boycott as 'a peaceful and moderate protest', and asserted that 'there seems to be a concerted campaign to entice or kidnap Catholic children and deprive them of their faith'.[87]

Not all Catholics, however, agreed with these opinions. At a Catholic social study congress in Dublin one lecturer, Mr Donal Barrington, said that the boycotters were doing an unjust and terrible thing, adding that that was not his own opinion alone, but 'the opinion of all intelligent Catholics, priests and laymen' with whom he had discussed the matter.[88] The Church of Ireland bishop and rector stated that they had had many messages from Roman Catholics deploring the boycott.[89] I have heard of Catholics who travelled many miles out of their way to buy goods from the two Protestant shopkeepers in Fethard. I have been told of one Catholic organisation whose national council

82. *Ibid.*, 27 May 1957.   83. *Ibid.*, *Standard*, 21 June 1957.
84. Statement by Fr Stafford, C.C., in *Irish Times*, 8 July 1957.
85. *Irish Times*, 3 July 1957.
86. According to Fr Stafford's statement: *ibid.*, 8 July 1957.
87. *Ibid.*, 1 July 1957.   88. *Ibid.*, 26 June 1957.
89. *Ibid.*, 7 June, 5 July 1957.

was appealed to by Bishop Staunton for support, but which, after a hot debate, refused it.

The most eminent, however, of the lay Catholics who condemned the boycott was the Taoiseach, Mr de Valera. On 4 July 1957—four days after the Bishop of Galway's sermon—he was asked in the Dail by Dr Noel Browne if he would make a statement on the Fethard-on-Sea boycott. Mr de Valera replied:

I have made no public statement because I have clung to the hope that good sense and decent neighbourly feeling would, of themselves, bring this business to an end. I cannot say that I know every fact, but if, as head of the government, I must speak, I can only say, from what has appeared in public, that I regard this boycott as ill-conceived, ill-considered and futile for the achievement of the purpose for which it seems to have been intended; that I regard it as unjust and cruel to confound the innocent with the guilty; that I repudiate any suggestion that this boycott is typical of the attitude or conduct of our people; that I am convinced that 90 per cent. of them look on this matter as I do; and that I beg of all who have regard for the fair name, good repute and well-being of our nation to use their influence to bring this deplorable affair to a speedy end.

I would like to appeal also to any who might have influence with the absent wife to urge her to respect her troth and her promise and to return with her children to her husband and her home.[90]

These words, measured and dignified though they were, could not by themselves bring the boycott to an end. It was not indeed within the government's power to do so, for it could not force individuals to do business with other individuals if they did not wish to, and the boycott seems to have continued until some time in the autumn.[91] Nor did Mr de Valera change the opinions of all on the other side. The Bishop of Galway issued a statement defending his description of the boycott as peaceful and moderate, pointing out that no injury to life, limb or property had been reported to the police, and that the Catholic people had not refused necessaries of life to those boycotted. 'It is not against

90. *Dail Debates,* CLXIII, 731.
91. I have seen no statement of when the boycott came to an end. It was reported as still continuing in *Irish Times,* 12 Aug. 1957.

charity or justice', he added, 'to refuse special favours, such as one's money or custom, to those whom one regards as responsible for, or approving of, a grave offence.'[92] But at least Mr de Valera made the government's position clear, and his words, coming at the moment they did, appeared as a formal rebuke to the Bishop of Galway.

One final episode to be discussed is the revival of agitation for the general Sunday opening of public houses. It was explained in a previous chapter that in 1948–50 the Licensed Vintners' and Grocers' Association had carried on an agitation with this object, but that it had been brought to a sharp halt by a strongly-worded statement from the hierarchy in June 1950.[93] At the beginning of 1955, however, the association reopened the question by submitting a memorandum to the Minister for Justice.[94] The association rested its case largely on the increasing frequency with which exemptions were being granted to the existing law. Under the Intoxicating Liquor Act 1927, district justices were entitled to grant exemption orders, permitting sales to local people as well as to *bona fide* travellers. In the nineteen-forties, it seems, this loophole in the law was little availed of. But in the nineteen-fifties, applications for exemption orders became more and more frequent, and were more and more often granted by district justices. By 1954, the secretary of the Licensed Vintners' Association could claim that 'this development . . . has reached such a point of frequency and increasingly widespread application as to constitute a substantial *"fait accompli"* in the matter of Sunday opening'.[95] The association's case, in short, was that the existing Sunday opening law was so often being dispensed with in practice that there was no longer the same justification for maintaining it in theory.

The association's memorandum reached the Department of Justice when the second inter-party government was in office. There can be little doubt what the department's reaction would have been if General MacEoin, who had been Minister for Justice in the first inter-party government, had received the same portfolio in the second. General MacEoin's attitude on this as on

---

92. *Ibid.*, 8 July 1957.   93. See above, pp. 174–8.
94. *Licensed Vintner and Grocer* (XX, 9) Feb. 1955, 5.
95. *Ibid.* (XX, 6) Christmas number 1954, 7.

other political matters was simple: if the hierarchy had once spoken, then it should be obeyed and the question was closed. He made his outlook clear when the question of Sunday opening was raised in the Fine Gael Ard-Fheis of 1955. 'The hierarchy', he was reported as saying, 'had spoken in no uncertain terms on the proposal and he would like to know if there was any publican who would encourage the Minister for Justice to go ahead and oppose the positive teaching of those who were entitled to teach.'[96] General MacEoin, however, was not now Minister for Justice: in the second inter-party government he was given the portfolio of Defence, and the Department of Justice was assigned to one of the Labour members of the government, Mr James Everett. Mr Everett was a different kind of person from General MacEoin. He was a life-long official of the Irish Transport and General Workers' Union, with a record of service going back to the militant days of the union when its members were hoisting red flags on requisitioned creameries.[97] On one occasion he himself is said to have put a picket on a convent with which his union was in dispute.[98] So, without necessarily labelling Mr Everett as anti-clerical, one could say that he was less likely to regard a statement from the hierarchy as closing a question than General MacEoin had been.

Mr Everett gave his decision when, in November 1955, an independent deputy supporting the government, Mr Jack McQuillan, introduced a motion calling for amendment of the licensing laws 'so as to enable rural dwellers to enjoy the same facilities as are at present afforded to city residents'.[99] This was an oblique way of saying that the Sunday opening laws should be the same in the countryside as in the four county boroughs. An interesting debate followed, in which deputies from all parties called for a change in the law, and no one mentioned the fact that the bishops had condemned any change in the law only five years before.[100] Mr Everett, replying, said that in his opinion the licensing laws must be revised, and proposed that a commission

96. *Ibid.* (XX, 10) March 1955, 5.
97. J. D. Clarkson, *Labour and Nationalism in Ireland,* 435, 445.
98. 'Backbencher' in *Irish Times,* 25 Feb. 1967.
99. *Dail Debates,* CLIII, 492 (2 Nov. 1955).
100. *Ibid.,* 492–504, 628–68 (2 and 9 Nov. 1955).

be set up to examine the question.[101] His proposal was accepted without a division.

The commission was established on 4 July 1956, and completed its report on 18 July 1957.[102] The weight of the evidence given before it favoured a change in the law. The Gardai (i.e. the police) complained of the difficulties in enforcing the law as it stood, and gave evidence of the connection between the *bona fide* traffic and road accidents.[103] A district justice gave evidence of the extent to which illegal trading on Sunday existed.[104] The contention of the Licensed Vintners' Association that exemption orders were greatly on the increase was borne out by official statistics.[105] It was not surprising, therefore, that the commission unanimously recommended a change in the law with regard to Sunday opening. The majority and minority reports differed in the precise hours they recommended, but they agreed in proposing that the *bona fide* traffic be abolished, and that general opening on Sundays be introduced. Even the member of the commission representing the Pioneer Association, Mr John K. Clear, concurred in this.[106] As he stated in an observation attached to the majority report: 'There is a case to be made for the opening of all public houses throughout the country for some period on Sundays in order to remove abuses which arise from the *Bona Fide* clause, Area Exemption Orders, and widespread illegal trading.'[107] The Pioneers had come a long way since they organised such massive opposition to Mr Corry's proposal to introduce uniform Sunday opening in 1948.[108]

The hierarchy, however, proved unimpressed by the volume of support for general Sunday opening. After their meeting of June 1959, the bishops issued a statement attacking the commission's proposals:

101. *Ibid.,* 664–5.

102. *Reports of the Commission of Inquiry into the operation of the laws relating to the sale and supply of intoxicating liquor, 1957,* 3, 25.

103. *Ibid.,* 6–8.   104. *Ibid.,* 8.   105. *Ibid.*

106. Mr Clear is named as the Pioneers' representative in *Licensed Vintner and Grocer* (XXII, 2) July 1956, 1.

107. *Reports of the Commission, op. cit.,* 27. That Mr Clear, in supporting the majority report, spoke for the Pioneers was made clear in *Pioneer* (X, 9) Sept. 1957, 18.

108. See above, p. 176.

... The abolition of *bona fide* trading if carried out, may be beneficial, but the benefits accruing from the change must be very seriously diminished by the recommendation to extend the opening hours all over the country on week days . . . and on Sundays. . . .

It cannot escape the attention of any responsible person that a relaxation of the law must seriously affect our people, more especially the youth of both sexes.

Increased facilities for obtaining intoxicating liquor by the extension of the general opening hours will inevitably lead to a greater extension of alcoholism which in modern conditions has most serious moral and social effects in the increase of delinquency and in widespread danger to life on the roads.

It is noteworthy that representatives of both the licensed trade and the trade employees did not favour an extension of the hour for closing.

Other countries are feeling it necessary to adopt more stringent legislation in the public interest. The arguments adduced in the 1957 Irish Commission for what is called a policy of liberalisation are altogether unconvincing.

The Bishops cannot believe that the vast and very reasonable majority of our decent people has shown any desire whatever for a relaxation of the law. On the contrary, the Christian sense of our people would welcome restriction and especially a genuine enforcement of law.

The evidence of the Gardai before the Commission proves that the existing laws have not been impartially enforced.

The proposal of the Commission to permit universally the sale and supply of intoxicating liquor on Sundays, especially the proposal to permit opening immediately after Mass, strikes at what is most sacred in the life of our people. The rightful observance of the Lord's Day has been one of the most powerful factors in preserving intact the Catholic life of Ireland.

While the concern of the Bishops is primarily the moral and religious aspect of the proposed legislation, nonetheless, the bishops are acutely aware of the economic ills that must result from extended facilities for the consumption of intoxicating liquor.

At a time when each successive government is urging on our people the very grave need for thrift, hard work, and increased productivity, the recommendations of the majority of the Commission, insofar as they will make for increased drinking, are ill-advised and deeply hurtful to our economic life, domestic, social, and national.

The Irish hierarchy confidently hopes that legislation when it is introduced, will not weaken the moral fibre of our nation, and will respect the deep-seated convictions of our Catholic people.[109]

This statement is phrased with more restraint than that of 1950. The bishops no longer say that general opening of public houses would be a violation of ecclesiastical law and that even to agitate for it is sinful. But their demands remain essentially the same. They oppose any extension of the Sunday opening hours. To the argument that the existing law is widely evaded, their reply is, not that it should be altered, but that it should be more strictly enforced.

The Fianna Fail government, however, did not prove disposed to listen to the hierarchy. In the autumn of 1959 it introduced an Intoxicating Liquor Bill based on the majority report of the commission. On the second reading Mr Lemass, who was now Taoiseach, dealt with the hierarchy's views. He fully acknowledged the hierarchy's right to speak on the subject. 'This is a matter', he said, 'upon which the views of religious authorities are entitled to receive here very great weight indeed, because there are moral as well as social aspects involved.'[110] But having conceded their right to be heard, he went on to controvert their arguments. He did not agree that extending the hours of opening would lead to an increase in drunkenness. He was informed that abuse came not from long hours of drinking but from illegal drinking, and his personal belief was that when people could enter a public house legally the inducement to excessive drinking would be diminished.[111] He was prepared to make only one concession to the hierarchy's point of view. 'In the case of Sunday opening hours', he explained, 'we received representation from the Church authorities urging us to keep in mind the undesirability of making arrangements which would conflict in any way

109. *Irish Catholic Directory, 1960*, 688–9 (23 June 1959).
110. *Dail Debates*, CLXXVIII, 391 (25 Nov. 1959).   111. *Ibid.*, 392.

with the duty of attendance at religious services.'[112] The government was, accordingly, making one change in the recommendations of the commission—instead of allowing public houses to open at 12.30 p.m. on Sundays, the opening hour would be one o'clock.[113]

In the course of debate, even this concession disappeared. Many rural deputies complained that a one o'clock opening time on Sunday was too late for their constituents.[114] In many country parishes, last mass was at 11 or 11.30, and, they represented, it would be a hardship to their constituents to hang around for three quarters of an hour or more after the end of mass, waiting for the pubs to open at one. The government was sufficiently impressed by this argument to move an amendment in committee changing the opening hour on Sunday to 12.30.[115] Thus the only point on which the government had been willing to yield to the hierarchy's wishes was speedily withdrawn. The Intoxicating Liquor Bill 1959 was a largely uncontroversial measure which caused no great stir while it was passing through the legislature. But in the history of Church-State relations it marks a significant landmark. For it provides the only example so far recorded of a recommendation from the hierarchy being simply rejected by an Irish government.

In a previous chapter it was suggested that the late forties and early fifties marked a period of increasing 'integralism', in which various movements to make Ireland more totally Catholic, each according to its own vision of what being totally Catholic entailed, secured considerable support.[116] But even at that time, there were signs of resistance to such trends.[117] In the period covered by this chapter, these counter-pressures were growing, and Irish Catholics were looking increasingly critically at measures which were supposed to be maintaining Catholic values. The tide had turned, and integralism was now on the wane. It remains to be seen what further changes would be brought by the nineteen-sixties.

---

112. *Ibid.,* 387.   113. *Ibid.*

114. On my calculation, nineteen deputies made this complaint on the second reading debate, and only one spoke out for the 1 p.m. opening hour: *ibid.,* 108–763 *passim* (18 Nov.–2 Dec. 1959).

115. *Ibid.,* CLXXX, 1092 (24 March 1960).

116. See above, p. 158.   117. See above, p. 193.

CHAPTER XI

QUIESCENCE AND A MOVE TO NEW ISSUES, 1959–70

After the tensions recorded in the last chapter, Church-State relations in Ireland settled down to a period of quiescence, and the first half of the nineteen-sixties was generally characterised by harmony. Bishop Browne of Galway on one occasion obliquely criticised Irish support for United Nations intervention in the Congo.[1] Bishop Lucey of Cork on a number of occasions attacked the government for an economic policy which, he claimed, discriminated against the small farmers of the west,[2] and was once chided by a minister for criticism which 'does not instil in the public respect for the civil authority'.[3] But this was all that there was to record in the way of public disagreements between churchmen and statesmen, and on the whole, the early nineteen-sixties were exceptionally uneventful in the history of Church-State relations.

The harmony was illustrated by the evolution of the Catholic social movement. This movement remained, if organisations and publications are listed, as active as ever. *An Ríoghacht* petered out at about this time, but *Muintir na Tíre* remained vigorous, as did the Christus Rex Society and the Social Study Conference. But the movement seemed to be growing less ideological, less concerned to promote what was taken to be a specifically Catholic view of things. Vocational organisation was no longer pressed. The last

---

1. *Irish Independent*, 22 Nov. 1961.
2. Dr Lucey's concern on this matter was expressed as far back as 1954: see his minority report in *Commission on Emigration and other Population Problems, 1948–54, Reports*, 335–63. Since then he has returned to the question repeatedly. For an unfriendly but well-referenced account of Dr Lucey's social views see M. Sheehy, *Is Ireland Dying?*, 184–98.
3. *Dail Debates*, CXCV, 1053 (17 May 1962: speech of Mr Jack Lynch, Minister for Industry and Commerce.)

article on the topic that I have seen appeared as far back as 1958,[4] and the Catholic Societies Vocational Organisation Conference, which had been an active pressure group in the early nineteen-fifties, became dormant about 1960.[5] Some of the best-known institutions for the propagation of Catholic social teaching dropped the word 'Catholic' from their title. In 1966 the Catholic Workers' College was renamed the College of Industrial Relations,[6] and the same year the Dublin Institute of Catholic Sociology changed its name to the Dublin Institute of Adult Education.[7]

Instead of promoting a ready-formed corpus of doctrine, the Catholic social movement appeared increasingly concerned with empirical investigation of the actual needs of the Irish people. *Muintir na Tire* sponsored the Limerick Rural Survey, which was the first sociological study of an Irish rural area since the work of the Harvard anthropologists, Arensberg and Kimball, in the nineteen-thirties.[8] Bishops began to send priests for academic training in sociology, and a high proportion of the small band of trained sociologists in Ireland now are priests—Mgr Jeremiah Newman and Father Liam Ryan of Maynooth, for instance, and Father James Kavanagh and Father Conor Ward of University College Dublin. Other priests and bishops became known for their practical social action. Father Thomas Fehily was a pioneer of social work among the long-neglected itinerants.[9] Father James McDyer revitalised a decaying Donegal parish by his co-operative farming and marketing schemes.[10] Bishop Birch of Ossory established the Kilkenny Social Service Centre and transformed the efficiency of voluntary social services in his diocese.[11] The changing viewpoint

4. Rev. J. Newman, 'Vocational organisation and the co-operative movement', *Christus Rex* (XII, 3) July 1958, 171–84.
5. Information from a former president of the conference, Mr W. F. Phillips.
6. E. Kent, S.J., 'Education for industrial relations', *Studies* (LV, no. 218) Summer 1966, 139.
7. *Irish Catholic Directory, 1967,* 791 (under date 6 Oct. 1966).
8. Rev. J. Newman (ed.), *The Limerick Rural Survey, 1958–64.*
9. For an account of the work of the Dublin Itinerant Settlement Committee, of which Fr Fehily is chairman, see the statement from the Archbishop of Dublin, Dr McQuaid, in *Irish Times,* 1 Dec. 1969.
10. For Fr McDyer's work see *Irish Times,* 22 Jan. 1964; T. P. Coogan, *Ireland since the Rising,* 225–7; A. Bestic, *The Importance of Being Irish,* 43–8.
11. For Dr Birch see T. P. Coogan, *op. cit.,* 242–5; D. Connery, *The Irish,* 149; *Hibernia,* 14 March 1969 and correspondence in subsequent issues.

of Catholics with an interest in social questions can be seen by anyone who browses through a run of *Christus Rex*. In the early years after its foundation in 1947, contributors to this journal seemed more anxious to pass moral judgments than to spend time amassing the facts. By the nineteen-sixties, however, they were more concerned to provide factual information. The volume for 1964, for instance, contained articles on 'employment prospects in the Republic', 'merits and problems of planning', 'modern research into attitudes towards work', and a survey of young people's recreation habits in an Irish town.

As the Catholic social movement in Ireland became more involved in empirical investigation, so denunciations of excessive State intervention died away. For investigation showed that in many ways the State in Ireland stepped in not too much but too little. There were whole groups for whom not enough was done: the aged, the mentally handicapped, the subsistence farmers of the western seaboard, the itinerants. An example of the changing outlook is provided by the Social Study Conference, which in 1966 chose as the topic for its summer school 'The Christian and State Welfare'. Ten or fifteen years before, such a topic would have led to one speech after another denouncing the evils of State control. In 1966, however, the speakers discussed, in matter-of-fact terms, the merits and deficiencies of existing State services, and several made recommendations for their extension.[12] Bishops, too, began to call for an increase, not a decrease, in State intervention. As early as 1959, Bishop Philbin of Clonfert suggested that the State should intervene more actively in the land market, so as to buy out inefficient farmers.[13] In the same year, Bishop Rogers of Killaloe argued that the State should give more financial aid to secondary education.[14] In 1964, Bishop Birch of Ossory appealed in a pastoral letter for more generous treatment of the aged by public as well as private interests.[15] In 1966, Archbishop Walsh of Tuam called for more financial aid from the State to the over-

---

12. Most of the papers were later published in *Christus Rex* (XXI, 3) July 1967. See also *Irish Times*, 4 Aug. 1966.
13. *Irish Catholic Directory, 1960*, 702 (25 Sept. 1959).
14. *Ibid., 1961*, 663 (8 Dec. 1959).
15. *Irish Times*, 17 Feb. 1964.

burdened local authorities.[16] Even Bishop Lucey of Cork, in his campaign on behalf of the small farmers of the west, was arguing not for an end of government intervention in the economy, but for a change in its nature.[17] All these appeals implied a recognition that the State was a beneficent force in Ireland, and they made a contrast with the tone of episcopal pronouncements about State power only a decade previously.

Even clearer evidence that Irish Catholic attitudes to social questions had really changed can be found in explicit repudiations, by Catholics in the nineteen-sixties, of what had been done by Catholics in the nineteen-forties and fifties. In the Jesuit periodical *Studies* for winter 1964, an article appeared by the economist Mr Garret FitzGerald (now a Fine Gael front-bencher) which caused considerable interest. Mr FitzGerald's theme was 'seeking a national purpose', and in the course of his argument he remarked: 'In some respects the thinking of the Catholic Church in Ireland has lagged far behind Catholic thought elsewhere. This has been particularly notable in relation to such matters as social welfare. One cannot resist the conclusion that in the 1930's and 1940's the Irish Church took a wrong turning in its thinking on these matters.'[18] About the same time a Fine Gael deputy, Mr Declan Costello (son of the Taoiseach of the mother and child scheme era) said in a talk at the Dublin Institute of Catholic Sociology: 'Social conditions in this country were evidence that Catholic influence on government policies had, on the whole, been preventative rather than positive. There was a danger that Catholic social principles might sometimes be used, unjustifiably, to support an unjust *status quo*. In the name of Catholic social principles movements towards social reform had been criticised and whilst condemning the reformer, the conditions which he sought to reform are condoned.'[19] One can hardly doubt that Mr Costello had in mind the mother and child episode in which his father had played so prominent a part.

One disclaimer of the past has come from a specially exalted

16. *Ibid.*, 14 Sept. 1966
17. For a good example see his speech at Kilcrohane: *Irish Weekly Independent*, 19 May 1960.
18. *Studies* (LIII, no. 212) Winter 1964, 345.
19. *Irish Times*, 7 Nov. 1964.

quarter. In a lecture at Queen's University Belfast in March 1966, Cardinal Conway, the Archbishop of Armagh, spoke on the proper role of the State. He affirmed the principle that the State should allow the maximum of freedom that was compatible with the common good, but stressed that the application of this principle varied greatly with the character of the society in question. To attempt nowadays, for instance, to reduce the State to the role which it had in the eighteenth century would produce chaos and untold hardship. He added that changes in the application of the doctrine could also take place as a result of a deeper understanding of the factual situation. He went on:

Even as recently as the 1940s it was not at all clear what effect on essential human liberties, even liberty of thought, the increasing invasion of the State into the field of economics would have. The experience in Russia and in pre-war Germany and Italy suggested to many people throughout a wide spectrum of political and economic thought that there was a close connection between increased State control of the economy and totalitarianism.

Even today not everything is clear in this important field; it may be some time yet before we can fully measure the effect on human liberty and initiative of increasing central control. Nevertheless, I think it is true to say that people understand this problem more clearly now than they did 20 years ago, and that some of the fears which were widely held at that time now appear to have been exaggerated.[20]

The Cardinal did not specifically say who the people were who had exaggerated fears of State control twenty years ago. But as he had lived through, and participated in, the controversies which had wracked Ireland on that very issue there can be little question of whom he had in mind. He must have been thinking of those Irish exponents of Catholic social teaching (including some of the bishops) who had made such alarmist forecasts of the dangers of State power in Ireland.

The movement towards consensus was not entirely on the side of the Church; it could also be found on the side of the State. This movement must not be exaggerated: the complaints

20. *Irish Independent,* 4 March 1966.

made in the nineteen-forties about the 'bureaucratic' nature of Irish administration, its self-sufficiency, its reluctance to consult and its impatience with outside interest groups, are still echoed today.[21] In recent years there have been several acrimonious disputes between government departments and the interest groups in their respective fields. The Department of Health at one time refused to receive any communications from the Irish Medical Association.[22] The Department of Agriculture has been for years on bad terms with the National Farmers' Association.[23] The Department of Education has antagonised several of the teachers' and managers' associations.[24] Nonetheless, with the development of economic planning after 1958, there was a multiplication of consultative bodies in Ireland, and by the nineteen-sixties there seemed some sign that the structures recommended by the Vocational Organisation Commission in 1944 were at last coming into existence. The National Industrial Economic Council, established in 1963, which includes representatives of the State and of both employers and workers, bears some resemblance to the National Industrial Conference which the Vocational Organisation Commission had proposed.[25] The Joint Industrial Boards which the commission had proposed for each industry are in some degree paralleled by the Adaptation Councils which have been established in twenty-four Irish industries.[26] The National Agricultural Council established in

21. For a sustained and well-documented example see C. McCarthy, *The Distasteful Challenge*. Mr McCarthy, who is secretary of an important trade union and a member of numerous government-sponsored committees, is well placed to observe Irish administrators at work.

22. This dispute occurred while Mr Sean MacEntee was Minister for Health: for its origins see *Journal of the Irish Medical Association*, June 1960, 178.

23. An outline history of this dispute can be found in the *Irish Times* annual reviews, 2 Jan. 1967, 1 Jan. 1968, 2 Jan. 1969, 1 Jan. 1970.

24. I have not kept a complete file of complaints against the department, which have been numerous in recent years, but here are a few examples: from the Irish National Teachers' Organisation, *Irish Times*, 14 April 1969; from the Association of Secondary Teachers in Ireland, *ibid.*, 1 Oct. 1968; from Protestants in West Cork, *ibid.*, 28 Nov. 1968; from the Teaching Brothers' Association, *Studies* (LVII, no. 227) Autumn 1968, 274–83. I make no judgment on the merits of the department's case in these disputes: I simply record the fact that the department has, justly or unjustly, come under fire from a remarkable proportion of the interest groups in its field.

25. G. FitzGerald, *Planning in Ireland*, 158–9. 26. *Ibid.*, 61, 66.

1967 may, if the dispute between the Department of Agriculture and the National Farmers' Association can be resolved, come to play a part similar to that proposed by the Vocational Organisation Commission for a National Agricultural Conference.[27] If there is no longer any talk about the need for vocational organisation in Ireland, part of the reason may be that more vocational organisation exists.

The early sixties, then, saw the end of the tension between 'bureaucratic' and 'vocational' outlooks which had so bedevilled Church-State relations in the forties and fifties. On the one side, exponents of Catholic social teaching ceased to denounce the State for its bureaucratic characteristics. On the other side, the ministers and civil servants who manned the State apparatus seemed to lose some of their old mistrust for vocational bodies. The result was a period of unwonted harmony in Church-State relations.

In the second half of the nineteen-sixties, the harmony has not been quite so complete. Since 1965 there has been some revival, if not of controversy between Church and State, at least of disagreement between individual churchmen on the one hand and individual politicians on the other. These disagreements have occurred in four different areas: education, censorship, constitutional reform, and housing. It would be premature to attempt a full discussion of these issues at this moment. Some of the controversies are still going on, and the outcome cannot yet be seen. Some of the principals are still too closely involved for it to be fair to approach them for interview. But an outline of the controversies in these four areas, in so far as they can be followed in published documents, will be offered in the next few pages.

The most surprising item in this list of controversies is education. For forty years, the Department of Education had treated suggestions for altering the educational system with extreme caution. In the nineteen-sixties, however, it has been quite suddenly transformed, and, under a succession of energetic ministers, has initiated adventurous new policies in every field. It has

27. *Ibid.*, 164.

sponsored the first scientific study of Irish educational needs,[28] and has followed this up by establishing a development branch in the department.[29] At primary level, it has proposed drastic changes in the curriculum,[30] and has also introduced a policy of amalgamating one- and two-teacher schools into larger units.[31] At university level, it has greatly increased the financial aid available for students,[32] and has made proposals for merging Trinity College and University College Dublin.[33] It is at post-primary level (to use the term which the Irish government has invented to cover both secondary and technical schools) that the most sweeping changes have been put in train. Here the government has, for the first time, given grants to owners of secondary schools for the building and extension of schools.[34] It has introduced a scheme for post-primary education to ensure that children are not debarred from receiving such education through lack of means.[35] It has initiated schemes for co-operation between secondary and vocational schools in areas where the existing schools are too small to provide a complete coverage of subjects on their own.[36] It has set up comprehensive schools in areas which were inadequately served by existing secondary and vocational schools.[37]

These changes have entailed a sudden increase of State intervention in a field where the Church has always been powerful, and it would be too much to expect that they could be put through entirely without controversy. The reforms in post-primary education appear to have run into opposition from the religious orders which own most of the secondary schools.

28. *Investment in Education. Report of the Survey Team Appointed by the Minister for Education in October 1962.*

29. *Seanad Debates,* LXII, 1077 (9 Feb. 1967: speech of Mr Donogh O'Malley, Minister for Education).

30. *Irish Times,* 14 Dec. 1968, 1–3 July 1969.

31. Announced by the then Minister for Education, Mr George Colley, on 21 July 1965: *Dail Debates,* CCXVII, 1968.

32. Under the Local Authorities (Higher Education) Act 1968.

33. *Irish Times,* 19 April 1967.

34. S. O'Connor, 'Post primary education', *Studies* (LVII, no. 227) Autumn 1968, 233–51. This article, by an Assistant Secretary in the Department of Education, is a major source of information for educational policy and aroused widespread interest when it was published.

35. *Irish Times,* 12 Sept. 1966.   36. S. O'Connor, *op. cit.,* 233, 239.

37. *Ibid.*

Most of the controversy has taken place behind closed doors and it is not easy to obtain a picture of what the points at issue have been, but every now and again some corner of the argument has been exposed to the public. In 1967 the then Minister for Education, Mr Donogh O'Malley, burst out in the Senate about his difficulties:

No one is going to stop me introducing my scheme next September. I know I am up against opposition and serious organised opposition but they are not going to defeat me on this. I shall tell you further that I shall expose them and I shall expose their tactics on every available occasion whoever they are. . . .

I had a deputation recently and a reverend gentleman as he went out the door . . . said jocosely but there was malice in his joke: 'You will never catch us. We will always be ahead of you.' It was our Divine Lord who said: 'Suffer little children to come unto me.' There will be a lot of suffering if that is the mentality that prevails in Ireland. I am surprised and I am disillusioned because no Minister for Education came into this Department with more goodwill than I did and I was very surprised. Maybe some day I shall tell the tale and no better man to tell it. I shall pull no punches. Christian charity how are you.[38]

In 1968, an article by an Assistant Secretary of the Department of Education in *Studies* drew a sharp rejoinder from the Teaching Brothers' Association, who accused the department of 'nationalisation by stealth'.[39] At the end of that year Mr O'Malley's successor as Minister for Education, Mr Brian Lenihan, had a brief but sharp public controversy with the Council of Managers of Catholic Secondary Schools, in which teachers' salaries provided the ostensible issue but in which more fundamental questions about the balance of power between managers and the State loomed in the background.[40]

On one occasion public controversy occurred between a minister and a bishop. This happened in 1965–6, and the participants were Mr George Colley, who then held the portfolio of Education, and Bishop Browne of Galway. The issue between

38. *Seanad Debates*, LXII, 1090 (9 Feb. 1967).
39. *Studies* (LVII, no. 227) Autumn 1968, 282.
40. *Irish Times*, 7, 10, 17 and 18 Dec. 1968.

them was the department's policy of amalgamating small rural schools. The bishop based his objections to this policy mainly on educational grounds: that the small rural schools fostered a sense of community; that their educational record was just as good as that of larger schools; that amalgamation of small schools would entail many children travelling long distances by bus, which was bad for their health. He also, however, raised the question of ecclesiastical authority, by complaining that there had been no discussion with 'those who were recognised as having a responsibility in education'. The hierarchy, he said, had not been consulted, and a letter from them expressing disapproval of the policy of amalgamation had been left unacknowledged by the minister. Mr Colley, however, stood his ground. He argued that his proposals were educationally sound, and denied that he had implemented them without consultation. He had, he said, informed the Catholic Clerical Managers' Association of his intentions, and had received no objection from them. While it was true that he had not replied to the hierarchy's letter, he had received a deputation from the Irish bishops, and 'it was not true to say they opposed his policy. It is true to say there are certain members of the hierarchy who are opposed to my policy, but there are only certain members, and not the hierarchy as a whole'.[41]

The significant feature of the controversy between Mr Colley and the Bishop of Galway, however, is that it was an isolated episode. On the whole, the Irish bishops have been notable for the cordiality with which they have welcomed the reforming plans of the Department of Education. Cardinal Conway said in 1966: 'The national aim of providing the best possible post-primary education is not merely welcome, but has the enthusiastic support of the Church. Indeed, this has been made clear to the responsible authorities time and again since the policy was first put forward a few years ago.'[42] Bishop Rogers of Killaloe, speaking only a few days after an exchange between the Bishop of Galway and Mr Colley, denied that there was any clash between Church and State in education, and added that 'given

41. For this controversy see *Irish Times*, 13 Sept. 1965; *Irish Independent*, 22 Sept., 7 Oct. 1965; and *Irish Times*, 7 Feb. 1966.
42. *Irish Times*, 27 Jan. 1966.

goodwill and co-operation, there should be no difficulty in seeing the Minister's excellent schemes come to fruition'.[43] The Archbishop of Dublin, Dr McQuaid, speaking in October 1967, described the minister's aim of enlarging the facilities for education as 'welcome and very praiseworthy', and added that 'it is a policy that I have always advocated'.[44] The introduction of comprehensive schools in areas with inadequate post-primary facilities was, I have been informed in interview by Cardinal Conway, welcomed from the first by the hierarchy. The provision of building grants for secondary schools was, I am informed on the same high authority, not merely not opposed by the hierarchy but sought by it. The bishops have remained aloof in the controversy between the Department of Education and the owners of secondary schools, and at primary level they have recently initiated a reform of their own. A statement from the hierarchy in June 1969 announced that a scheme would be prepared for associating the parents of children at primary school with the work of the school.[45] It remains to be seen what this will amount to in practice, but it could lead to the introduction into primary education of the element of democratic local control which has hitherto been so notably lacking.[46]

Particularly interesting was the hierarchy's reaction to the plan, announced by Mr O'Malley in April 1967, for merging Trinity College and University College Dublin. The government's reason for proposing this plan was primarily economic: both institutions received financial aid from the government; the sums demanded were becoming increasingly burdensome; and the crux came when both colleges applied for large grants to enable them to build new engineering schools. At that point, the government decided that some kind of unification was necessary to bring such expensive duplication to an end.[47] But though the motives for the government's decision were largely economic, Mr O'Malley was well aware that it had other im-

---

43. *Irish Catholic Directory*, 1967, 723 (11 Feb. 1966).
44. *Irish Times*, 14 Oct. 1967.
45. *Ibid.*, 19 June 1969.
46. See above, pp. 17, 256.
47. The economic arguments were most fully explained by Mr Brian Lenihan, Mr O'Malley's successor as Minister for Education: see *Irish Times*, 28 Oct. 1968.

M

plications. In announcing the plan, he said that it would end 'a most insidious form of partition on our own doorstep', and he foresaw the new university as being 'interdenominational'.[48]

Historical precedent suggested that the hierarchy would not take kindly to such a plan. It had always discouraged Catholics from attending Trinity College, and in recent years, as we saw in the last chapter, its attitude had appeared to be hardening. Indeed there had been reaffirmations of its position from two bishops within the few weeks previous to Mr O'Malley's announcement.[49] An interdenominational merger between Trinity and U.C.D. would seem, on the face of it, to be little better from the hierarchy's point of view than allowing Catholics to enter Trinity directly. A few years previously, when such an amalgamation was suggested by a U.C.D. professor,[50] it was condemned by Cardinal D'Alton as meaning a union of incompatibles.[51]

In 1967, however, the bishops proved more flexible than their previous traditions would have led one to expect. The first public comment came from Cardinal Conway, who said that the plan 'contained a number of good ideas', and 'could make a positive step towards a rationalisation of the situation in all its aspects'.[52] The hierarchy at its first meeting after the announcement of the plan issued a non-committal communique which at least expressed no objection in principle to a merger of the two university colleges. The communique stated: 'The Bishops considered the question of university education in Ireland in the light of the recent statement by the Minister for Education. They welcomed the efforts being made towards a satisfactory solution of this question; they felt bound to point out that any sound system of university education in Ireland must be one which respected the fundamental religious and moral principles of our people.'[53]

48. *Irish Times*, 19 April 1967.
49. By Archbishop McQuaid of Dublin in an article published in *Sunday Independent*, 12 Feb. 1967; by Bishop Philbin of Down and Connor in *Commission on Higher Education, 1960–67, I: Presentation and Summary of Report*, 49–50, which was published in March 1967: see *Irish Times*, 22 March 1967.
50. *Irish Weekly Independent*, 3 April 1958: speech by Professor J. J. O'Meara.
51. *Ibid.*, 26 June 1958: speech at Maynooth.
52. *Irish Times*, 22 April 1967.   53. *Ibid.*, 21 June 1967.

At the time of writing, the fate of the merger plan is still uncertain. Opinion in both Trinity College and University College Dublin has hardened against it, and representatives of the two institutions have worked out an alternative plan, allowing for a looser association between them.[54] In the meantime, however, the hierarchy's attitude to Trinity has undergone an important evolution. In June 1970, it was announced that the bishops were seeking approval from Rome for the repeal of the statute prohibiting the attendance, without special permission, of Catholic students at Trinity. The occasion for this change in policy was stated to be 'the substantial agreement on basic issues that has been reached between the National University of Ireland and Trinity College', but Cardinal Conway, at the press conference announcing the decision, made clear that it was 'the conclusion of a process of re-thinking' which had been going on among the bishops since 1965.[55] When it is remembered how adamant the bishops had been, only a few years previously, on the subject of Trinity College, the change in attitude is remarkable. It is perhaps the most striking instance of the new flexibility which the hierarchy has been displaying in recent years.

A second area in which there has been some controversy between churchmen and statesmen has been censorship. The key figure here has been Mr Brian Lenihan, Minister for Justice between 1964 and 1968, who carried through sweeping changes. Mr Lenihan started with the film censorship which, at the end of 1964, was under fire in the press for the increasing severity of its decisions.[56] Mr Lenihan responded by replacing the Appeal Board, whose term of office was about to come to an end, with a new and more liberal-minded team.[57] The results were soon apparent in the film censor's statistics. Whereas in 1964, exhibitors had bothered to take only 18 films to the Appeal Board, and had had their appeals allowed in only six of these cases, in 1965 they took 69 films to the Appeal Board, and had their

54. *Ibid.*, 25 April 1970.
55. *Ibid.*, 26 June 1970. Rome's approval for the lifting of the statute was announced a few weeks later: *ibid.*, 7 Sept. 1970.
56. *Irish Times*, 21 Nov. 1964; *Sunday Independent*, 22 and 29 Nov. 1964.
57. *Sunday Independent*, 29 Nov. 1964.

appeals accepted, wholly or in part, in 37 cases.[58] The real innovation of the new Appeal Board was to give certificates for limited viewing, that is, for audiences above a given age. This had always been legally possible, but the film censor, and the previous Appeal Board, had been reluctant to use their power to grant such certificates: their argument, it seems, had been that to allow a film to be advertised with a limited certificate would only make it more attractive.[59] But the result of this policy had been that if a film had not been judged suitable for even the most juvenile audience, then it could not be shown in Ireland at all. Under the new regime, adult films could be shown to adult audiences.

From films, Mr Lenihan moved on to books. Since the reconstruction of the Censorship of Publications Board in 1956–7, book bannings in Ireland had aroused much less controversy than before,[60] but there was still one defect in the situation. This was that, though the censors might now be fairly liberal, they could not remove the ban on books which had been condemned by their more rigorous predecessors. In 1967, therefore, Mr Lenihan introduced a bill which provided for the removal of the ban on books after twenty years, unless the ban was specifically re-imposed.[61] This relaxation caused so little controversy that, while the bill was passing through the Dail, the minister found it possible to go further, and the act as passed provided for the unbanning of books after twelve years.[62] The result was the release of over 5,000 titles,[63] and re-bannings since have been extremely rare.[64]

These changes provoked some episcopal comment. In February 1965, just after the reconstruction of the film censorship Appeal Board, Archbishop McQuaid of Dublin told a meeting of the National Film Institute: 'Our good, ordinary people

58. Fergus Linehan, 'Films', in *Irish Times*, 14 Feb. 1966.
59. This was implied in a speech by Mr Lenihan: see Des Hickey, *Sunday Independent*, 22 Nov. 1964.
60. See above, p. 316.
61. *Dail Debates*, CCXXVIII, 680 (10 May 1967).
62. *Ibid.*, 1445 (24 May 1967).
63. M. Adams, *Censorship*, 199.
64. I have noted only one instance reported in the press: J. P. Donleavy, *The Ginger Man*. See *Irish Times*, 18 April 1969.

demand from the civil authority that we shall be protected from the public activities of those who neither accept nor practise the natural and the Christian moral law.'[65] The timing of this statement might seem to indicate a fear that the civil authority was not sufficiently protecting the people from those 'who neither accept nor practise the natural and the Christian moral law.' In May 1966, Bishop Lucey of Cork gave his views on book censorship. Far from thinking the existing censorship too strict, he considered it insufficient. The existing machinery provided for the banning of books, but exacted no other penalty from pornographers, and it operated only after a book had been published. The bishop suggested that it be made an offence to publish corrupting works. This, he said, would 'make authors, publishers and booksellers take a long, cool look at what they would put before the public and think twice about taking the risk that can be securely and profitably taken as things are'.[66] Dr Lucey's statement came soon after the first newspaper report that the literary censorship was to be reformed,[67] and may have been an attempt to ensure that, when change came, it would come in what he considered the right direction.

Neither of these episcopal statements, however, had any effect on government policy, and they appear to have been quite isolated. Nor were all clerics on the same side. Among the influences which made possible the relaxation of censorship laws was the work of some younger priests, such as Father Peter Connolly of Maynooth and Father John Kelly, S.J., who produced, in clerically-managed periodicals such as *Studies* and the *Furrow*, temperate and balanced reviews of films or books which happened to be banned in Ireland. Father Connolly explained his strategy in an article published in 1964:

The real aim of whatever articles I published . . . was to bypass the kind of anti-censorship wars which . . . in my opinion, are wholly outmoded. Carried on valiantly by *The Bell* writers in the 'forties those wars had pushed 'liberal' litterateurs and conservative Irish readers farther and farther apart and pinned them down on extreme wings. It was time to try something else. This formula was to offer

65. *Ibid.,* 18 Feb. 1965.   66. *Ibid.,* 16 May 1966.
67. *Sunday Independent,* 8 May 1966.

positive appreciations of contemporary films and books which would simply ignore polemics about our censorship. It would demonstrate to Irish readers that in face of modern novels or films of whatever kind it was not necessary to bury one's head in the sand nor on the other hand to sacrifice one jot of moral principle. . . . In this way we hoped for a gradual growth of the climate of Catholic opinion which would make a juvenile standard of censorship—though not all censorship—untenable.

Father Connolly found that this approach was generally successful. 'For the one Parish Priest who told you that you were undermining the simple faith of the people', he wrote, 'a score of priests and as many lay-people showed they were reassured in theirs.'[68]

There was one aspect of censorship which Mr Lenihan did not tackle. This was the prohibition on books and periodicals which advocate 'the unnatural prevention of conception'. In introducing his Censorship of Publications Bill, Mr Lenihan explained that to alter the law here might involve amending other legislation as well, such as the Criminal Law Amendment Act of 1935 which had forbidden the sale and import of contraceptives, and that he thought it better to leave the question aside for the moment.[69] But though there has been no change in the text of the law on this point, there has been a marked change in its application in recent years. The world-wide debate among Catholics on the ethics of contraception has spilled over into Ireland, and both sides of the case are now freely argued in books, television and the newspapers. Indeed so many Irish newspapers and periodicals have now carried letters or articles putting the case for contraception—as well as ones putting the other side— that, if the law were strictly enforced, it would probably appear that the majority of Irish publications have broken it. The *Sunday Independent,* the *Sunday Press,* the *Irish Times,* and the weekly periodical *Woman's Way* can perhaps be singled out for the frankness with which this topic has been treated in their columns. But the Censorship Board has never molested them and they continue to flourish.

68. *Hibernia,* Feb. 1964, 9.
69. *Dail Debates,* CCXXVIII, 684 (10 May 1967).

The third subject on which some politicians have received criticism from some churchmen has been constitutional reform. The current Irish constitution was adopted in 1937 and has not been amended since 1941, and it is reasonable to suppose that it may no longer be as well suited to Ireland's needs as it once was. In 1966, therefore, the then Taoiseach, Mr Lemass, arranged for an all-party committee of the Dail to be set up to review it.[70] The committee's report, published at the end of 1967, comprised a rather random collection of recommendations of varying importance, most of which need not concern us here, but one of its suggestions—that proposing an amendment to Article 41, on the family—is certainly relevant. The committee examined the section of Article 41 which provides that 'no law shall be enacted providing for the grant of a dissolution of marriage'. It noted that this prohibition had been criticised for ignoring 'the wishes of a certain minority of the population who would wish to have divorce facilities and who are not prevented from securing divorce by the tenets of the religious denominations to which they belong'. It remarked that the prohibition was 'a source of embarrassment to those seeking to bring about better relations between North and South', since divorce existed in Northern Ireland, and it referred to 'the more liberal attitude now prevailing in Catholic circles in regard to the rites and practices of other religious denominations, particularly since the Second Vatican Council'. The committee concluded that the clause was unnecessarily rigid, and proposed its replacement by an alternative on lines such as the following: 'In the case of a person who was married in accordance with the rites of a religion, no law shall be enacted providing for the grant of a dissolution of that marriage on grounds other than those acceptable to that religion.' Such an amendment, it believed, would meet with no objection from any quarter.[71]

The committee's hopes that there would be no objection were soon shattered. Cardinal Conway was the first bishop to comment. He began by remarking that 'although in most countries official commissions normally consult interested bodies before

70. *Irish Times*, 4 April, 3 Sept. 1966.
71. *Report of the Committee on the Constitution, December, 1967*, 43–4.

drawing up their reports, there has not been the slightest consultation of the Catholic hierarchy in this case'. He went on:

The proposal would involve the setting up of divorce courts in the Republic. In the beginning they would be limited in scope but, inevitably, this would only be the first step. Everyone knows how these things spread once the gates are opened. Already, within 24 hours, one national newspaper has suggested that there should be divorce for all.

One must have the greatest possible respect for the tenets of our fellow-Christians. Yet, in fact, comparatively few of them believe in divorce, and still fewer of them want it. Even these few have little difficulty in securing a divorce elsewhere, and many of them have done so. One may ask whether what inconvenience there is, affecting very few, would justify such a radical and far-reaching break with our national traditions.

One thing is certain. Once the first divorce law has been introduced it will only be a matter of time till it is extended to apply to everybody. I am sure that Irish husbands and wives will ponder very carefully on what the committee's proposal to open the gates to divorce will almost inevitably lead to in terms of family life.[72]

The Archbishop of Dublin, Dr McQuaid, referred to the subject a few weeks later, in his lenten regulations:

Recently a proposal has been put forward by an informal committee to allow certain facilities for civil divorce in some instances.

Civil divorce, as a measure which purports to dissolve a valid marriage, is contrary to the law of God.

The experience of other countries has proved that civil divorce produces the gravest evils in society.

The effort, even if well-intentioned, to solve hardships within marriage by civil divorce has invariably resulted for society in a series of greater sufferings and deeper evils.[73]

72. *Irish Times,* 15 Dec. 1967.
73. *Ibid.,* 26 Feb. 1968.

Dr Hanly, the Bishop of Elphin, and Dr Lucey, the Bishop of Cork, are among other members of the hierarchy who have protested against the proposal.[74]

It is unlikely that any Irish government would adopt the committee's recommendation on this matter. Quite apart from the bishops' objections, the wording proposed by the committee would raise legal difficulties. The committee contained no Protestants, and evidently consulted no Protestant authorities. Had it done so, it would have discovered that it is not always easy to find out what, if any, are the grounds for a dissolution of marriage acceptable to a particular denomination. If the amendment proposed by the committee were to be accepted, the Irish courts might find themselves plunged into assessing the matrimonial doctrines of the various reformed Churches.

Episcopal comment on the Report of the Committee on the Constitution was, however, just as interesting for what it did not say as for what it said. For the committee's proposals in regard to Article 41 were not the only ones in which bishops might have been expected to show an interest. The committee also discussed the clauses of Article 44 which acknowledge 'the special position of the Holy Catholic Apostolic and Roman Church' and recognise certain other religious denominations by name. It stated: 'These provisions give offence to non-Catholics and are also a useful weapon in the hands of those who are anxious to emphasise the differences between North and South. They are also defective in that they make no provision for religious denominations which did not exist in Ireland at the time the Constitution came into operation, in contrast to later provisions of the Article which apply universally to all denominations.' It went on to say that the documents of the Second Vatican Council show that the Catholic Church 'does not seek any special recognition or privilege as compared with other religions', and it recommended that these provisions be deleted.[75] Now this recommendation provoked no public comment whatever from any ecclesiastic. It could be suspected that the hierarchy had no desire to stand over Article 44, and that, in the

---

74. *Irish Catholic Directory, 1969,* 732 (25 Feb. 1968).
75. *Report of the Committee on the Constitution, December, 1967,* 47–8.

event of a revision of the constitution, these clauses could be deleted without opposition.

Subsequent events have increased this suspicion to a certainty. In September 1969 the Taoiseach, Mr Jack Lynch, in the course of a radio interview suggested that Article 44 might be amended.[76] On this occasion, Church leaders not only made no protests: they openly endorsed what Mr Lynch had said. Cardinal Conway stated: 'I personally would not shed a tear if the relevant subsections of Article 44 were to disappear.'[77] A few days later, after the autumn meeting of the Catholic hierarchy, it was officially stated that the bishops had discussed the proposed removal of Article 44 from the constitution, and that 'they had agreed that a recent statement made by Cardinal Conway represented the bishops' views'.[78] It is now, probably, only a matter of time before Article 44 is amended and the acknowledgement of the 'special position' of the Catholic Church removed from the constitution.

These three controversies of the later nineteen-sixties—on education, censorship and constitutional reform—prove, perhaps even more decisively than the quiescence of the earlier nineteen-sixties, how rapidly Ireland has been changing. For all three of them occurred only because politicians took up questions which they had previously been reluctant to touch. No politician had previously suggested the removal of the specifically 'Catholic' features of the constitution: the last controversy on the matter had occurred when *Maria Duce* complained that the constitution was not Catholic enough. No previous minister had liberalised the censorship so drastically as Mr Lenihan: the reconstitution of the Censorship Board by Mr Everett and Mr Traynor in 1956-7 had only been a first step.[79] No previous government had been prepared to make any but the most cautious changes in the education system: as a senior member of Fianna Fail has put it to me, politicians were afraid that they would 'stir up the Church'. Yet the reaction of the bishops to these unprecedented forays has been conspicuous for its moderation. Only the proposal to amend Article 41 so as to provide limited facilities for

76. *Irish Times,* 22 Sept. 1969.   77. *Ibid.,* 23 Sept. 1969.
78. *Ibid.,* 10 Oct. 1969.   79. See above, p. 316.

divorce has aroused much criticism. The suggestion that Article 44 might be amended has been specifically approved. Voices raised against censorship reform have been few and faint. In education, the hierarchy has not merely acquiesced in, but co-operated with, changes which are bound to reduce the Church's influence.

In one final controversy to be mentioned here, which has developed only while this book was in preparation, the clergy concerned have done more than merely acquiesce in changes proposed by the politicians: they have tried to push the politicians into going further. The argument has arisen over the housing shortage in Dublin. Despite a great deal of construction in the last forty years, there are still many families, especially in the city centre, who are desperately in need of better housing. Yet the government, in the face of this problem, has allowed the building industry to use much of its resources in constructing new office blocks, which are springing up all over Dublin, and often adjacent to areas of particularly bad housing. Among those who have led the protest against this policy have been several priests. Father Austin Flannery, O.P., has produced programmes on the housing crisis for Radio Eireann.[80] Father Michael Sweetman, S.J., has been prepared to share a platform with a communist, Mr Michael O'Riordan, to denounce the government's inaction.[81] Father Sean McCarron, S.J., has also criticised the government, pointing out that adequate housing is essential if people are to lead a moral family life.[82] These interventions have been none too welcome to government spokesmen, and Father Sweetman was publicly attacked in the Dail by the then Minister for Local Government, Mr Kevin Boland.[83] It will be noted that Father Flannery, Father Sweetman and Father McCarron all belong to religious orders, and it is impossible to say how far they speak for the general body of the clergy in Dublin. It is also too early to say what effect, if any, their efforts will have on government policy. But it is an

80. The text of one of these programmes was published in *Irish Press*, 4 May 1968.
81. A. Bestic, *The Importance of Being Irish*, 3.
82. *Irish Times*, 28 July 1969.
83. *Dail Debates*, CCXXXIV, 1096–9 (8 May 1968).

interesting and (in Ireland) novel experience to find priests criticising a government from a radical social standpoint.

To sum up, the nineteen-sixties saw more notable changes in Church-State relations than any previous decade covered by this book. The 'integralist' outlook which caused such tension in the forties and fifties disappeared. The divergence between 'bureaucratic' and 'vocational' viewpoints died away. Churchmen became strikingly more relaxed in their attitude to the State. They ceased to utter warnings against the encroachments of State power: indeed, they were more likely to criticise the State for doing too little than too much. And yet this transformation took place without fuss. The State continued to pay as much respect to the Church as ever. To give one example, the government is invariably represented, usually by the Taoiseach himself, when a new bishop is consecrated. Relations between ministers and bishops seem usually to have been cordial, and such controversies as have occurred have been few in number and limited in nature. It has been a revolution by consent.

The next question that arises is: why did this transformation take place? Something can be attributed to the personal factor. The hierarchy now contains many men who are a generation younger than the bishops who fought the battles of the late forties and early fifties, and who have a more moderate and flexible outlook. Prelates such as Dr Morris of Cashel, Dr Birch of Ossory, Dr Harty of Killaloe and Dr Russell of Waterford come to mind. The leadership given by Cardinal Conway, who became Archbishop of Armagh in 1963, appears to have been more flexible than that of his predecessor Cardinal D'Alton. On the other side, the retirement of Mr de Valera from active politics in 1959 appeared to release a log-jam among the politicians. His successor, Mr Sean Lemass (Taoiseach from 1959 to 1966), was not so many years younger in age, but seemed to belong to a different generation in outlook. He had a critical, questing mind, continually re-examining old assumptions and looking for better ways to do things. Under him a new generation of young and energetic ministers came to the fore: Mr Charles Haughey, Dr Patrick Hillery, Mr Donogh O'Malley, Mr Brian Lenihan, Mr George Colley and others. Like their leader, they were always ready to re-examine established assumptions, and if, say, education or censorship were shaken up during this period, this is partly due to the innovating spirit of the ministers concerned.

The outlook of the new generation of leaders in Church and State was interestingly illustrated in two interviews, with Cardinal Conway and with Mr Lemass, published during 1969. To a remarkable degree the two men said the same things. Mr Lemass, when asked 'Is the influence of the Church on Irish politics greatly exaggerated?' replied:

Oh, yes. As Taoiseach I never had the slightest problem in this regard, nor do I recollect any occasion when the Church tried to pressurise me in an area affecting government policy. Once or twice members of the hierarchy came to me to express anxiety about certain minor developments that were taking place, mainly in the context of the appointment of individuals in whom they had not much confidence, but never to the extent of pressing for a change.

I felt they were expressing their concern as citizens with certain things that were happening but they never made any attempt to impose their views on me. Once or twice I was in doubt as to what the reaction of the Church might be to some proposals and I went along to discuss them with members of the hierarchy; but this was merely to clarify my own mind. . . . These were such cases as the Adoption Bill and the Succession Bill which might affect Church interests.[84]

Cardinal Conway, interviewed on Irish television, was reported to have said that 'the hierarchy had almost as much to do with the Stormont Government as it had with the Government in the Republic'. He added that 'the notion that Ireland was governed from Maynooth was fantastic. It bore no relation to reality. He and the bishops knew no more about 95 per cent of government business than what appeared in the newspapers. Naturally, both in the North and in the South, there was contact in certain matters such as education, but the relations between the hierarchy and the government in the Republic were the normal kind of

84. *Irish Press,* 27 Jan. 1969. The Adoption Bill to which Mr Lemass referred was presumably not the original measure of 1952, which went through long before he became Taoiseach, but an amending measure passed in 1964.

relations between a government and Church Authorities'.[85] Whether the impression given by Cardinal Conway and Mr Lemass is entirely accurate is a question that we shall have to raise in the final chapter, but it is interesting that the two leaders seemed equally anxious to stress how limited is the role played by the Church.

To suggest, however, that the changes of the last few years were due merely to the personal qualities of the leaders in Church and State would be much too simple an explanation. For the question would still arise: what were the conditions which permitted this more flexible and innovating leadership to develop? Part of the answer can be found in changes which have affected the Catholic Church as a whole. For it is a commonplace that the last decade has been almost revolutionary in world catholicism. The innovations of Pope John XXIII (1958–63) and of the Second Vatican Council (1962–5) had effects which are still being worked out, and it would be natural to expect that in so intensely Catholic a country as Ireland these effects should have been particularly strong. Three examples can be given of how developments in Ireland have simply paralleled developments in world catholicism.

One is the growth of the ecumenical movement. The desire of Pope John XXIII and of the Second Vatican Council to encourage good will among Christians has had its echo in Ireland, where ecumenical contacts have developed rapidly in the last six years.[86] For the most part these events are irrelevant to a study of Church and State, but their influence has spilled over into the political field. This was most obvious in the report of the Dail Committee on the Constitution, which referred to the ecumenical movement to justify its recommendations for amending Articles 41 and 44.

A second example of how developments in Irish catholicism have paralleled developments elsewhere can be found in the growing freedom of discussion within the Church. The Second

85. Interview on Telefis Eireann, reported in *Irish Times*, 26 July 1969.
86. The growth of Catholic participation in the ecumenical movement can best be followed by examining the chronicle sections of the *Irish Catholic Directory*. There is a notable increase in the number of ecumenical events reported from 1964 on.

Vatican Council encouraged Catholics to speak their minds frankly;[87] the process has been carried to lengths which even the most liberal of the Council Fathers must find disconcerting. The most obvious example is the debate over contraception, which, as already mentioned, has been pursued just as vigorously in Ireland as elsewhere. The reaction of bishops to this climate of freer discussion has been, on the whole, not to denounce it, but to participate in it. Among the prelates who have allowed themselves to be interviewed on television have been Cardinal Conway, Archbishop Morris of Cashel, Bishop Philbin of Down and Connor, Bishop Birch of Ossory, Bishop Harty of Killaloe, Bishop Herlihy of Ferns, Bishop Lennon of Kildare and Leighlin, and Bishop Browne of Galway.[88] Archbishop McQuaid of Dublin has so far been too shy to expose himself to this kind of interview; but he has opened a press office,[89] and in recent years appears to have taken greater trouble to explain his actions to the public.[90] This climate of freer discussion has doubtless affected clerical attitudes to politics. One of the bishops involved in the health-service controversies of the nineteen-fifties has remarked to me that nowadays they might be more prepared to trust the laity. The willingness of the hierarchy to accept recent reforms in education is perhaps an example of this greater trust in the laity being displayed.

A third field in which trends in world catholicism can be seen reflected in Ireland is that of Catholic social teaching. In 1961 Pope John XXIII published an encyclical on social questions, *Mater et Magistra*, which was the first comprehensive treatment of social questions by a pope since Pius XI's encyclical

---

87. See especially the Dogmatic Constitution on the Church, paragraph 37: W. Abbott, S.J. (ed.), *The Documents of Vatican II*, 64–5.

88. I have compiled this list with the aid of two friends connected with Telefís Éireann. We have tried to make it as complete as possible: I hope that no bishop has been inadvertently omitted.

89. *Irish Times*, 16 March 1965.

90. e.g. his statement of the reasons for the removal of a controversial crib in Dublin Airport church, *Irish Times*, 4 Jan. 1965; and his article explaining the reasons for the ban on Catholics attending Trinity: *Sunday Independent*, 12 Feb. 1967. The latter article turned out to be simply a repetition of a pastoral letter of 1961; but it is interesting that Dr McQuaid considered it desirable to reply to criticisms of the ban, which were becoming increasingly frequent at that time.

Quadragesimo Anno of 1931. There are some marked differences of emphasis between the two documents. John XXIII, for instance, scarcely mentions vocational organisation; and when he does so it is only to give the warning that vocational groups must not develop the defects of bureaucracy.[91] He agrees with Pius XI on the principle of subsidiarity—that a larger association should not 'arrogate to itself functions which can be performed efficiently by smaller and lower societies'[92]—but he goes on to say that in modern conditions this still entails leaving the most extensive powers in the hands of the State:

Recent advances in scientific knowledge and productive techniques give to the public authority much more power than it formerly had to remedy lack of balance, whether between different sectors in the economy, or between different parts of the same country, or even between the different peoples of the world. It has more power also to control the disorders which arise out of the unpredictable fluctuations in the economy and effectively to prevent the emergence of mass unemployment. Governments have the care of the common good and in these conditions it is urgently necessary for them to intervene more frequently in economic matters, on a wider scale than formerly and with better organisation; and, to this end, to establish the laws, offices, means and methods of action appropriate to these tasks.[93]

If we find, then, that Irish Catholics have ceased to press for vocational organisation, or that they are less afraid than they used to be of State power, the development is not a purely local one: it mirrors the trend in the social teaching of the popes.

To explain recent changes in Irish catholicism, however simply as a reflection of changes in world catholicism would, not meet all the facts of the case. For it is generally agreed that, towards the end of the nineteen-fifties, Ireland as a whole, and not just Irish society in its religious aspect, passed some kind of turning-point. It is easy to illustrate the consensus on this matter because, by some coincidence, there has been a spate of general

91. *Mater et Magistra,* paragraph 65.
92. *Ibid.,* paragraph 53.
93. *Ibid.,* paragraph 54. I am using the translation in the Catholic Social Guild publication, *The Social Thought of John XXIII.*

works on Ireland in the last four years, and all the authors concerned stress this point. Mr T. P. Coogan takes 1957 as the watershed year;[94] Mr Tony Gray and Professor Oliver MacDonagh prefer 1959;[95] Mr Garret FitzGerald appears to suggest 1958.[96] Mr Donald Connery and Mr Alan Bestic offer no exact date as beginning the transformation, but they are so impressed with its existence that they organise their books round a description of it.[97]

There is considerable agreement between these authors, also, on the nature of the turning-point. Mr Connery speaks of a move from inertia to ferment.[98] Mr Bestic notes more frankness of discussion and less sensitivity to outside criticism.[99] Mr Charles McCarthy says that 'there has been a remarkable change in our society in recent years, a growth of frankness, a growth of moral maturity'.[100] Mr T. P. Coogan says: 'In the last few years an enormous psychological change has occurred in Ireland. The conviction that things could be improved has dawned on a people conditioned to believe that they could only get worse.'[101] Mr Garret FitzGerald speaks of 'a transformation of the economy of the Republic and, most important of all perhaps, a transformation of the outlook of the Irish people'.[102] There seems general consensus, then, that the change is a psychological one, and that the Irish people have become more optimistic, more adventurous, more self-confident and more ready to accept criticism from themselves and from others.

What are the causes of this psychological transformation of a people? The most comprehensive list is provided by Mr Connery, who has written one of the best of the recent spate of books on Ireland. He suggests five factors. One of these—the liberalisation of the Roman Catholic Church initiated by Pope John XXIII— we have already dealt with. The others are: the shift from isolationism to outward-looking national policies (by which

94. T. P. Coogan, *Ireland since the Rising*, esp. 104–5.
95. Tony Gray, *The Irish Answer*, 88; O. MacDonagh, *Ireland*, 132.
96. G. FitzGerald, *Planning in Ireland*, 41.
97. D. Connery, *The Irish*; A. Bestic, *The Importance of Being Irish*.
98. D. Connery, *op. cit.*, 29.
99. A. Bestic, *op. cit.*, 3–5.
100. C. MacCarthy, *The Distasteful Challenge*, 112.
101. T. P. Coogan, *op. cit.*, 105.   102. G. FitzGerald, *op. cit.*, 41.

Mr Connery means the Irish involvement in United Nations peace-keeping, the application to join the Common Market, and a more relaxed attitude to the communist world, shown in new trade relationships with communist nations); the sweeping in of all manner of foreign influences (by which he means the increase in the number of foreign-owned factories, the increase in tourism, the loosening grip of the censors and the greater professionalism of Irish journalism); the advent of television; and the economic improvement which has created both confidence and new demands.[103]

The last two of these factors deserve a little more discussion. Television has been a growing influence in Ireland from the early fifties, since the British programmes could be received over a considerable portion of the country, including the main population centre, Dublin. But its real importance for Irish culture has come with the opening of a national television service, Telefis Eireann, on New Year's Day 1962. Television is a medium which requires controversy. A newspaper can get away with a single, slanted presentation of views for years on end; but a television discussion will be intolerably dull unless the participants disagree with each other. Telefis Eireann has come to realise that this applies to religious discussions as much as to any others, and as time has gone on it has allowed increasing freedom of discussion on religious topics. Out of many possible examples, two may be mentioned. One was Mr Michael Viney's programme, 'Too Many Children?' broadcast late in 1966, in which Dublin mothers discussed frankly their attitudes to family planning.[104] The other is Mr Gay Byrne's *Late Late Show*, put on every Saturday night throughout most of the year, which is Telefis Eireann's most popular discussion programme, and which often tackles religious topics.[105] If there is much more public discussion among Irish Catholics than there used to be, it cannot entirely be attributed to the influence of the Vatican Council; the indigenous factor of a local television service must be taken into account as well.

103. D. Connery, *op. cit.*, 37–43.
104. Described in *ibid.*, 170–2.
105. For a report of one especially controversial programme see *Sunday Press*, 3 April 1966.

Mr Connery's last point—the effects of economic improvement —is perhaps his most important. It is all the more important because of the background of catastrophic depression from which it has sprung. The early and middle fifties were, economically, most discouraging years for Ireland. Economic growth was slow, inflation was serious, and emigration was high[106]— and all this was made more galling by the fact that the rest of Europe, including Ireland's nearest neighbour Britain, seemed to be riding a wave of prosperity. Then in 1956 came a balance-of-payments crisis, the imposition of ferocious fiscal measures by the government in an attempt to solve the problem, and an actual decline in national output.[107] The shock to the national morale proved almost mortal. Mr Coogan writes: 'I remember only too vividly the depressing experience of saying goodbye seemingly every week to yet another bank clerk, lawyer, student, carpenter or whatever—all of them emigrating. "This bloody country is finished" was a phrase heard with dirgelike regularity.'[108] Mr FitzGerald states: 'The severity of the psychological impact of this crisis can scarcely be overstated, for it provoked doubts in some minds even as to the viability of an independent Irish State, and led some people to throw up secure jobs in order to seek their fortunes in other countries which seemed, unlike the Ireland of those years, to have a future for them and their children.'[109] Professor MacDonagh recalls: 'In certain regions—the northwest midlands and northeast Connacht, for example—the sense of decay and premonitions of doom were overwhelming in the mid 1950s; it was all too easy to see here the first stages of a general depopulation, in which moreover, unlike the nineteenth-century exodus, there seemed no hope of subsequent resurrection.'[110] In 1957 emigration reached a figure only just short of the total number of births for that year.[111]

That Ireland turned the corner is generally attributed to the advice of a young and newly-appointed Secretary of the Department of Finance, Mr T. K. Whitaker, who, with the authority of the Fianna Fail government newly returned to office, elabor-

106. G. FitzGerald, *Planning in Ireland*, 8–9.   107. *Ibid.*, 14–15.
108. T. P. Coogan, *Ireland since the Rising*, 107.
109. G. FitzGerald, *op. cit.*, 15.
110. O. MacDonagh, *Ireland*, 130.   111. G. FitzGerald, *op. cit.*, 17.

ated the First Programme for Economic Expansion which was published in 1958. Its target was a modest one—a growth rate of two per cent per annum—but even that was an improvement for a country whose growth rate had been nil, and by showing how this target might be attained he helped to restore national morale.[112] In the event Ireland did even better than he had forecast, and the growth rate in the years 1959–63 was not two per cent but four per cent,[113] with proportionately good results for the national morale. Since 1965 the Irish economy has had a more chequered career, but at least the corner has been turned, and it is some consolation in more recent troubles that Ireland is no longer the exception but that many other countries are having their difficulties too.

The tonic effect on the national psychology of the economic recovery since 1958 has had effects in every aspect of the national life. Its impact can be traced in Church-State relations as elsewhere. If the State has been more prepared to intervene in the field of education, for instance, this is partly because, with the growth of the economy, there is more money available; it is also because, with the growth of economic planning, there is more realisation of the economic benefits of educational efficiency. The Second Programme for Economic Expansion, published in 1963–4, contains a section on education.[114] And one reason why there has been so little criticism of State intervention from exponents of Catholic social teaching in Ireland in recent years may be that, with the advent of the First Programme, State action in the economic sphere has achieved a great success. It is not only *Mater et Magistra* which has made State intervention more respectable in Ireland; developments in Ireland itself have had the same effect.

One can agree with all Mr Connery's points in accounting for the psychological transformation of Ireland in recent years, and yet wonder if some deeper factor may not also be at work. A notable feature of Irish history ever since the great famine of

112. For accounts of Mr Whitaker's plan and its effects see T. P. Coogan, *op. cit.*, 106–8; O. MacDonagh, *op. cit.*, 131–3; G. FitzGerald, *op. cit.*, 15–52.
113. Derived from G. FitzGerald, *op. cit.*, 45.
114. *Second Programme for Economic Expansion*, Part II, 193–206.

1845–8 has been the series of sudden transformations which the country has undergone, at intervals of roughly a generation. The famine itself was the first and greatest of these watersheds, with its enormous human loss at the time, and its enduring effect on the national morale, shown by the unique phenomenon of a continuous population decline lasting for over a century. Then about 1880, there was another watershed, when a long period of pessimistic resignation and of ineffective political leadership came to an end, and a period of greater toughness began, in which a younger generation of leaders such as Parnell, Davitt and John Dillon led the country to victory in the land war and nearly achieved home rule. They and their followers in due course grew old and relatively satisfied, and after 1916 they in their turn were swept aside, as another generation pushed through a political revolution. It does seem, as Professor Mac-Donagh has pointed out, that in Irish history there are clearly-marked points at which one generation supersedes another.[115] If this is so, then another such generational take-over was overdue by the end of the fifties. We have already suggested, in an earlier chapter, that the growing tensions which were detectable in the late forties and early fifties may have been due to a conflict of generations.[116] Perhaps what happened in the late fifties was that the younger generation finally took control. This was the first generation to have grown to maturity since independence, a fact which may help to account for its psychological characteristics of poise, adventurousness and self-assurance. All this is only speculative, and it would not be easy to prove, but the psychological watershed which Ireland passed at the end of the fifties is so remarkable that factors of short-term effect seem insufficient to account for it. Certainly in Church-State relations it seems to have marked the beginning of a new era.

115. O. MacDonagh, *op. cit.,* 132.
116. See above, p. 194.

CHAPTER XII

CONCLUSION

This final chapter will be devoted to the question: what does the evidence assembled in this book prove about the influence of the Catholic hierarchy on State policy in Ireland?

It is worth stressing at the outset that the influence which we are examining has been fairly rarely exercised. Most contacts between bishops on the one hand, and civil servants or ministers on the other, are likely to be at the level of administrative detail. The Department of Education seeks the approval of a bishop for the amalgamation of schools lying in different parishes. A bishop writes to the Department of Local Government over planning permission for a school or a church. The Department of Health seeks the assistance of a bishop in an argument which it is having with a religious order over conditions of work for lay staff in a hospital run by the order. This is the kind of question on which, I am given to understand, interaction between bishops and government departments is likely to be most frequent.[1] On questions of policy, contact appears to be much rarer. Archbishop D'Alton of Armagh claimed, at the time of the mother and child scheme crisis, that 'since a native Government was established, the bishops have intervened very rarely'.[2] His successor, Cardinal Conway, has stated that he and the bishops 'knew no more about 95 per cent of government business than appeared in the newspapers', and has added that the bishops have almost as much contact with the government in Northern Ireland as with that of the Republic.[3] Mr Lemass, the former Taoiseach, has spoken in interview of bishops coming to see him 'once or twice', and of his going to see them 'once or

1. An impression built up from my interviews with bishops, ministers and civil servants.
2. *Irish Catholic Directory*, *1952*, 681 (under date 18 June 1951). See above, p. 247.
3. *Irish Times*, 26 July 1969. See above, p. 393.

twice',[4] which does not suggest a high frequency of contact when it is remembered that he was Taoiseach for over seven years, from 1959 to 1966. One bishop has remarked to me in interview that generally the first that the bishops know about a new policy is when a white paper is published, by which time the government's views are to some degree settled and it is late in the day to exert influence.

These comments from highly-qualified sources seem to be borne out by what can be gleaned by a researcher. A rough indication of the frequency with which the bishops' influence has been felt on policy can be given by listing those items of legislation in the framing of which the bishops, or some of them, are known to have taken an interest. I append a list of those measures in regard to which I have evidence that, at any stage, one or more bishops were consulted or made representations. The list is as follows:

Censorship of Films Act 1923[5]
Censorship of Publications Act 1929[6]
Legitimacy Act 1930[7]
Vocational Education Act 1930[8]
The Constitution of Ireland, 1937[9]
Public Health Bill 1945[10]
Health Act 1947[11]

4. *Irish Press*, 27 Jan. 1969. See above, p. 353.
5. The responsible minister stated that this measure followed a visit to him from a deputation representing various bodies including 'the Catholic Church in Ireland.' This would presumably mean the hierarchy. See above, p. 39.
6. The historian of censorship has found evidence of some slight contact between hierarchy and government at a very early stage in the framing of this measure: M. Adams, *Censorship*, 20, 25.
7. This measure was asked for by the bishops: see above, p. 43.
8. The bishops secured a private assurance that vocational schools would not poach on the field of secondary schools: see above, p. 38.
9. There are some indications that Church authorities were consulted on the wording of certain articles: see above, p. 56. The Church of Ireland Archbishop of Dublin was consulted on the wording of Article 44—see G. Seaver, *John Allen Fitzgerald Gregg, Archbishop*, 127—and it would be surprising if no Catholic bishop were consulted as well.
10. The parliamentary secretary responsible for the bill consulted the Archbishop of Dublin about it: see above, p. 138.
11. The hierarchy protested against this measure, but only after it had been passed: see above, p. 143.

Intoxicating Liquor (Amendment) Bill 1948[12] (private member's bill)

Adoption Act 1952[13]

Vital Statistics and Registration of Births, Marriages and Deaths Act 1952[14]

Health Act 1953[15]

Agriculture (An Foras Talúntais) Act 1958[16]

Intoxicating Liquor Act 1960[17]

Charities Act 1961[18]

Adoption Act 1964[19]

Succession Act 1965[20]

This makes a total of sixteen measures. The number of statutes enacted by the Irish parliament since 1923 has been about 1,800.

This list will, it is true, underrepresent the involvement of the Irish hierarchy in policy in two ways. First, it includes only items

12. Publicly condemned by the hierarchy: see above, p. 177.

13. This measure was introduced only after a committee of the hierarchy had expressed approval of such a proposal, given certain safeguards, and the Archbishop of Dublin was consulted constantly while it was being framed: see above, pp. 275–6.

14. My evidence in this case is only inference. One bishop mentioned to me that there had been consultation on the law of marriage, and a glance through the statute book suggested that this was the most likely measure to have provided the occasion for such consultation. As it altered the statutory duties laid on clergymen officiating at marriages, it would be only reasonable if the Churches were consulted.

15. The hierarchy protested against this measure as it was passing through the Dail: see above, p. 285.

16. The form taken by this act was influenced by the protests made from many quarters, including some bishops, to earlier proposals for an Agricultural Institute: see above, pp. 308–11.

17. The bishops publicly criticised the recommendations of the commission of inquiry into the liquor laws on which this measure was based: see above, pp. 327–9.

18. Mentioned to me in interview by a bishop. The measure included clauses regulating bequests for religious purposes, so it was reasonable that consultation with the Churches should take place.

19. Mentioned in interview by Mr Lemass, *Irish Press*, 27 Jan. 1969. See above, p. 353. The fact that consultation with the bishops had occurred could be inferred from the speech of the Minister for Justice, Mr Charles Haughey, introducing the bill. He remarked that there had been discussions with 'social workers, persons in adoption societies, various religious authorities and so on': *Dail Debates*, CCV, 976 (6 Nov. 1963).

20. Mentioned in interview by Mr Lemass, *Irish Press*, 27 Jan. 1969. See above, p. 353.

of legislation, and so omits other important policy decisions in which bishops took an interest, but which were not embodied in statute. The educational changes of the sixties, for instance, on several of which the hierarchy was consulted,[21] do not appear in the list because, on the whole, they did not entail legislation. The mother and child scheme does not appear on the list either, because it was not a statute, but an outline of regulations in implementation of a statute.

Again, the list underrepresents the involvement of the bishops because it is probably incomplete. In compiling it, I have had to rely on gleanings from published documents and on the recollections of those whom I have interviewed, and neither source is likely to be comprehensive. I can name a number of measures where consultation between government and hierarchy would appear to have been probable, but where I have no evidence that it actually took place. The Criminal Law Amendment Act 1935 (which forbade the sale of contraceptives), the Children Act 1941 (which regulated the reformatories and industrial schools run by religious orders), and perhaps the Intoxicating Liquor Acts of 1924, 1927 and 1943 are examples. The Dance Halls Act 1935 may be another: as was mentioned in an earlier chapter, one clerical writer believes this act to have resulted from representations from some of the bishops, though I have no more direct evidence that such representations were made.[22]

Nonetheless, when all these provisos are made, it does not seem likely that contact between government and bishops at the level of policy is at all frequent. To put it in quantitative terms, one might guess that, since 1923, there have been three or four dozen items of legislation or other questions of policy on which government and bishops have been in consultation. This would work out at an average of not more than one such issue a year.

Not only is contact between ministers and bishops on matters of policy infrequent, but when it does occur it appears to be generally amicable. This was brought home to me when, at a late stage in this research, I interviewed Dr McQuaid, the Arch-

---

21. See above, pp. 340–1.   22. See above, p. 50.

bishop of Dublin. Dr McQuaid summed up his twenty-nine years' experience as archbishop by saying that ministers had always accorded him courtesy and cordial co-operation, and that what struck him most on looking back was the absence of contention. Dr McQuaid's judgment is emphatic, and yet perhaps it is no more than one would expect. Preceding pages have offered few instances of overt conflict between bishops and ministers, and in a country so homogeneous as Ireland, this was only natural. Churchmen and statesmen were moulded by the same culture, educated at the same schools, quite often related to each other. In these circumstances the chances for conflict were cut to a minimum.

Granted all this, however, the question still arises: if conflict does occur, which is the more influential party? In the event of disagreement, whose view is more likely to prevail, the bishop's or the minister's? Two opposing answers to this question are sometimes met. The first is to assert that the Catholic hierarchy stands in relation to the government in the same position as any other interest group. The bishops' opinions, according to this view, will be listened to by the government, and, if they seem reasonable—or if they seem likely to be popular with the electorate—may well be accepted. But the final decision is taken by the government, and the hierarchy is not essentially in any different position from the Irish Congress of Trade Unions, or the Federation of Irish Industries, or any other body believed to speak for a considerable number of citizens. This is a point of view which I have met most often in private conversation, particularly with members of Fianna Fail, who are inclined to claim that it represents the attitude of their own party. But it can occasionally be found in print. Mr Sean MacBride, for instance, in debate with an Ulster Unionist who argued that the Republic was governed by the hierarchy, replied: 'Surely the leaders of the Church everywhere were entitled to express views concerning legislation which would affect them, just as trade unionists and other bodies had the right to do the same.'[23]

This theory, however, does not seem fully to accord with the facts. To begin with, it does not square with the self-image of

23. *Irish Times,* 24 April 1954: speech at Kilkenny.

the Irish Catholic hierarchy, whose words have been surprisingly peremptory on occasions. To cite a few examples:

The hierarchy must regard the Scheme proposed by the Minister for Health as opposed to Catholic social teaching.[24]

Where there has been no existing and long-standing custom, to open public houses on Sundays even for a few hours would be a serious violation of . . . ecclesiastical law. So long as this ecclesiastical law remains it would be sinful to agitate for their opening.[25]

Acting then in virtue of the authority conferred on us by our sacred office, we declare that it is a mortal sin for a Catholic to become or remain a member of an organisation or society, which arrogates to itself the right to bear arms.[26]

Or to quote the comment of an individual bishop on the intervention against the Health Bill in 1953:

When the bishops in this country took a stand not so long ago on the Health Bill, they were not acting as a mere pressure group: they were not exercising the democratic right they undoubtedly had as citizens to make representations directly to the Government. They intervened on the higher ground that the Church is the divinely appointed guardian and interpreter of the moral law. . . . In a word their position was that they were the final arbiters of right and wrong even in political matters.[27]

These are not the words of a private interest group making submissions to a government whose ultimate supremacy is recognised: they are the words of men who believe that they have an authority of their own, independent of the State, and which they may use even to give guidance to the State.

Nor does the view that the hierarchy is merely one interest group among others accurately portray how politicians in fact behave. Even members of Fianna Fail administrations, whatever

24. Ruling on the mother-and-child scheme: see below, Appendix B, p. 427.
25. Statement of 20 June 1950: see above, p. 178.
26. Statement of 18 Jan. 1956: see above, p. 321.
27. Speech by Bishop Lucey of Cork at Killarney, 12 April 1955: see above p. 312.

some of them may claim in private, do not treat the hierarchy as being on a par with other interest groups. When the hierarchy sent their protest against the Health Bill to the newspapers in April 1953, the effect on Mr de Valera was electric. He dropped all his engagements, drove off to see the Primate, and asked for the letter to be withdrawn. One could not imagine his treating a letter from the Irish Trade Union Congress, or from a manufacturers' or farmers' organisation, with such concern. Again, on the legal adoption question, Fianna Fail, no less than the inter-party government, proved reluctant to legislate until the hierarchy had given the all clear. And on education, it is only in the changed climate of the last few years that Fianna Fail has been willing to put through a programme of reform: until recently, Fianna Fail was just as wary as were other parties of arousing the hierarchy. As for Mr MacBride, whatever he may have said in debate with an Ulster Unionist, his own conduct in 1951 shows that he did not then put the hierarchy on a level with the trade unions. As he said during the debate on Dr Browne's resignation: 'All of us in the Government who are Catholics are ... bound to give obedience to the rulings of our Church.'[28]

The analogy between the hierarchy and other interest groups breaks down because, in a mainly Catholic country, the Catholic hierarchy has a weapon which no other interest group possesses: its authority over men's consciences. Most politicians on all sides of the house are committed Catholics, and accept the hierarchy's right to speak on matters of faith or morals. Even politicians who are personally indifferent on religious matters will recognise that the majority of the electorate are believers, and will act accordingly.[29] Mr Sean O'Faolain made the point at the time of the mother and child controversy:

If a Prime Minister in England were informed by the Archbishop of Canterbury that a proposed law would be condemned by the Church of England, he would deplore it, but he would not be afraid of any effects other than political effects. If our Taoiseach were informed thus

28. See above, p. 232.
29. Two ex-ministers whom I have met have told me that they are not believing Catholics. Neither of them ever avowed this in public.

by the Protestant Archbishop of Dublin he would measure the effects in the same way. And likewise with most other institutions, religious or secular. But when the Catholic Church, through its representatives, speaks, he realises, and the Roman Catholic public realises, that if they disobey they may draw on themselves this weapon whose touch means death.[30]

Mr O'Faolain had put his point in extravagant language, but he had made an essential distinction. The Catholic hierarchy is in a position matched by no other interest group in Ireland.

The opposing view of the hierarchy's position is to assert that Ireland is a theocratic State, in which the hierarchy has the final say on any matter in which it wishes to intervene. This theory was advanced in the Ulster Unionist pamphlet *Southern Ireland— Church or State?*, and was adopted for a moment by the *Irish Times* in the heat of the mother and child controversy. It is also the main theme of Paul Blanshard's book *The Irish and Catholic Power*. A certain amount of evidence can be found for it. The extreme caution shown by successive governments about legislating in the fields of, say, legal adoption or education without the prior approval of the hierarchy might seem to indicate that the politicians accepted the overriding authority of the bishops in these areas. Some of the statements made by ministers at the time of the mother and child episode would also appear to fit a theocratic-State interpretation. Mr Costello, for instance, when informing the Archbishop of Dublin that the government had abandoned the mother and child scheme, stated 'that decision expresses the complete willingness of the government to defer to the judgment . . . given by the hierarchy', and in the parliamentary debate which followed he stated that 'I, as a Catholic, obey my Church authorities and will continue to do so, in spite of the *Irish Times* or anything else'.[31]

All the same, the total record does not show that Irish governments automatically defer to the hierarchy on any point on which the hierarchy chooses to speak. The clearest example is the Sunday-opening question, where the advice given by the hier-

---

30. See above. p. 249.
31. For these, and other such statements by ministers, see above, p. 232.

archy was in the end simply rejected by the government of the day. On the health services issue, Fianna Fail governments evaded the hierarchy's protest against the Health Act 1947, and then hammered out a compromise after its protests against the Health Bill in 1953. Even the mother and child episode does not prove all that it might seem at first sight to demonstrate. Ministers certainly accepted the hierarchy's ruling with alacrity, but the situation at the time must be recalled: Dr Browne had exasperated his cabinet colleagues, some of them already disliked his mother and child scheme, and when it came to the crisis they were not prepared to save him from the trouble he had caused for himself among the bishops. The episode proves nothing about how they might have reacted if the hierarchy had opposed some measure which ministers unanimously favoured.

Neither of these opposing views, then, fully fits the facts. The hierarchy is more than just one interest group among many; but it is not so powerful that Ireland must be considered a theocratic State. Some middle view needs to be worked out.

An important feature of the hierarchy's power is that it is not a constant, of equal importance on all subjects and at all periods. Perhaps the best way of answering the question 'how much power has the Irish hierarchy?' is to seek to isolate the variables which affect its influence. One such variable, it may be suspected, is the degree of unity within the hierarchy on the topic in question. Common sense would suggest that the bishops speak with more assurance, and are more likely to make themselves heeded, if they are united on an issue than if their policy is a compromise between divergent points of view. The importance of this factor can certainly be seen in the nineteenth century. In 1845-50 a majority of the Catholic hierarchy opposed the government's plans for the establishment of non-denominational university colleges, but the government was emboldened to persevere in its intentions by the knowledge that a very large minority of the hierarchy favoured its plans.[32] In more recent years, however, it is much harder to obtain evidence of divergences of opinion

---

32. For the fullest account of this episode see T. W Moody and J. C. Beckett, *Queen's Belfast, 1845-1949*, I, 22-78.

within the hierarchy. Unanimity in public is required from the bishops by ecclesiastical legislation. The statutes of the National Council of 1956 include the sentence: 'No bishop is permitted to approve or condemn a law proposed by the civil government which affects several dioceses, until the other bishops concerned have examined the law.'[33] Similar or stronger phrases can be found in the statutes of 1875, 1900 and 1927.[34] The result is that the importance of internal divisions in the hierarchy is a factor which can only be guessed at. It would be interesting to know, for instance, whether the more conciliatory attitude of the hierarchy in recent years to State intervention in education is due to a change of opinion among the bishops as a whole, or whether it is the result of an intransigent group being overborne by the moderates. The rather divergent tone of the public statements by, say, Cardinal Conway on the one hand and Bishop Browne on the other suggests that there may be two parties; but at present this can only be speculation. It will have to be left to future researchers, with access to the archives, to assess how important divisions within the hierarchy have been.

Even in the present state of the evidence, however, three variables affecting the influence of the hierarchy may be discerned. One is that the hierarchy's influence may to some extent be affected by which party is in power. The importance of this factor must not be exaggerated. In the early years of the State, as was shown in Chapter II, there was a high degree of consensus among all parties as to what should be done by the State in order to support traditional Catholic standards of morality. In the forties and fifties, Fianna Fail and inter-party administrations reacted similarly on many issues. Neither was anxious to legislate for legal adoption until the hierarchy had clarified its attitude. Both found it expedient to retreat from the original plans for an Agricultural Institute, in face of a wide-ranging coalition of opponents which included some bishops. On the Sunday opening question, opinion in all parties seems to have evolved at much the same rate, so that a general acquiescence in the hierarchy's opinion

33. *Acta et Decreta Concilii Plenarii . . . 1956*, decree 63.
34. *Acta et Decreta Synodi Plenariae . . . 1875*, decree 247; *Acta et Decreta Synodi Plenariae . . . 1900*, decree 390; *Acta et Decreta Concilii Plenarii . . . 1927*, decree 97.

in 1950 had become general willingness to ignore it by 1959. Even on the health services issue, where the difference between inter-party and Fianna Fail administrations is most apparent, much of the difference seems to be due to the internal tensions of the inter-party government. Dr Browne had lost the confidence of his cabinet colleagues and so they were not prepared to defend him against the bishops; if he had been in better standing with his fellow-ministers, their attitude to the hierarchy might have been less compliant.

Nonetheless, the distinction between Fianna Fail on the one hand and the remaining parties on the other cannot be ignored. Fianna Fail was, after all, founded by men who had been excommunicated for their part in the Civil War of 1922–3, and it would be surprising if this experience had left no mark on their attitude to ecclesiastical authority. I have noticed the contrast most in private conversation, where senior members of Fianna Fail are inclined to boast of the independence which they have shown towards the hierarchy, while Fine Gael veterans take pride in the loyalty with which they have accepted the hierarchy's decisions. But the difference has been perceptible also in their public attitudes. In the nineteen-thirties, Fine Gael was closer to the hierarchy in its views on the I.R.A. or the Spanish Civil War than was Fianna Fail. In 1955, after the Archbishop of Dublin expressed his disapproval of the forthcoming Yugoslav football match, the inter-party government withdrew those facilities within its control but a Fianna Fail front-bencher conducted the official welcome for the visiting team. Even on the health services issue, when every allowance is made for the exasperation which Dr Browne aroused among his colleagues, the fact remains that the inter-party government showed an alacrity in deferring to the hierarchy's wishes which was never displayed by Fianna Fail. The difference may be only one of emphasis, but Fianna Fail administrations have proved somewhat more aloof from the hierarchy than administrations formed by other parties.

A second variable to be taken into account is period. Previous chapters will have shown that there was a considerable difference in the activity shown by bishops between one period and another. Three main phases may be discerned, the dividing lines between them occurring about the end of the nineteen-thirties and the end of the nineteen-fifties. The political influence of the hierarchy has been least apparent in the most recent of these periods. Indeed these last few years have been notable mainly for the acceptance by the bishops of changes which at an earlier date they would probably have opposed. Censorship of books and films has been relaxed with little complaint. The special position accorded to the Catholic Church in the constitution—a provision which at the time of its introduction in 1937 was considered by some Church authorities not to go far enough—is now likely to be removed, and the hierarchy has expressly disclaimed any interest in its retention. Above all, in the field of education, where for so long the hierarchy had shown the greatest sensitivity to any encroachments by the State, it has now accepted changes which inevitably entail an increase in State control. The great changes in Irish society during recent years have left their mark on the bishops as on everyone else, and they appear readier to trust the laity (including State officials) than they were in the past.

In the first of the three periods—that lasting till the late thirties—there is somewhat more evidence of episcopal interests impinging on State policy. The main preoccupation of the bishops in those years was the maintenance of traditional standards of morality, and this was reflected in the trend of State legislation. Divorce was prohibited, the sale of contraceptives banned, dance halls regulated, and a censorship established for books and films. However, though these measures undoubtedly gratified the bishops, there is no evidence that the hierarchy had to apply pressure to secure them, or even that it specifically asked for all of them. There was such general agreement in Irish society on the necessity of such measures that there was little need for the bishops to intervene directly. During this first period, then, episcopal influence on State policy was not obtrusive.

It is in the middle period—the forties and fifties—that the political activity of the Irish bishops was most obvious. To a great extent this reflected the stage of development reached by the Catholic social movement in Ireland. In the previous period, churchmen had been less interested in social questions; in the most recent period they have been less confident that, in such matters, they know the right answers. But in the forties and fifties, many of them believed that in the concept of 'vocationalism' hey

N

had a solution to the ills of Ireland, and they pushed it with naive energy. Bishop Dignan of Clonfert produced his plan for the reorganisation of social services; Bishop Browne of Galway presided over the commission which produced the Vocational Organisation Report. Several bishops attacked Mr Dillon's proposals for an Agricultural Institute, and one criticised Mr Norton's social welfare scheme. The hierarchy as a body sought on three occasions to modify the structure of State health services.

But the greater readiness of bishops to speak out on political issues in this period was not simply a by-product of the Catholic social movement. There was a wide range of topics on which they proved ready to express opinions. Several expressed anxiety at any softness towards communism, and Archbishop McQuaid of Dublin tried to stop a football match against Yugoslavia in 1955. A committee of the hierarchy laid down conditions for the passage of adoption legislation. Bishop Browne of Galway justified the Fethard-on-Sea boycott. The hierarchy as a whole opposed the agitation for Sunday opening of licensed premises. Ireland seemed to be going through a disturbed period, in which established attitudes were being increasingly questioned, and in which conservative sections of society—such as the bishops—felt their values threatened. The clash between those forces which in a previous chapter were labelled 'integralist', and the resistances which they built up, was at its greatest in these years.

It does not follow that, because the bishops were unusually active in this period, they were therefore unusually effective in influencing government policy. On the contrary, they took some hard knocks in these years. Bishop Dignan's social welfare plan was peremptorily rejected. Bishop Browne's vocational organisation report was shelved. Archbishop McQuaid's attempt to mediate in the school strike of 1946 was rebuffed. The hierarchy as a whole saw its advice on the licensing laws rejected, and was far from totally successful in its attempts to secure modifications in the health services. But although the bishops may not have been entirely effective in this middle period, the range of issues on which they spoke, and the vigour with which they expressed their views, meant that they were a more obvious factor in Irish politics than either earlier or later.

A third variable affecting the power of the hierarchy is the nature of the topic on which it is seeking to exert influence. Episcopal influence has probably been at its strongest in the field of education. The system taken over from the British was unique in the world for the degree of clerical control which it permitted, and it has been jealously guarded by the hierarchy. It is only in recent years, under the impact of financial pressures and of a more liberal climate of opinion, that the bishops have consented to its modification. Another area in which episcopal influence has been strong has been on questions of personal morality. The Censorship of Publications Act 1929 and the Dance Halls Act 1935, for instance, whether or not specifically asked for by the hierarchy, followed many complaints from bishops about the influx of evil literature and the evils surrounding dance halls. On legal adoption, it was accepted on all sides, by reformers as well as opponents, that this was the kind of issue on which the hierarchy was entitled to speak, and the government did not legislate until after the hierarchy had expressed its approval.

On the other hand, the hierarchy is at its weakest where strong national feeling is involved. Catholics who are prepared to subordinate their own judgment to that of the bishops on, say, education may not be prepared to do so when they believe a national issue to be at stake. This was shown during the Civil War, when republicans defied the hierarchy's condemnation, and again when the I.R.A. continued its operations despite the hierarchy's condemnations of 1931 and 1936. A quainter illustration of the same principle may be found during the war years, when the government used its powers of censorship on episcopal pastorals. The de Valera government, in many ways so deferential to the Church, was prepared, when it believed that national security was at stake, to treat bishops with no more ceremony than other citizens.

Apart from issues where national feeling was aroused, the hierarchy was most likely to have difficulty in getting its views accepted if it intervened on an issue where public opinion was not accustomed to hearing it speak. On the health services, for instance, the hierarchy had never intervened before 1947, so its *locus standi* in the matter was not established by custom. The reason, of course, was that the hierarchy had not previously seen any need to speak on this subject; but the fact that it had not done so probably made ministers, officials and the general public psychologically more resistant to intervention when it came. Again, on Sunday opening, the hierarchy was combating long-standing habits. The bishops, in their statements of 1950 and 1959, argued that the existing law, far from being relaxed, ought to be tightened and more strictly enforced. But it was far too late in the nineteen-fifties to start taking such a line. Irishmen had for generations been accustomed to their Sunday drink, and were not going to give it up now.

The extent of the hierarchy's influence in Irish politics, then, is by no means easy to define. The theocratic-State model on the one hand, and the Church-as-just-another-interest-group model on the other, can both be ruled out as over-simplified, but it is by no means easy to present a satisfactory model intermediate between these two. The difficulty is that the hierarchy exerts influence not on a *tabula rasa* but on a society in which all sorts of other influences are also at work. Party traditions can affect the bishops' power; so can change in the climate of opinion; so can the nature of the issues on which they are seeking to exert pressure. The best answer to the question 'how much influence does the hierarchy possess in Irish politics?' is that no simple answer is possible: it depends on the circumstances. This may seem an answer disappointingly lacking in precision, but it corresponds to the reality of things: any more definite answer would do violence to the evidence.

APPENDIX A

THE MOTHER AND CHILD SCHEME, 1950

Since this scheme, which plays so important a part in the preceding narrative, has never been published, the text will be reproduced here. Readers can then form their own judgment on whether it merited the criticisms which were made at the time. The original document is a cyclostyled typescript of 28 foolscap pages, dated June 1950, and headed 'Department of Health. Proposals for a Mother and Child Health Service under Part III of the Health Act, 1947'. The text is reproduced here exactly as in the original, with the omission of a three-page analytical table of contents.

I have to thank the Secretary of the Irish Medical Association for letting me see a copy of the scheme.

PROPOSALS FOR A MOTHER AND CHILD HEALTH SERVICE

1. Part III of the Health Act, 1947, provides that each health authority shall make arrangements for the safeguarding of the health of women in respect of motherhood and for their education in that respect. It also provides that each health authority shall do in respect of children who are not pupils of any school, and of pupils of schools to which the Act applies, the following things:—

(a) safeguard and improve their health and physical condition;

(b) arrange for their medical inspection at schools or other places;

(c) provide for their education in matters relating to health;

(d) provide for treatment of their illnesses and defects; and

(e) ascertain cases of mental deficiency.

2. Section 28 of the Act provides that the Minister for Health may make Regulations as to the manner in which and the extent to which health authorities are to exercise their powers under Part III of the Act.

3. Tentative schemes as set out in this memorandum have been prepared by the Minister as the basis on which Regulations will be made by him under the Act.

4. The general pattern of the service throughout the country will be the same. There will, however, be some difference between the scheme for county boroughs and the scheme for other areas. The memorandum outlines in the first instance the proposals for county boroughs and later indicates the main differences between them and the proposals for other areas.

SUGGESTED MOTHER AND CHILD HEALTH SERVICE SCHEME FOR COUNTY BOROUGHS

Scope

5. In general, the scheme will provide for safeguarding the health of women in respect of motherhood and for attendance to the health of children up to 16 years of age. No portion of the scheme is compulsory and facilities under the scheme will be provided by health authorities only with the consent of the persons concerned or, in the case of children, the consent of parents or guardians. There will be no means test.

6. It will be the aim to include provision in the scheme for the following matters:—

(a) maternity care (including ante-natal and post-natal care and attendance at confinement);

(b) gynaecological care for women in respect of motherhood;

(c) neo-natal care of the infant;

(d) health care of the pre-school child;

(e) health care of pupils of schools to which the Act applies;

(f) health care of the child who has left school;

(g) hospital, specialist and laboratory facilities;

(h) dental care for women in respect of motherhood and for children; and

(i) ascertainment of cases of mental deficiency.

7. Persons who do not avail themselves of the general practitioner facilities provided under the scheme will not be debarred from participation in any other branch of the service. They will, however, be responsible for the payment of their private doctor's fee.

Administration

8. The Corporations of county boroughs, as health authorities, are responsible for the making of the arrangements envisaged under Part III of the Health Act, 1947, in so far as their respective county boroughs are concerned.

9. The chief medical officer in each of the county boroughs will be responsible for the immediate direction and supervision of the scheme. All aspects of the health services in so far as they cover mothers and children will be integrated to form a unified service under his control. He will ensure that a close liaison is maintained between the projected service and all other branches of the health services. Admissions to hospital, in the case of children and women coming under the scheme, will generally be provided for by the chief medical officer, in accordance with special arrangements which must necessarily be made to ensure the smooth working of the scheme. In cases of urgency, however, it is proposed that any doctor may secure the admission of a person to hospital and report the matter later to the chief medical officer.

10. It is proposed that medical care for children (as detailed later) will be provided by district medical officers who will be remunerated by capitation payments. To facilitate the provision of this care and the improved functioning of the existing Medical Assistance Service (as provided under the Public Assistance Act, 1939) it is proposed that each county borough will be divided into district health units (dispensary districts) on a re-organised basis. The existing number of district health units will be increased and each district will be served by one or more district medical officers. Where more than one district medical officer is employed, the district health unit will be divided into sub-units, each served by a district medical officer who will be responsible for domiciliary medical care for patients in his sub-unit who are eligible for Medical Assistance, other than women and children to the extent to which they are catered for under the Mother and Child Health Service Scheme. The medical officer in each unit or sub-unit will attend at the district health centre (dispensary) at arranged days and times for attendance on patients in the category just mentioned. He will afford any necessary attention at the health centre to any such

patient resident in the district health unit, even though such person may not actually reside in the sub-unit in which the medical officer is responsible for domiciliary medical care for Medical Assistance patients. Every 2 or 3 or more district health units will form a Mother and Child Health Service District. The district medical officers serving in a Mother and Child Health Service District will provide a general medical care service for children resident in the district. Parents or guardians may register their children for medical care with any of the district medical officers serving in the Mother and Child Health Service District in which they are resident. This arrangement will ensure a reasonably wide choice of doctor, for general medical care for children, in each Mother and Child Health Service District.

11. It is proposed that certain built up areas which lie outside, but immediately adjoin, the county boroughs and are urban in character, e.g. housing areas at Spanglehill and Garranabraher in Cork and Donnycarney North in Dublin, will be catered for under the scheme for the county boroughs. Some dispensary districts are at present situated partly in county boroughs and partly in adjoining rural areas. The position regarding the rural portions of such districts will be considered when the re-organisation of dispensary districts in the county boroughs has taken place.

12. It is visualised that Dublin County Borough (including certain adjoining areas) will be divided into approximately 25 district health units. The total number of district medical officers will be about 85. The district health units will be amalgamated to form 9 or 10 Mother and Child Health Service Districts. The number of district medical officers in each Mother and Child Health Service District from whom a choice of doctor will be possible for medical care for children will vary between 7 and 10.

13. It is visualised that the county boroughs (including certain adjoining areas) of Cork, Limerick and Waterford will be divided into 4, 3 and 2 district health units respectively. The number of district medical officers will be about 13, 8 and 5 respectively. Cork County Borough will form one or two Mother and Child Health Service Districts. The number of district medical officers from whom a choice will be possible will depend on whether the county borough comprises one or two Mother and Child Health Service Districts. The county boroughs of Limerick and Waterford will form single Mother and Child Health Service Districts and the number of district medical officers from whom a choice will be possible will be 8 and 5 respectively.

Specialist Services

14. Specialist services will be provided by hospitals participating in the service, and/or by specialists appointed by the health authority for the purposes of the scheme. Specialist services will normally be provided at hospitals and at central clinics and they will ordinarily be made available on the 'reference-appointment' system only. Medical practitioners will normally refer patients for specialist care through the chief medical officer. Specialists will be called upon to provide domiciliary care only in exceptional circumstances.

Hospital Care

15. Hospital care will be provided in local authority hospitals and in voluntary hospitals which are prepared to co-operate in the service.

Laboratory Services

16. It is proposed to develop laboratory services generally and to provide that any person eligible for care under the scheme may obtain such services free of direct charge.

Dental Services

17. Dental attention will be afforded at a central clinic, or clinics, by staff employed by the health authority.

Care for Women in respect of Motherhood

18. This part of the service will provide for ante-natal, intra-natal and post-natal care, and for gynaecological care for women in respect of motherhood.

19. In Dublin it is hoped to make special arrangements under which the maternity hospitals will provide care, as far as possible, for women in respect of motherhood.

20. In the county boroughs (including certain adjoining areas) of Cork, Limerick and Waterford care for women in respect of motherhood will be provided, as far as possible, by staff attached to the appropriate local authority hospital. This staff will normally consist of an obstetrician-gynaecologist and such other medical, nursing and midwifery staff as may be required. Clinics will be held at out-patient departments of the hospitals and/or other appropriate centres. Antenatal, post-natal and gynaecological care will be provided at the clinics. Cases which present difficulty, or which require gynaecological

care which cannot be afforded at the ordinary clinic, will be referred to the obstetrician-gynaecologist either at the hospital, or at special clinics, which will be conducted by him. Women will be encouraged to attend regularly at the appropriate clinics for ante-natal care and they will, where necessary, be visited in their homes by the midwives or other suitably qualified nurses. Domiciliary visits by midwives or nurses will enable them to familiarise themselves with the domestic surroundings in cases in which the patient is to be confined at home, and to give advice on the making of appropriate arrangements regarding the lying-in room. A midwife or nurse attached to the hospital staff will conduct the normal domiciliary confinement. If any difficulty arises she will call in a medical officer attached to the hospital. Cases in which major difficulty is anticipated at the confinement will be confined in hospital under the supervision of the obstetrician-gynaecologist. The obstetrician-gynaecologist will be called upon to provide domiciliary obstetrical care only in exceptional circumstances, e.g. in the case of severe post-partum shock and haemorrhage. Owing to the shortage of maternity beds priority in relation to confinements in hospital may, for the present, have to be given to cases in which difficulty is anticipated and to cases where conditions are unsuitable for confinement in the home. Additional beds which it is hoped to provide will have the effect of easing the situation regarding hospital accommodation.

Health Care of Children

21. The health care proposed for children will vary, to a certain extent, according to the following groups into which children may be divided:—

    (*a*) Neo-natal infants (i.e. infants under 6 weeks);

    (*b*) Pre-school children over 6 weeks;

    (*c*) Pupils of schools to which the Act applies; and

    (*d*) Children who have left school.

In particular instances it may be necessary to provide, for children in one group, a type of medical care which is normally applicable only to children in another group, but, in general, the care proposed for the children in each group is as set out in the following paragraphs.

(*a*) Neo-natal infants

22. In Dublin County Borough (including certain adjoining areas) it is hoped to make special arrangements under which the maternity

hospitals will provide health care for neo-natal infants participating in the service.

23. In the county boroughs (including certain adjoining areas) of Cork, Limerick, and Waterford the staffs attached to the local authority hospital will provide any necessary care for infants born in the hospital, or in the county borough area generally. Special units will be provided at the hospitals for the care of premature or sick infants. Infants discharged from hospital, or born outside the hospital, will be visited regularly by a nurse. The nurse will call on the services of a medical officer if his services are considered necessary. In addition to visiting infants in their homes at the request of the nurse, medical officers attached to the hospitals will carry out general examinations of infants either in their homes or at infant welfare clinics held at appropriate centres. It is hoped that there will be at least two such examinations of each infant during the neo-natal stage—one as soon as possible after birth and the other in or about the 6th week of life. Specialist treatment and advice will be given as required at the hospital or at special clinics.

(b) Pre-school child over 6 weeks

24. Provisions for the care of this group will include:—

    (i) routine domiciliary visiting;

    (ii) general medical care;

    (iii) periodic medical examination; and

    (iv) ascertainment of cases of mental deficiency.

(i) *Routine domiciliary visiting*

25. Routine domiciliary visiting will be carried out by the public health nurse. It will be her duty to recommend parents or guardians to seek medical care for such children as appear to her to require it. Parents or guardians will be encouraged to bring their children regularly to the clinics conducted by the district medical officers and to the periodic medical examinations. The number of visits which will be paid by the nurse will vary with the age and the needs of the particular child.

(ii) *General medical care*

26. Special arrangements will be made, where necessary, for certain measures such as vaccination against smallpox and immunisation

against diphtheria] and whooping cough, and for the holding of periodic medical examinations. The provision of any other medical care, at general practitioner level, will be a matter for the district medical officer. He will be required to conduct clinics, at the district health centre (but at times different from the times of the Medical Assistance clinics) to which parents or guardians may bring children who are registered with him for medical care. He will be assisted at these clinics by a public health nurse. The district medical officer will be required, at the request of parents or guardians, to visit sick infants in their homes and to provide any appropriate treatment. It will be his duty to make arrangements for specialist and hospital care as required. He will also be required to provide, for children registered with him, appropriate medical care which may be considered necessary as a result of the periodic medical examinations (see paragraph 27).

(iii) Periodic medical examination

27. Periodic medical examinations will be conducted by medical officers employed on a whole-time or part-time basis by the health authority. This service will supplement the normal medical care provided by the district medical officer. It will be the aim to have each child medically examined at least once a year.

(c) Pupils of schools to which the Act applies

28. The provisions for children in this group will be similar to those for pre-school children over 6 weeks, except that routine domiciliary visiting by the public health nurse will not be carried out. The existing system of school medical inspection, suitably reorganised, will comprise the provision for the medical examination of children.

(d) Children who have left school

29. Provisions, similar to those for pupils of schools, will be made for children up to the age of 16 years who are not pupils of any school. Medical examination sessions for these children on the lines of those referred to in paragraph 27 will be held at suitable intervals.

Dissemination of Information and Advice on Matters relating to the Health of Mothers and Children

30. The health authorities will conduct publicity campaigns to stress the necessity for positive health measures and such campaigns will be suitably co-ordinated with the publicity campaign of the Department of Health.

Supply of Nutritional Aids, Medicines, Drugs and Medical, Surgical, Dental and Ophthalmic or other Appliances

31. Approved aids, medicines, drugs or appliances will normally be made available at the central health clinics or dispensaries on the recommendations of the medical staff employed in connection with the scheme. Details of the procedure to be adopted in this matter have yet to be drawn up.

Voluntary Health Agencies

32. The activities of voluntary health agencies, which will be prepared to be associated with the activities of health authorities, will be encouraged and assisted.

Records

33. Health authorities will make arrangements for the keeping of records in connection with the scheme. The record forms or cards will be simple in design and will be designed to facilitate the extraction by modern methods of statistical data. Medical personnel participating in the service will in particular be required to keep records of the illnesses of their patients.

MAIN DIFFERENCES BETWEEN THE SCHEME FOR COUNTY BOROUGHS AND THE SCHEME FOR OTHER AREAS

34. Existing dispensary districts vary considerably in area and population and are, in many cases, unsuitable units for the purposes of the Medical Assistance Service and the Mother and Child Health Service. A reorganisation of dispensary districts will, therefore, be necessary. Pending this reorganisation, which will be carried out as soon as possible, the introduction of a domiciliary medical care service for all children in areas other than the county boroughs will be deferred. It is accordingly necessary to distinguish between—

(a) the proposals which are common to both the interim period (i.e., the period prior to the reorganisation of dispensary districts) and the final period (i.e., the period after the reorganisation of dispensary districts);

(b) the proposals which relate to the interim period only; and

(c) the proposals which relate to the final period only.

(a) Interim and Final Periods

35. Midwives or other suitably qualified nurses employed by the local authority (but not normally attached to hospital staffs) will provide the maternity care for women which, in the county boroughs, will be provided by midwives and nurses attached to the hospital. Each area will have the services of an obstetrician-gynaecologist who will provide a service similar to that provided by the obstetrician-gynaecologist attached to the appropriate hospital in Cork, Limerick and Waterford. The obstetrician-gynaecologist will conduct special clinics at appropriate centres. A small neo-natal unit will, wherever practicable, be provided in each county hospital for the treatment of cases needing special attention. Medical care of the infant in the neo-natal period at general practitioner level will be a matter for the doctor providing the maternity care service for the mother. Gynaecological care at general practitioner level for women in respect of motherhood will be afforded by the district medical officers, except in cases where the provision of such care is a matter for a private practitioner participating in the maternity care portion of the service in the interim period (see paragraphs 36, 52, 55 and 56). Women needing specialist attention will be catered for by the obstetrician-gynaecologist at the county hospital or at clinics held at other appropriate centres.

(b) Interim Period only

36. Maternity care at general practitioner level will be provided by district medical officers and by private general practitioners who are willing to participate in the scheme. Doctors will be remunerated for this work by capitation payments as detailed later (see paragraphs 52 and 58). A choice of doctor will be possible from any of the medical practitioners participating in the service.

37. The provision of domiciliary medical care for children (other than those eligible for Medical Assistance) will be deferred pending the reorganisation of dispensary districts. District medical officers will, however, provide a health care service for all children at the district health centre or depot. They will be remunerated for this work by a lump sum payment (see paragraph 59). During the interim period dispensary medical officers will continue to be responsible for domiciliary medical care for children eligible for Medical Assistance.

(c) *Final Period*

38. Such maternity care and gynaecological care in respect of motherhood, as may suitably be given by general practitioners, will be provided by district medical officers. They will generally be remunerated for this work by capitation payments. Mother and Child Health Service Districts will be formed, as in the county boroughs, and a choice of doctor will be possible from any of the district medical officers resident in each district.

39. General medical care for children will be provided, as in the case of the county boroughs (paragraph 26), by district medical officers. They will be remunerated for this work by capitation payments, if a choice of doctor is possible, and by a lump sum payment (see paragraph 63 (*a*)) if no choice of doctor is possible.

PROPOSED PAYMENTS TO GENERAL PRACTITIONERS, RANGE OF SERVICE, ETC., UNDER THE MOTHER AND CHILD HEALTH SERVICE

40. It has already been indicated that the scheme proposed in respect of county boroughs will differ in certain respects from the scheme proposed for areas other than the county boroughs. It is necessary, therefore, to distinguish between the conditions of service, etc., which will apply:—

(A) In county boroughs; and

(B) In areas other than county boroughs in:—

    (i) both the interim and final periods;

    (ii) the interim period only; and

    (iii) the final period only.

A. COUNTY BOROUGHS

Salary as dispensary medical officer and medical officer of health

41. The salary as dispensary medical officer and medical officer of health will be unaltered in the case of existing officers. In view of the

reduction which will take place in the volume of Medical Assistance work to be performed by dispensary medical officers, consequent on the appointment of an increased number of medical officers, future appointees will enter the Medical Assistance Service on a salary scale of £322 10s. × £16 2s. 6d. × £483 15s. per annum (i.e. £300 × £15 × £450 per annum plus 7½% temporary bonus)—the salary as medical officer of health remaining unaltered.

Fees payable from other sources

42. The rates of fees payable from other sources will not be affected.

Additional appointments

43. The additional appointments required under the proposed scheme will be made initially on a temporary basis. An appointee will, in addition to duties under the Mother and Child Health Service, be required to undertake duties as district medical officer and dispensary medical officer. In the making of these temporary appointments a preference will be given to doctors already practising in the districts to which appointments relate.

Maternity and gynaecological care for patients eligible for Medical Assistance

44. Such maternity care and gynaecological care in respect of motherhood as is at present afforded by dispensary medical officers for patients eligible for Medical Assistance, will cease to be the responsibility of the dispensary medical officers, as it is proposed that this work will be undertaken by the maternity hospitals in Dublin County Borough and by local authority hospital staffs in the other county boroughs.

Capitation fees in respect of a general medical care service for children

45. In view of the intention to permit the exercise of a choice of doctor in respect of general medical care for children under the Mother and Child Health Service Scheme it is proposed that remuneration will take the form of capitation payments. Medical officers will, of course, be already in receipt of a fixed salary in respect of duties, considerably more limited than at present, as dispensary medical officers, and in arriving at the suggested capitation fees to be paid to medical officers regard has been had to this fact. The district medical officers will

provide the general medical care service for children from the age of 6 weeks to 16 years. The remuneration payable for this work will be a capitation fee of 10/- per child per annum.

Limitation on lists

46. It is intended that a maximum upper limit will be fixed regarding the number of children which any individual district medical officer may accept on his list for the general medical care service. A figure of 1,600 to 1,800 is suggested. This figure may require revision when experience has been gained as to the working of the scheme.

Choice of doctor and choice of patient

47. As already indicated parents or guardians will have a choice of doctor from among the district medical officers serving in the Mother and Child Health Service District in which they are resident. Doctors will be entitled to refuse to accept particular children for inclusion on their lists, except those children who fail to find a doctor willing to accept them and whom the local authority finds it necessary to allocate to a particular doctor. A doctor will be entitled to have a child removed from his list, after the expiration of a given period of notice, provided that the parents or guardians of the child have been able to secure acceptance of the child for another doctor's list, or that, failing this, the health authority has allocated the child to another doctor.

Range of service to be afforded under the general medical care service for children

48. The range of responsibility under the general medical care service will comprise attendance on request of a parent or guardian at the patient's home and the affording of any necessary medical care including the making of arrangements for hospital or specialist care where required; the affording of any necessary medical care or advice at sessions held at the appropriate district health centre; and the provision of treatment found necessary, as a result of the periodic medical examinations (see paragraphs 27, 28 and 29). The clinical sessions referred to will be held on such days and at such hours as may be fixed by the health authority after discussions with the medical officers. They will be held at times different from the times of the Medical Assistance clinics.

B. AREAS OTHER THAN THE COUNTY BOROUGHS

(i) *Interim and final periods*

49. Certain aspects of the conditions of service which will apply to medical practitioners participating in the service in the county boroughs will apply also to medical practitioners operating in areas other than the county boroughs in the interim and final periods, viz:—

    (*a*) salary as dispensary medical officer and medical officer of health (see paragraph 41);

    (*b*) fees payable from other sources (see paragraph 42); and

    (*c*) additional appointments (see paragraph 43).

50. Due to the differences between the schemes proposed for the county boroughs and other areas there will be certain differences between the conditions of service applicable to doctors participating in the service in areas other than the county boroughs and the conditions of service applicable to doctors serving in the county boroughs. These differences are set out in the following paragraphs.

Maternity care

51. Maternity care at general practitioner level for patients who are at present eligible for Medical Assistance will cease to be the responsibility of the dispensary medical officer as part of his duties under the Medical Assistance Service. Such care will in future be provided under the Mother and Child Health Service and it is proposed that a choice of doctor will be afforded, wherever possible, for all women wishing to avail of the service. (This choice, in the interim period, will be made possible from district medical officers and private medical practitioners who are willing to participate in the service. In the final period choice of doctor will be made possible from district medical officers only.)

Capitation fees in respect of maternity care service where a choice of doctor is afforded

52. In view of the proposal to permit, where practicable, the exercise of a choice of doctor for women in respect of maternity care under the scheme, it is proposed that remuneration will take the form of capitation payments. Medical officers will, of course, be already in receipt of a fixed salary in respect of duties, considerably more limited than at present, as dispensary medical officers, and in arriving at the suggested capitation fee to be paid to district medical officers regard has been had

to this fact. It is proposed that the capitation fee will be £4 per case. This fee will be payable both in the interim and final periods.

Lump sum addition to salary in respect of maternity care service where a choice of doctor is not afforded

53. In areas where a choice of doctor is not afforded and the service is restricted to a particular district medical officer, remuneration will take the form of a lump sum addition to the medical officer's existing salary. The amount of the lump sum will be fixed in conformity with a graduated scale which will vary in accordance with the populations of the districts in question. Details of this scale will be drawn up as soon as all aspects of this matter have been fully examined. It is expected that there will not be many areas in which a choice of doctor will not be possible. This provision will apply both in the interim and final periods.

Capitation payments to private medical practitioners participating in the maternity care service

54. As this provision will only be made in the interim period details will be found in relation thereto in paragraph 58.

Range of service to be provided under the maternity care service

55. The number of medical and obstetrical examinations required by individuals will vary but as a general rule an initial medical and obstetrical examination will be afforded at or about the 16th week of pregnancy and a further examination at or about the 36th week together with such other examinations and ante-natal care as the doctor thinks necessary or as may be requested by the midwife. Ante-natal care at an earlier stage than the 16th week will be required in certain cases. The doctor will be responsible for the general supervision of the midwife in relation to the discharge of her duties (including the giving of instructions to the midwife regarding urine testing where the midwife is regarded as suitable to discharge this work); attendance at an abortion or other emergency; attendance at the confinement (if, in the opinion of the doctor, it is required, or if he is summoned to the confinement by the midwife in attendance) and medical care of the mother and child during the post-natal period (up to 6 weeks), including a post-natal examination of the mother at or about the 6th week after the confinement, and such gynaecological care during the pregnancy and post-natal period as may suitably be given by general practitioners. It is intended that the fee to be paid or payment to be made as indicated in paragraphs 52 and 53 will cover the services

outlined above. Details of a reduced scale of fees to apply in cases where the full range of care is not given will be drawn up later, but, normally if a doctor can prove that he could not render any particular part of the proposed services for reasons outside his own control no loss of portion of the fee will be involved.

Gynaecological care

56. As intimated in paragraph 55, such gynaecological care during the pregnancy and post-natal period (6 weeks), as may suitably be given by a general practitioner, will be a matter for the doctor (district medical officer or private practitioner) providing the maternity care service. Any other gynaecological care in respect of motherhood, which may suitably be given by a general practitioner, will be a matter for the district medical officer. It will be the duty of the doctor (district medical officer or private practitioner) providing gynaecological care to make arrangements for specialist and hospital care as required.

57. Until such time as experience of the scheme in actual operation has indicated how district medical officers can best be remunerated for gynaecological work not covered by the fees payable in respect of maternity care, they will each be allowed a lump sum of £20 per annum. This payment takes into account the present obligation on medical officers (in their capacity as dispensary medical officers) to afford medical care for patients eligible for Medical Assistance. The proposed payment will apply both in the interim and final periods unless a change has been decided upon in the meantime.

(ii) *Interim Period*

Capitation payments to private medical practitioners participating in the maternity care service

58. Provision will be made in the interim period whereby private medical practitioners will be enabled to participate in the maternity care service. Women will be entitled to choose a doctor from among the district medical officers or other medical practitioners participating in the service. Private medical practitioners will be employed on a capitation rate payment of £5 10s. 0d. per case.

Medical care and advice at district health centres or depots

59. Pending the introduction of a general domiciliary medical care service for all children it is proposed that parents or guardians will be entitled to seek medical care or advice for their children from district medical officers at the district health centres or depots. It is intended

that district medical officers will be remunerated for this work by a lump sum payment of £30 per annum. This payment takes into account the existing obligation on medical officers (in their capacity as dispensary medical officers) to afford medical care and advice in the case of children eligible for Medical Assistance.

Domiciliary medical care for children

60. Pending the introduction of a general domiciliary medical care service for all children, such care for children whose parents or guardians are eligible for Medical Assistance will be provided by the dispensary medical officers as at present.

(iii) *Final period*

General medical care service for children

61. Domiciliary medical care for children will be introduced to supplement the medical care service made available at district health centres and depots.

62. Certain aspects of the conditions of service which will apply to district medical officers participating in the general medical care service for children in the county boroughs will also apply to district medical officers operating in areas other than the county boroughs in the final period, viz.—

(*a*) capitation fees in respect of a general medical care service for children (see paragraph 45);

(*b*) limitation on lists (see paragraph 46);

(*c*) choice of doctor and choice of patient (see paragraph 47); and

(*d*) range of service to be afforded under the general medical care service for children (see paragraph 48).

63. The following provisions which will not be applicable to district medical officers serving in the county boroughs will apply to district medical officers providing the general medical care service for children in other areas, viz.—

(*a*) *Lump sum additions to salary in certain cases in respect of affording of general medical care for children*

In districts where a choice of doctor is not afforded for the general medical care service for children, remuneration will take the form of a lump sum addition to salary fixed in conformity with a graduated scale which will vary in accordance with the population of the district in question. It is expected that there will not be many districts in which a choice of doctor will not be possible.

(b) Cessation of lump sum payment to district medical officers in respect of the affording of medical care and advice at district health centres or depots

In the interim period pending the introduction of a general domiciliary medical care service for all children, parents or guardians will be entitled, as mentioned in paragraph 59, to medical care or advice for their children at district health centres or depots. Sessions at district health centres or depots will continue in the final period but the special payment of £30 per annum to each district medical officer, provided for in the interim period, will cease to be paid, as the capitation fees, or lump sum additions to salary as the case may be, to be paid in the final period for general medical care for children, will include payment in respect of the clinical sessions to be held at the district health centres or depots.

Care for women in respect of motherhood

64. In the final period such medical care for women in respect of motherhood as may suitably be given by general practitioners will be provided by district medical officers.

MISCELLANEOUS

65. The right of district medical officers to engage in private practice will not be affected.

66. Doctors participating in the service will not be entitled to demand or accept any fee or other remuneration (other than that provided by the local authority) in respect of any services afforded in accordance with the provisions of the scheme.

67. Estimates of the average earnings from public funds of medical officers under the present system and under the proposed system are given in appendices A and B. Appendix A deals with medical officers in the county boroughs and Appendix B with medical officers in areas other than the county boroughs. In neither case is any account taken of earnings from private practice. Appendix C contains notes with a bearing on Appendices A and B.

APPENDIX A

COUNTY BOROUGHS

Components of estimated earnings from public funds of medical officers	Existing Medical Officers		Future Appointees
	Present Position	Position after general medical care for children scheme has come into operation	
Salary as dispensary medical officer (including temporary bonus of 7½%)	£376 5s. 0d. × £16 2s. 6d. —£537 10s. 0d.	£376 5s. 0d. × £16 2s. 6d. —£537 10s. 0d.	£322 10s. 0d. × £16 2s. 6d. —£483 1s. 0d.
Salary as medical officer of health (including temporary bonus of 7½%) (inclusive) (average)	£42 0s. 0d.	£42 0s. 0d.	£42 0s. 0d.
Fees from other sources, e.g. vaccination, medical certification, etc. (average)	£333 0s. 0d.	£250 0s. 0d.	£250 0s. 0d.
Fees for domiciliary medical care for children (average)	—	£700 0s. 0d.	£700 0s. 0d.
Total average annual emoluments (exclusive of private practice)			
(a) With minimum dispensary medical officer salary	£751 5s. 0d.	£1,368 5s. 0d.	£1,314 10s. 0d.
(b) With maximum dispensary medical officer salary	£912 10s. 0d.	£1,529 10s. 0d.	£1,475 15s. 0d.

APPENDIX B

AREAS OTHER THAN THE COUNTY BOROUGHS

Components of estimated earnings from public funds of medical officers	Existing medical officers			Future appointees	
	Present Position	Interim Period, i.e., before domiciliary medical care for children is introduced	Final Period, i.e., after domiciliary medical care for children has been introduced	Interim Period	Final Period
Salary as dispensary medical officer (including temporary bonus of 7½%)	£376 5s. 0d. × £16 2s. 6d. — £537 10s. 0d.	£367 5s. 0d. × £16 2s. 6d. — £537 10s. 0d.	£376 5s. 0d. × £16 2s. 6d. — £537 10s. 0d.	£322 10s. 0d. × £16 2s. 6d. — £483 15s. 0d.	£322 10s. 0d. × £16 2s. 6d. — £483 15s. 0d.
Salary as medical officer of health (inclusive) (average) (including temporary bonus of 7½%)	£60 0s. 0d.	£60 0s. 0d.	£60 0s. 0d.	£60 0s. 0d.	£60 0s. 0d.
Fees from other sources, e.g. vaccination, medical certification, etc. (average)	£172 0s. 0d.	£172 0s. 0d.	£109 0s. 0d.	£172 0s. 0d.	£109 0s. 0d.
Capitation fees from maternity care service (average)	—	£154 0s. 0d.	£245 0s. 0d.	£154 0s. 0d.	£245 0s. 0d.

Lump sum payment for affording medical care and advice for children at district health centres or depots	—	£30 0s. 0d.	—	£30 0s. 0d.	—
Lump sum payment for affording gynaecological care	—	£20 0s. 0d.	£20 0s. 0d.	£20 0s. 0d.	£20 0s. 0d.
Capitation fees from domiciliary medical care service for children (average)	—	—	£424 0s. 0d.		£424 0s. 0d.
Total average annual emoluments (exclusive of private practice): *(a)* with minimum dispensary medical officer salary	£608 5s. 0d.	£812 5s. 0d.	£1,234 5s. 0d.	£758 10s. 0d.	£1,180 10s. 0d.
(b) with maximum dispensary medical officer salary	£769 10s. 0d.	£973 10s. 0d.	£1,395 10s. 0d.	£919 15s. 0d.	£1,341 15s. 0d.

APPENDIX C

(*a*) The reduction shown in certain instances in Appendices A and B in the estimated average earnings of district medical officers from vaccination, etc., arises from the fact that a greater number of medical officers will be participating in the service in the future.

(*b*) It will be noted that the average earnings from capitation fees in respect of the maternity care service in areas other than the county boroughs (Appendix B) are less in the interim period than in the final period. This arises from the proposal that the maternity care service in the final period will be provided only by district medical officers and that private medical practitioners will not be participating in the service at that stage.

APPENDIX B

CORRESPONDENCE RELEASED BY DR NOEL BROWNE ON HIS RESIGNATION AS MINISTER FOR HEALTH, 1951

This correspondence was published in full in the three Dublin morning newspapers of 12 April 1951. It was shortly afterwards reproduced, along with other material, in the Ulster Unionist pamphlet *Southern Ireland—Church or State?*, but it has not since been republished. It seems worth reproducing here in full for two reasons. The first is that it is important source material for the narrative above, especially in Chapter VII. The second is that it will provide those readers who have no personal recollection of the episode with an opportunity to appreciate the impact which Dr Browne's revelations made. Such readers must remember that, until this time, there had been very little discussion of, or information about, Church-State relations in Ireland. They can imagine for themselves the interest which this unprecedented flood of material provoked.

The text as presented here follows that in *The Irish Times* of 12 April 1951.

MR. SEAN MACBRIDE'S LETTER TO DR. BROWNE

Dear Dr. Browne,

Following upon your own declarations and the indications given by me, I had hoped that it would not have been necessary to write this letter. Unfortunately, by reason of the situation which has arisen, and for which I fear you are largely responsible, I have no alternative, as leader of Clann na Poblachta, but to request you to transmit, as soon as possible, your resignation as Minister for Health to the Taoiseach.

You will no doubt realise that, in the light of the events that have happened, it would not now be possible for you to implement successfully the Mother and Child health service, which is urgently required and which both the Government and the Clann have undertaken to provide. The prolongation of the present situation can only further delay the provision of the service, and is, in my view, highly detrimental not merely to the Clann, but also to the national interest. The creation of a situation where it is made to appear that a conflict exists between the spiritual and temporal authorities is always undesirable; in the case of Ireland, it is highly damaging to the cause of national unity, and should have been avoided.

In my view, the creation of this situation and the long delays that have occurred in the provision of the service were as unnecessary as they were damaging to the national interest, to the Government, and to Clann na Poblachta.

As the leader of a new party which has taken a share in responsibility for the management of the country's affairs, I feel that I owe to the nation, to the Government, and to the Clann, the duty of ensuring that any Minister for whom I am responsible, discharges his duties with that high standard of conduct which is required in Government.

Lest it be sought to represent, as has been done studiously for some time past, in the Press and elsewhere, that my actions indicate in some respect opposition to mother and child health services, I wish to state categorically that the establishment, with the minimum delay, of such services in the freest sense of the word and with the least impediment possible, has been my earnest wish. My complaint is that situations are being created unnecessarily which can only cause delays and added difficulties.

In my view the principle involved in the provision of such services is simply that lack or inadequacy of means should not deprive any mother or child from receiving the best possible medical care and attention that money and science can provide. In giving effect to this principle all impediments and irritations associated with the 'red ticket' and 'means test' systems can, and must, be completely removed; on this score there would be general agreement.

Within the framework of the principle indicated above, I feel certain, as I have previously pointed out to you, that the present difficulties can be resolved.

It should be borne in mind that out of the moneys provided by the Oireachtas, the more money is available for the provision of better and more complete health services for the lower income groups the better these services will be. While I see no particular merit in collecting taxes from a man earning, say, £15 a week or less, to provide free medical services for a man with, say, an income of £1,000 a year or more, I fully realise that, even in the case of wealthy people, a long illness or expensive treatment may cause an undue financial burden. Accordingly, the scheme to be provided must be sufficiently flexible and easy of access to ensure that even wealthy people can, in such cases, participate.

I should like to assure you that, in reaching the decision that has compelled me to write this letter, I have sincerely sought to eliminate from my mind the other events, not connected with the mother and child services, which have rendered our collaboration increasingly difficult in the course of the last year. I can assure you that these events will not preclude me from extending to you my fullest co-operation in the future for the achievement of the tasks which Clann na Poblachta undertook if you are prepared to co-operate to this end.

I am sorry that you should have embarked upon the course of action which has resulted in this situation. In a substantial portion of the time during which we collaborated in the Clann and in the Government, you did valuable work for which you deserve the thanks and gratitude, of the Clann and of myself. This debt of gratitude, coupled with what I thought was your lack of experience, were factors which prompted me to allow the situation to develop further than I should have. I can only hope that mature consideration, and possibly, too, wiser counsels, will enable you to continue to work in the Clann with a full sense of responsibility and loyal co-operation.

Yours sincerely,

Sean MacBride.

A copy of this letter is being sent to the Taoiseach for his information.

Mr. MacBride's letter to Taoiseach

10th April, 1951.

Dear Taoiseach,

I enclose a copy of a letter which I have sent by hand to-night to Dr. Browne, Minister for Health, requesting him to tender his resignation to you.

As the formation of the Inter-Party Government is a new concept in our Parliamentary history, it is well that I should set out the considerations that have compelled me to adopt this course.

I take the view that, as the leader of one of the parties in the Government, it is part of my responsibility to be in a position to assure the Taoiseach at all times that the members of the party which I have the honour to lead in the Government are trustworthy of the confidence of the Government, the Oireachtas, and the people, and are capable of discharging their duties effectively. As I can no longer give you this assurance in regard to Dr. Browne, for the reasons stated in my letter to him, I deemed it to be the proper course to request him to transmit his resignation to you.

I am sure that you and the other members of the Government will greatly regret the circumstances which have compelled me to adopt this course. Dr. Browne did good work in the Government for which he deserves full credit, and it is most unfortunate that he should have behaved, in recent times, in a manner which compelled me to take the action I have taken.

I hope that Dr. Browne may benefit by the experience he has gained, and that, at some time in the future, he may again be in a position to render service to the country.

Yours sincerely,

(Signed) Sean MacBride,
Minister for External Affairs.

DR. BROWNE'S REPLY TO MR. MACBRIDE

Dr. Noel Browne sent the following reply to the letter from Mr. MacBride, which requested Dr. Browne to resign his position as Minister for Health:

Dear Mr. MacBride,

I received at a late hour last night your letter calling for my resignation. Your action did not surprise me, as it was in full conformity with the standards of behaviour which I have learned to expect from you. As I informed you on last Saturday, I proposed to resign on the following day (Sunday).

I explained at the executive meeting on Sunday and by a statement to the Press that I had deferred my action pending an outcome of the negotiations which had been initiated by the Trade Union Congress with a view to reaching a solution which would meet the views of the Hierarchy and still enable a non-means test scheme to be introduced. It was only for this reason that I deferred my resignation.

Your letter is a model of the two-faced hypocrisy and humbug so characteristic of you. Your references to a conflict between the spiritual and temporal authorities will occasion a smile among the many people who remember the earlier version of your kaleidoscopic self.

On the other side is your envenomed attack on me at the executive meeting last Sunday because, among other charges of my political inexperience, I had allowed myself to be photographed with the Protestant Archbishop of Dublin. This puerile bigotry is scarcely calculated to assist the cause of national reunification which you profess to have at heart.

Your references to my immaturity are surely gratuitous. My experience of democratic politics began only a few weeks subsequent to your own. I did not, however, have much to unlearn.

I have had a bitter experience of your cruel and authoritarian mind. It is my fervent hope that the destiny of this country will never be fully placed in your hands, because it would, in my view, mean the destruction of all those ideals which are part and parcel of Christian democracy.

Again, may I comment on your reference to 'that high standard of conduct which is required in government'. Inside the Cabinet and outside in conversations with you I have protested against the making of appointments on a corrupt basis and against other irregularities. May I instance as one example the reasons for my resignation from the Standing Committee. Your defence when these matters were raised at our party executive meeting by a former member was that 'unsavoury matters are inseparable from politics'. This view I cannot accept.

I entered politics because I believed in the high-minded principles which you were expounding on political platforms. I do you no injustice when I state that I have never observed you hearken to any of these principles when practical cases came before us. I have tried to analyse your curious philosophy not very successfully. Expediency is your sole yardstick, and to expediency you are prepared to subordinate all principles sacred and profane.

I have to-day sent to the general secretary my resignation from the Clann na Poblachta Party. I have bidden farewell to your unwholesome brand of politics. Despite my experiences at your hand, I am not so cynical as to believe that you typify the ordinary politically conscious person in this country. May God forbid that you should.

I am, as demanded by you, to-day sending my resignation to the Taoiseach.

Yours faithfully,

Noel C. Browne.

BISHOP OF FERNS TO TAOISEACH

10th October, 1950.

Dear Taoiseach,

The Archbishops and Bishops of Ireland, at their meeting on October 10th, had under consideration the proposals for Mother and Child health service and other kindred medical services. They recognise that these proposals are motivated by a sincere desire to improve public health, but they feel bound by their office to consider whether the proposals are in accordance with Catholic moral teaching.

In their opinion the powers taken by the State in the proposed Mother and Child Health Service are in direct opposition to the rights of the family and of the individual and are liable to very great abuse. Their character is such that no assurance that they would be used in moderation could justify their enactment. If adopted in law they would constitute a ready-made instrument for future totalitarian aggression.

The right to provide for the health of children belongs to parents, not to the State. The State has the right to intervene only in a subsidiary capacity, to supplement, not to supplant.

It may help indigent or neglectful parents; it may not deprive 90% of parents of their rights because of 10% necessitous or negligent parents.

It is not sound social policy to impose a state medical service on the whole community on the pretext of relieving the necessitous 10 per cent from the so-called indignity of the means test.

The right to provide for the physical education of children belongs to the family and not to the State. Experience has shown that physical or health education is closely interwoven with important moral questions on which the Catholic Church has definite teaching.

Education in regard to motherhood includes instruction in regard to sex relations, chastity and marriage. The State has no competence to give instruction in such matters. We regard with the greatest apprehension the proposal to give to local medical officers the right to tell Catholic girls and women how they should behave in regard to this sphere of conduct at once so delicate and sacred.

Gynaecological care may be, and in some other countries is, interpreted to include provision for birth limitation and abortion. We have no guarantee that State officials will respect Catholic principles in regard to these matters. Doctors trained in institutions in which we have no confidence may be appointed as medical officers under the proposed services, and may give gynaecological care not in accordance with Catholic principles.

The proposed service also destroys the confidential relations between doctor and patient and regards all cases of illnesses as matter for public records and research without regard to the individual's right to privacy.

The elimination of private medical practitioners by a State-paid service has not been shown to be necessary or even advantageous to the patient, the public in general or the medical profession.

The Bishops are most favourable to measures which would benefit public health, but they consider that instead of imposing a costly bureaucratic scheme of nationalised medical service the State might well consider the advisability of providing the maternity hospitals and other institutional facilities which are at present lacking and should give adequate maternity benefits and taxation relief for large families.

The Bishops desire that your Government should give careful consideration to the dangers inherent in the present proposals before they are adopted by the Government for legislative enactment and, therefore, they feel it their duty to submit their views on this subject to you privately and at the earliest opportunity, since they regard the issues involved as of the gravest moral and religious importance.

I remain, dear Taoiseach,

> Yours very sincerely,
>
> (Sgd.) James Staunton,
>
> Bishop of Ferns,
>
> Secretary to the Hierarchy.

John A. Costello, T.D.,
Taoiseach.

Note:—The letter of October 10th, 1950, from the Hierarchy was handed by the Taoiseach to the Minister about November 9th. The Minister at once prepared a detailed reply and within a few days sent it to the Taoiseach for transmission to the Hierarchy. Some days after the receipt of the letter of March 8th, 1951, from His Grace the Archbishop of Dublin, the Minister learnt for the first time that the Taoiseach had not transmitted this reply to the Hierarchy. The Minister's reply was in terms similar to his memorandum which was sent to the Hierarchy on March 27th last.

O

ARCHBISHOP TO THE MINISTER

Archbishop's House,
Dublin, N.E.3.
8th March, 1951.

Dear Minister,

I beg to thank you for your letter of the 6th inst. received by me to-day, enclosing a pamphlet which purports to explain the proposed Mother and Child Health Service.

I welcome any legitimate improvement of medical services for those whose basic family wage or income does not readily assure the necessary facilities.

And, if proof be needed of my attitude, I may be permitted to point to many actions of my Episcopate, in particular to the work of the Catholic Social Service Conference founded by me, more especially its Maternity Welfare Centres.

I regret, however, that, as I stated, on the occasion when on behalf of the Hierarchy, I asked you to meet me with Their Lordships of Ferns and Galway, I may not approve of the Mother and Child Health Service, as it is proposed by you to implement the Scheme.

Now, as Archbishop of Dublin, I regret that I must reiterate each and every objection made by me on that occasion, and unresolved, either then or later, by the Minister for Health.

Inasmuch as I was authorised to deal with the Taoiseach, on behalf of the Hierarchy, I have felt it my duty to send to the Taoiseach to-day, for his information, a copy of this letter.

I shall report to the Hierarchy, at its General Meeting, the receipt to-day of your letter, with enclosed pamphlet.

I am,
Yours sincerely,
(Sgd.) John C. McQuaid,
Archbishop of Dublin,
Primate of Ireland.

Noel C. Browne, Esq., T.D., M.B.,
The Minister for Health,
The Custom House, Dublin.

MR. McGILLIGAN TO DR. BROWNE

14 Marta, 1951.

Dear Minister,

I have been considering the official minute referred to in your letter of the 6th March regarding capitation fees for General Practitioners under the Mother and Child Health Service. The Scheme, as previously submitted, proposed that the domiciliary care of children would be afforded by District Medical Officers only. The proposal now submitted to allow Private General Practitioners to participate in the Scheme for domiciliary care of children is an entirely new feature.

The latest Scheme also proposes to provide immediately for domiciliary care of children in areas outside the four County Boroughs. There is also a new feature as you will see by referring to paragraph 4 of your Department's official minute (H,1949 Ilgheathach) of the 3rd August, 1949. That paragraph said that the introduction of domiciliary care for children in rural areas was being deferred until the existing dispensary districts throughout the country would have been redistributed—a process that would take some time. The immediate introduction of this Service in rural areas will make the Scheme much more costly in the earlier years than was previously estimated.

I consider it necessary that the authority of the Government should be got for the revised Scheme now submitted, in view of the two completely new features in it. The question of the appropriate capitation fees to be paid can be deferred until the revised Scheme has been approved, though I should say that from such examination as I have been able to make, the capitation fees proposed for Private General Practitioners are unduly high by camparison with those proposed for District Medical Officers.

Yours sincerely,

(Sgd.) P. McGilligan.

Noel C. Browne, Esq., T.D.,
Minister for Health.

TAOISEACH TO MINISTER

Roinn an Taoisigh,
Baile Atha Cliath,
15 Marta, 1951.

Dear Dr. Browne,

As I indicated to you yesterday afternoon, I am gravely concerned at the contents of the letter, dated 8th March, which His Grace the Archbishop of Dublin wrote to you, consequent upon your sending His Grace a pamphlet on the proposed Mother and Child Health Service.

In that letter His Grace said:—

'I regret, however, that as I stated on the occasion when, on behalf of the Hierarchy, I asked you to meet me with Their Lordships of Ferns and Galway, I may not approve of the Mother and Child Health Service, as it is proposed by you to implement the Scheme.

'Now, as Archbishop of Dublin, I regret that I must reiterate each and every objection made by me on that occasion, and unresolved either then or later, by the Minister for Health.'

In reply to the letter which His Grace wrote to me when forwarding me a copy of his letter to you, I stated that His Grace's views would receive respectful and earnest consideration.

I understand that you have not replied to His Grace's letter. I am afraid you do not appear to realise the serious implications of the views expressed in that letter, since you have, by advertisement and otherwise, continued to publicise the scheme to which objections have been taken. Such action might well seem to be defiance of the Hierarchy.

I should also like to recall to you the letter, dated 10th October, 1950, which His Lordship the Bishop of Ferns addressed to me on behalf of the Hierarchy, setting forth in detail objections to the Mother and Child Health Service as proposed by you. As you have been aware, I have so far refrained from replying to that letter. I have postponed sending a formal reply in the hope that you would have been able to achieve a satisfactory adjustment of the matters in controversy. Your letter forwarding a copy of your scheme to the Archbishop of Dublin, and His Grace's reply thereto intimating his intention of reporting on the matter to the Hierarchy, have, however, now made it difficult for me further to postpone replying to the letter from the Bishop of Ferns.

I have no doubt that all my colleagues and, in particular, yourself would not be party to any proposals affecting moral questions which would or might come into conflict with the definite teaching of the Catholic Church. Having regard to the views expressed in the letters received from the Hierarchy, I feel that you should take steps at once to consult Their Lordships so as to remove any grounds for objection on their part to the Mother and Child Health Service and to find a mutually satisfactory solution of the difficulties which have arisen.

I can assure you that immediate steps will be taken to dispose of any financial matters which may be outstanding in regard to the proposed service on the understanding that the objections raised by the Hierarchy have been resolved. Indeed I may say that to my mind the financial questions which may remain outstanding are altogether insignificant and susceptible of speedy solution once the larger issues raised in the correspondence from members of the Hierarchy are settled.

I need hardly add that the Government are strongly in favour of a Mother and Child Service, and are anxious that it should be made operative as soon as possible, and trust that your further negotiations will enable this desirable object to be achieved.

Yours sincerely,
(Sgd.) John A. Costello.

Dr. Noel Browne, T.D.,
Minister for Health.

DR. BROWNE TO TAOISEACH

Oifig an Aire Slainte,
Baile Atha Cliath,
19 Marta, 1951.

Dear Taoiseach,

Am I correct in thinking from the terms of your letter of March 15th that you are under the impression that the Hierarchy are opposed to the Mother and Child Health Protection Scheme? May I point out that this impression, if held by you, is certainly not borne out by the following facts.

In the first place you will recall that, following my interview with His Grace the Archbishop of Dublin and Their Lordships of Galway and Ferns at the Archbishop's House on the 11th October last, I gave you to understand I was quite satisfied in my mind that the misapprehensions which were referred to by His Grace and Their Lordships at that meeting were satisfactorily disposed of by myself, with the exception of the one outstanding point concerning health education, on which point I gave unequivocal guarantees to His Grace and Their Lordships that everything possible which could be done to allay their fears in this regard I would most willingly carry out, if necessary, in forthcoming amending legislation to the 1947 Health Act. To reinforce my impression that that interview with His Grace and Their Lordships had concluded on a very satisfactory note for all concerned, you will recall that you personally assured me, following a meeting which you had with His Grace on the 12th October last, that you were in a position to corroborate His Grace's and Their Lordships' satisfaction with the explanations which I gave in relation to their misapprehensions concerning the Scheme. In particular, you gave me to understand that His Grace and Their Lordships were completely satisfied on the score of my guarantee concerning the educational problem.

I would like to add, in addition, that, since sending this brochure concerning the Mother and Child Scheme to all the members of the Hierarchy, I have received acknowledgments from a number of the Bishops, including incidentally His Lordship of Galway, who was present at the meeting of 11th October last. In none of these acknowledgments is there any suggestion of an objection to the Scheme except in the letter from His Grace the Archbishop of Dublin. Since the receipt of your letter I have been in communication with a member of the Hierarchy, who further assures me that, so far as he is aware, the Hierarchy as such have expressed no objection to the Mother and Child Scheme whatsoever on the grounds of faith and morals.

I would be interested to know whether your withholding of approval to the Mother and Child Scheme is due either to the supposed opposition of the Hierarchy to the Scheme or to the possible opposition of any individual member of the Hierarchy. I would be glad if you would treat this matter as extremely urgent, in view of the fact that I must complete, as you yourself have suggested, my further investigations of these misapprehensions with the minimum of delay.

Yours sincerely,

(Sgd.) Noel C. Browne.

An Taoiseach,
Tithe an Rialtais,
Baile Atha Cliath.

Mr. Costello's reply

Roinn an Taoisigh,
Baile Atha Cliath,
21st March, 1951.

Dear Dr. Browne,

I am in receipt of your letter of the 19th instant. The answers to the queries which you put to me are substantially contained in my letter to you of the 15th instant.

In that letter I recalled to you the letter of the 10th October, 1950, which His Lordship the Bishop of Ferns, as Secretary to the Hierarchy, and on behalf of the Hierarchy, addressed to me. That letter, having stated that 'The Archbishops and Bishops of Ireland at their meeting on October 10th had under consideration the proposals for Mother and Child Health Services and other kindred medical services' and that 'they feel bound by their office to consider whether the proposals are in accordance with Catholic moral teaching,' went on to say, 'In their opinion, the powers taken by the State in the proposed Mother and Child Health Service are in direct opposition to the rights of the family and of the individual and are liable to very great abuse.' That letter proceeded to give in some detail the Bishops' views and objections concerning such substantial moral questions as—the right of the State to supplement, not to supplant; the right of parents in regard to their children's health; improved facilities rather than a scheme of nationalised medical service; and the preservation of correct confidential relations between doctor and patient.

The letter concluded with an expression of the Bishops' desire that the Government should give careful consideration to the dangers inherent in the proposals. That letter was delivered to me as Head of the Government by the Archbishop of Dublin on behalf of the Hierarchy, only some time after your interview with the Archbishop of Dublin and the Bishops of Galway and Ferns. If, in the letter delivered to the Government, the Hierarchy continued to speak of the dangers inherent in the proposals, one cannot easily understand your opinion that you had completely satisfied the Archbishop of Dublin and the Bishops of Galway and Ferns concerning the removal of these dangers. On the contrary, the Government has received no assurance whatever from the Hierarchy as to its confidence in the scheme. The letter delivered to the Government emanated from the whole Hierarchy, and must be regarded as still expressing the Hierarchy's views until a contrary expression has been received from the Hierarchy.

My concern is not with any impressions I may or may not have— but is with that letter which officially records in formal terms the views of the Hierarchy and with the letter of the 8th March, 1951, which His Grace the Archbishop of Dublin addressed to you when you sent him a pamphlet on the proposed Mother and Child Health Service, and in which he reiterated the objections to the scheme which he stated to you were still unresolved.

As I have already indicated, I am at a loss to understand how you could feel satisfied that you had, at your interview on the 11th October last with His Grace the Archbishop and Their Lordships of Galway and Ferns, satisfactorily disposed of their objections. I certainly never stated to you, as you suggest, that I was in a position to corroborate His Grace's and Their Lordships' satisfaction with the explanation which you gave in connection with their objections to the scheme. In view of what I had been told by His Grace at my interview with him I certainly could have given you no such assurance. Out of consideration for you and in an earnest desire to help you in the difficulties which the Hierarchy see in your scheme, I offered my personal help to you as intermediary with the Hierarchy to try to smooth those difficulties and resolve their objections, which I felt could be done by appropriate amendments of the scheme and amending legislation if necessary. To illustrate how it might be possible to meet some of the objections I suggested that you might introduce into the Health Bill, 1950, then before the Dail, an amendment of Section 21 of the Health Act, 1947, by deleting from the section the words 'and for their education in respect thereof.'

That you are seriously in error in thinking that you had satisfied His Grace and Their Lordships at your interview is amply borne out by the letter of the 8th March last to you from His Grace the Arch-bishop of Dublin when he specifically stated, in the passages quoted in my recent letter to you, that on the occasion of your interview he stated that he could not approve of the scheme. In that letter His Grace, as Archbishop of Dublin, reiterated each and every objection made on the occasion of the interview with you and which he said were 'unresolved either then or later' by you.

My withholding of approval of the scheme is due to the objections set forth in the letter to me from the Secretary of the Hierarchy, written on behalf of the Hierarchy, and to the reiteration of their objections by His Grace the Archbishop of Dublin, as Archbishop of Dublin.

My letter to you of the 15th instant was a request to you to have those objections resolved.

Yours sincerely,

(Sgd.) John A. Costello.

Noel C. Browne, Esq., T.D.,
Minister for Health,
Department of Health,
Custom House, Dublin.

MINISTER'S REPLY

Oifig an Aire Slainte,
Baile Atha Cliath,
21 Marta, 1951.

Dear Taoiseach,

I should have thought it unnecessary to point out that from the beginning it has been my concern to see that the Mother and Child Scheme contained nothing contrary to Catholic moral teaching. I hope I need not assure you that as a Catholic I will unhesitatingly and immediately accept any pronouncement from the Hierarchy as to what is Catholic moral teaching in reference to this matter.

I see no reason, however, in your letter of the 21st instant to change the opinion I expressed in mine of the 19th instant. For the reasons set out in that letter I am not satisfied that the Hierarchy are opposed to the Scheme on grounds of Faith and Morals. I note that you have not addressed yourself to any of these reasons except that you do not admit that following upon your interview with His Grace the Archbishop of Dublin on October 12, 1950, you assured me that His Grace and Their Lordships of Ferns and Galway were satisfied. My recollection of that is fortified by the note which I made of your statement to me on that occasion and the recollection of other persons to whom I then conveyed your statement.

Have you overlooked the fact that the letter from His Lordship the Bishop of Ferns is dated October 10th, that is to say the day *before* my interview with His Grace and Their Lordships? I assumed that this is the letter which His Grace the Archbishop of Dublin referred to when he spoke to me on my way into the conference to meet Their Lordships of Ferns and Galway and which he said it was proposed to hand to you on the following day. In fact the first mention you made to me of the receipt of the letter was on November 9th, 1950, and which in your letter of the 21st instant you stated you received 'only some time after your interview'.

I took the view that this letter, which had already been discussed, and in my view satisfactorily discussed, was given to you merely as a matter of record. I intended the reply which I gave to you and which substantially represented the case I made to His Grace and Their Lordships to be likewise for record. I was under the impression that you had sent it as a reply to the letter of His Lordship the Bishop of Ferns and I was horrified to learn for the first time only a few days ago that you had in fact never sent it.

If, however, as you now say in your letter of 21st instant, you understood that His Grace and Their Lordships were not satisfied after the interview of 11th October, that belief on your part is quite inconsistent with your subsequent conduct in the matter. In particular, you allowed the Scheme to develop without ever suggesting that the objections of His Grace the Archbishop of Dublin and Their Lordships of Ferns and Galway were still unresolved, and you never discussed that aspect of the matter with me or questioned me about it until 14th instant. You are quoted by a circular issued by the Irish Medical Association on December 12th as asserting: 'It was his considered opinion that neither the Dail nor Senate would approve any amendment of the Act or Regulations which would envisage the omission of a free service for all in connection with the Scheme.'

Furthermore, in your interview with the Irish Medical Association on December 12th, 1950, there was no suggestion of any difficulty in the way of the implementation of the Scheme other than those raised by the Irish Medical Association. It seems strange that at this late hour when the discussions with the Irish Medical Association have reached a crucial point that you advance, as the only remaining objection to the Scheme, the one which of all possible objections—namely, the supposed opposition of the Hierarchy—should have first been satisfactorily disposed of before any steps were taken in furtherance of the Mother and Child Scheme, and which I, naturally, would have been most anxious to dispose of if I did not believe, as I did and still believe, that matters were satisfactorily arranged at the interview which I had with His Grace the Archbishop of Dublin and Their Lordships of Ferns and Galway on October 11th last.

Yours sincerely,
(Sgd.) Noel C. Browne.

An Taoiseach,
Tithe an Rialtais,
Baile Atha Cliath.

TAOISEACH TO DR. BROWNE

Roinn an Taoisigh,
Baile Atha Cliath,
22nd March, 1951.

Dear Dr. Browne,

I have your reply of the 21st March, 1951, to my letter of the same date. I did not in that letter address myself to the reasons which you had advanced in support of your suggestion that the Hierarchy are not opposed to the Mother and Child Scheme as outlined by you. I did not do so because it is for the Hierarchy alone to say whether or no the Scheme contained anything contrary to Catholic moral teaching. It is clear from the letter which His Grace the Archbishop of Dublin addressed to you on the 8th March, 1951, that the objections put forward on the occasion of your interview with him and with Their Lordships of Ferns and Galway on the 11th October last were 'unresolved either then or later'. It is clear from the same letter that His Grace sent me a copy of it, inasmuch as he was authorised to deal with me 'on behalf of the Hierarchy'.

My actions in regard to this matter since I received the letter from His Lordship the Bishop of Ferns on the 10th October last have beer entirely actuated by what I conceived to be a friendly desire to help a colleague and I take it somewhat amiss to find misconstrued m endeavours to have the objections to the Scheme which had been advanced on behalf of the Hierarchy satisfactorily resolved.

In the hope that these objections could be satisfactorily disposed of I refrained from replying to the letter from His Lordship the Bishop of Ferns of the 10th October. I explained to His Grace the Archbishop of Dublin my reasons for so refraining and he communicated these to the Hierarchy. I need hardly say that I accept unreservedly your statement that you would abide by any pronouncement from the Hierarchy as to what is Catholic moral teaching in reference to this matter.

Yours sincerely,

(Sgd.) John A. Costello.

Dr. Noel Browne, T.D.,
Minister for Health.

MINISTER TO TAOISEACH

Oifig an Aire Slainte,
Baile Atha Cliath,
24 March, 1951.

Dear Taoiseach,

In accordance with our telephone conversation of the 22nd March, 1951, I herewith enclose the Memorandum which you requested me to furnish for transmission to His Lordship of Ferns on behalf of the Hierarchy. In doing this I am acting also in accordance with the suggestion of His Grace the Archbishop of Dublin with whom I discussed the matter on 22nd March, 1951. He appears to fully appreciate the extreme urgency of the serious situation which had developed within the Cabinet and of its likely implications to its future.

I would ask that you be good enough to forward without delay this Memorandum for the early consideration and decision of the Hierarchy on the question contained therein. I am assured by His Grace, Dr McQuaid, that he is using his every endeavour to ensure the earliest possible consideration and decision of Their Lordships on this matter.

I would be obliged if you would send me a copy of the correspondence which you enclose with this Memorandum.

Yours sincerely,

(Sgd.) Noel C. Browne.

An Taoiseach,
Tithe an Rialtais,
Baile Atha Cliath.

LETTER TO BISHOP

Department of the Taoiseach,
Dublin.
28 March, 1951.

Dear Dr. Browne,

I am enclosing a copy of a letter which I have addressed to His Lordship the Bishop of Ferns when transmitting for the consideration

and decision of the Hierarchy the memorandum which you sent me
on the 24th March, 1951, containing your observations on matters
relating to the Mother and Child Scheme which were referred to in
a letter dated 10th October, 1950, addressed to me by His Lordship
the Bishop of Ferns as Secretary to the Hierarchy.

Yours sincerely,

(Sgd.) John A. Costello,

Dr Noel Browne, T.D.,
Minister for Health,
Custom House, Dublin.

Roinn an Taoisigh.
27th March, 1951.

My Lord Bishop,
 I beg to enclose a memorandum of observations of the Minister
for Health on various matters relating to the Mother and Child
Scheme referred to in a letter dated the 10th October, 1950, addressed
to me by Your Lordship as Secretary to the Hierarchy.

 May I be allowed to state that since the receipt by me from His
Grace of Dublin of their Lordships' letter my colleagues and I have
given anxious consideration to the objections made by the Hierarchy
to the Scheme advocated by the Minister for Health.

 His Grace of Dublin has on many occasions seen me in the interval
and kindly agreed to inform the Standing Committee that the Government would readily and immediately acquiesce in a decision of the
Hierarchy concerning faith and morals.

 If I have not answered earlier and in detail the letter of the Hierarchy
I trust that it will be understood that both His Grace of Dublin and I
believed it to be much more advantageous in the special circumstances
of the case to await developments.

 Within recent weeks the publication by the Minister for Health of
a brochure explaining his scheme called forth from His Grace of
Dublin an immediate reply in which His Grace reiterated each and
every objection already made by him to the Scheme.

 After an interview with His Grace in which the Minister had been
again warned of His Grace's objections and had himself asked for an
early decision of the Hierarchy the Minister for Health forwarded to
me the enclosed memorandum.

His Grace of Dublin has kept me accurately informed of these latter circumstances and has kindly agreed to request Your Lordship as the Most Reverend Secretary to include the Minister's observations on the agenda of the forthcoming meeting of the Hierarchy.

I am, my Lord,

Respectfully and sincerely,

(Sgd.) John A. Costello.

Most Rev. James Staunton, D.D.,
Secretary to the Hierarchy,
Wexford.

MEMORANDUM

Memorandum of observations of the Minister for Health on various matters relating to the Mother and Child Scheme referred to in a letter, dated 10th October, 1950, addressed to the Taoiseach by the Most Rev. J. Staunton, D.D., Bishop of Ferns, Secretary to the Hierarchy.

With reference to the letter dated 10th October from His Lordship the Bishop of Ferns, on behalf of the Hierarchy of Ireland, and handed to the Taoiseach by His Grace the Archbishop of Dublin, the Minister for Health desires to state that he has given the most earnest consideration to the many points mentioned therein, but as these points are of such importance, he feels that it is necessary for him to reply at some length.

He first desires to thank the members of the Hierarchy for their acknowledgment that the proposals for the service in question are based on a sincere desire to improve the public health. He feels he need not assure the Hierarchy that the proposals have no other object than to secure that improvement.

* * *

It appears to the Minister from the letter of the Hierarchy that the fundamental objection of the Hierarchy to the scheme is based on the misapprehension that there will be compulsion on mothers or children to avail of the scheme or portion of it. As the Minister stated to His Grace the Archbishop of Dublin, and Their Lordships of Ferns and Galway, at the interview on October 11th, which they accorded to him, there is no such compulsion. Every parent will be free to avail of it or not as he or she thinks fit, just as State-aided primary schools are provided for such as wish to attend them, but there is no compulsion on any parent to send a child to such schools.

If the members of the Hierarchy were re-assured on this matter of compulsion, the Minister feels that the apprehension which is the ground for their objection to the Scheme would be removed. Nevertheless, he feels that it may not be out of place to repeat here observations he made to His Grace the Archbishop of Dublin, and Their Lordships of Ferns and Galway, at the interview referred to concerning some of the remaining points in the letter of the Hierarchy.

In the second paragraph of that letter, it is stated that, in the opinion of the Archbishops and Bishops, the powers taken by the State in the proposed Service are in direct opposition to the rights of the family and of the individual, and are liable to very great abuse. In this connection, the Minister begs to draw Their Lordships' attention to the fact that medical charities, and later the Public Assistance systems of medical relief for the poorer classes of the community, covering about one-third of the population, have for a very long time past provided a fairly comprehensive maternity and child health service, and so far as he can ascertain there was never any complaint that there was anything in these systems which constitutes an invasion of the rights of the family or of the individual. The only fundamental difference in principle between the existing Public Assistance system of medical relief and the proposed Mother and Child Service is that there was a means test for the former and that it will be eliminated in the latter. There will, of course, be other differences—better and more extensive hospital treatment facilities, for instance, will be provided which were absent before; but the difference will not be fundamental except in the matter of the means test. The Minister presumes that the elimination of the means test could not be a factor which weighed with the Hierarchy in arriving at the opinion quoted above.

The letter from the Hierarchy goes on to state that the right to provide for the health of children belongs to parents. The Minister, naturally, is in complete agreement with that view. The Scheme, he submits, does not, however, invade or interfere with that right. Parents will still be free to exercise it if they so wish. It merely places at the disposal of parents a means of providing for the health of their families. There is a close parallel here with the position in regard to education. The Constitution (Art. 42) recognises the right and duty of parents to provide for the education of their children. In order to provide parents with the means of fulfilling their obligations in this regard, the Constitution requires the State to provide free primary education, but does not oblige parents to send their children to State schools, though it does require that children should receive a certain minimum education. In the case of the Mother and Child Scheme, there is no compulsion of any sort in regard to minimum health requirements.

*   *   *

The letter goes on to state that 'it is not sound social policy to impose a State medical service on the whole community on the pretext of relieving the necessitous 10% from the so-called indignity of a means test'. In regard to this, the Minister respectfully desires to draw attention to the following points:

1. A State medical service is not being imposed on the community. A service is merely being made available to all, which, as the Minister had mentioned earlier, any individual is entitled to avail of or not, either in whole or in part, as he or she thinks fit.

2. There is no pretext of relieving 'the necessitous 10%'. What is being done is that for the first time a good medical service is being made available to all sections of the community, not solely to save the necessitous from 'the so-called indignity of the means test', though this is one of the objects of the Scheme, but also because of the high mortality rate in this country amongst mothers and children.

3. 'The necessitous 10%,' if the right to medical care under the Public Assistance Acts is the criterion, really amounts to over 30% of the population, but all are aware that there is a considerable section of the community outside that category which is unable to afford proper medical care for their children, or can provide for that care for an ailing child only by inordinate sacrifices on the part of other members of the family.

4. The existing service for the treatment of infectious diseases is available to all free and without a means test. This service covers the whole range of treatment (including X-rays, institutional treatment, drugs, etc.) for such diseases as tuberculosis, and all

fevers. The omission of a means test from the Mother and Child Service, therefore, does not introduce a new principle.

* * *

The principle enunciated in the next paragraph of the letter from the Hierarchy—that 'the right to provide for the physical education of children belongs to the family and not to the State'—is also enshrined in the Constitution (Art. 42). The family, however, may delegate certain aspects of that right as it does to teachers and others in charge of youth. Though certain aspects of physical education involve important moral questions, there is a large field of physical and health instruction into which moral issues do not enter; for example, habits of personal cleanliness, care of teeth, training in carriage and deportment, remedial exercises for deformed limbs. The aspects which have moral implications will continue under the new Scheme to be in the care of the family or the members of the medical profession who have care of them at present. The Minister proposes to return to this matter later in the Memorandum.

Education in regard to motherhood may include instruction in sex relationship, chastity and marriage. It also includes, however, such matters as correct diet during pregnancy, an avoidance of certain forms of work and certain social habits—for example, smoking during that time. It is only the latter type of education which is to be provided under the Scheme, and care will be taken to ensure that the regulations governing its operation will include nothing of an objectionable nature under this heading. The Minister desires to repeat the assurances which he gave in this meeting with His Grace the Archbishop of Dublin and Their Lordships of Ferns and Galway on the 11th October, that he would provide such safeguards in matters of health education as would meet the requirements of the Hierarchy.

In order to ensure, however, that the Scheme, when put into operation, will contain nothing in regard to this matter or to the matter referred to in the preceding paragraph, which the Hierarchy feels to be open to objection, the Minister is prepared to submit to the Hierarchy for their approval the draft, when available, of that part of the regulations which will deal with these matters. Alternatively, he is prepared to consider any other course in regard to them which the Hierarchy might suggest.

* * *

The gynaecological care visualised in the Scheme refers primarily to conditions arising out of difficult or mismanaged pregnancies. It is within the bounds of possibility that doctors engaged in the provision of such care may recommend treatments or procedures which are contrary to Catholic teaching, and consequently the Minister thinks that this may be an appropriate place to state the position in regard to the recruitment of medical personnel generally.

The Constitution (Art. 44) prohibits the State from imposing any disabilities or making any discrimination on the grounds of religious profession, belief or status. Accordingly, it would not be possible to recruit for the purposes of the Scheme, any more than it is possible at present to recruit for the local authority service, only such doctors as had been trained in medical schools in which the medical education is in accordance with Catholic principles. At general practitioner level, however, it will be possible to provide under the Scheme, in all but a few areas, a choice of doctor. It is proposed in the Scheme that all general practitioners are free to participate in the Scheme if they so wish as well as the local district medical officers. Those people who desire to avail of the Scheme will be able to avail of that choice in a manner which may not only provide them with the family doctor they have always been attending but with a choice which will provide reasonable assurances that only treatment in accordance with Catholic principles will be given. The same applies in the matter of medical advice. The position will, therefore, be better than it is at the moment in regard to the one-third who, under the Public Assistance system, are tied to one doctor because of their poverty. At the specialist level, the position will be no less satisfactory than it is at present.

There is the additional safeguard that, unlike the neighbouring island, this country is predominantly Catholic and its medical profession is predominantly Catholic, also.

*   *   *

A good deal has been said and written about the confidential relationship between the doctor and the patient, and the danger of the destruction of that relationship in any State or local authority scheme. Already the local authority provides numerous public health services, including diagnosis and treatment of venereal disease and tuberculosis and many other infectious diseases. Similarly there are medical inspections of school children. In addition, general medical care in respect of all diseases is provided by dispensary doctors. All these services necessitate the keeping of records, and the Minister is not aware that this has led to any violation of the doctor-patient relationship. The Mother and Child Scheme will not introduce any new principle in this regard. Even outside the local authority service every hospital and doctor keep records of the ailments of their patients, and in most cases these are available in the doctor's home or in a hospital to such lay persons as receptionists and clerks. The Minister feels that the doctor-patient relationship would not be impaired under the scheme.

In regard to the next point in the letter from the Hierarchy—namely, that 'the elimination of private medical practitioners by a State-paid service has not been shown to be necessary, or even advantageous, to the patient, the public in general or the medical profession'—the Minister submits that the scheme will not result in the elimination of private medical practitioners. As is set out above, the scheme is open to all practitioners who desire to participate in it, and these practitioners, whether they participate in the scheme or not, will continue to treat all persons who decide not to avail of the scheme and all those who will be outside the scope of the scheme.

*   *   *

The original scheme was drafted on the basis that it would be operated by district medical officers. The Minister made it clear, however, from the outset that the scheme was tentative, and from an early stage he was prepared to give all private medical practitioners an opportunity of participating in the scheme if they wish to do so, and, if a sufficient number intimate their willingness to come in, the scheme will be amended so as to enable them to take part in it. This should remove any possible objection on the ground that the scheme might tend to reduce the amount of traditional private medical practice. It will also allow those members of the public who decide to make use of the scheme to have the service of their family doctor if he is a participant in the scheme.

Further, the high level of mother and child mortality in this country appears to indicate a need for an immediate and drastic improvement in the present facilities and it was the considered view of the Oireachtas in passing the Health Act of 1947 that such improvement could best be effected by the introduction of a free Mother and Child Service, in the interests of the public in general. The Scheme should, incidentally, prove advantageous to the medical profession as well as to the public because it will bring to the doctors persons who hitherto, because of lack of means or because of ignorance, did not avail of their services to the extent to which they should.

The letter from the Hierarchy then mentions 'the advisability of providing the maternity hospitals and other institutional facilities which are at present lacking' and that the State 'should give adequate maternity benefits and taxation relief for large families'.

The Minister has in fact for the past three years been promoting a very large building programme designed to provide maternity hospitals and other institutional facilities which are at present lacking. The various measures which are being taken are within the knowledge of individual members of the Hierarchy in regard to their own areas.

In regard to maternity benefits, the new National Insurance legislation giving effect to the proposals contained in the White Paper on Social Security marks an important advance in the direction mentioned in the letter from the Hierarchy.

*   *   *

Taxation relief for large families is already given under the Income Tax code, and has the effect that a married man with two children whose sole income is from employment pays no Income Tax unless his income is above the £10 10s. a week level. The Income Tax exemption, rises by about £1 a week, above that figure in respect of each additional child, so that a man with eight children pays no Income Tax unless he has about £16 10s. a week. The Minister also desires to draw attention to the provisions of the Children's Allowances Act of 1944 and the Infectious Diseases Regulations. Under the former Act, children's allowances are payable without any means test irrespective of the means of the family if that family contains qualified children within the meaning of the Act. With regard to the latter Regulations, there are over 40 diseases in respect of which, during the last three or four years, diagnostic, institutional and treatment facilities have been available quite free to all those anxious to avail themselves of the services irrespective of income level and for which there is no means test. So far as the Minister is aware, no objection has been taken to these Schemes.

In regard to the last paragraph of the letter from the Hierarchy, the Minister respectfully desires to draw attention to the fact that in introducing the Mother and Child Health Service Scheme, the Government is merely giving effect to an Act of the Oireachtas passed in 1947.

To remove any possible misunderstanding about the basis of the matter, the Minister desires to emphasise that Part III of the Health Act, 1947, which became law on the 13th August, 1947, provides for the introduction of a Mother and Child Service, and determines the broad outlines of such service. The draft scheme has been prepared to conform with, and in fact does conform with, the provisions of the 1947 Act.

In view of the foregoing observations and in view, particularly, of the fact that the Mother and Child Scheme is in no sense compulsory and that whatever guarantees the Hierarchy desire in the matter of instruction will be unreservedly given, the Minister respectfully asks whether the Hierarchy considers that the Mother and Child Scheme is contrary to Catholic moral teaching.

Department of Health,
Custom House,
Dublin.

ARCHBISHOP TO TAOISEACH

Archbishop's House,
Dublin.
5th April, 1951.

My dear Taoiseach,

At our Standing Committee Meeting on the 3rd instant, and again at our General Meeting yesterday, the 4th instant, in St. Patrick's College, Maynooth, long and careful consideration was given by the Hierarchy to the memorandum which you had forwarded in your letter of 27th March from the Minister for Health on his Mother and Child Health Scheme.

I have the honour to transmit to you the reply of the Hierarchy, representing the unanimous decision of the General Meeting of the Archbishops and Bishops.

I have been deputed to sign the enclosed reply on behalf of the Hierarchy.

I beg to remain, my dear Taoiseach,

Yours respectfully and sincerely,
John C. McQuaid,
Archbishop of Dublin,
Primate of Ireland.

John A. Costello, Esq., T.D., S.C.,
The Taoiseach.

Archbishop's House,
Dublin.
5th April, 1951.

Dear Taoiseach,

The Archbishops and Bishops have considered very carefully your letter of 27th March, 1951, and the memorandum submitted by the Minister for Health in reply to their letter to you of 10th October, 1950.

The Archbishops and Bishops wish first to point out that, on 7th October, 1947, they sent to the Head of the Government a letter in which they expressed grave disapproval of certain parts of the then recently enacted Health Act, 1947, especially those dealing with Mother and Child services. In Sections 21–28 the public authority was given the right and duty to provide for the health of all children, to treat their ailments, to educate them in regard to health, to educate women in regard to motherhood, and to provide all women with gynaecological care. They pointed out that to claim such powers for the public authority, without qualification, is entirely and directly contrary to Catholic teaching on the rights of the family, the rights of the Church in education, the rights of the medical profession and of voluntary institutions. The then Taoiseach replied, deferring a fuller answer to our comments on the ground that the constitutionality of the Act was being called into question.

The Archbishops and Bishops desire to express once again approval of a sane and legitimate Health Service, which will properly safeguard the health of Mothers and Children.

The Hierarchy cannot approve of any scheme which, in its general tendency, must foster undue control by the State in a sphere so delicate and so intimately concerned with morals as that which deals with gynaecology or obstetrics and with the relations between doctor and patient.

Neither can the Bishops approve of any scheme which must have for practical result the undue lessening of the proper initiative of individuals and associations and the undermining of self-reliance.

The Bishops do not consider it their duty to enter into an examination of the detailed considerations put forward by the Minister for Health in his memorandum, save in so far as they wish to point out the fallacy of treating the proposed Mother and Child Health Scheme on a basis of parity with the provision by the State of minimum primary education, or the prevention of infectious diseases or a scheme of children's allowances.

It is to be noted that the proposed Scheme fails to give clear evidence of the details of implementation. The Scheme, as set forth in vague, general terms, has the appearance of conferring a benefit on the mothers and children of the whole nation.

The Hierarchy must regard the Scheme proposed by the Minister for Health as opposed to Catholic social teaching:

Firstly—In this particular Scheme the State arrogates to itself a function and control, on a nationwide basis, in respect of education, more especially in the very intimate matters of chastity, individual and conjugal. The Bishops have noted with satisfaction the statement of the Minister for Health that he is willing to amend the Scheme in this particular. It is the principle which must be amended, and it is the principle which must be set forth correctly, in a legally binding manner and in an enactment of the Oireachtas. The Bishops believe that this result cannot be achieved except by the amendment of the relevant sections of the Health Act, 1947.

Secondly—In this particular Scheme, the State arrogates to itself a function and control, on a nationwide basis, in respect of health services, which properly ought to be and actually can be, efficiently secured, for the vast majority of the citizens, by individual initiative and by lawful associations.

Thirdly—In this particular Scheme, the State must enter unduly and very intimately into the life of patients, both parents and children, and of doctors.

Fourthly—To implement this particular Scheme, the State must levy a heavy tax on the whole community, by direct or indirect methods, independently of the necessity or desire of the citizens to use the facilities provided.

Fifthly—In implementing this particular Scheme by taxation, direct or indirect, the State will, in practice, morally compel the citizens to avail of the services provided.

Sixthly—This particular Scheme, when enacted on a nation-wide basis, must succeed in damaging gravely the self-reliance of parents, whose family-wage or income would allow them duly to provide of themselves medical treatment for their dependents.

Seventhly—In implementing this particular Scheme, the State must have recourse, in great part, to ministerial regulations, as distinct from legislative enactments of the Oireachtas.

Finally, the Bishops are pleased to note that no evidence has been supplied in the letter of the Taoiseach that the proposed Mother and Child Health Scheme advocated by the Minister for Health enjoys the support of the Government. Accordingly, the Hierarchy have firm confidence that it will yet be possible, with reflection and calm consultation, for the Government to provide a Scheme which, while it affords due facilities for those whom the State, as guardian of the common good, is rightly called upon to assist, will nonetheless respect, in its principles and implementation, the traditional life and spirit of our Christian people.

We have the honour to remain, dear Taoiseach,

Yours respectfully and sincerely,

(Signed on behalf of the Hierarchy of Ireland)

John C. McQuaid,

Archbishop of Dublin,

Primate of Ireland.

John A. Costello, Esq., T.D., S.C.,
The Taoiseach,
Government Buildings,
Dublin.

APPENDIX C

THE LETTER OF THE IRISH HIERARCHY ON THE HEALTH BILL, APRIL 1953

This appendix contains the text of the letter from the hierarchy to the Catholics of Ireland on the Health Bill 1952, discussed above in Chapter IX. As was explained there, the letter was in the end collected back from the newspaper offices and not published. However, it remained in the hands of the press long enough for copies to be made and I have seen versions of it from two completely different sources, differing only in paragraphing and punctuation. I have followed the paragraphing and punctuation of what seemed to me the more carefully-executed of the two copies. The text is as follows:—

On the instructions of the Irish Hierarchy, we beg to enclose a copy of a public statement addressed to the Faithful in regard to the Health Bill, 1952.

We remain,

Yours sincerely,

William McNeely,

Bishop of Raphoe,

James Fergus,

Bishop of Achonry,

Secretaries.

The Irish Hierarchy has had under consideration the Health Bill, 1952. In fulfilment of our teaching office and in harmony with the frequently expressed desire of our Holy Father, the Pope, that the individual and the family should be protected against the inroads of state interference, we consider it advisable to issue the following statement to the Faithful:

We are entirely in favour of a Health Service which will give the best possible medical and hospital treatment to all our people, without unduly interfering with the rights of individuals, families, the medical profession, and voluntary institutions, and without unduly lessening personal responsibility and initiative.

We are glad to note that the present Bill proposes to repeal Part III of the Health Act, 1947, Sections 21–28, against which we objected in 1947, 1950 and 1951 on moral and religious grounds. These sections claimed dangerous powers for the Public Health Authority: the power to treat all the illnesses and the defects of children without any recognition of the existence or rights of their parents, the power to educate all women in respect of motherhood and the power to provide gynaecological treatment for all women. Our Catholic people are aware that Catholic doctrine in regard to sex-relations, chastity and marriage is, nowadays, violently opposed; that gynaecological care in many countries means provision for birth control, and abortion in so-called Health clinics; and that health education often involves the claim to direct the child according to pernicious Freudian and materialistic principles. Yet the 1947 Act provided no safeguard that Catholic mothers and children will have the right to be treated or educated according to Catholic principles. We are glad that these Sections of the Act are to be repealed.

Further, we are pleased to note that Section 4 of the 1952 Bill recognises, in general terms, the principles of freedom and excludes compulsory examination and treatment which was involved in Sections 25, 32, 38 and 50 of the 1947 Act.

It is necessary for us, however, to point out that in certain points the Bill is not in harmony with Catholic teaching.

(A) According to Catholic teaching each individual has the primary responsibility to provide for his own health and the father has the responsibility to provide for the health of his family.

The Health Bill, 1952, on the other hand, proceeds on the assumption that the Public Authority is responsible for the treatment of all mothers in child-birth and for the institutional and specialist services for seven-eighths of the population in all cases of sickness and disease. To transfer to the State the responsibility and duty of individuals and families must lower their sense of personal responsibility and seriously weaken the moral fibre of the people.

The Constitution of Ireland in Article 42 (1) 'guarantees to respect the inalienable right and duty of parents to provide according to their means, for the religious and moral, intellectual, physical and social education of their children'. Physical education of children means, not merely the training of the child in matters of hygiene and health but also caring for its health by nutrition and treating its illnesses and defects.

(B) Again it is a principle of Catholic teaching that the State should not assume immediate control in social and economic spheres except when it is clearly demanded by the common good. When any particular social function can be efficiently discharged by individuals or private associations the role of the State should be mainly one of co-ordination and assistance. This principle is clearly set forth by Pope Pius XI in his well-known Encyclical *Quadragesimo Anno*. 'It is an injustice, a grave evil and a disturbance of right order for a larger and higher association to arrogate to itself functions which can be discharged by smaller and lower societies. This is a fundamental principle of social philosophy unshaken and unchangeable. Of its nature the true aim of all social activity should be to help members of the social body but never to destroy or absorb them.'

The present Bill, however, extends considerably the already wide field of medical service which is directly operated and controlled by the State. Instead of helping citizens, by graded subvention according to their means, to obtain treatment from the Doctor and Hospital of their choice it provides that citizens will be treated in whatever institutions the public official may decide. It sets up a centralised bureaucratic system in the matter of most intimate concern, health and life.

The Public Health Authority which will administer the service is not an independent local body representative of varied interests. It is an official entirely subordinate to the Minister. This Bill gives the Minister, for the time being, an extremely wide power to make regulations for every detail of the service so that he could in time seriously modify the system of Doctor-patient relationship, medical practice and hospital administration.

The Bill does not guarantee that women will have the freedom of choice of doctor for maternity service as was promised in the preliminary White Paper. Even in England the State Medical Service allows every person to choose his doctor. The Bill does not give to patients the right to use the State subsidy in the hospital of their choice as in New Zealand. It tends towards the elimination of the voluntary hospitals and the establishment of a monopoly of State hospitals. This taken with the present tendency to make specialists and consultants full time State servants, forbidden to practise outside State hospitals, is calculated to have a detrimental effect on the future of our medical schools. The Bill, as it stands, gives power to public authorities to provide and maintain medical schools thereby bringing the State into medical education.

All these measures constitute a big step towards the complete socialisation of medicine, the gravity of which is emphasised by the fact that it is only part of a general trend of the State to extend its control in various branches of social and economic life.

(C) The Bill contains no safeguard that patients will not be obliged to accept treatment in obstetrics, gynaecology, psychiatry, from men who are imbued with materialistic principles or advocate practices contrary to the Natural law.

We sincerely hope that the Health Bill 1952 will be so amended as to bring it into harmony with the principles of freedom and responsibility which are fundamental in the life and faith of a people.

Signed on behalf of the Irish Hierarchy.

John Cardinal D'Alton,
Archbishop of Armagh,
Primate of All Ireland,
Chairman,

William McNeely,
Bishop of Raphoe,

James Fergus,
Bishop of Achonry,
Secretaries.

SOURCES

1. *Material on Ireland*

A. INTERVIEWS

The following were kind enough to give me interviews in connection with this research:

The Right Reverend Mgr Cecil Barrett (Vice-Chairman, Catholic Protection and Rescue Society of Ireland).

Mr Gerald Boland (Minister for Justice, 1939–48, 1951–4).

The Most Reverend Michael Browne (Bishop of Galway, 1937).

Dr Noel Browne, T.D. (Minister for Health, 1948–51).

Mr H. Byrne (formerly Chairman of the Social Committee, Adoption Society (Ireland)).

His Eminence William Cardinal Conway (Archbishop of Armagh, 1963–).

Mr John A. Costello (Taoiseach, 1948–51, 1954–7).

Dr James Deeny (formerly Chief Medical Adviser, Department of Health).

Mr James Dillon (Minister for Agriculture, 1948–51, 1954–7).

Dr Oliver FitzGerald (Editor of the *Journal of the Medical Association of Eire* and the *Journal of the Irish Medical Association*, 1944–52).

Mr Christopher Gore-Grimes (formerly Secretary, Irish Association of Civil Liberties).

Mr Vincent Grogan (formerly Supreme Knight, Knights of St Columbanus).

Mr A. J. E. Hartford (formerly Vice-President, Adoption Society (Ireland)).

Rev. John Horgan, C.S.Sp. (for information on the late Fr Denis Fahey, C.S.Sp.)

Rev. Edmond Kent, S.J. (formerly Superior, College of Industrial Relations, Dublin).

The Most Reverend Cornelius Lucey (Coadjutor-Bishop of Cork, 1951–2, Bishop of Cork, 1952–   ).

Mr Sean MacBride (Minister for External Affairs, 1948–51).

General Sean MacEoin (Minister for Justice, 1948–51, Minister for Defence, 1954–7).

Mr Patrick McGilligan (Minister for Industry and Commerce, 1924–32 and Minister for External Affairs 1927–32, Minister for Finance, 1948–51, Attorney-General, 1954–7).

The Right Reverend Mgr Peter McKevitt (Professor of Sociology, Maynooth, 1937–53).

Dr T. F. MacNamara (formerly Secretary, Limerick branch of the Irish Medical Association).

The Most Reverend John C. McQuaid (Archbishop of Dublin, 1940–   ).

Dr E. G. T. MacWeeney (Medical Inspector in the Departments of Local Government and Health, 1936–50).

Mr Donal Nevin (Mr Nevin has held a succession of important positions under the Irish Trade Union Congress and the Irish Congress of Trade Unions).

Mr T. C. J. O'Connell (formerly a member of the Executive Committee of the Irish Medical Association).

Mrs V. E. Penney (formerly Secretary, Adoption Society (Ireland)).

The Most Reverend William Philbin (Bishop of Clonfert, 1954–62, Bishop of Down and Connor, 1962–   ).

Mr W. F. Phillips (formerly President of *An Rioghacht,* and formerly Chairman of the Catholic Societies Vocational Organisation Conference).

Mr T. Roseingrave (formerly Chairman of the Catholic Societies Vocational Organisation Conference).

Dr Andrew Ryan (President of the Irish Medical Association, 1946–8).

The Right Reverend Mgr Arthur Ryan (P.P., St Brigid's, Belfast, and a noted Irish theologian).

The late Dr James Ryan (Minister for Agriculture, 1932–47, Minister for Health and Minister for Social Welfare, 1947–8, 1951–4, Minister for Finance, 1957–65).

The late Dr F. C. Ward (Parliamentary Secretary to the Minister for Local Government and Public Health, 1932–46).

Also six civil servants, to whom I am equally grateful but who would probably prefer, in the tradition of their service, to remain anonymous.

As well as interviewing the thirty-nine informants just listed, I have had many conversations with other well-informed people both clerical and lay. Some important items of oral evidence cited in this book have come from informants other than those listed above.

B. Unpublished Documents

In the possession of the Irish Medical Association:

Department of Health, Proposals for a Mother and Child Health Service under Part III of the Health Act, 1947 (i.e. the mother and child scheme). (Cyclostyled.)

Report of conference held at the Department of Health on the 24th October, 1950, between the Minister for Health and a deputation appointed by the Association to discuss proposals in connection with a Mother and Child Health Scheme under Part III of the Health Act 1947. (Cyclostyled.)

In the possession of a doctor formerly prominent in the Irish Medical Association:

The Mother and Child Scheme. Is it Needed? (Cyclostyled document circulated in Clann na Poblachta about the end of 1950.)

In the possession of Mr Sean MacBride:

A number of typescript or duplicated documents on the affairs of Clann na Poblachta, November 1950–June 1951.

In the possession of the National Library of Ireland:

Vocational Organisation Commission. Minutes of Evidence. (Twenty volumes: N.L.I. MSS 922–41. Mostly cyclostyled.)

In the possession of Mrs V. E. Penney, formerly Secretary, Adoption Society (Ireland):

Hon. Secretary's annual reports for 1949–53 (typescript).

Memorandum for Most Reverend Dr. D'Alton in connection with— (1) the aims of the Adoption Society Ireland, (2) the lines of suggested legislation to fulfil these aims. (Typescript, 1950.)

C. THESES

Judge, Jerome Joseph, *The Labour Movement in the Republic of Ireland*, Ph.D., University College Dublin, 1955.

Keatinge, N. P., *The Formulation of Irish Foreign Policy*, Ph.D., Trinity College Dublin, 1968.

Manning, Maurice, *The Blueshirts*, M.A., University College Dublin, 1967.

Miller, David W., *The Politics of Faith and Fatherland: The Catholic Church and Nationalism in Ireland, 1898–1918*, Ph.D., Chicago, 1968.

Pyne, Peter P., *The Third Sinn Fein Party, 1923–1926*, M.A., University College Dublin, 1968.

D. IRISH GOVERNMENT PUBLICATIONS

(I cite these under the headings, and with the catalogue numbers, used in the *Catalogues of Government Publications*.)

Oireachtas publications:

Acts of the Oireachtas. Annual volumes. P.P. 1.

Bills. (I have found it easiest to consult these in the National Library of Ireland, where bills as printed at different stages, and the amendments thereto, are bound in annual volumes.)

Dail Eireann Debates. P.P. 3.

Seanad Eireann Debates. P.P. 4.

Department of Education:

Presentation and Summary of Report of the Commission on Higher Education. E.59. (1967.)

Department of Finance:

Programme for Economic Expansion. F.57. (1958.)
Second Programme for Economic Expansion, Parts I and II. F.57/1 and 2. (1963–4.)

Central Statistics Office:

Census of Population, 1946. I.40/23-32.
Census of Population, 1961. I.40/40-8.
Statistical Abstract. Annual: I.74.

Department of Justice:

Reports of An Bord Uchtala (i.e. the Adoption Board). Annual since 1953. J.64.

Department of Local Government and Public Health:

Reports, to 1945. K.24.

Department of Health:

Reports, from 1945. K.60. (Although the Department of Health did not split off from the Department of Local Government until 1947, its first report covers events from 1945.)
Outline of Proposals for the Improvement of the Health Services. K.51. (i.e. the 1947 white paper.)
Proposals for Improved and Extended Health Services, July, 1952. K.63. (i.e. the 1952 white paper.)
Advisory Body on Voluntary Health Insurance Scheme. Report. K.72.
The Health Services and their Further Development. K.87. (i.e. the 1966 white paper.)
Quarterly Returns of Marriages, Births, and Deaths. T.2.

Department of Social Welfare:

Reports, from 1947. K.59.
Social Security—White Paper containing Government Proposals (October, 1949). K.54.

Miscellaneous:

Dail Eireann. Copies of the Public Notices of the Results of the Elections and of the Transfers of Votes in respect of: (a) *General Election, 1948,* (b) *General Election, 1951,* (c) *By-elections, 1944 to 1952 (inclusive).* M.51/3.

P

Reports:

Report and Minutes of Evidence of the Intoxicating Liquor Commission. R.21. (1926.)

Report of the Committee on Evil Literature. R.34. (1927.)

Report of the Commission on Technical Education. R.39. (1927.)

Second House of the Oireachtas Commission. Report. R.60. (1936.)

Commission on Vocational Organisation. Report. R.76. (Dated 1943 on the cover, but published in 1944.)

Report of the Tribunal appointed by the Taoiseach on the 7th day of June, 1946, pursuant to resolution passed on the 5th day of June, 1946, by Dail Eireann and Seanad Eireann. R.78. (On Dr Ward's case.)

Commission on Youth Unemployment, 1951. Report. R.82.

Commission on Emigration and Other Population Problems, 1948–54. Reports. R.84.

Reports of the Commission of Inquiry into the operation of the laws relating to the sale and supply of intoxicating liquor, 1957. R.86.

Report of the Committee on the Constitution, December, 1967. R.107.

Registrar-General's Office:

Annual Reports, to 1952. T.3.

Reports on Vital Statistics, from 1953. T.3.

E. NEWSPAPERS, PERIODICALS AND ANNUALS

Place of publication of all items is Dublin, unless otherwise stated.

(i) *Newspapers, periodicals and annuals consulted for an extended period.*

Administration. Quarterly, 1953– . Examined since publication began.

Annual Register, London. Annual, 1758– . Chapters on Ireland examined since 1900.

The Bell. Irregular, but generally monthly, 1941–54. Examined for the period of publication.

Catholic Bulletin. Monthly, 1911–39. Examined for 1922–35.

Catholic Protection and Rescue Society. Annual Reports, 1914– . Examined since publication began.

Christus Rex, Maynooth. Quarterly, 1947– . Examined since publication began.

Comhar. Monthly, 1942– . Examined for April–September 1951.
Congress of Irish Unions. Annual Meetings, 1945–59. Examined for 1945–51.

Fiat. Irregular, 1945?–62? I have used the file in the National Library of Ireland, which is not quite complete, and have also obtained certain issues from other sources.

Furrow, Maynooth. Monthly, 1950– . Examined since publication began.

Hibernia. Generally monthly, 1937– . Examined since 1961.

Ireland To-Day. Monthly, 1936–8. Examined for the period of publication.

Irish Catholic Directory. Annual, 1836– . Sections on Irish ecclesiastical events examined since 1905.

Irish Ecclesiastical Record, Maynooth. Monthly, 1864–1968. Examined for 1916–68.

Irish Farmers' Journal. Weekly, 1950– . Examined for 1954–7.

Irish School Weekly, 1904–54. Examined for 1944–6.

Irish Trade Union Congress and Labour Party, Reports of Annual Meetings, 1916–17; *Irish Labour Party and Trade Union Congress, Reports of Annual Meetings,* 1918–22; *Irish Labour Party and Trade Union Congress, Annual Reports,* 1923–30; *The Labour Party, Annual Reports,* 1930–41; *The Labour Party, Reports of the Administrative Council,* 1942–. Examined for 1916–65.

Irish Trade Union Congress, Annual Reports, 1930–59. Examined for 1945–51.

Irish Weekly Independent, 1893–1960. Examined for 1911–60.

Journal of the Irish Free State Medical Union, 1937–41; *Journal of the Medical Association of Eire,* 1941–50; *Journal of the Irish Medical Association,* 1951– . Monthly. Examined for 1939–53, and for particular points thereafter.

The Licensed Vintner and Grocer. Monthly, 1934– . Examined for 1947–62.

Muintir na Tire Official Handbook, Tipperary, 1941–9; *Rural Ireland,* Tipperary, 1950– . Annual. Examined since publication began.

The Pioneer. Monthly, 1948– . Examined for 1948–60.

The Round Table, London. Quarterly, 1910– . Examined for 1922–67.

The Standard. Weekly, 1928– . Examined for 1942–57, and previous to 1942 for particular points.

Studies. Quarterly, 1912– . Examined since publication began.

The Tablet, London. Weekly, 1840– . Examined for April–June 1951.

(ii) *Dublin daily papers extensively consulted*

(I did not attempt to examine any daily paper systematically for an extended period. My method of work was to reconstruct the outline of events from weeklies, especially the *Irish Weekly Independent* and the *Standard*. If these sources gave me sufficient information for my purposes, I used them as my authorities and have cited them in my footnotes. If I needed further information, I went to the dailies.)

Dublin Evening Mail
Irish Independent
Irish Press
Irish Times.

(iii) *Newspapers, periodicals and annuals consulted on particular points or for particular articles.*

Church History, Chicago, XXXIII, Dec. 1964, for: Emmet Larkin, 'Socialism and Catholicism in Ireland'. (On the period 1910–14.)

Economic and Social Review, I, 1 and 2, 1969–70, for: Peter Pyne, 'The Third Sinn Fein Party, 1923–1926'.

Guardian, Manchester, 8–11 Jan. 1964, for four articles by Peter Lennon on 'Censorship in Ireland'.

History, London, XLIII, no. 148, June 1958, for: T. W. Moody, 'The Irish university question of the nineteenth century'.

Irish Journal of Medical Science, 6th series, no. 199, July 1942, for: T. W. T. Dillon, 'The statistics of tuberculosis'.

Irish Law Times Reports, for cases in 1943, 1945 and 1950.

Irish Monthly, LXXVIII, no. 924, June 1950, for: J. Waldron, '*An Rioghacht*: a retrospect'.

Irish National Teachers' Organisation. Annual Directory and Irish Educational Year Book for 1940, for information on the I.N.T.O.'s part in securing changes in the Labour party constitution.

Irish Theological Quarterly, Maynooth, XIX, 1952, for: Most Rev. C. Lucey, 'The moral aspect of means tests'.

Ibid., XXVIII, 1961, for: Rev. Enda McDonagh, 'Church and State in the constitution of Ireland'.

Liberty, IX, 1–3, Jan.-March 1954, for articles on the Dublin Institute of Catholic Sociology, the Catholic Workers' College, and *An Rioghacht*.

Limerick Leader, Limerick, 1946–7, for articles by Dr James McPolin.

Midland Herald, Mullingar, Feb.-April 1950, for details of Westmeath County Council meetings.

Political Studies, Oxford, II, 2, June 1954, for Basil Chubb, 'Vocational representation and the Irish Senate'.

Social Compass, The Hague, XI, 3/4, 1964, for C. K. Ward, 'Socio-religious research in Ireland'.

Thom's Directory of Ireland, 1928, 1958, for information on technical instruction and vocational education committees.

University Review, V, 2, Summer 1968, for Michael McInerney, 'Noel Browne: Church and State'.

Westmeath Examiner, Mullingar, Feb.-April 1950, for details of Westmeath County Council meetings.

Westmeath Independent, Athlone, Feb.-April 1950, for details of Westmeath County Council meetings.

(iv) *Scrapbooks*

I have also had the benefit of using certain scrapbooks of newspaper cuttings kindly lent to me by their owners:

A scrapbook in the possession of the late Dr F. C. Ward containing cuttings on health policy, 1945-6.

A series of scrapbooks in the possession of Mrs V. E. Penney covering very fully the activities of the Adoption Society (Ireland) from 1948 to 1953.

F. Books and Pamphlets

Place of publication of all items is Dublin, unless otherwise stated.

Some of the rarer items I found only in the Catholic Central Library, Merrion Square, Dublin, and these I have identified with the initials 'C.C.L.'

Acta et Decreta Synodi Plenariae Episcoporum Hiberniae habitae apud Maynutiam, an. MDCCCLXXV, 1877.

Acta et Decreta Synodi Plenariae Episcoporum Hiberniae habitae apud Maynutiam, an. MDCCCC, 1906.

Acta et Decreta Concilii Plenarii Episcoporum Hiberniae quod habitum est apud Maynutiam . . . 1927, 1929.

Acta et Decreta Concilii Plenarii quod habitum est apud Maynooth . . . 1956, 1960. (This volume, unlike its predecessors for the Councils of 1875, 1900 and 1927, was put on sale only to the clergy and is not to be found in public libraries. It is, however, not difficult for a layman to secure access to a copy, if he uses his initiative.)

Adams, Michael, *Censorship: the Irish Experience*, 1968.

Akenson, Donald H., *The Irish Education Experiment: the National System of Education in the Nineteenth Century*, London, 1970.

Arensberg, Conrad M., *The Irish Countryman*, London, 1937.

Arensberg, Conrad M., and Kimball, Solon T., *Family and Community in Ireland*, Cambridge, Mass., 2nd edn., 1968.

Atkinson, Norman D., *Irish Education: a History of Educational Institutions*, 1969.

Barrett, Cecil J., C.C., *Adoption*, 1952.

Barrington, Donal, *The Church, the State and the Constitution*, 1959. (Catholic Truth Society of Ireland pamphlet.)

Bestic, Alan, *The Importance of Being Irish*, London, 1969.

Beth, Loren P., *The Development of Judicial Review in Ireland, 1937–1966*, 1967.

Blanchard, Jean, *Le Droit Ecclesiastique Contemporain d'Irlande*, Paris, 1958.

Blanchard, Jean, *The Church in Contemporary Ireland*, 1963.

Blanshard, Paul *The Irish and Catholic Power*, London, 1954.

Boylan, Rev. Patrick, *Catholicism and Citizenship in Self-Governed Ireland*, 1922. (Irish Messenger Social Action series: pamphlet.)

Bromage, Mary C., *De Valera and the March of a Nation*, London, 1956.

Browne, Rev. M., *Disabilities of the Catholic Church in Ireland*, n.d. [1930?] (Catholic Truth Society of Ireland pamphlet.)

Cahill, Rev. E., S.J., *Freemasonry and the Anti-Christian Movement*, 1929.

Cahill, Rev. E., S.J., *Ireland's Peril*, 1930. (Pamphlet published by An Rioghacht.)

Catholic Social Worker's Handbook, 2nd edn., 1947.

Catholic Societies Vocational Organisation Conference, *The Vocational Organisation Commission. A Synopsis*, 1945; 2nd edn., 1953.

Chubb, Basil, *The Government and Politics of Ireland*, Oxford, 1970.

Chubb, Basil (ed.), *A Source Book of Irish Government*, 1964.

Clarkson, J., Dunsmore, *Labour and Nationalism in Ireland*, New York, 1925.

Collins, John, *Local Government*, 2nd edn., revised by Desmond Roche, 1963.

Collis, W. R. F., *The State of Medicine in Ireland*, 1943.

Comerford, Rev. F., C.S.Sp., *Late Fr. Denis Fahey, C.S.Sp. An Appreciation*, n.p., n.d. [1954?] (Pamphlet: C.C.L.)

Connell, K. H., *Irish Peasant Society*, Oxford, 1968.

Connery, Donald S., *The Irish*, London, 1968.

Coogan, Timothy Patrick, *Ireland since the Rising*, London, 1966.

Coogan, Timothy Patrick, *The I.R.A.*, London, 1970.

D'Alton, John Cardinal, *The Church and Freedom*, n.d. [1952?] (Catholic Truth Society of Ireland pamphlet.)

Dignan, Most Rev. J., *Catholics and Trinity College*, n.d. [1934?] (Catholic Truth Society of Ireland pamphlet.)

Dignan, Most Rev. J., *Social Security. Outlines of a Scheme of National Health Insurance*, Sligo, 1945.

Duffy, Patrick, *The Lay Teacher*, n.d. [1967].

Earl, Lawrence, *The Battle of Baltinglass*, London, 1952.

Edwards, Owen Dudley (ed.), *Conor Cruise O'Brien Introduces Ireland*, London, 1969.

Fahey, Rev. Denis, C.S.Sp., *The Church and Farming*, Cork, 1953.

Fahey, Rev. Denis, C.S.Sp., *The Kingship of Christ, according to the principles of St Thomas Aquinas*, 1931.

Fahey, Rev. Denis, C.S.Sp., *The Kingship of Christ and the Conversion of the Jewish Nation*, 1953.

Fahey, Rev. Denis, C.S.Sp., *Money Manipulation and Social Order*, 1944.

Fahey, Rev. Denis, C.S.Sp., *The Mystical Body of Christ in the Modern World*, 1st edn., 1935, 2nd edn., 1938, 3rd edn., 1939.

Fahey, Rev. Denis, C.S.Sp., *The Mystical Body of Christ and the Reorganisation of Society*, Cork, 1945.

Fahey, Rev. Denis, C.S.Sp., *The Rulers of Russia*, 1938.

Fahey, Rev. Denis, C.S.Sp., *The Social Rights of Our Divine Lord Jesus Christ, the King*, adapted from the French of Rev. A. Philippe, C.SS.R., 1932.

Farley, Desmond, *Social Insurance and Social Assistance in Ireland*, 1964.

Fennell, Desmond (ed.), *The Changing Face of Catholic Ireland*, London, 1968.

FitzGerald, Garret, *Planning in Ireland*, Dublin and London, 1968.

FitzGerald, Garret, *State-Sponsored Bodies*, 2nd edn., 1963.

Fleming, Lionel, *Head or Harp*, London, 1965.

Garvin, Thomas, *The Irish Senate*, 1969.

Gorham, Maurice, *Forty Years of Irish Broadcasting*, 1967.

Gray, Tony, *The Irish Answer*, London, 1966.

Handbook of the Catholic Social Service Conference, 1945. (In C.C.L.)

Hawkins, John, *The Irish Question Today*, London, 1941. (Fabian Society, Research Series no. 54.)

Hensey, Brendan, *The Health Services of Ireland*, 1959.

Hogan, James, *Could Ireland Become Communist?*, Cork, n.d. [1935].

Horgan, John J., *Parnell to Pearse*, 1948.

Humphreys, Alexander J., *New Dubliners. Urbanization and the Irish Family*, London, 1966.

Hurley, Michael, S.J. (ed.), *Irish Anglicanism, 1869–1969*, 1970.

Inglis, Brian, *West Briton*, London, 1962.

Irish Christian Front, n.d. [1936]. (Pamphlet: in National Library of Ireland.)

Jackson, John Archer, *The Irish in Britain*, London, 1963.

Jeffares, A. Norman, and Cross, K. G. W., *In Excited Reverie. A Centenary Tribute to William Butler Yeats 1865–1939*, London, 1965.

Kaim-Caudle, P. R., *Social Policy in the Irish Republic*, London, 1967.

Kelly, J. M., *Fundamental Rights in the Irish Law and Constitution*, 2nd edn., 1967.

Kerr, James P., *A Catechism of Catholic Social Principles*, 1st edn., 1916.

Larkin, Emmet, *James Larkin, Irish Labour Leader, 1876–1947*, London, 1965.

Leon, D., *Advisory Bodies in Irish Government*, 1963.

The Liberal Ethic, 1950. (*Irish Times* pamphlet.)

Lyons, F. S. L., *The Fall of Parnell, 1890–91*, London, 1960.

Lyons, F. S. L., *John Dillon*, London, 1968.

McCarthy, Charles, *The Distasteful Challenge*, 1968.

MacDonagh, Oliver, *Ireland*, Englewood Cliffs, N.J., 1968.

McDowell, R. B., *Public Opinion and Government Policy in Ireland, 1801–1846*, London, 1952.

McElligott, T. J., *Education in Ireland*, 1966.

McKenna, Lambert, S.J., *The Church and Labour*, 1914.

McKevitt, Rev. Peter, *The Plan of Society*, 1944.

MacManus, Francis, (ed.), *The Years of the Great Test, 1926–39*, Cork, 1967.

McQuaid, Most Rev. John C., *Wellsprings of the Faith*, 1956.

Manual of the Guilds of Regnum Christi, 1934. (In C.C.L.)

Maria Duce, *Memorandum to Hierarchy, Public Bodies, T.D's and Senators*, n.p., n.d. [1950]. (Leaflet, in C.C.L.)

Mescal, John, *Religion in the Irish System of Education*, 1957.

Moody, T. W., and Beckett, J. C., *Queen's, Belfast, 1845–1949: the History of a University*, London, 2 vols., 1959.

Moss, Warner, *Political Parties in the Irish Free State*, New York, 1933.

Newman, Jeremiah (ed.), *The Limerick Rural Survey, 1958–64*, Tipperary, 1964.

Newman, Jeremiah, *Studies in Political Morality*, 1962.

Nowlan, Kevin B., *The Politics of Repeal*, London, 1965.

Nowlan, Kevin B., and Williams, T. Desmond (eds.), *Ireland in the War Years and After, 1939–51*, 1969.

O'Brien, John A. (ed.), *The Vanishing Irish*, London, 1954.

O'Connell, T. J., *History of the Irish National Teachers' Organisation, 1868–1968*, n.d. [1969].

O'Connor, Frank, *My Father's Son*, London, 1968.

O'Duffy, Eoin, *Crusade in Spain*, n.d. [1938].

O'Faolain, Sean, *The Irish*, London, 1st edn., 1947.

O'Faolain, Sean, *An Irish Journey*, London, 1941.

O'Faolain, Sean, *Vive Moi! An Autobiography*, London, 1965.

O'Leary, Cornelius, *The Irish Republic and its Experiment with Proportional Representation*, Notre Dame, Ind., 1961.

O'Riordan, Rev. M., *Catholicity and Progress in Ireland*, London, 1906.

O'Sullivan, Donal, *The Irish Free State and its Senate*, London, 1940.

Paul-Dubois, L., *Contemporary Ireland*, 1908.

Philbin, Most Rev. William, *The Irish and the New Europe*, 1962.

Philbin, Most Rev. William, *Neighbourliness*, 1958.

Philbin, Most Rev. William, *Patriotism*, 1958.

Phillips, W. Alison, *The Revolution in Ireland, 1906–1923*, London, 2nd edn., 1926.

Plater, Charles, S.J., *The Priest and Social Action*, London, 1914. (Contains one chapter on Ireland.)

Plunkett, Sir Horace, *Ireland in the New Century*, London, 1904.

Rahilly, Alfred, *A Guide to Books for Social Students and Others*, 1916.

Rohan, Dorine, *Marriage Irish Style*, Cork, 1969.

Rumpf, Erhard, *Nationalismus und Sozialismus in Irland*, Meisenheim am Glan, 1959.

Ryan, W. P., *The Pope's Green Island*, London, 1912.

Rynne, Stephen, *Father John Hayes*, 1960.

Seaver, George, *John Allen Fitzgerald Gregg, Archbishop*, London and Dublin, 1963.

Seoighe, Mainchín, *Maraíodh Seán Sabhat aréir*, 1964.

Sheehy, Michael, *Is Ireland Dying?*, London, 1968.

Southern Ireland—Church or State?, Belfast, n.d. [1951].

Toner, Jerome, O.P., *Rural Ireland: Some of its Problems*, 1955.

Ussher, Arland, *The Face and Mind of Ireland*, London, 1949.

White, Terence de Vere, *Kevin O'Higgins*, London, 1948.

Young, Filson, *Ireland at the Cross Roads*, London, 1903.

2. *Comparative material on other countries*

A. Newspapers, Periodicals and other Serials

Documentation Catholique, Paris. Fortnightly, 1919– . Examined for 1946–55.
International Labour Review, Geneva. Monthly, 1921– . Examined for 1938–65.
International Social Security Association, Bulletin, Geneva. Irregular, 1948– . Examined for 1948–55.
Irish News, Belfast. Daily, 1855– . Examined for information on the Mater Hospital dispute, Aug.–Oct. 1947.
Northern Ireland, Parliamentary Debates. Official Report. House of Commons, xxxi (1947–8). Examined for information on the Mater Hospital dispute.
Presenza, Milan, 1, 2, July 1969, for: 'Padre Gemelli, dieci anni dopo'.

B. Books and Pamphlets

Abbott, Walter, M., S.J. (ed.), *The Documents of Vatican II*, London, 1966.
Abell, Aaron I., *American Catholicism and Social Action: A Search for Social Justice, 1865–1950*, Garden City, N.Y., 1960.
Alix, Christine, *Le Saint-Siège et les Nationalismes en Europe, 1870–1960*, Paris, 1962.
Binchy, D. A., *Church and State in Fascist Italy*, London, 1941.
Bosworth, William, *Catholicism and Crisis in Modern France*, Princeton, N.J., 1962.
Brown, Robert Douglas, *The Battle of Crichel Down*, London, 1955.
Calvez, Jean-Yves, S.J., and Perrin, Jacques, S.J., *The Church and Social Justice*, London, 1961.
Catholic Education Council for England and Wales, *The Case for Catholic Schools*, London, 1951.
Catholic Social Guild, *A Code of Social Principles*, prepared by the International Union of Social Studies, Oxford, 1st edn. 1929., 2nd edn., 1937, 3rd edn., 1952.
Catholic Social Guild, *The Social Thought of John XXIII*, Oxford, 1964.
Daniel-Rops, Henri, *A Fight for God, 1870–1939*. London, 1966.

Diamant, Alfred, *Austrian Catholics and the First Republic*, Princeton, N.J., 1960.

Durand, Paul, *La Politique Contemporaine de Sécurité Sociale*, Paris, 1953.

Eckstein, Harry, *Pressure Group Politics. The Case of the British Medical Association*, London, 1960.

Einaudi, Mario, and Goguel, François, *Christian Democracy in Italy and France*, Notre Dame, Ind., 1952.

Elbow, Matthew H., *French Corporative Theory, 1789–1948*, New York, 1953.

Filthaut, E., O.P., *Deutsche Katholikentage 1848–1958 und soziale Frage*, Essen, 1960.

Fogarty, Michael P., *Christian Democracy in Western Europe, 1820–1953*, London, 1957.

Friedlander, Walter A., *Individualism and Social Welfare: an Analysis of the System of Social Security and Social Welfare in France*, New York, 1962.

Galant, Henry C., *Histoire Politique de la Sécurité Sociale Française, 1945–52*, Paris, 1955.

Gestel, C. van, O.P., *La Doctrine Sociale de l'Eglise*, Brussels, 3rd edn., 1964.

Gilson, Etienne (ed.), *The Church Speaks to the Modern World: the Social Teachings of Leo XIII*, Garden City, N.Y., 1954.

International Social Security Association, *Ninth General Meeting, Rome, 3 to 8 October 1949. Proceedings, Reports and National Monographs, Resolutions and Conclusions*, Geneva, 1950. (Report II is on 'Protection of Mother and Child by means of Social Security.')

Jennings, W. I., *Cabinet Government*, 1st edn., London, 1936.

Kornitzer, Margaret, *Child Adoption in the Modern World*, London, 1952.

Lindsey, Almont, *Socialized Medicine in England and Wales*, London, 1962.

McLaughlin, Terence P., C.S.B. (ed.), *The Church and the Reconstruction of the Modern World: the Social Encyclicals of Pius XI*, Garden City, N.Y., 1957.

Mathieu, Marie-Hélène, et al., *Perspectives Chrétiennes sur l'Adoption*, Paris, 1962.

Mayer, Henry (ed.), *Catholics and the Free Society: an Australian Symposium*, Melbourne, 1961.

Messner, Joseph, *Social Ethics*, St. Louis, 1949.

Moody, Joseph N. (ed.), *Church and Society: Catholic Social and Political Thought and Movements, 1789–1950*, New York, 1953.

A National Health Service, Cmd. 6502, London, 1944.

Nichols, James Hastings, *Democracy and the Churches*, Philadelphia, 1951.

Plas, Michel van der, *Uit het Rijke Roomsche Leven: een documentaire over de jaren 1925–1935*, Utrecht, n.d. [1963].

Plater, Charles, S.J., *The Priest and Social Action*, London, 1914.

Premoli, Orazio M., *Contemporary Church History (1900–1925)*, London, 1932.

Purdy, W. A., *The Church on the Move. The Characters and Policies of Pius XII and John XXIII*, London, 1966.

Quinn, Herbert F., *The Union Nationale. A Study in Quebec Nationalism*, Toronto, 1963.

Richardson, J. Henry, *Economic and Financial Aspects of Social Security*, London, 1960.

Rovan, Joseph, *Le Catholicisme Politique en Allemagne*, Paris, 1956.

Scholl, S. H. (ed.), *150 Ans de Mouvement Ouvrier Chrétien en Europe de l'Ouest, 1789–1939*, Louvain and Paris, 1966.

Semaines Sociales de France, XXXVIIIᵉ Session, *Santé et Société*, Lyon, 1951.

La Sicurezza Sociale, XXIII Settimana Sociale dei Cattolici d'Italia, Bologna, 24–29 Settembre 1949, Rome, 2nd edn., 1963.

Social Insurance and Allied Services. Report by Sir William Beveridge, Cmd. 6404, London, 1942.

United States Department of Health, Education and Welfare, *Social Security Programs throughout the World*, Washington, 1961.

Vaussard, Maurice, *Histoire de la Démocratie Chrétienne. France–Belgique-Italie*, Paris, 1956.

Verkade, Willem, *Democratic Parties in the Low Countries and Germany*, Leiden, 1965.

Williams, Philip, *Crisis and Compromise: Politics in the Fourth Republic*, London, 1964.

INDEX

449